Secretary of State North Carolina

The Legislative Manual and Political Register of the State of North Carolina

Secretary of State North Carolina

The Legislative Manual and Political Register of the State of North Carolina

ISBN/EAN: 9783744728744

Printed in Europe, USA, Canada, Australia, Japan

Cover: Foto ©Suzi / pixelio.de

More available books at **www.hansebooks.com**

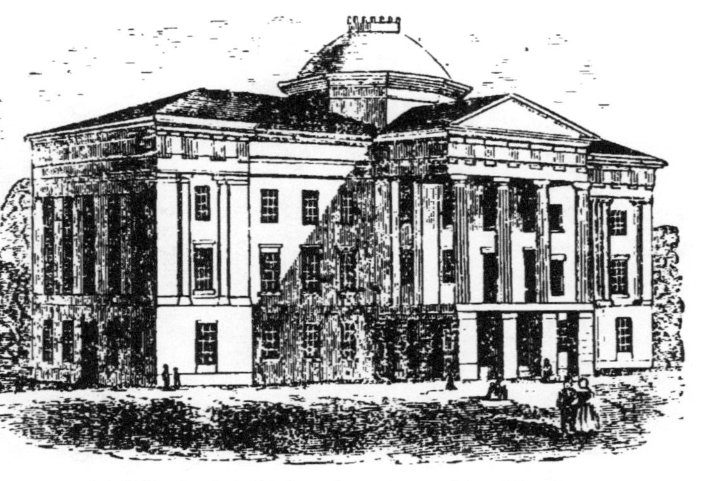

CAPITOL BUILDING, RALEIGH, N. C.

THE LEGISLATIVE MANUAL

AND

POLITICAL REGISTER

OF THE

State of North Carolina,

FOR THE YEAR 1874.

COMPRISING THE

CONSTITUTION OF THE UNITED STATES AND OF THE STATE OF NORTH CAROLINA; A MAP SHOWING THE COUNTIES AND THE CONGRESSIONAL DISTRICTS; A CALENDAR OF CHRONOLOGICAL EVENTS, WITH LISTS AND TABLES FOR REFERENCE.

"Facts alone are wanting in life. Plant nothing else, and root out everything else. Facts alone can influence the minds and actions of men."—*Dickens.*

Compiled by authority of the General Assembly of North Carolina, under the direction of

W. H. Howerton,

Secretary of State.

By JOHN H. WHEELER, late Treasurer of the State, and Author of the History of North Carolina.

RALEIGH:

JOSIAH TURNER, JR., STATE PRINTER AND BINDER.

1874.

RESOLUTION IN RELATION TO A "NORTH CAROLINA MANUAL."

SECTION 1. *Resolved by the Senate, the House of Representatives concurring,* That the Secretary of State shall cause to be printed at once, and again next winter, and biennially thereafter, "A Manual of North Carolina," containing the Constitution of the United States, the Constitution of North Carolina, with the names of all the Governors and other executive officers of the State, Judges of the Supreme and Superior Courts, members and officers of the two Houses of the General Assembly, with such other chronological and statistical information as he may deem useful. *Resolved further,* That each publication shall cover one thousand copies, to be distributed as follows: Four to each Senator and Representative, one to each officer of the two Houses, one to each State officer, including Judges of the Supreme and Superior Courts, one to the Governor of each State one to each Superior Court Clerk for the use of their offices, and there to remain, ten copies to the State Library, and the residue to be equally distributed in the several counties of the State to such parties as the said Secretary may elect. *Resolved further,* That in no edition of said "Manual" after the first shall any name be reprinted except the names of those actually in office,

SEC. 2. This resolution shall be in full force after its ratification.

Ratified this 10th day of February, A. D. 1874.

PREFACE.

A Legislative Manual and Political Register for the State of North Carolina is herewith presented, for the first time, in the history of the State.

The want of such a compilation is felt by every citizen in the State.

In very many of the States of the Union, such a work is annually published by public patronage, and is much esteemed as affording a ready reference to names, dates and facts, which are inaccessible to some, of difficulty to many, and important to all.

The compiler feels grateful to many patriotic citizens of North Carolina for aid afforded. In the collection of so many names and facts, and the compilation of so large an array of figures, it is to be expected that some errors will occur. Much labor and pains have been taken to guard against them; errors will creep in, however, and the compiler will be grateful to any one who may detect them, and communicate the facts, that they may be avoided in future editions. It is to be hoped, however, that should some errors occur, they will be so small as not to mislead the observant reader, or impair the usefulness of the work.

In future editions, (as the work is, by law, to be prepared for each succeeding Legislature,) such errors will be avoided; and by improvement in matter and embellishments in mode, this work more worthy of its distinguished subject, and the patronage of its patriotic citizens.

JOHN H. WHEELER.

TABLE OF CONTENTS.

No. I.

Chronological Table, Dates and Events.

JANUARY.

Days of Mo.	Day of Wk.	Sun Rises.	Sun Sets.	CHRONOLOGICAL EVENTS.
1	Th.	7 11	4 57	1620, Slaves first brought to Virginia.
2	Fr.	7 11	4 58	Jan. 1, 1863, Proc. of Emancipation issued by Presd't Lincoln.
3	Sat.	7 11	4 59	1776, Norfolk, Va., burnt by British.
4	Sun	7 11	5 00	Second Sunday after Christmas.
5	Mo.	7 11	5 01	2d, 1821, Florida acquired by treaty.
6	Tu.	7 11	5 02	
7	We.	7 11	5 03	4th, 1822, First Cotton Factory at Lowell, Mass.
8	Th.	7 11	5 03	1863, Gov. Branch died.
9	Fr.	7 11	5 04	4th, 1801, David L. Swain born.
10	Sat.	7 11	5 05	8th, 1815, Battle of New Orleans.
11	Sun	7 11	5 06	First Sunday after Epiphany.
12	Mo.	7 10	5 07	10th, 1836, U. S. Government free from debt, $28,000,000 surplus
13	Tu.	7 10	5 08	[revenue distributed.
14	We.	7 10	5 09	1861, Florida seceded from the Union.
15	Th.	7 10	5 10	1862, Sens. Polk and Johnson, of Mo., expelled from U. S. Sen.
16	Fr.	7 09	5 11	11th, 1861, Alabama seceded.
17	Sat.	7 09	5 11	1871, Admiral H. H. Bell, U. S. N., of N. C., drowned in Japan.
18	Sun	7 09	5 13	1861, Georgia seceded from Union.
19	Mo.	7 09	5 14	1783, treaty of Versailles.
20	Tu.	7 08	5 15	1852, Perry's expedition to Japan.
21	We.	7 08	5 16	
22	Th.	7 07	5 17	1872, Governor Thomas Bragg died.
23	Fr.	7 07	5 18	22, 1764, Mason and Dixon line between Ches. and Del. Bays.
24	Sat.	7 06	5 19	23, 1844, William Gaston died.
25	Sun	7 06	5 20	Third Sunday after Epiphany.
26	Mo.	7 05	5 21	1861, Louisiana seceded from Union.
27	Tu.	7 04	5 22	1781, 17th, Battle of Cowpens.
28	We.	7 03	5 24	1835, Dr. Jos. Caldwell died.
29	Th.	7 03	5 25	1837, 15th, Wilkes' expedition sailed.
30	Fr.	7 02	5 26	1869, Terrible fire at Chicago.
31	Sat.	7 02	5 27	1729, Carolinas divided into North and South Carolina.

FEBRUARY.

Days of Mo.	Days of Wk.	Sun Rises.	Sun Sets.	CHRONOLOGICAL EVENTS.
1	Sun	7 07	5 27	1864, Col. H. M. Shaw killed in battle near Newbern, N. C.
2	Mo.	7 06	5 28	1873, St. John's College at Oxford opened.
3	Tu.	6 59	5 29	1781, Gen. Wm. Davidson killed in battle at Catawba River.
4	We.	6 58	5 30	1804, Lewis and Clark cross the Rocky Mountains.
5	Th.	6 57	5 31	1801, U. S. Military Academy at West Point, N. Y.
6	Fr.	6 56	5 32	1827, Hon. Charles R. Thomas born.
7	Sat.	6 56	5 33	1867, Geo. Peabody gives $2,000,000 for Educa. pur. to South.
8	Sun	6 54	5 34	Sexagesima Sunday.
9	Mo.	6 53	5 35	1862, Roanoke Island taken by Burnside.
10	Tu.	6 52	5 36	1848, Judge Daniel, of Supreme Court, died.
11	We.	6 51	5 37	1840, Hugh L. White died.
12	Th.	6 50	5 38	1302, Mariner's compass discovered by a Neapolitan.
13	Fr.	6 49	5 39	1452, Printing discovered by a German.
14	Sat.	6 48	5 40	
15	Sun	6 47	5 41	Quinquagesima Sunday.
16	Mo.	6 46	5 42	
17	Tu.	6 45	5 43	1818, 19th, Governor Caldwell born.
18	We.	6 44	5 44	1834, William Wirt died.
19	Th.	6 43	5 45	1861, Jeff. Davis inaugurated President of Conf. States.
20	Fr.	6 42	5 46	1854, Robert Strange died.
21	Sat.	6 41	5 47	1871, Geo. W. Mordecai died.
22	Sun	6 40	5 48	1732, George Washington born.
23	Mo.	6 38	5 49	1848, John Quincy Adams died in Capitol at Washington.
24	Tu.	6 37	5 49	1870, Anson Burlingame died in Russia.
25	We.	6 36	5 50	
26	Th.	6 36	5 51	1776, Battle of Moore's Creek Bridge, N. C.
27	Fr.	6 33	5 54	1844, Explosion of cannon on U. S. frigate Princeton.
28	Sat.	6 31	5 55	1837, Cilley killed by Graves in a duel at Bladensburg.

MARCH.

Days of Mo.	Days of Wk.	Sun Rises.	Sun Sets.	CHRONOLOGICAL EVENTS.
1	Sun	6 29	5 58	Second Sunday in Lent.
2	Mo.	6 28	5 58	1867, Nebraska admitted, (37th State.)
3	Tu.	6 27	5 59	1779, Battle of Brier Creek, Ashe defeated,
4	We.	6 25	5 59	1789, First Congress of U. S. under Con., met at Philadelphia.
5	Th.	6 24	6 00	
6	Fr.	6 23	6 01	
7	Sat.	6 22	6 02	1862, Merrimack sinks the Cumberland in Hampton Roads.
8	Sun	6 22	6 03	Third Sunday in Lent. 1863, Battle of Pea Ridge, Arkansas.
9	Mo.	6 20	6 04	1868, Andrew Johnson impeached.
10	Tu.	6 18	6 05	1837, Davidson College opened.
11	We.	6 17	6 06	1865, Fayetteville occupied by Sherman.
12	Th.	6 15	6 07	1831, Hon. Francis E. Shober born.
13	Fr.	6 12	6 07	
14	Sat.	6 11	6 08	1862, Newbern taken by Burnside.
15	Sun	6 10	6 08	1781, Battle of Guilford Court House.
16	Mo.	6 08	6 10	1873, Rev. W. Barringer died.
17	Tu.	6 07	6 11	1862, John Tyler died at Richmond.
18	We.	6 06	6 11	
19	Th.	6 04	6 12	
20	Fr.	6 03	6 13	1862, Winton burnt by U. S. troops.
21	Sat.	6 02	6 14	1865, General Schofield occupied Goldsboro'.
22	Sun	6 00	6 15	Fifth Sunday in Lent.
23	Mo.	5 59	6 16	
24	Tu.	5 57	6 17	
25	We.	5 55	6 17	
26	Th.	5 54	6 18	1865, Gen. Stoneman occupied Boon, Watauga county.
27	Fr.	5 53	6 18	
28	Sat.	5 51	6 19	
29	Sun	5 50	6 19	Palm Sunday. 1847, Vera Cruz taken by United States.
30	Mo.	5 48	6 20	
31	Tu.	5 47	6 21	1850, John C. Calhoun died at Washington City.

APRIL.

Days of Mo.	Days of Wk.	Sun Rises.	Sun Sets.	CHRONOLOGICAL EVENTS.
1	We.	5 44	6 23	1819, First passage across Atlantic by steam, (steamer Savannah.)
2	Th.	5 43	6 24	1743, Jefferson born.
3	Fr.	5 41	6 25	1767, Jackson born in Mecklenburg county, N. C.
4	Sat.	5 40	6 26	1865, Richmond evacuated—U. S. troops in possession.
5	Sun	5 39	6 27	Easter Sunday.
6	Mo.	5 37	6 28	1862, Battle of Shiloh.
7	Tu.	5 34	6 29	
8	We.	5 33	6 30	1866, Civil war closed: date of Proc. by Pres. declari'g war end'd.
9	Th.	5 32	6 31	1865, Gen. R. E. Lee surrendered to Gen. Grant at Appo. C. H.
10	Fr.	5 30	6 32	1858, Thomas H. Benton died.
11	Sat.	5 29	6 32	1865, Gen. Stoneman occupied Salisbury.
12	Sun	5 27	6 33	1777, Henry Clay born.
13	Mo.	5 26	6 33	1865, Gen. Sherman with U. S. army occupy Raleigh.
14	Tu.	5 25	6 34	1861, Fort Sumter taken by Confederates.
15	We.	5 25	6 35	1865, Abraham Lincoln died—shot by Booth.
16	Th.	5 24	6 36	1861, Virginia secedes from Union.
17	Fr.	5 22	6 36	1654, Shakespeare born.
18	Sat.	5 21	6 37	1847, Battle of Cerro Gordo.
19	Sun	5 20	6 38	
20	Mo.	5 19	6 39	1861, Civil war opened—date of Proclamation as to blockade.
21	Tu.	5 18	6 40	1836, Gov. H. G. Burton died.
22	We.	5 16	6 40	1867, R. M. Saunders died.
23	Th.	5 15	6 41	1861, U. S. Branch Mint at Charlotte seized by Confederates.
24	Fr.	5 14	6 42	1828, Gen. R. B. Vance born.
25	Sat.	5 13	6 43	
26	Sun	5 12	6 44	1865, Johnson surrendered.
27	Mo.	5 10	6 45	1822, U. S. Grant born.
28	Tu.	5 09	6 45	1870, Capitol floor at Richmond fell. Many killed.
29	We.	5 09	6 46	1871, Gov. Charles Manly died.
30	Th.	5 08	6 46	1789, Washington inaugurated as President of United States.

MAY.

Days of Mo.	Days of Wk	Sun Rises.	Sun Sets.	CHRONOLOGICAL EVENTS.
1	Fr.	5 07	6 47	
2	Sa.	5 06	6 48	
3	Sun	5 05	6 48	Fourth Sunday after Easter.
4	Mo.	5 04	6 49	1873, Jas. L. Orr died in Russia.
5	Tu.	5 03	6 50	1854, Missouri compromise repealed.
6	We.	5 02	6 51	1861, Tennessee and Arkansas secede from Union.
7	Th.	5 01	6 52	1849, Charles Fisher died ; 1873, Judge Chase died.
8	Fr.	5 00	6 52	1845, General Jackson died ; 1846, Battle of Palo Alto.
9	Sa.	5 00	6 53	
10	Sun	4 58	6 54	1865, Jefferson Davis taken prisoner in Georgia.
11	Mo.	4 57	6 55	1866, George E. Badger died.
12	Tu.	4 56	6 56	1780, Charleston surrendered ; 1865, Jas. C. Johnston died.
13	We.	4 56	6 56	1846, War declared to exist between U. S. and Mexico.
14	Th.	4 55	6 57	
15	Fr.	4 54	6 58	1873, Court House of Washington County burnt.
16	Sa.	4 53	6 59	1771, Battle of Alamance.
17	Sun	4 53	7 00	1870, John H. Bryan died at Raleigh.
18	Mo.	4 53	7 00	1868, Impeachment against Andrew Johnson failed.
19	Tu.	4 52	7 01	1847, Treaty of Peace with Mexico.
20	We.	4 51	7 02	1775, Dec. of Ind. at Charlotte ; 1861, N. C. seceded.
21	Th.	4 50	7 03	1865, W. W. Holden appointed Provisional Governor of N. C.
22	Fr.	4 50	7 04	1865, Governors Vance and Letcher prisoners.
23	Sa.	4 49	7 05	
24	Sun	4 49	7 05	
25	Mo.	4 48	7 06	
26	Tu.	4 48	7 07	
27	We.	4 48	7 08	1844, First Telegraph sent in U. S. from Balt. to Washington.
28	Th.	4 47	7 09	
29	Fr.	4 46	7 09	1790, Rhode Island ratifies U. S. Constitution (last State.)
30	Sa.	4 46	7 09	
31	Sun	4 46	7 09	Trinity Sunday.

JUNE.

Days of Mo.	Days of Wk.	Sun Rises.	Sun Sets.	CHRONOLOGICAL EVENTS.
1	Mo.	4 44	7 12	1862, Battle of Seven Pines; 1864, Battle of Cold Harbor.
2	Tu.	4 44	7 11	1868, James Buchanan died.
3	We.	4 44	7 11	1861, Stephen A. Douglas died.
4	Th.	4 43	7 11	1845, War declared against Mexico.
5	Fr.	4 43	7 12	
6	Sa.	4 43	7 13	
7	Sun	4 43	7 14	First Sunday after Trinity.
8	Mo.	4 43	7 14	1867, Gen. William A. Blount died at Raleigh.
9	Tu.	4 43	7 15	
10	We.	4 43	7 15	1861, Battle of Bethel; 1869, Pacific Railroad completed.
11	Th.	4 43	7 16	
12	Fr.	4 43	7 16	1831, Capitol at Raleigh burnt by accident.
13	Sa.	4 43	7 17	
14	Sun	4 43	7 17	Second Sunday after Trinity.
15	Mo.	4 43	7 17	1849, James K. Polk died.
16	Tu.	4 43	7 18	1871, Jas. B. Shepard, of Raleigh, died; 1826, Hon J. Pool born.
17	We.	4 44	7 18	1775, Battle of Bunker Hill.
18	Th.	4 44	7 18	1812, War declared against England; 1815, Battle of Waterloo.
19	Fr.	4 44	7 18	1867, Maximilian shot in Mexico.
20	Sa.	4 44	7 18	
21	Sun	4 45	7 18	Third Sunday after Trinity.
22	Mo.	4 45	7 19	1780, Battle at Ramsour's Mill, near Lincolnton.
23	Tu.	4 45	7 19	1807, The British ship Leopard fires into U. S. ship Chesapeake.
24	We.	4 45	7 19	
25	Th.	4 46	7 19	1870, Hon. David Heaton died.
26	Fr.	4 46	7 19	
27	Sa.	4 46	7 19	1857, Dr. Elisha Mitchell died.
28	Sun	4 47	7 19	1778, Battle of Monmouth.
29	Mo.	4 47	7 19	1852, Henry Clay died; 1837, Nathaniel Macon died.
30	Tu.	4 48	7 19	1868, Hon. J. R. J. Daniel died.

JULY.

Days of Mo.	Days of Wk	Sun Rises.		Sun Sets.		CHRONOLOGICAL EVENTS.
1	We.	4	48	7	19	1778, Constitution of United States rejected by N. C.
2	Th.	4	49	7	19	1690, Battle of the Boyne.
3	Fr.	4	49	7	19	1862, Col Stokes died at Richmond of wounds received in battle.
4	Sa.	4	50	7	19	1584, First landing of English in America on Roanoke Island.
5	Sun	4	50	7	19	1826, Adams and Jefferson died.
6	Mo.	4	51	7	18	1831, Munroe died.
7	Tu.	4	51	7	18	
8	We.	4	52	7	18	1792, Washington City selected as the Capiatl of U. S.
9	Th.	4	52	7	18	1850, General Z. Taylor died.
10	Fr.	4	53	7	18	1447, Columbus born.
11	Sa.	4	53	7	17	1804, Alex. Hamilton killed in a duel by Burr.
12	Sun	4	54	7	17	Sixth Sunday after Trinity.
13	Mo.	4	54	7	16	1854, San Juan del Norte, or Greytown, destroyed by Capt. Hol-
14	Tu.	4	55	7	16	[lins of United States frigate Cyane
15	We.	4	56	7	15	
16	Th.	4	57	7	15	
17	Fr.	4	57	7	14	1863, Gen. J. J. Pettigrew died of wounds near Winchester, Va.
18	Sa.	4	58	7	14	
19	Sun	4	59	7	13	Seventh Sunday after Trinity.
20	Mo.	5	00	7	12	1812, Hon. Thos. S. Ashe born.
21	Tu.	5	00	7	12	1861. Battle of Manassas (1st.)
22	We.	5	00	7	11	
23	Th.	5	01	7	11	
24	Fr.	5	02	7	11	1862, Martin Van Buren died.
25	Sa.	5	03	7	09	
26	Sun	5	04	7	08	Eighth Sunday after Trinity.
27	Mo.	5	04	7	08	1866, Atlantic Cable laid.
28	Tu.	5	05	7	07	1863, Battle of Boon's Mills,—Ransom drives back U. S. troops.
29	We.	5	06	7	06	
30	Th.	5	07	7	05	
31	Fr.	5	08	7	04	

AUGUST.

Days of Mo.	Days of Wk	Sun Rises.	Sun Sets.	CHRONOLOGICAL EVENTS.
1	Sa.	5 08	7 04	
2	Sun	5 09	7 03	Ninth Sunday after Trinity.
3	Mo.	5 10	7 02	1834, John Stanly died.
4	Tu.	5 11	7 01	1857, J. C. Dobbin died; 1858, Atlantic Cable landed in U. S.
5	We.	5 12	7 00	
6	Th.	5 12	6 59	
7	Fr.	5 13	6 58	1853, Intense heat in United States; 400 died in New York.
8	Sa.	5 14	6 57	1796, Jay's treaty ratified by Senate.
9	Sun	5 15	6 56	1842, Ashburton Treaty.
10	Mo.	5 16	6 55	
11	Tu.	5 16	6 52	
12	We.	5 17	6 52	1847, Louis D. Wilson died in Mexico.
13	Th.	5 18	6 51	1851, Nicaragua route opened to Pacific.
14	Fr.	5 19	6 50	
15	Sa.	5 20	6 49	1769, Napoleon Bonaparte born.
16	Sun	5 20	6 47	1780, Battle of Camden—Gates defeated by Cornwallis.
17	Mo.	5 21	6 46	1862, Warren Winslow died.
18	Tu.	5 22	6 45	1812, U. S. frigate Constitution captures British frigate Guerrier
19	We.	5 23	6 44	1867, Cable between Cuba and Florida laid.
20	Th.	5 23	6 43	
21	Fr.	5 24	6 41	
22	Sa.	5 24	6 40	1830, Court House in Winton, Hertford Co., N. C. destroyed by
23	Sun	5 25	6 39	[an incendiary.
24	Mo.	5 26	6 38	1814, Washington City taken by the British.
25	Tu.	5 27	6 36	1774, First Legislature in N. C. independent of the Crown.
26	We.	5 28	6 35	1775, Royal Governor Martin retreats from North Carolina.
27	Th.	5 28	6 35	1867, Professor Faraday died; 1866, John M. Morehead died.
28	Fr.	5 29	6 32	1868, David L. Swain died.
29	Sa.	5 30	6 31	
30	Sun	5 31	6 30	Thirteenth Sunday after Trinity.
31	Mo.	5 31	6 28	

SEPTEMBER.

Days of Mo.	Days of Wk	Sun Rises.	Sun Sets.	CHRONOLOGICAL EVENTS.
1	Tu.	5 31	6 27	1873, Hon. D. M. Barringer died.
2	We.	5 33	6 26	
3	Th.	5 33	6 25	1783, England recognizes the Independence of the U. S.
4	Fr.	5 34	6 23	
5	Sa.	5 35	6 22	1802, Gov. Spaight killed at Newbern in a duel, by Jno. Stanly.
6	Sun	5 36	6 20	Fourteenth Sunday after Trinity.
7	Mo.	5 37	6 19	1861, Hon. Willie P. Mangum died.
8	Tu.	5 38	6 17	1781, Battle of Eutaw Springs. 1847, Battle of Molina del Rey.
9	We.	5 39	6 16	1813, Perry's victory on Lake Erie.
10	Th.	5 39	6 14	1869, Hon. John Bell, of Tennessee, died.
11	Fr.	5 40	6 13	1777, Battle of Brandywine.
12	Sa.	5 41	6 11	
13	Sun	5 42	6 10	1781 Gov. Burke seized by Fanning and taken to Br. officers.
14	Mo.	5 42	6 08	1862, Hon. Wm. S. Ashe killed on Rail Road, Wilmington.
15	Tu.	5 43	6 07	1847, City of Mexico taken by U. S. Troops under Scott.
16	We.	5 43	6 05	1834, Hon. A. M. Waddell born.
17	Th.	5 44	6 04	1787, Constitution of United States formed at Philadelphia.
18	Fr.	5 45	6 03	1862, Gen. L. O'B. Branch killed in battle at Sharpsburg.
19	Sat.	5 46	6 01	1872, Mt. Cenis tunnel opened.
20	Sun	5 47	6 00	Sixteenth Sunday after Trinity.
21	Mo.	5 48	5 58	
22	Tu.	5 49	5 55	
23	We.	5 50	5 54	
24	Th.	5 51	5 54	1794, Whiskey insurrection in Pennsylvania.
25	Fr.	5 52	5 54	
26	Sat.	5 53	5 49	
27	Sun	5 53	5 49	Seventeenth Sunday after Trinity.
28	Mo.	5 53	5 48	1830, Hon. A. S. Merrimon born.
29	Tu.	5 54	5 46	1873, Admiral Winslow, United States Navy, died.
30	We.	5 54	5 45	1825, Hon. Sion H. Rogers born.

OCTOBER.

Days of Mo.	Days of Wk	Sun Rises.	Sun Sets.	CHRONOLOGICAL EVENTS.
1	Th.	5 56	5 42	1873, Water Works organized in Wilmington.
2	Fr.	5 57	5 41	1860, Prince of Wales at Washington.
3	Sat.	5 58	5 39	1780, Major Andre hung at Tappan.
4	Sun	5 59	5 38	1777, battle of Germantown; Gen. Nash killed.
5	Mo.	6 00	5 36	1826, Hon. Matt. W. Ransom born.
6	Tu.	6 01	5 35	
7	We.	6 02	5 34	1780, Battle of King's Mountain.
8	Th.	6 02	5 34	1869, Franklin Pierce died; 1872, Chicago fire.
9	Fr.	6 02	5 32	1872, W. H. Seward died. 1868, Howell Cobb died.
10	Sat.	6 03	5 31	1868, Jesse A. Bynum died.
11	Sun	6 04	5 29	1492, America discovered by Columbus.
12	Mo.	6 05	5 28	
13	Tu.	6 06	5 27	
14	We	6 07	5 25	1841, Gov. Owen died.
15	Th.	6 08	5 24	
16	Fr.	6 09	5 22	1870, Robt. B. Gilliam, of Granville, died.
17	Sat	6 10	5 21	
18	Sun	6 11	5 20	1781, battle of Yorktown.
19	Mo.	6 12	5 19	1864, Gen. S. D. Ramsour died of wounds received at Cedar Ck.
20	Tu.	6 13	5 17	1861, battle of Edward's Ferry, Va., Gen. Baker killed.
21	We.	6 14	5 16	1868, Hon. David Outlaw, of Bertie, died.
22	Th.	6 15	5 15	
23	Fr.	6 16	5 14	
24	Sat.	6 16	5 12	1852, Daniel Webster died.
25	Sun	6 17	5 11	
26	Mo.	6 18	5 10	1828, Hon. W. M. Robbins born.
27	Tu.	6 19	5 09	1866, Francis L. Hawks died.
28	We.	6 20	5 08	1871, Thos. Ewing, of Ohio, died; 1861, Missouri seceded.
29	Th.	6 21	5 07	1857, Wm. Hill, Secretary of State, died.
30	Fr.	6 21	5 06	1861, First telegram from Atlantic to Pacific.
31	Sat.	6 22	5 05	

NOVEMBER.

Days of Mo.	Days of Wk.	Sun Rises.	Sun Sets.	CHRONOLOGICAL EVENTS.
1	Sun	6 23	5 04	
2	Mo.	6 24	5 03	1795, Jas. K. Polk born in N. C.
3	Tu.	6 25	5 02	
4	We.	6 26	5 01	
5	Th.	6 27	5 00	1872, Thomas Sully died.
6	Fr.	6 28	4 59	
7	Sat.	6 29	4 58	
8	Sun	6 30	4 57	
9	Mo.	6 31	4 57	
10	Tu.	6 32	4 56	1865, Wirtz hung in Washingtou for treason.
11	We.	6 33	4 55	1836, Gen. Joseph Graham died.
12	Th.	6 34	4 54	1865, Preston King, of New York, commits suicide.
13	Fr.	6 35	4 54	
14	Sat.	6 36	4 53	
15	Sun	6 37	4 53	
16	Mo.	6 38	4 52	
17	Tu.	6 39	4 51	1861, U. S. steamer San Jacinto, Capt. Wilkes, arrived at Fort[ress Monro, with Mason and Slidell, prisoners on board.
18	We	6 40	4 51	
19	Th.	6 41	4 50	1873, Hon. Nathaniel Boyden died.
20	Fri.	6 42	4 50	1861, Kentucky seceded.
21	Sat.	6 43	4 49	1789, N. C. ratifies the Constitution of the United States.
22	Sun	6 44	4 49	1800, Congress met at Washington for first time.
23	Mo.	6 45	4 48	
24	Tu.	6 46	4 48	
25	We	6 47	4 47	
26	Th.	6 48	4 46	
27	Fri.	6 49	4 45	
28	Sat.	6 50	4 43	
29	Sun	6 51	4 42	
30	Mo.	6 52	4 41	

DECEMBER.

Days of Mo.	Days of Wk	Sun Rises.	Sun Sets.	CHRONOLOGICAL EVENTS.
1	Tu.	6 53	4 46	Annual meeting of the Grand Lodge, of N. C.
2	We.	6 54	4 46	1859, John Brown hung at Harper's Ferry, Va.
3	Th.	6 55	4 46	1805, Battle of Austerlitz.
4	Fri.	6 55	4 46	1873, Gen. Alfred Dockery died.
5	Sat.	6 56	4 46	
6	Sun	6 57	4 46	1870, Hon. Bedford Brown died.
7	Mo.	6 58	4 46	1787, Delaware ratifies U. S. Constitution, (first State.)
8	Tu.	6 59	4 46	1848, First gold deposited in Mint from California.
9	We.	6 59	4 47	1775, Battle of Great Bridge, near Norfolk, Va.
10	Th.	7 00	4 47	1787, Pennsylvania ratifies the Constitution.
11	Fri.	7 01	4 47	1776, Constitution of North Carolina formed at Halifax.
12	Sat.	7 02	4 47	1873, Edwin Forrest died.
13	Sun	7 03	4 47	1814, Hartford Convention met.
14	Mo.	7 04	4 47	1799, Washington died.
15	Tu.	7 04	4 48	
16	We.	7 04	4 48	1862, Battle of Goldsboro', Clingman drives Foster back.
17	Th.	7 05	4 48	1830, Bolivar died.
18	Fri.	7 06	4 49	1865, Hon. Thomas Corwin, of Ohio, died.
19	Sat.	7 06	4 49	1787, New Jersey ratifies the Constitution of United States.
20	Sun	7 07	4 50	1857, Gen. David Newland, of Burke, committed suicide.
21	Mo.	7 07	4 51	1620, Pilgrims land at Plymouth.
22	Tu.	7 07	4 51	1860, South Carolina secedes from the Union.
23	We.	7 08	4 52	1807, Embargo laid in United States.
24	Th.	7 08	4 52	1814, Treaty of Ghent.
25	Fri.	7 09	4 53	1851, Library of Congress burnt. Christmas.
26	Sat.	7 09	4 54	
27	Sun	7 10	4 54	1776, Battle of Trenton.
28	Mo.	7 10	4 55	
29	Tu.	7 10	4 55	
30	We.	7 11	4 55	
31	Th.	7 11	4 56	1775, battle of Quebec; Montgomery killed.

NO. II.

Constitution of the United States.

CONSTITUTION.

WE, the people of the United States, in order to form a more perfect union, establish justice, insure domestic tranquility, provide for the common defense, promote the general welfare, and secure the blessings of liberty to ourselves and our posterity, do ordain and establish this Constitution for the United States of America.

ARTICLE I.

SECTION 1. All legislative powers herein granted shall be vested in a Congress of the United States, which shall consist of a Senate and House of Representatives.

SECTION 2. The House of Representatives shall be composed of members chosen every second year by the people of the several States, and the electors in each State shall have the qualifications requisite for electors of the most numerous branch of the State Legislature.

No person shall be a representative who shall not have attained the age of twenty-five years, and been seven years a citizen of the United States, and who shall not, when elected, be an inhabitant of that State in which he shall be chosen.

Representatives and direct taxes shall be apportioned among the several States which may be included within this Union, according to their respective numbers, which shall be determined by adding to the whole number of free persons, including those bound to service for a term of years, and excluding Indians not taxed, three-fifths of all other persons. The actual enumeration shall be made within three years after the first meeting of the Congress of the United States, and within every subsequent term of ten years, in such manner as they shall by law direct. The number of Representatives shall not exceed one for every thirty thousand, but each State shall have at least one Representative; and until such enumeration shall be made, the State of *New Hampshire* shall be entitled to choose three, *Massachusetts* eight, *Rhode Island and Providence Plantations* one, *Connecticut* five, *New York* six, *New Jersey* four, *Pennsylvania* eight, *Delaware* one, *Maryland* six, *Virginia* ten, *North Carolina* five, *South Carolina* five, and *Georgia* three.

When vacancies happen in the representation from any State, the executive authority thereof shall issue writs of election to fill such vacancies.

The House of Representatives shall choose their Speaker and other officers, and shall have the sole power of impeachment.

SECTION 3. The Senate of the United States shall be composed of two Senators from each State, chosen by the Legislature thereof, for six years; and each Senator shall have one vote.

Immediately after they shall be assembled in consequence of the first election, they shall be divided as equally as may be into three classes. The seats of the

Senators of the first class shall be vacated at the expiration of the second year: of the second class, at the expiration of the fourth year, and of the third class, at the expiration of the sixth year, so that one-third may be chosen every second year; and if vacancies happen by resignation or otherwise, during the recess of the Legislature of any State, the executive thereof may make temporary appointments until the next meeting of the legislature, which shall then fill such vacancies.

No person shall be a Senator, who shall not have attained to the age of thirty years, and been nine years a citizen of the United States, and who shall not, when elected, be an inhabitant of that State for which he shall be chosen.

The Vice President of the United States shall be president of the Senate, but shall have no vote unless they be equally divided.

The Senate shall choose their other officers, and also a President *pro tempore* in the absence of the Vice President, or when he shall exercise the office of President of the United States.

The Senate shall have the sole power to try all impeachments. When sitting for that purpose, they shall be on oath or affirmation. When the President of the United States is tried, the Chief Justice shall preside; and no person shall be convicted without the concurrence of two-thirds of the members present.

Judgment in cases of impeachment shall not extend further than to removal from office, and disqualification to hold and enjoy any office of honor, trust or profit under the United States: but the party convicted shall nevertheless be liable and subject to indictment, trial, judgment and punishment, according to law.

SECTION 4. The times, places, and manner of holding elections for Senators and Representatives shall be prescribed in each State by the legislature thereof; but the Congress may at any time by law make or alter such regulations, except as to the places of choosing Senators.

The Congress shall assemble at least once in every year, and such meeting shall be on the first Monday in December, unless they shall by law appoint a different day.

SECTION 5. Each house shall be the judge of the elections, returns, and qualification of its own members, and a majority of each shall constitute a quorum to do business; but a smaller number may adjourn from day to day, and may be authorized to compel the attendance of absent members, in such manner and under such penalties, as each house may provide.

Each house may determine the rules of its proceedings, punish its members for disorderly behavior, and with the concurrence of two-thirds, expel a member.

Each House shall keep a journal of its proceedings, and from time to time publish the same, excepting such parts as may in their judgment require secrecy, and the yeas and nays of the members of either house on any question shall, at the desire of one-fifth of those present, be entered on the journal.

Neither house, during the session of Congress, shall without the consent of the other, adjourn for more than three days, nor to any other place than that in which the two houses shall be sitting.

SECTION 6. The Senators and Representatives shall receive a compensation for their services, to be ascertained by law, and paid out of the Treasury of the United States. They shall in all cases except treason, felony and breach of the peace, be privileged from arrest during their attendance at the session of their respective houses, and in going to and returning from the same; and for any speech or debate in either house, they shall not be questioned in any other place.

No Senator or Representative shall, during the time for which he was elected, be appointed to any civil office under the authority of the United States, which shall have been created, or the emoluments whereof shall have been increased during such time; and no person holding any office under the United States, shall be a member of either house during his continuance in office.

SECTION 7. All bills for raising revenue shall originate in the House of Representatives; but the Senate may propose or concur with amendments as on other bills.

Every bill which shall have passed the House of Representatives and the Senate, shall, before it become a law, be presented to the President of the United States; if he approve he shall sign it, but if not he shall return it, with his objections to that house in which it shall have originated, who shall enter the objections at large on their journal, and proceed to reconsider it. If after such reconsideration two-thirds of that house shall agree to pass the bill, it shall be sent, together with the objections, to the other house, by which it shall likewise be reconsidered, and if approved by two-thirds of that house, it shall become a law. But in all cases the votes of both houses shall be determined by yeas and nays, and the names of the persons voting for and against the bill shall be entered on the journal of each house respectively. If any bill shall not be returned by the President within ten days (Sundays excepted) after it shall have been presented to him, the same shall be a law, in like manner as if he had signed it, unless the Congress by their adjournment prevent its return, in which case it shall not be a law.

Every order, resolution, or vote to which the concurrence of the Senate and House of Representatives may be necessary (except on a question of adjournment) shall be presented to the President of the United States; and before the same shall take effect, shall be approved by him, or being disapproved by him, shall be repassed by two-thirds of the Senate and House of Representatives, according to the rules and limitations prescribed in the case of a bill.

SECTION 8. The Congress shall have power to lay and collect taxes, duties, imposts and excises, to pay the debts and provide for the common defense and general welfare of the United States; but all duties, imposts and excises shall be uniform throughout the United States:

To borrow money on the credit of the United States;

To regulate commerce with foreign nations, and among the several States, and with the Indian tribes;

To establish an uniform rule of naturalization, and uniform laws on the subject of bankruptcies throughout the United States;

To coin money, to regulate the value thereof, and of foreign coin, and fix the standard of weights and measures;

To provide for the punishment of counterfeiting the securities and current coin of the United States;

To establish post offices and post roads;

To promote the progress of science and useful arts, by securing for limited times to authors and inventors the exclusive right to their respective writings and discoveries;

To constitute tribunals inferior to the Supreme Court;

To define and punish piracies and felonies committed on the high seas, and offences against the law of nations;

To declare war, grant letters of marque and reprisal, and make rules concerning captures on land and water;

To raise and support armies, but no appropriation of money to that use shall be for a longer term than two years;

To provide and maintain a navy;

To make rules for the government and regulation of the land and naval forces;

To provide for calling forth the militia to execute the laws of the Union, suppress insurrections and repel invasions;

To provide for organizing, arming and disciplining the militia, and for governing such part of them as may be employed in the service of the United States, reserving to the States respectively, the appointment of the officers, and the authority of training the militia according to the discipline prescribed by Congress;

To exercise exclusive legislation in all cases whatsoever, over such district (not exceeding ten miles square) as may, by cession of particular States, and the acceptance of Congress, become the seat of government of the United States, and to exercise like authority over all places purchased by the consent of the legislature of the State in which the same shall be, for the erection of forts, magazines, arsenals, dockyards, and other needful buildings;—and

To make all laws which shall be necessary and proper for carrying into execution the foregoing powers, and all other powers vested by this Constitution in the Government of the United States, or in any department or officer thereof.

SECTION 9. The migration or importation of such persons as any of the States now existing shall think proper to admit, shall not be prohibited by the Congress prior to the year one thousand eight hundred and eight, but a tax or duty may be imposed on such importation, not exceeding ten dollars for each person.

The privilege of the writ of habeas corpus shall not be suspended, unless when in cases of rebellion or invasion the public safety may require it.

No bill of attainder or ex post facto law shall be passed.

No capitation, or other direct tax shall be laid, unless in proportion to the census or enumeration hereinbefore directed to be taken.

No tax or duty shall be laid on articles exported from any State.

No preference shall be given by any regulation of commerce or revenue to the ports of one State over those of another; nor shall vessels bound to, or from one State, be obliged to enter, clear, or pay duties in another.

No money shall be drawn from the treasury, but in consequence of appropriations made by law; and a regular statement and account of the receipts and expenditures of all public money shall be published from time to time.

No title of nobility shall be granted by the United States; and no person holding an office of profit or trust under them, shall, without the consent of the Congress, accept of any present, emolument, office, or title of any kind whatever, from any king, prince, or foreign State.

SECTION 10. No state shall enter into any treaty, alliance, or confederation; grant letters of marque and reprisal; coin money: emit bills of credit; make anything but gold and silver coin a tender in payment of debts; pass any bill of attainder, ex post facto law, or law impairing the obligation of contracts, or grant any title of nobility.

No State shall, without the consent of the Congress, lay any imposts or duties on imports or exports, except what may be absolutely necessary for executing its inspection laws; and the net produce of all duties and imposts, laid by any State on imports or exports, shall be for the use of the treasury of the United States; and all such laws shall be subject to the revision and control of the Congress.

No State shall, without the consent of Congress, lay any duty of tonnage, keep troops or ships of war in time of peace, enter into any agreement or compact with another State, or with a foreign power, or engage in war, unless actually invaded, or in such imminent danger as will not admit of delay.

ARTICLE II.

SECTION 1. The executive power shall be vested in a President of the United States of America. He shall hold his office during the term of four years, and together with the Vice President, chosen for the same term, be elected as follows:

Each State shall appoint, in such manner as the legislature thereof may direct, a number of electors, equal to the whole number of Senators and Representatives to which the State may be entitled in the Congress; but no Senator or Representative, or person holding an office of trust or profit under the United States shall be appointed an elector.

The electors shall meet in their respective States, and vote by ballot for two persons, of whom one at least shall not be an inhabitant of the same State with themselves. And they shall make a list of all the persons voted for, and of the number of votes for each; which list they shall sign and certify, and transmit, sealed, to the seat of the government of the United States, directed to the President of the Senate. The President of the Senate shall, in the presence of the Senate and House of Representatives, open all the certificates, and the votes shall then be counted. The person having the greatest number of votes shall be the President, if such number be a majority of the whole number of electors appointed; and if there be more than one who have such a majority, and have an equal number of votes, then the House of Representatives shall immediately choose by ballot one of them President; and if no person have a majority, then from the five highest on the list the said House shall in like manner choose the President. But in choosing the President, the votes shall be taken by States, the representation from each State having one vote; a quorum for this purpose shall consist of a member or members from two-thirds of the States, and a majority of all the States shall be necessary to a choice. In every case, after the choice of the President, the person having the greatest number of votes of the electors, shall be the Vice President. But if there should remain two or more who have equal votes, the Senate shall choose from them by ballot the Vice President.*

The Congress may determine the time of choosing the electors, and the day on which they shall give their votes; which day shall be the same throughout the United States.

No person except a natural born citizen, or a citizen of the United States, at

*This clause of the Constitution has been amended. See 12th article of the amendments.

the time of the adoption of this Constitution shall be eligible to the office of President; neither shall any person be eligible to that office, who shall not have attained to the age of thirty-five years, and been fourteen years a resident within the United States.

In case of the removal of the President from office, or of his death, resignation, or inability to discharge the powers and duties of the said office, the same shall devolve on the Vice President, and the Congress may by law provide for the case of removal, death, resignation or inability both of the President and Vice President, declaring what officer shall then act as President, and such officer shall act accordingly, until the disability be removed, or a President shall be elected.

The President shall, at stated times, receive for his service a compensation which shall be neither increased nor diminished during the period for which he shall have been elected, and he shall not receive within that period any other emolument from the United States, or any of them.

Before he enter on the execution of his office, he shall take the following oath or affirmation:

"I do solemnly swear (or affirm) that I will faithfully execute the office of President of the United States, and will, to the best of my ability, preserve, protect, and defend the constitution of the United States."

SECTION 2. The President shall be commander-in-chief of the army and navy of the United States, and of the militia of the several States, when called into the actual service of the United States; he may require the opinion, in writing, of the principal officer in each of the executive departments, upon any subject relating to the duties of their respective offices, and he shall have power to grant reprieves and pardons for offenses against the United States, except in cases of impeachment.

He shall have power, by and with the advice and consent of the Senate, to make treaties, provided two-thirds of the senators present concur; and he shall nominate, and by and with the advice and consent of the Senate, shall appoint ambassadors, other public ministers and consuls, judges of the Supreme Court, and all other officers of the United States, whose appointments are not herein otherwise provided for, and which shall be established by law; but the Congress may by law vest the appointment of such inferior officers as they may think proper, in the President alone, in the courts of law or in the heads of departments.

The President shall have power to fill up all vacancies that may happen during the recess of the Senate, by granting commissions which shall expire at the end of their next session.

SECTION 3. He shall from time to time give to the Congress information of the state of the Union, and recommend to their consideration such measures as he shall judge necessary and expedient; he may on extraordinary occasions, convene both houses or either of them, and in case of disagreement between them, with respect to the time of adjournment, he may adjourn them to such time as he shall think proper; he shall receive ambassadors and other public ministers; he shall take care that the laws be faithfully executed, and shall commission all of the officers of the United States.

SECTION 4. The President, Vice President, and all civil officers of the United States, shall be removed from office on impeachment for, and conviction of treason, bribery, or other high crimes and misdemeanors.

ARTICLE III.

SECTION 1. The judicial power of the United States shall be vested in one Supreme Court, and in such inferior courts as the Congress may from time to time ordain and establish. The judges both of the supreme and inferior courts, shall hold their offices during good behavior, and shall at stated times receive for their services a compensation which shall not be diminished during their continuance in office.

SECTION 2. The judicial power shall extend to all cases, in law and equity, arising under this Constitution, the laws of the United States, and treaties made or which shall be made, under their authority; to all cases affecting ambassadors, other public ministers, and consuls; to all cases of admiralty and maritime jurisdiction; to controversies to which the United States shall be a party; to controversies between two or more States; between a State and citizens of another State; between citizens of different States; between citizens of the same State claiming lands under grants of different States, and between a State or the citizens thereof, and foreign States, citizens or subjects.

In all cases affecting ambassadors, other public ministers and consuls, and those in which a State shall be a party, the Supreme Court shall have original jurisdiction. In all the other cases before mentioned, the Supreme Court shall have appellate jurisdiction, both as to law and fact; with such exceptions, and under such regulations as the Congress shall make.

The trial of all crimes, except in cases of impeachment, shall be by jury; and such trial shall be held in the State where the said crimes shall have been committed; but when not committed within any State, the trial shall be at such place or places as the Congress may by law have directed.

SECTION 3. Treason against the United States shall consist only in levying war against them, or in adhering to their enemies, giving them aid and comfort. No person shall be convicted of treason unless on the testimony of two witnesses to the same overt act, or on confession in open court.

The Congress shall have power to declare the punishment of treason, but no attainder of treason shall work corruption of blood or forfeiture except during the life of the person attainted.

ARTICLE IV.

SECTION 1. Full faith and credit shall be given in each State to the public acts, records, and judicial proceedings of every other State. And the Congress may by general laws prescribe the manner in which such acts, records and proceedings shall be proved, and the effect thereof.

SECTION 2. The citizens of each State shall be entitled to all privileges and immunities of citizens in the several States.

A person charged in any State with treason, felony, or other crime, who shall flee from justice, and be found in another State, shall, on demand of the executive authority of the State from which he fled, be delivered up, to be removed to the State having jurisdiction of the crime.

No person held to service or labor in one State, under the laws thereof, escaping into another, shall, in consequence of any law or regulation therein, be discharged from such service or labor, but shall be delivered up on claim of the party to whom such service or labor may be due.

SECTION 3. New States may be admitted by the Congress into this Union; but no new State shall be formed or erected within the jurisdiction of any other State; nor any State be formed by the junction of two or more States, or part of States, without the consent of the legislatures of the States concerned as well as of the Congress.

The Congress shall have power to dispose of and make all needful rules and regulations respecting the territory or other property belonging to the United States; and nothing in this Constitution shall be so construed as to prejudice any claims of the United States, or of any particular State.

SECTION 4. The United States shall guaranty to every State in this Union a republican form of government, and shall protect each of them against invasion, and on application of the legislature, or of the executive, (when the legislature cannot be convened,) against domestic violence.

ARTICLE V.

The Congress, whenever two-thirds of both houses shall deem it necessary, shall propose amendments to this Constitution, or, on the application of the legislatures of two-thirds of the several States, shall call a convention for proposing amendments, which in either case, shall be valid to all intents and purposes, as part of this Constitution, when ratified by the legislatures of three-fourths of the several States, or by conventions in three-fourths thereof, as the one or the other mode of ratification may be proposed by the Congress; provided that no amendment which may be made prior to the year one thousand eight hundred and eight, shall in any manner affect the first and fourth clauses in the ninth section of the first article; and that no State, without its consent, shall be deprived of its equal suffrage in the Senate.

ARTICLE VI.

All debts contracted and engagements entered into, before the adoption of this Constitution, shall be as valid against the United States under this Constitution, as under the confederation.

This Constitution, and the laws of the United States which shall be made in pursuance thereof, and all treaties made, or which shall be made, under the authority of the United States, shall be the supreme law of the land; and the judges in every State shall be bound thereby, anything in the Constitution or laws of any State to the contrary notwithstanding.

The Senators and Representatives before mentioned, and the members of the several State legislatures, and all executive and judicial officers, both of the United States and of the several States, shall be bound by oath or affirmation, to support this Constitution; but no religious test shall ever be required as a qualification to any office or public trust under the United States.

ARTICLE VII.

The ratification of the conventions of nine States shall be sufficient for the establishment of this Constitution between the States so ratifying the same.

Done in convention by the unanimous consent of the States present, the seventeenth day of September in the year of our Lord one thousand seven hundred and eighty-seven, and of the independence of the United States of America the twelfth. In witness whereof we have hereunto subscribed our names.

GEO. WASHINGTON,
Presid't and deputy from Virginia.

NEW HAMPSHIRE.
JOHN LANGDON,
NICHOLAS GILMAN,

MASSACHUSETTS.
NATHANIEL GORHAM,
RUFUS KING.

CONNECTICUT.
WM. SAML. JOHNSON,
ROGER SHERMAN,

NEW YORK.
ALEXANDER HAMILTON.

NEW JERSEY.
WIL. LIVINGSTON,
DAVID BREARLEY,
WM. PATERSON,
JONA. DAYTON.

PENNSYLVANIA.
B. FRANKLIN,
THOMAS MIFFLIN,
ROBT. MORRIS,
GEO. CLYMER,
THOS. FITZSIMONS,
JARED INGERSOLL,
JAMES WILSON,
GOUV. MORRIS.

DELAWARE.
GEO. READ,
GUNNING BEDFORD, JR.,
JOHN DICKINSON,
RICHARD BASSET,
JACO. BROOM.

MARYLAND.
JAMES McHENRY,
DAN. OF ST. THOMAS JENIFER.
DANL. CARROLL.

VIRGINIA.
JOHN BLAIR,
JAMES MADISON, JR.

NORTH CAROLINA.
WM. BLOUNT,
RICH'D DOBBS SPAIGHT,
HU. WILLIAMSON.

SOUTH CAROLINA.
J. RUTLEGE.
CHAS. COATESWORTH PINCKNEY,
CHARLES PINCKNEY,
PIERCE BUTLER.

GEORGIA.
WILLIAM FEW,
ABR. BALDWIN.

Attest: WILLIAM JACKSON, *Secretary.*

AMENDMENTS.

[The following amendments were proposed at the first session of the first Congress of the United States, which was begun and held at the city of New York, on the 4th of March, 1789, and were adopted by the requisite number of States.—1 vol. Laws of U. S., p. 72.]

[The preamble and resolution following, preceded the original proposition of the amendments, and, as they have been supposed by a high equity judge, (8 Wendell's reports, p. 100,) to have an important bearing on the construction of those amendments, they are here inserted. They will be found in the journals of the first session of the first Congress.

Congress of the United States, begun and held at the city of New York, on Wednesday, the 4th of March, 1789. The conventions of a number of the States having, at the time of their adopting the Constitution, expressed a desire, in order to prevent misconstruction or abuses of its powers, that further declaratory and restrictive clauses should be added; and as extending the ground of public confidence in the government, will best insure the beneficent ends of its institution,—

RESOLVED, By the Senate and House of Representatives of the United States of America, in Congress assembled, two-thirds of both houses concurring, that the following articles be proposed to the legislatures of the several States, as amendments to the constitution of the United States, all or any of which articles, when ratified by three-fourths of said legislatures, to be valid to all intents and purposes as part of said Constitution, namely:]

ARTICLE I.

Congress shall make no law respecting an establishment of religion, or prohibiting the free exercise thereof; or abridging the freedom of speech, or of the press; or the right of the people peaceably to assemble, and to petition the government for a redress of grievances.

ARTICLE II.

A well regulated militia, being necessary to the security of a free State, the right of the people to keep and bear arms shall not be infringed.

ARTICLE III.

No soldier shall, in time of peace, be quartered in any house, without the consent of the owner, nor in time of war, but in a manner to be prescribed by law.

ARTICLE IV.

The right of the people to be secure in their persons, houses, papers, and effects, against unreasonable searches and seizures, shall not be violated, and no warrants shall issue, but upon probable cause, supported by oath or affirmation, and particularly describing the place to be searched, and the persons or things to be seized.

ARTICLE V.

No person shall be held to answer for a capital, or otherwise infamous crime, unless on a presentment or indictment of a grand jury, except in cases arising in the land or naval forces, or in the militia, when in actual service in time of war or public danger; nor shall any person be subject for the same offense to be twice put in jeopardy of life or limb; nor shall be compelled in any criminal case to be a witness against himself, nor be deprived of life, liberty, or property, without due process of law; nor shall private property be taken for public use, without just compensation.

ARTICLE VI.

In all criminal prosecutions, the accused shall enjoy the right to a speedy and public trial, by an impartial jury of the State and district wherein the crime shall have been committed, which district shall have been previously ascertained by law, and to be informed of the nature and cause of the accusation; to be confronted with the witnesses against him; to have compulsory process for obtaining witnesses in his favor, and to have the assistance of counsel for his defense.

ARTICLE VII.

In suits at common law, where the value in controversy shall exceed twenty dollars, the right of trial by jury shall be preserved, and no fact tried by a jury shall be otherwise re-examined in any court of the United States, than according to the rules of the common law.

ARTICLE VIII.

Excessive bail shall not be required, nor excessive fines imposed, nor cruel and unusual punishments inflicted.

ARTICLE IX.

The enumeration in the Constitution, of certain rights shall not be construed to deny or disparage others retained by the people.

ARTICLE X.

The powers not delegated to the United States by the Constitution, nor prohibited by it to the States, are reserved to the States respectively, or to the people.

[The following amendment was proposed at the second session of the third Congress. It is printed in the laws of the United States, 1st vol., p. 73, as article XI.]

ARTICLE XI.

The judicial power of the United States shall not be construed to extend to any suit in law or equity, commenced or prosecuted against one of the United States by citizens of another State, or by citizens or subjects of any foreign State.

ARTICLE XII.

The electors shall meet in their respective States and vote by ballot for President and Vice President, one of whom, at least, shall not be an inhabitant of the same State with themselves; they shall name in their ballots the person voted for as President, and in distinct ballots the person voted for as Vice President, and they shall make distinct lists of all persons voted for as President, and of all persons voted for as Vice President, and of the number of votes for each; which lists they shall sign and certify, and transmit sealed to the seat of government of the United States, directed to the President of Senate. The President of the Senate shall, in the presence of the Senate and House of Representatives, open all the certificates, and the votes shall then be counted; the person having the greatest number of votes for President shall be the President, if such number be a majority of the whole number of electors appointed; and if no person have such majority, then from the persons having the highest numbers not exceeding three on the list of those voted for as President, the House of Representatives shall choose immediately, by ballot, the President. But in choosing the President, the votes shall be taken by States, the representation from each State having one vote; a quorum for this purpose shall consist of a member or members from two-thirds of the States, and a majority of all the States shall be necessary to a choice. And if the House of Representatives shall not choose a President whenever the right of choice shall devolve upon them, before the fourth day of March, next following, then the Vice President shall act as President, as in the case of the death or other constitutional disability of the President.

The person having the greatest number of votes as Vice President, shall be the Vice President, if such number be a majority of the whole number of electors appointed, and if no person have a majority, then from the two highest numbers on the list, the Senate shall choose the Vice President; a quorum for the purpose shall consist of two-thirds of the whole number of Senators, and a majority of the whole number shall be necessary to a choice. But no person constitutionally ineligible to the office of President shall be eligible to that of Vice President of the United States.

ARTICLE XIII.

SECTION 1. Neither slavery nor involuntary servitude, except as a punishment for crime, whereof the party shall have been duly convicted, shall exist within the United States, or any place subject to their jurisdiction.

SECTION 2. Congress shall have power to enforce this article by appropriate legislation.

ARTICLE XIV.

SECTION 1. All persons born or naturalized in the United States, and subject to the jurisdiction thereof, are citizens of the United States and of the State wherein they reside. No State shall make or enforce any law which shall abridge the privileges or immunities of citizens of the United States, nor shall any State deprive any person of life, liberty or property without due process of law, nor deny to any person within its jurisdiction the equal protection of the laws.

SECTION 2. Representatives shall be apportioned among the several States according to their respective numbers, counting the whole number of persons in each State, excluding Indians not taxed. But when the right to vote at any election for the choice of electors for President and Vice President of the United States, Representatives in Congress, the executive and judicial officers of a State, or the members of the Legislature thereof, is denied to any of the male inhabitants of such State, being twenty-one years of age, and citizens of the United States, or in any way abridged, except for participation in rebellion or other crime, the basis of representation therein shall be reduced in the proportion which the number of male citizens shall bear to the whole number of male citizens twenty-one years of age in such State.

SECTION 3. No person shall be a Senator or Representative in Congress, or elector of President or Vice President, or hold any office, civil or military, under the United States, or under any State, who, having previously taken an oath as a member of Congress, or as an officer of the United States, or as a member of any State Legislature, or as an executive or judicial officer of any State, to support the Constitution of the United States, shall have engaged in insurrection or rebellion against the same, or given aid or comfort to the enemies thereof; but Congress may, by a vote of two-thirds of each House, remove such disability.

SECTION 4. The validity of the public debt of the United States, authorized by law, including debts incurred for payment of pensions and bounties for services in suppressing the insurrection or rebellion, shall not be questioned. But neither the United States nor any State shall assume or pay any debt or obligation incurred in aid of insurrection or rebellion against the United States, or any claim for the loss or emancipation of any slave; but all such debts, obligations and claims shall be held illegal and void.

SECTION 5. The Congress shall have power to enforce, by appropriate legislation, the provisions of this article.

ARTICLE XV.

SECTION 1. The right of the citizens of the United States to vote shall not be denied or abridged by the United States or by any State on account of race, color or previous condition of servitude.

SECTION 2. The Congress shall have power to enforce this article by appropriate legislation.

NO. III.

List of Executive Officers.

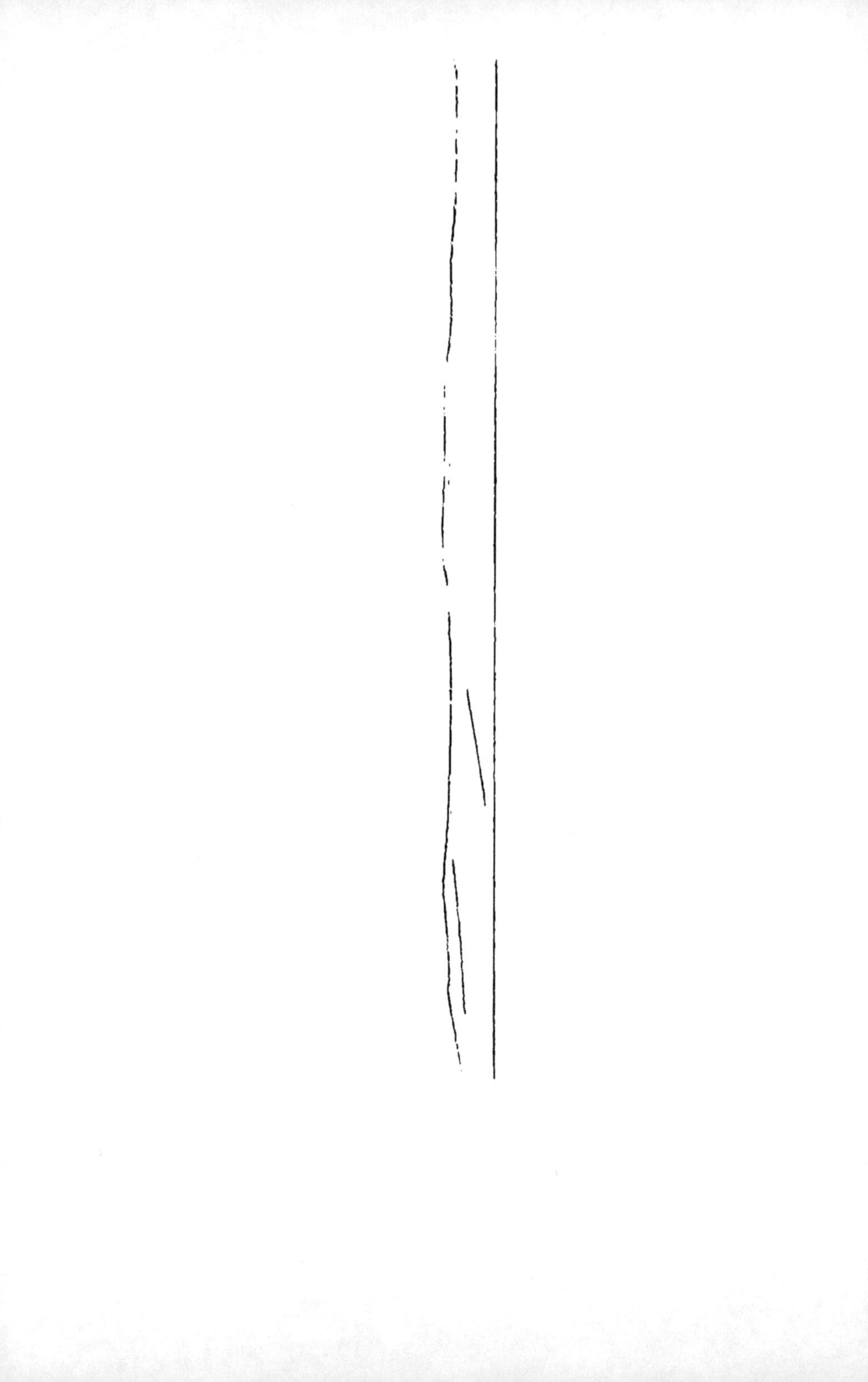

No. IV.

AREA OF EACH STATE IN SQUARE MILES AND POPULATION OF EACH AND EVERY SQUARE MILE.

No.	STATES.	AREA.	POPULATION PER SQUARE MILE.	
1	Alaska	577,390	Massachusetts	157
2	Texas	237,321	Rhode Island	133
3	California	188,982	Connecticut	98
4	Oregon	95,274	New York	84
5	Minnesota	83,531	New Jersey	80
6	Missouri	67,380	Maryland	73
7	Virginia and West Virginia	61,352	Pennsylvania	63
8	Florida	59,268	Ohio	58
9	Georgia	58,000	Delaware	52
10	Michigan	56,243	Indiana	39
11	Illinois	55,405	New Hampshire	35
12	Iowa	55,045	Vermont	34
13	Wisconsin	53,924	Illinois	30
14	Arkansas	52,188	Kentucky	30
15	Alabama	50,722	South Carolina	28
16	Mississippi	47,156	Virginia	26
17	Louisiana	46,413	Tennessee	24
18	New York	46,000	North Carolina	22
19	Pennsylvania	46,000	Maine	20
20	Tennessee	45,509	Alabama	19
21	North Carolina	50,000	Georgia	18
22	Ohio	39,964	Missouri	17
23	Kentucky	37,680	Louisiana	15
24	Indiana	33,809	Wisconsin	14
25	Maine	30,000	Michigan	13
26	South Carolina	24,500	Iowa	12
27	Maryland	9,356	Arkansas	8
28	New Hampshire	9,280	Texas	2
29	Vermont	9,056		
30	New Jersey	8,320		
31	Massachusetts	7,800		
32	Connecticut	4,674		
33	Delaware	2,100		
34	Rhode Island	1,306		

No. V.

RATIO OF REPRESENTATIVES IN CONGRESS.

In 1789 the House, by Constitution, had 65 Members.

DATE.	RATIO.	MEMBERS.
1793	33,000	105
1803	33,000	141
1813	35,000	181
1823	40,000	212
1833	47,000	243
1843	70,000	223
1853	93,000	233
1863	126,000	243
1873	135,000	283

No. VI.

List of Members of the Continental and United States Congress, etc.

LIST OF MEMBERS

OF THE

CONTINENTAL AND U. S. CONGRESS TO DATES WITH BIOGRAPHICAL SKETCHES.

The Continental Congress first met at Philadelphia, September 5th, 1774. In January, 1785, it met at New York, which continued to be the place of meeting until the adoption of the constitution. General Washington was inaugurated President at this place, on 30th April, 1789.

MEMBERS FROM NORTH CAROLINA TO THE CONTINENTAL CONGRESS BEFORE THE ADOPTION OF THE CONSTITUTION.

	From	To
Ashe, John B.	1787	1788
Bloodworth, Timothy	1786	1787
Blount, William	1782	1783
	1786	1787
Burke, Thomas	1777	1781
Burton, Robert	1787	1788
Caswell, Richard	1774	1776
Cumming, William	1784	1784
Harnett, Cornelius	1777	1780
Hawkins, Benjamin	1781	1784
	1786	1787
Hewes, Joseph	1774	1777
	1779	1780
Hill, Whitmill	1778	1781
Hooper, William	1774	1777
Johnston, Samuel	1780	1782
Jones, Allen	1779	1780
Jones, Willie	1780	1781
Nash, Abner	1782	1784
	1785	1786
Penn, John	1775	1776
	1777	1880
Sitgreaves, John	1784	1785
Sharpe, William	1779	1782
Spaight, Richard D.	1783	1785
Swan, John	1787	1788
Williams, John	1778	1779
Williamson, Hugh	1782	1785
	1787	1788
White, Alexander	1786	1788

MEMBERS OF SENATE OF UNITED STATES FROM NORTH CAROLINA.

	In.	Out.
Abbott, Jos. C.	1867	1871
Badger, George E.	1846	1855
Biggs, Asa	1854	1858
Bragg, Thos.	1849	1851
Bloodsworth, Timothy	1795	1801
Branch, John	1823	1829
Brown, Bedford	1829	1841
Clingman, T. L.	1859	1861
Franklin, Jesse	1799	1805
	1807	1813
Graham, William A.	1841	1843
Hawkins, Benjamin	1789	1795
Haywood, William H.	1843	1846
Iredell, James	1828	1831
Johnston, Samuel	1789	1793
Locke, Francis	1814	1815
Macon, Nathaniel	1815	1828
Maugum, W. P.	1831	1837
	1841	1847
	1848	1853
Martin, Alexander	1793	1799
Merrimon, A. S.	1873	1879
Pool, John	1867	1873
Ransom, Matt W.	1872	1877
Reid, D. S.	1854	1859
Stokes, Montfort	1816	1823
Stone, David	1801	1807
	1813	1814
Strange, Robert	1837	1841
Turner, James	1805	1816

MEMBERS OF THE HOUSE OF REPRESENTATIVES FROM N. C.

Name	In.	Out.
Alexander, Evan	1805	1809
Alexander, Nathaniel	1803	1805
Alston, Willis	1799	1803
Alston, Willis, Jr.	1803	1815
	1825	1831
Arrington, A. H.	1841	1845
Ashe, John B.	1790	1793
Ashe, William S.	1849	1853
Ashe, Thos. S.	1873	1875
Biggs, Asa	1845	1847
Barringer, Daniel L.	1826	1835
Barringer, Daniel M.	1843	1849
Bethune, Laughlin	1831	1833
Blackledge, William	1803	1809
	1811	1813
Bleckledge, Wm. S.	1821	1823
Bloodworth, Timothy	1790	1791
Blount, Thomas	1793	1799
	1805	1809
	1811	1812
Boyden, Nathaniel	1847	1849
Branch, John	1831	1833
Branch, L. O'B.	1855	1861
Bryan, Nathan	1795	1798
Bryan, John H.	1825	1829
Bryan, Joseph H.	1815	1819
Burgess, Dempsey	1795	1798
Burton, Hutchins G.	1819	1824
Bynum, Jesse A.	1833	1841
Boyden, Nathaniel	1847	1849
Caldwell, Green W.	1841	1843
Caldwell, Joseph P.	1849	1851
Carson, Samuel P.	1825	1833
Clark, James W.	1815	1817
Clark, Henry S.	1845	1847
Cobb, C. L.	1871	1875
Cocaran, James	1809	1813
Conner, H. W.	1821	1841
Crane, Butler	1853	1861
Crudup, Josiah	1821	1823
Culpepper, John	1807	1809
	1813	1817
	1819	1821
	1823	1825
Clingman, Thomas L.	1843	1845
	1847	1859
Daniel, J. R. J.	1841	1853
Davidson, William	1818	1821
Dawson, William J.	1793	1795
Deweese, J. T.	1867	
Dobbin, James C.	1845	1847
Deberry, Edmund	1829	1831
	1833	1845
	1849	1851
Dockery, Alfred	1845	1847
	1851	1853
Dockery, O. H.	1867	1871
Dickens, Samuel	1816	1817
Donnell, R. S.	1847	1849
Dixon, Joseph	1799	1801
Dixon, Joseph H.	1871	1872

Name	In.	Out.
Dudly, Edward B.	1829	1831
Edwards, Weldon N.	1816	1827
Fisher, Charles	1819	1821
	1839	1841
Forney, Daniel M.	1815	1818
Forney, Peter	1813	1815
Franklin, Jesse,	1795	1797
Franklin, Meshack	1807	1815
French, John R.	1867	1871
Gaston, William	1813	1817
Gatlin, Alfred M.	1823	1825
Gillespie, James	1793	1799
	1803	1805
Gilmer, John A.	1857	1861
Graham, James	1833	1843
	1845	1847
Grove, William B.	1791	1803
Hall, Thomas H.	1817	1825
	1827	1835
Hawkins, M. T.	1831	1841
Heaton, David	1867	
Henderson, Archibald	1799	1803
Hill, John	1839	1841
Hill, William H.	1799	1803
Hines, Richard	1825	1827
Holland, James	1795	1797
	1801	1811
Holmes, Gabriel	1825	1829
Hooks, Charles	1816	1817
	1819	1825
Jones, A. H.	1867	
Johnson, Charles	1801	1802
Kenan, Thomas	1805	1811
Kennedy, William	1803	1805
	1809	1811
	1812	1815
King, William R.	1811	1816
Lash, J. T.	1867	
Leach, Jas. M.	1858	1860
	1869	1875
Lock, Matthew	1793	1799
Long, John	1821	1829
Love, William C.	1815	1817
Macon, Nathaniel	1791	1805
Mangum, W. P.	1823	1826
Manning, John Jr.,	1871	
McBride, Archibald	1809	1813
McDowell, Jos.	1793	1795
	1797	1799
McFarland, Duncan	1805	1807
McKay, James J.	1831	1849
McNeil, Archibald	1821	1823
	1825	1827
Mebane, Alexander	1793	1794
Mitchell, Anderson	1842	1843
Montgomery, William	1835	1841
Momford, George	1817	1819
Morehead, James T.	1851	1853
Murfree, William H.	1813	1817
Outlaw, George	1824	1828
Outlaw, David	1847	1853

HOUSE OF REPRESENTATIVES.—Continued.

Name	In.	Out.
Owen, Jas.	1817	1819
Paine, R. T.	1855	1857
Pettigrew, E.	1835	1837
Pearson, Joseph	1809	1815
Pickens, Israel	1811	1817
Potter, Robert	1829	1831
Puryear, R. C.	1853	1855
Purviance, Samuel D.	1803	1805
Rayner, Kenneth	1839	1845
Reade, E. G.	1855	1857
Rencher, Abraham	1829	1839
	1841	1843
Reid, David S.	1843	1847
Rogers, Sion H.	1853	1855
	1871	1873
Robbins, W. M.	1873	1875
Ruffin, Thos.	1853	1861
Saunders, R. M.	1821	1827
	1841	1845
Sawyer, Lemuel	1807	
	1817	
	1825	
Sawyer, S. T.	1837	1839
Scales, A. M.	1857	1859
Settle, Thomas	1817	1819
Sevier, John	1790	
Shadwick, William	1796	
Shepard, Charles B.	1837	
Sheperd, William B.	1827	
Sheperd, A. H.	1829	
	1841	
	1847	
Shober, F. E.	1869	
Smith, James S.	1817	
Smith, W. A.	1873	
Smith, W. N. H.	1859	1861
Slocumb, Jesse	1817	
Speight, Jesse	1827	
Spaight, R. D.	1798	
Spaight, R. D. Jr.,	1823	
Stanford, Richard	1797	
Stanly, John	1801	
	1809	
Stanly, Edward	1837	
	1849	
Steele, John	1790	
Stewart, James	1818	
Stone, David	1799	
Tatum, Abs.	1795	
Tate, Magnus	1815	
Thomas, Charles R.	1871	1875
Turner, Daniel	1827	
Vance, Robert B.	1812	
Vance, R. B. Jr.,	1873	1875
Vance, Zebulon B.	1858	1861
Venable, Abraham W.	1847	
Waddell, A. M.	1871	1875
Walker, Felix	1817	
Washington, Wm. H.	1841	
Williams, Benjamin	1793	
Williams, Lewis	1815	
Williams, Marmaduke	1803	
Williams, Robert	1797	
Williamson, Hugh	1790	
Winslow, Warren	1855	1861
Winston, Joseph	1793	
	1803	
Wynns, Thomas	1802	
Yancy, Bartlett	1813	

MEMBERS NOW IN CONGRESS, JAN. 1, 1874.

SENATORS.

MATT WHITAKER RANSOM, of Northampton county, (post office, Weldon,) was born in Warren county, North Carolina, in 1826; received an academic education; graduated from the University of North Carolina in 1847; studied law and was admitted to the bar on graduating in 1847; is a lawyer and planter; was elected attorney-general of North Carolina in 1852, and resigned in 1855; was a member of the Legislature of North Carolina in 1858, 1859, and 1860; was a Peace Commissioner from the State of North Carolina to the Congress of Southern States at Montgomery, Alabama, in 1861; entered the confederate army, serving as lieutenant-colonel, colonel, brigadier-general, and major-general, and surrendered at Appomattox; was elected to the United States Senate as a Democrat in January, 1872, and took his seat April 24, 1872. His term of service will expire March 3, 1877.

AUGUSTUS S. MERRIMON, of Raleigh, was born in Buncombe county, on September 30th, 1830; self educated; studied law; admitted to bar in 1852. Elected in 1860 a member of the Legislature, as a whig; solicitor of the 8th circuit in 1862, which he held during the war; in 1866 elected a Judge of the Superior Court, which he soon resigned: in 1872 was the Conservative candidate for Governor of the State; elected in 1872 Senator to Congress for 6 years from March 4, 1873.

REPRESENTATIVES.

First District.—Beaufort, Bertie, Camden, Chowan, Currituck, Gates, Hertford, Hyde, Martin, Pamlico, Pasquotank, Perquimans, Pitt, Tyrrell, Dare and Washington.

CLINTON L. COBB, of Elizabeth City, was born at Elizabeth City, North Carolina, August 25, 1842; he attended school until he was thirteen years of age, and then went into a counting-room: studied law, and was admitted to the bar in 1867; was a candidate for the Legislature in 1866 ,but was defeated on the Howard amendment; was an independent candidate for Congress in 1868, but withdrew in favor of J. R. French; was elected to the Forty-first Congress, and was re-elected to the Forty-second Congress as the regular Republican candidate by 5,000 majority over T. Morgan, independent Republican: re-elected to Forty-third Congress by 1,429 votes over David Carter.

Second District.—Craven, Edgecombe, Greene, Jones, Lenoir, Wayne, Wilson, Northampton, Warren and Halfax counties.

CHARLES R. THOMAS, of Newbern, was born in Carteret County, North Carolina, February 7, 1827; graduated at the University of North Carolina in June, 1849; studied and practiced law; was elected one of the judges of the superior court in April, 1868, and resigned on his election to the Forty-second Congress:

HOUSE OF REPRESENTATIVES—CONTINUED.

was re-elected to the Forty-third Congress as a Republican, receiving about 2,000 majority over L. W. Humphrey, Democrat; re-elected to Forty-third Congress by 8,445 majority over Kitchen.

Third District.—Bladen, Brunswick, Columbus, Cumberland, Carteret, Harnett, Duplin, Moore, New Hanover, Onslow and Sampson counties.

ALFRED MOORE WADDELL, of Wilmington, was born at Hillsborough, North Carolina, September 16, 1834; educated at Bingham's School and Caldwell Institute, at Hillsborough, and graduated at the University of North Carolina in the class of 1853; studied law and practices the profession; was clerk of a court of equity from 1858 until 1861; was a delegate to the National Conservative Convention at Baltimore in 1866 which nominated Bell and Everett: owned and edited the "Wilmington Daily Herald" from May, 1860, to May, 1861; served in the confederate army as lieutenant-colonel of cavalry; and was elected to the Forty-second Congress as a Democrat by a majority of 351 over O. H. Dockery, Republican; elected to Forty-third Congress by 731 votes over McKay.

Fourth District.—Chatham, Franklin, Granville, Johnston, Nash, Orange and Wake Counties.

WILLIAM A. SMITH, of Princeton, was born in Warren County, January 9th, 1828; early education at Old Fields Schools, till 14, when he was employed on the Raleigh and Gaston Railroad; here he worked for two years when he went to Alabama, Louisiana and Texas; returning to North Carolina, he settled in Johnston County; in 1861 was elected a member of the Convention which voted the State out of the Union; in 1864 elected to the Legislature; in 1865 elected member of the Convention authorized by President Johnson; in 1870 elected to the State Senate; in 1868 was called to the Presidency of the North Carolina Railroad from Goldsboro' to Charlotte; appointed President of the Yadkin River Road from Salisbury to Wadesboro', and Receiver of the Western North Carolina Railroad from Salisbury to Old Fort; in 1872 elected to Congress by 732 votes over Hon. Sion H. Rogers.

Fifth District.—Alamance, Randolph, Guilford, Rockingham, Davidson, Stokes, Person and Caswell Counties.

JAMES M. LEACH, of Lexington, was born in Randolph County, North Carolina; received a classical education; studied law and practices the profession; was a member of the House of Commons of North Carolina, by re-elections, for ten years; was a Presidential elector on the Fillmore ticket in 1856; was elected to the House of Representatives of the United States in 1858; was a member of the Confederate Congress of 1864–'65; was elected to the State Senate of North Carolina twice after the war; and was elected to the Forty-second Congress as a Conservative, receiving 12,541 votes against 11,302 votes for W. L. Scott, Republican; elected to Forty-third Congress by 258 votes over Hon. Thomas Settle.

Sixth District.—Anson, Cabarrus, Catawba, Gaston, Lincoln, Mecklenburg, Montgomery, Richmond, Robeson, Stanly and Union Counties.

THOMAS S. ASHE, of Wadesboro', Anson County, North Carolina, was born July 21, 1812; educated at the University of North Carolina, where he graduated in 1832; studied law; admitted to the bar in 1835; was elected to the House in 1842, and to the Senate in 1854; was elected Solicitor in 1847 in Wilmington District; member of the Confederate Congress in 1861, and of the Confederate Senate

HOUSE OF REPRESENTATIVES—CONTINUED.

in 1864; was Democratic candidate for Governor in 1868, and defeated by Gov. Holden; was elected in 1872 to Congress, by a majority of 2,149 votes over Hon. O. H. Dockery.

Seventh District.—Alexander, Alleghany, Ashe, Davie, Iredell, Forsythe, Rowan, Surry, Watauga, Wilkes and Yadkin counties.

WILLIAM M. ROBBINS, Statesville, Iredell County, was born in Randolph County, October 26th, 1828; educated at Randolph Macon College, graduated in 1851, taking first honor; elected Senator in General Assembly in 1868 and 1870, and in 1872 elected to Congress by a majority of 1,613 votes over D. M. Furches.

Eighth District.—Caldwell, Cherokee, Cleaveland, Clay, Buncombe, Burke, Henderson, Haywood, Jackson, McDowell, Macon, Madison, Mitchell, Polk, Rutherford, Swain, Transylvania and Yancey Counties.

R. B. VANCE, Asheville, Buncombe County; was born April 24th, 1828; educated in the schools of the County; farmer by profession; first political appearance is the present; elected to Congress in 1872 by a majority of 2,555 over Wm. G. Candler, Esq., attorney at law; in confederate service and rose from rank of a Captain to that of Brigadier General.

No. VII.

Population of States and Territories of the United States from 1790 to 1870.

No. VIII.

MOVEMENT OF POPULATION WEST BY COUNTIES FROM 1790 TO 1870.

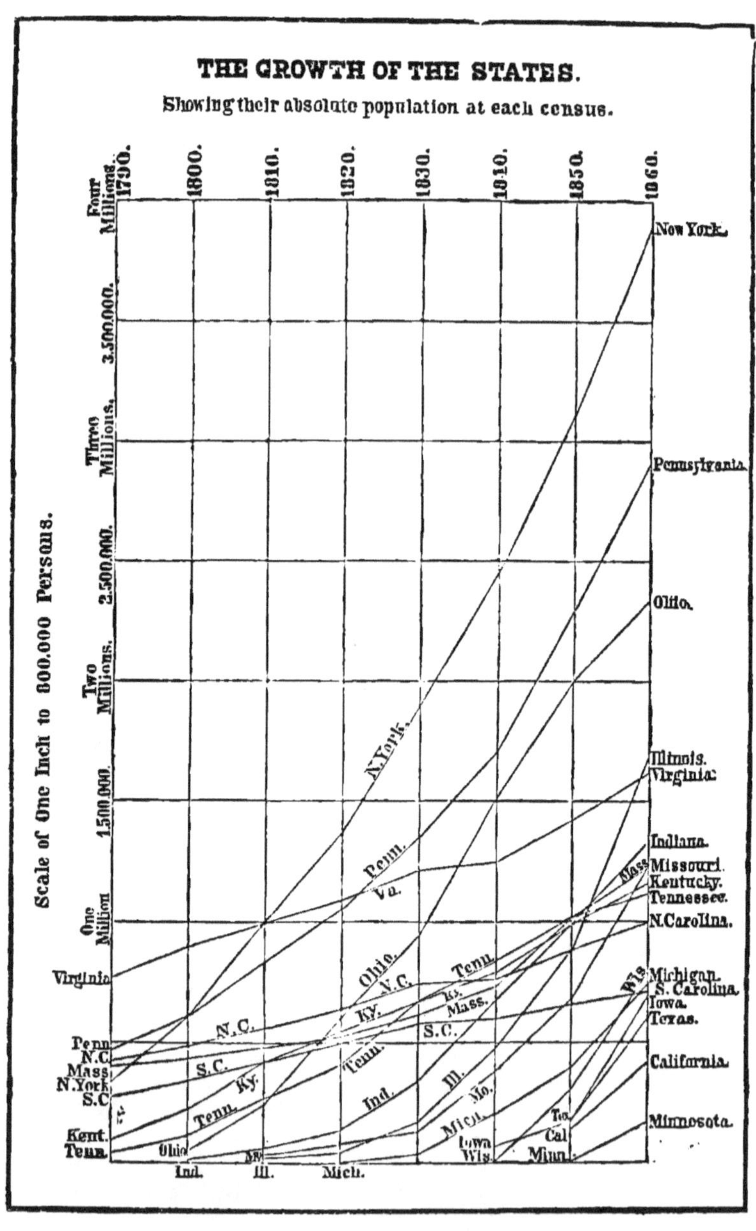

No. IX.

Movement of Representatives in Congress from 1789 to 1870, etc.

t to the present.

…sus, .	7th Census, 1850.	8th Census, 1860.	9th Census. 1870.	
0.	93,423.	126,123.	134,675	
7	 7	 6	 8	
....	 2	 3	 4	
....	 2	 3	 4	
4	 4	 4	 4	
1	 1	 1	 1	
....	 1	 1	 2	
8	 8	 7	 9	
7	 9	 14	 19	
10	 11	 11	 13	
....	 2	 6	 9	
....	....	 1	 3	
10	 0	 9	 10	
4	 4	 5	 6	
7	 6	 5	 5	
6	 6	 5	 6	
10	 11	 10	 11	
3	 4	 6	 9	
....	....	 2	 3	
4	 5	 5	 6	
5	 7	 9	 13	
....	....	 1	 1	
....	....	 1	 1	
4	 3	 3	 3	
5	 5	 5	 7	
34	 33	 31	 33	
9	 8	 7	 8	
21	 21	 19	 20	
....	....	 1	 1	
24	 25	 24	 27	
2	 2	 2	 2	
7	 6	 4	 5	
11	 10	 8	 10	
....	 2	 4	 6	
4	 3	 3	 3	
15	 13	 8	 9	
....	....	 3	 3	
....	....	 6	 1	
222	234	243	292	members.
			10	delegates.
			302	total House.

No. X.

LEGISLATIVE DEPARTMENT OF THE VARIOUS POWERS OF THE WORLD.

COUNTRY.	LOWER HOUSE.	UPPER HOUSE.	RATIO.
Austria	203	122	98,000
Belgium	116	58	42,000
Brazil	122	60	62,000
Denmark	101	59	14,000
France	376	169	100,000
Great Britain	658	462	45,000
North German Confederation	280	43	100,000
Portugal	154	115	28,000
Prussia	432	255	52,000
Spain	350	306	35,000
Argentine Republic	54	28	22,000
Chili	98	20	26,000
Peru	86	36	33,000
Switzerland	128	44	20,000
United States	292	74	135,000

Statesman's Year Book, London, for 1868.

No. XI.

Constitution of North Carolina.

CONSTITUTION.

Established the 16th day of March, 1868.—Amendments ratified by the people, 7th day of August, 1873.

CHAPTER I.

PREAMBLE.

We, the people of the State of North Carolina, grateful to Almighty God, the Sovereign Ruler of Nations, for the preservation of the American Union, and the existence of our civil, political and religious liberties, and acknowledging our dependence upon Him, for the continuance of those blessings to us and our posterity, do, for the more certain security thereof, and for the better government of this State, ordain and establish this Constitution:

ARTICLE I.

DECLARATION OF RIGHTS.

That the great, general and essential principles of liberty and free government, may be recognized and established, and that the relations of this State to the Union and government of the United States, and those of the people of this State, to the rest of the American people, may be defined and affirmed, we do declare:

SECTION 1. *The equality and rights of men:* That we hold it to be self-evident that all men are created equal; that they are endowed by their Creator with certain unalienable rights; that among these are life, liberty, the enjoyment of the fruits of their own labor, and the pursuit of happiness.

SEC. 2. *Political power and government:* That all political power is vested in, and derived from the people; all government of right originates from the people, is founded upon their will only, and is instituted solely for the good of the whole.

SEC. 3. *Internal government of the State:* That the people of this State have the inherent, sole and exclusive right of regulating the internal government and police thereof, and of altering and abolishing their Constitution and form of government, whenever it may be necessary to their safety and happiness; but every such right should be exercised in pursuance of law, and consistently with the Constitution of the United States.

SEC. 4. *No right to secede:* That this State shall ever remain a member of the American Union; that the people thereof are part of the American nation; that there is no right on the part of this State to secede, and that all attempts from whatever source or upon whatever pretext, to dissolve said Union, or to sever said nation, ought to be resisted with the whole power of the State.

SEC. 5. *Allegiance:* That every citizen of this State owes paramount allegiance to the Constitution and Government of the United States, and that no law or ordinance of the State in contravention or subversion thereof, can have any binding force.

SEC. 6. *Public debt:* The State shall never assume or pay, or authorize the collection of, any debt or obligation, express or implied, incurred in aid of insurrection or rebellion against the United States, or any claim for the loss or emancipation of any slave.

SEC. 7. *Exclusive Privileges:* No man or set of men are entitled to exclusive or separate emoluments or privileges from the community but in consideration of public services.

SEC. 8. *Legislative, Executive, and Judicial power distinct:* The Legislative, Executive, and Supreme judicial powers of the government ought to be forever separate and distinct from each other.

SEC. 9. *Power of suspending laws:* All power of suspending laws, or the execution of laws, by any authority, without the consent of the Representatives of the people, is injurious to their rights, and ought not to be exercised.

SEC. 10. *Elections:* All elections ought to be free.

SEC. 11. *Criminal prosecutions:* In all criminal prosecutions, every man has the right to be informed of the accusation against him and to confront the accusers and witnesses with other testimony, and to have counsel for his defence, and not be compelled to give evidence against himself, or to pay costs, jail fees, or necessary witness fees of the defence, unless found guilty.

SEC. 12. *Answer to criminal charges:* No person shall be put to answer any criminal charge, except as hereinafter allowed, but by indictment, presentment, or impeachment.

SEC. 13. *Trial by jury:* No person shall be convicted of any crime but by the unanimous verdict of a jury of good and lawful men in open court. The Legislature may, however, provide other means of trial, for petty misdemeanors, with the right of appeal.

SEC. 14. *Bail:* Excessive bail should not be required, nor excessive fines imposed, nor cruel or unusual punishments inflicted.

SEC. 15. *Search Warrants:* General warrants, whereby any officer or messenger may be commanded to search suspected places, without evidence of the act committed, or to seize any person or persons not named, whose offence is not particularly described and supported by evidence, are dangerous to liberty and ought not to be granted.

SEC. 16. *Imprisonment for debt:* There shall be no imprisonment for debt in this State, except in cases of fraud.

SEC. 17. *No person to be imprisoned, &c., except by law:* No person ought to be taken, imprisoned or disseized of his freehold, liberties or privileges, or outlawed, or exiled, or in any manner deprived of his life, liberty, or property, but by the law of the land.

SEC. 18. *Habeas Corpus:* Every person restrained of his liberty, is entitled to a remedy to enquire into the lawfulness thereof, and to remove the same, if unlawful; and such remedy ought not to be denied or delayed.

SEC. 19. *Controversies respecting property:* In all controversies at law respecting property, the ancient mode of trial by jury is one of the best securities of the rights of the people, and ought to remain sacred and inviolable.

SEC. 20. *Freedom of the press:* The freedom of the press is one of the great bulwarks of liberty, and therefore ought never to be restrained, but every individual shall be held responsible for the abuse of the same.

SEC. 21. *Habeas Corpus:* The privileges of the writ of *habeas corpus* shall not be suspended.

SEC. 22. *Property qualification:* As political rights and privileges are not dependent upon, or modified by property, therefore no property qualification ought to affect the right to vote or hold office.

SEC. 23. *Representation and taxation:* The people of this State ought not to be taxed, or made subject to the payment of any impost or duty, without the consent of themselves, or their representatives in General Assembly, freely given.

SEC. 24. *Militia and standing armies:* A well regulated militia being necessary to the security of a free State, the right of the people to keep and bear arms shall not be infringed; and, as standing armies, in time of peace, are dangerous to liberty, they ought not to be kept up, and the military should be kept under strict subordination to, and governed by, the civil power.

SEC. 25. *Right to assemble, &c.:* The people have a right to assemble together to consult for their common good, to instruct their representatives, and to apply to the Legislature for redress of grievances.

SEC. 26. *Religious liberty:* All men have a natural and unalienable right to worship Almighty God according to the dictates of their own consciences, and no human authority should, in any case whatever, control or interfere with the rights of conscience.

SEC. 27. *Education:* The people have a right to the privilege of education, and it is the duty of the State to guard and maintain that right.

SEC. 28. *Elections should be frequent:* For redress of grievances, and for amending and strengthening the laws, elections should be often held.

SEC. 29. *Recurrence to first principles:* A frequent recurrence to fundamental principles, is absolutely necessary to preserve the blessings of liberty.

SEC. 30. *Hereditary honors, &c.:* No hereditary emoluments, privileges, or honors, ought to be granted or conferred in this State.

SEC. 31. *Perpetuities, &c.:* Perpetuities and monopolies are contrary to the genius of a free State, and ought not to be allowed.

SEC. 32. *Ex post facto laws:* Retrospective laws, punishing acts committed before the existence of such laws, and by them only declared criminal, are oppressive, unjust and incompatible with liberty, wherefore, no *ex post facto* law ought to be made. No law taxing retrospectively, sales, purchases, or other acts previously done, ought to be passed.

SEC. 33. *Slavery abolished:* Slavery and involuntary servitude, otherwise than for crime whereof the parties shall have been duly convicted, shall be, and are hereby forever prohibited within this State.

SEC. 34. *Boundaries of the State:* The limits and boundaries of the State shall be and remain as they now are.

SEC. 35. *Courts shall be open:* All courts shall be open, and every person for an injury done him in his lands, goods, person, or reputation, shall have remedy by due course of law, and right and justice administered without sale, denial, or delay.

SEC. 36. *Soldiers in time of peace:* No soldier shall, in time of peace, be quartered in any house without the consent of the owner; nor in time of war, but in a manner prescribed by law.

SEC. 37. *Other rights:* This enumeration of rights shall not be construed to impair or deny others, retained by the people; and all powers, not herein delegated, remain with the people.

ARTICLE II.

LEGISLATIVE DEPARTMENT.

SECTION 1. *Two branches:* The Legislative authority shall be vested in two distinct branches, both dependent on the people to-wit: a Senate and House of Representatives.

SEC. 2. *Time of meeting:* The Senate and House of Representatives shall meet biennially on the third Monday in November and when assembled, shall be denominated the General Assembly. Neither House shall proceed upon public business, unless a majority of all the members are actually present.

SEC. 3. *Senate:* The Senate shall be composed of fifty Senators biennially chosen by ballott.

SEC. 4. *Senatorial Districts:* Until the first session of the General Assembly which shall be had after the year eighteen hundred and seventy-one, the Senate shall be composed of members elected from districts constituted as follows :*

1*st District*—Currituck, Camden, Pasquotank, Hertford, Gates, Chowan and Perquimans shall elect two Senators.

2*d District*—Tyrrell, Washington, Martin, Dare, Beaufort and Hyde shall elect two Senators.

3*d District*—Northampton and Bertie shall elect one Senator.

4*th District*—Halifax shall elect one Senator.

5*th District*—Edgecombe shall elect one Senator.

6*th District*—Pitt shall elect one Senator.

7*th District*—Wilson, Nash and Franklin shall elect two Senators.

8*th District*—Craven shall elect one Senator.

9*th District*—Jones, Onslow and Carteret shall elect one Senator.

10*th District*—Duplin and Wayne shall elect two Senators.

11*th District*—Greene and Lenoir shall elect one Senator.

12*th District*—New Hanover shall elect one Senator.

13*th District*—Brunswick and Bladen shall elect one Senator.

14*th District*—Sampson shall elect one Senator.

15*th District*—Columbus and Robeson shall elect one Senator.

16*th District*—Cumberland and Harnett shall elect one Senator.

17*th District*—Johnston shall elect one Senator.

18*th District*—Wake shall elect one Senator.

19*th District*—Warren shall elect one Senator.

20*th District*—Orange, Person and Caswell shall elect two Senators.

21*st District*—Granville shall elect one Senator.

22*d District*—Chatham shall elect one Senator.

23*d District*—Rockingham shall elect one Senator.

24*th District*—Alamance and Guilford shall elect two Senators.

25*th District*—Randolph and Moore shall elect one Senator.

26*th District*—Richmond and Montgomery shall elect one Senator.

27*th District*—Anson and Union shall elect one Senator.

28*th District*—Cabarrus and Stanly shall elect one Senator.

29*th District*—Mecklenburg shall elect one Senator.

30*th District*—Rowan and Davie shall elect one Senator.

31*st District*—Davidson shall elect one Senator.

32*d District*—Stokes and Forsythe shall elect one Senator.

33*d District*—Surry and Yadkin shall elect one Senator.

34*th District*—Iredell, Wilkes and Alexander shall elect two Senators.

35*th District*—Alleghany, Ashe and Watauga shall elect one Senator.

---

*NOTE.—To prevent confusion, the Senatorial Districts and the apportionment of members for the House of Representatives, as laid off and made by the act of 1871-'72, chap. 52, are here inserted, instead of those originally provided for in the Constitution.

36th District—Caldwell, Burke, McDowell, Mitchell and Yancey shall elect two Senators.

37th District—Catawba and Lincoln shall elect one Senator.

38th District—Gaston and Cleveland shall elect one Senator.

39th District—Rutherford and Polk shall elect one Senator.

40th District—Buncombe and Madison shall elect one Senator.

41st District—Haywood, Henderson and Transylvania shall elect one Senator.

42d District—Jackson, Swain, Macon, Cherokee, Clay and Graham shall elect one Senator.

SEC. 5. *Senatorial Districts; Census:* The Senate districts shall be so altered by the General Assembly, at the first session after the return of every enumeration taken by order of Congress, that each Senate district shall contain, as nearly as may be, an equal number of inhabitants, excluding aliens and Indians not taxed, and shall remain unaltered until the return of another enumeration, and shall at all times consist of contiguous territory; and no county shall be divided into the formation of a Senate district, unless such county shall be equitably entitled to two or more Senators.

SEC. 6. *Apportionment of Representatives:* The House of Representatives shall be composed of one hundred and twenty Representatives, biennially chosen by ballot, to be elected by the counties respectively, according to their population, and each county shall have at least one Representative in the House of Representatives, although it may not contain the requisite ratio of representation; this apportionment shall be made by the General Assembly at the respective times and periods when the districts for the Senate are hereinbefore directed to be laid off.

SEC. 7. *Ratio of representation:* In making the apportionment in the House of Representatives, the ratio of representation shall be ascertained by dividing the amount of the population of the State, exclusive of that comprehended within those counties which do not severally contain the one hundred and twentieth part of the population of the State, by the number of Representatives, less the number assigned to such counties; and in ascertaining the number of the population of the State, aliens and Indians not taxed, shall not be included. To each County containing the said ratio and not twice the said ratio, there shall be assigned one Representatives to each county containing twice but not three times the said ratio, there shall be assigned two Representatives, and so on progressively, and then the remaining Representatives shall be assigned severally to the Counties having the largest fractions.

SEC. 8. *Apportionment, &c.:* Until the General Assembly shall have made the apportionment as herein provided, the House of Representatives shall be composed of members elected from the Counties in the following manner, to-wit:

(APPORTIONMENT OF 1872.)

The County of Wake shall elect four members; New Hanover, three: Buncombe, Caswell, Chatham, Craven, Cumberland, Davidson, Duplin, Edgecombe, Granville, Guilford, Halifax, Iredell, Johnston, Mecklenburg, Orange, Pitt, Randolph, Robeson, Rockingham, Rowan, Sampson, Warren, Wayne, Wilkes, two each; Alamance, Alexander, Alleghany, Anson, Ashe, Beaufort, Bertie, Bladen, Brunswick, Burke, Cabarrus, Caldwell, Camden, Carteret, Catawba, Cherokee, Chowan, Clay, Cleveland, Columbus, Currituck, Dare, Davie, Forsythe, Franklin, Gaston, Gates, Greene, Harnett, Haywood, Henderson, Hertford, Hyde, Jackson, Jones, Lenoir, Lincoln, Macon, Madison, Martin, McDowell, Mitchell, Montgomery, Moore, Nash, Northampton, Onslow, Pasquotank, Perquimans, Person, Polk, Richmond, Rutherford, Stanly, Stokes, Surry, Swain, Transylvania, Tyrrell, Union, Washington, Watauga, Wilson, Yadkin and Yancey, one member each.

SEC. 9. *Qualification of Senators:* Each member of the Senate shall be not less than twenty-five years of age; shall have resided in the State as a citizen two years, and shall have usually resided in the District for which he is chosen, one year immediately preceding his election.

SEC. 10. *Qualification of Representatives:* Each member of the House of Representatives shall be a qualified elector of the State, and shall have resided in the County for which he is chosen, for one year immediately preceding his election.

SEC. 11. *Election of Officers:* In the election of all officers, whose appointment shall be conferred upon the General Assembly by the Constitution, the vote shall be *viva voce*.

SEC. 12. *No power to grant divorces:* The General Assembly shall have power to pass general laws regulating divorces and alimony, but shall not have power to grant a divorce or secure alimony in any individual case.

SEC. 13. *Private laws, names, &c.:* The General Assembly shall not have power to pass any private law to alter the name of any person, or to legitimate any person not born in lawful wedlock, or to restore to the rights of citizenship any person convicted of an infamous crime, but shall have power to pass general laws regulating the same.

SEC. 14. *Notice, private laws:* The General Assembly shall not pass any private law, unless it shall be made to appear, that thirty days notice of application to pass such law shall have been given, under such direction, and in such manner as shall be provided by law.

SEC. 15. *Vacancies:* If vacancies shall occur in the General Assembly by death, resignation or otherwise, writs of election shall be issued by the Governor under such regulations as may be prescribed by law.

SEC. 16. *Laws to raise revenue:* No law shall be passed to raise money on the credit of the State, or to pledge the faith of the State directly or indirectly for the payment of any debt, or to impose any tax upon the people of the State, or to allow the counties, cities or towns to do so, unless the bill for the purpose shall have been read three several times in each house of the General Assembly, and passed three several readings, which readings shall have been on three different days, and agreed to by each House respectively, and unless the yeas and nays on the second and third readings of the bill shall have been entered on the Journal.

SEC. 17. *Entails:* The General Assembly shall regulate entails in such manner as to prevent perpetuities.

SEC. 18. *Journals:* Each House shall keep a journal of its proceedings, which shall be printed and made public immediately after the adjournment of the General Assembly.

SEC. 19. *Protest:* Any member of either House may dissent from, and protest against, any act or resolve, which he may think injurious to the public, or any individual, and have the reasons of his dissent entered on the Journal.

SEC. 20. *Officers of the House:* The House of Representatives shall choose their own Speaker and other officers.

SEC. 21. *President of the Senate:* The Lieutenant-Governor shall preside in the Senate, but shall have no vote, unless it may be equally divided.

SEC. 22. *Speaker pro tem:* The Senate shall choose its other officers and also a Speaker (*pro tempore*) in the absence of the Lieutenant-Governor, or when he shall exercise the office of Governor.

SEC. 23. *Style of enactment:* The style of the acts shall be, "The General Assembly of North Carolina do enact."

SEC. 24. *Powers of each House:* Each House shall be judge of the qualifications and elections of its own members, shall sit upon its own adjournment from day to day, prepare bills to be passed into laws, and the two Houses, may also jointly adjourn to any future day, or other place.

SEC. 25. *Bills, &c., read three times:* All bills and resolutions of a legislative nature shall be read three times in each House, before they pass into laws; and shall be signed by the presiding officers of both Houses.

SEC. 26. *Oath of members:* Each member of the General Assembly, before taking his seat, shall take an oath or affirmation that he will support the Constitution and laws of the United States, and the Constitution of the State of North Carolina, and will faithfully discharge his duty as a member of the Senate or House of Representatives.

SEC. 27. *Terms of office:* The terms of office for Senators and members of the House of Representatives shall commence at the time of their election; and the term of office of those elected at the first election held under this Constitution shall terminate at the same time as if they had been elected, at the first ensuing regular election.

SEC. 28. *Yeas and Nays:* Upon motion made and seconded in either House, by one-fifth of the members present, the yeas and nays upon any question shall be taken and entered upon the journals.

SEC. 79. *Election of members:* The election for members of the General Assembly shall be held for the respective districts, and counties, at the places where they are now held, or may be directed hereafter to be held, in such manner as may be prescribed by law, on the first Thursday in August, in the year one thousand eight hundred and seventy, and every two years thereafter. But the General Assembly may change the time of holding the elections. The first election shall be held when the vote shall be taken on the ratification of this Constitution by the voters of the State, and the General Assembly then elected, shall meet on the fifteenth day after the approval thereof by the Congress of the United States, if it fall not on Sunday, but if it shall so fall, then on the next day thereafter, and the members then elected shall hold their seats until their successors are elected at a regular election.

ARTICLE III.

EXECUTIVE DEPARTMENT.

SECTION 1. *Officers of Executive Department; Term of office:* The Executive Department shall consist of a Governor, (in whom shall be vested the Supreme executive power of the State) a Lieutenant-Governor, a Secretary of State, an Auditor, a Treasurer, Superintendent of Public Instruction, and an Attorney-General, who shall be elected for a term of four years, by the qualified electors of the State, at the same time and places, and in the same manner as members of the General Assembly are elected. Their term of office shall commence on the first day of January next, aftèr their election, and continue until their successors are elected and qualified: *Provided,* That the officers first elected shall assume the duties of their office ten days after the approval of this Constitution by the Congress of the United States, and shall hold their offices four years from and after the first day of January, 1869.

SEC. 2. *Qualification and age of Governor, and Lieutenant-Governor:* No person shall be eligible as Governor or Lieutenant-Governor, unless he shall have attained the age of thirty years, shall have been a citizen of the United States five years, and shall have been a resident of this State for two years next before the election; nor shall the person elected to either of these two offices be eligible to the same office more than four years in any term of eight years unless the office shall have been cast upon him as Lieutenant-Governor or President of the Senate.

SEC. 3. *Returns of Election:* The return of every election for officers of the Executive Department shall be sealed up and transmitted to the seat of government by the returning officers, directed to the Speaker of the House of Representatives, who shall open and publish the same in the presence of a majority of the members of both Houses of the General Assembly. The persons having the highest number of votes respectively, shall be declared duly elected; but if two or more be equal and higest in votes for the same office, then one of them shall be chosen by joint-ballot of both Houses of the General Assembly. Contested elections shall be determined by a joint vote of both Houses of the General Assembly, in such manner as shall be prescribed by law.

SEC. 4. *Oaths of office for Governor:* The Governor, before entering upon the duties of his office, shall, in the presence of the members of both branches of the General Assembly, or before any Justice of the Supreme Court, take an oath or affirmation, that he will support the Constitution and laws of the United States and of the State of North Carolina, and that he will faithfully perform the duties appertaining to the office of Governor to which he has been elected.

SEC. 5. *Residence and duties:* The Governor shall reside at the seat of government of this State, and he shall, from time to time, give the General Assembly information of the affairs of the State, and recommend to their consideration such measures as he shall deem expedient.

SEC. 6. *Reprieves, &c.:* The Governor shall have power to grant reprieves, commutations and pardons, after conviction, for all offences, (except in cases of impeachment) upon such conditions as he may think proper, subject to such regulations as may be provided by law relative to the manner of applying for pardons. He shall biennially communicate to the General Assembly each case of reprieve, commutation or pardon granted: stating the name of each convict, the crime for which he was convicted, the sentence and its date, the date of commutation, pardon, or reprieve, and the reasons therefor.

SEC. 7. *Reports of executive officers:* The officers of the Executive Department and of the Public Institutions of the State, shall at least five days previous to each regular session of the General Assembly, severally report to the Governor, who shall transmit such reports, with his message, to the General Assembly; and the Governor may, at any time, require information in writing from the officers in the Executive Department upon any subject relating to the duties of their respective offices, and shall take care that the laws be faithfully executed.

SEC. 8. *Commander-in-Chief of Militia:* The Governor shall be Commander-in-Chief of the militia of the State, except when they shall be called into the service of the United States.

SEC. 9. *Extra sessions of the General Assembly:* The Governor shall have power, on extraordinary occasions, by and with the advice of the Council of State, to convene the General Assembly in extra session by his proclamation, stating therein the purpose or purposes for which they are thus convened.

SEC. 10. *Governor shall nominate and appoint officers, &c.:* The Governor shall nominate, and, by and with the advice and consent of a majority of the Senators elect, appoint, all officers whose offices are established by this Constitution, or which shall be created by law, and whose appointments are not otherwise provided for, and no such officer shall be appointed or elected by the General Assembly.

SEC. 1. *Duties of Lieutenant-Governor; Compensation:* The Lieutenant-Governor shall be President of the Senate, but shall have no vote unless the Senate be equally divided. He shall, whilst acting as President of the Senate, receive for his services the same pay which shall for the same period, be allowed to the

Speaker of the House of Representatives, and he shall receive no other compensation except when he is acting as Governor.

SEC. 12. *Impeachment of the Governor; or vacancy:* In case of the impeachment of the Governor, his failure to qualify, his absence from the State, his inability to discharge the duties of his office, or in the case the office of Governor shall in any wise become vacant, the powers, duties and emoluments of the office shall devolve upon the Lieutenant-Governor until the disabilities shall cease, or a new Governor shall be elected and qualified. In every case in which the Lieutenant-Governor shall be unable to preside over the Senate, the Senators shall elect one of their own number President of their body; and the powers, duties, and emoluments of the office of Governor shall devolve upon him whenever the Lieutenant-Governor shall, for any reason, be prevented from discharging the duties of such office as above provided, and he shall continue as acting Governor until the disabilities be removed or a new Governor or Lieutenant-Governor shall be elected and qualified. Whenever, during the recess of the General Assembly, it shall become necessary for a President of the Senate to administer the government, the Secretary of State shall convene the Senate, that they may elect such President.

SEC. 13. *Duties of other executive officers:* The respective duties of the Secretary of State, Auditor, Treasurer, Superintendent of Public Instruction, and Attorney-General shall be prescribed by law. If the office of any of said officers shall be vacated by death, resignation, or otherwise, it shall be the duty of the Governor to appoint another until the disability be removed or his successor be elected and qualified. Every such vacancy shall be filled by election, at the first general election that occurs more than thirty days after the vacancy has taken place and the the person chosen, shall hold the office for the remainder of the unexpired term fixed in the first section of this article.

SEC. 14. *Council of State:* The Secretary of State, Auditor, Treasurer and Superintendent of Public Instruction, shall constitute, *ex officio*, the Council of State who shall advise the Governor in the execution of his office, and three of whom, shall constitute a quorum; their advice and proceedings in this capacity shall be entered into a Journal, to be kept for this purpose exclusively, and signed by the members present, from any part of which any member may enter his dissent; and such Journal shall be placed before the General Assembly when called for by either House. The Attorney-General shall be, *ex officio*, the legal adviser of the Executive Department.

SEC. 15. *Compensation:* The officers mentioned in this Article shall, at stated periods, receive for their services a compensation to be established by law, which shall neither be increased nor diminished during the time for which they shall have been elected, and the said officers shall receive no other emolument or allowance whatever.

SEC. 16. *Great Seal:* There shall be a seal of the State, which shall be kept by the Governor, and used by him, as occasion may require, and shall be called "the Great Seal of the State of North Carolina." All grants and commissions shall be issued in the name and by the authority of the State of North Carolina, sealed with "the Great Seal of the State," signed by the Governor and countersigned by the Secretary of State.

SEC. 17. *Bureau of Statistics, &c.;* There shall be established in the office of Secretary of State, a Bureau of Statistics, Agriculture and Immigration, under such regulations as the General Assembly may provide.

ARTICLE IV.

JUDICIAL DEPARTMENT.

SECTION 1. *Distinction between Law and Equity abolished; Issues;* The distinction between actions at law and suits in equity, and the forms of all such actions and suits shall be abolished, and there shall be in this State but one form of action, for the enforcement or protection of private rights or the redress of private wrongs which shall be denominated a civil action: and every action prosecuted by the people of the State as a party, against a person charged with a public offence, for the punishment of the same, shall be termed a criminal action. Feigned issues shall also be abolished and the fact at issue tried by order of Court before a jury.

SEC. 2. *Courts;* The Judicial power of the State shall be vested in a Court for the trial of Impeachments, a Supreme Court, Superior Courts, Courts of Justices of the Peace, and Special Courts.

SEC. 3. *Court of Impeachment;* The Court for the trial of Impeachments shall be the Senate. A majority of the members shall be necessary to a quorum, and the judgment shall not extend beyond removal from, and disqualification to hold, office in this State; but the party shall be liable to indictment and punishment according to law.

SEC. 4. *Power of Impeaching:* The House of Representatives solely, shall have the power of impeaching. No person shall be convicted without the concurrence of two-thirds of the Senators present. When the Governor is impeached the Chief Justice shall preside.

SEC. 5. *Treason, what it consists in:* Treason against the State shall consist only in levying war against it or adhering to its enemies, giving them aid and comfort. No person shall be convicted of treason unless on the testimony of two witnesses to the same overt act, or on confession in open court. No conviction of treason or attainder shall work corruption of blood or forfeiture.

SEC. 6. *Supreme Court;* The Supreme Court shall consist of a Chief Justice and four Associate Justices.

SEC. 7. *Terms of:* There shall be two terms of the Supreme Court held at the seat of Government of the State in each year, commencing on the first Monday in January, and first Monday in June, and continuing as long as the public interests may require.

SEC. 8. *Jurisdiction:* The Supreme Court shall have jurisdiction to review, upon appeal, any decision of the courts below, upon any matter of law or legal inference; but no issue of fact shall be tried before this court; and the court shall have power to issue any remedial writs necessary, to give it a general supervision and control of the inferior courts.

SEC. 9. *Claims against the State:* The Supreme Court shall have original jurisdiction to hear claims against the State, but its decisions shall be merely recommendatory; no process in the nature of execution shall issue thereon; they shall be reported to the next session of the General Assembly for its action.

SEC. 10. *Judicial Districts:* The State shall be divided into twelve judicial districts, for each of which a Judge shall be chosen, who shall hold a Superior Court in each county in said district, at least twice in each year, to continue for two weeks, unless the business shall be sooner disposed of.

SEC. 11. *Same:* Until altered by law, the following shall be the Judicial Districts:*

FIRST DISTRICT:—Northampton, Bertie, Hertford, Gates, Chowan, Perquimans, Pasquotank, Camden, Currituck, Dare.

SECOND DISTRICT:—Tyrrell, Washington, Hyde, Martin, Beaufort, Pitt, Edgecombe.

THIRD DISTRICT:—Wilson, Wayne, Craven, Onslow, Lenoir, Jones, Greene, Carteret.

FOURTH DISTRICT:—Robeson, Bladen, Columbus, Brunswick, New Hanover, Duplin.

FIFTH DISTRICT:—Harnett, Moore, Montgomery, Stanley, Union, Anson, Richmond, Cumberland, Sampson.

SIXTH DISTRICT:—Nash, Warren, Franklin, Johnston, Wake, Granville, Halifax.

SEVENTH DISTRICT:—Alamance, Guilford, Rockingham, Caswell, Person, Orange, Chatham, Randolph.

EIGHTH DISTRICT:—Surry, Yadkin, Davie, Rowan, Davidson, Forsythe, Stokes.

NINTH DISTRICT:—Polk, Rutherford, Cleveland, Lincoln, Gaston, Mecklenburg, Cabarrus.

TENTH DISTRICT:—Catawba, Alexander, Caldwell, Alleghany, Ashe, Wilkes, Iredell.

ELEVENTH DISTRICT:—Watauga, McDowell, Henderson, Buncombe, Madison, Yancey, Mitchell, Burke.

TWELFTH DISTRICT:—Graham, Cherokee, Clay, Macon, Swain, Jackson, Haywood, Transylvania.

SEC. 12. *Judges may exchange Districts:* Every Judge of a Superior Court shall reside in his District while holding his office. The Judges may exchange Districts

---

*NOTE.—The Judicial Districts as they are now arranged are inserted, instead of those provided for originally.

with each other with the consent of the Governor, and the Governor, for good reasons, which he shall report to the Legislature at its current or next session, may require any Judge to hold one or more specified terms of said Courts in lieu of the Judge in whose District they are.

SEC. 13. *Jurisdiction of Superior Courts:* The Superior Courts shall have exclusive original jurisdiction of all civil actions, whereof exclusive original jurisdiction is not given to some other Courts; and of all criminal actions, in which the punishment may exceed a fine of fifty dollars or imprisonment for one month.

SEC. 14. *Appellate Jurisdiction:* The Superior Courts shall have appellate jurisdiction of all issues of law or fact, determined by a Probate Judge or a Justice of the Peace, where the matter in controversy exceeds twenty-five dollars, and of matters of law in all cases.

SEC. 15. *Jurisdiction of the Clerks of the Superior Courts:* The Clerks of the Superior Courts shall have jurisdiction of the probate of deeds, the granting of letters testamentary and of administration, the appointment of guardians, the apprenticing of orphans, to audit the accounts of executors, administrators, and guardians, and of such other matters as shall be prescribed by law. All issues of fact joined before them shall be transferred to the Superior Courts for trial, and appeals shall lie to the Superior Courts from their judgments in all matters of law.

SEC. 16. *Trial by jury waived:* In all issues of fact, joined in any court, the parties may waive the right to have the same determined by jury, in which case the finding of the Judge upon the facts, shall have the force and effect of a verdict of a jury.

SEC. 17. *Special Courts:* The General Assembly shall provide for the establishment of Special Courts, for the trial of misdemeanors, in cities and towns, where the same may be necessary.

SEC. 18. *Clerk of Supreme Court:* The Clerk of the Supreme Court shall be appointed by the Court, and shall hold his office for eight years.

SEC. 19. *Clerk of Superior Court:* A Clerk of the Superior Court for each county, shall be elected by the qualified voters thereof, at the time and in the manner prescribed by law, for the election of members of the General Assembly.

SEC. 20. *Term of office:* Clerks of the Superior Courts shall hold their offices for four years.

SEC. 21. *Salaries, &c., of Judges and other officers:* The General Assembly shall prescribe and regulate the fees, salaries and emoluments of all officers provided for in this Article; but the salaries of the Judges shall not be diminished during their continuance in office.

SEC. 22. *What laws in force:* The laws of North Carolina, not repugnant to this Constitution, or to the Constitution and laws of the United States, shall be in force until lawfully altered.

SEC. 23. *Suits transferred* · Actions at laws, and suits in equity, pending when this Constitution shall go into effect, shall be transferred to the Courts having jurisdiction thereof, without prejudice by reason of the change, and all such actions and suits, commenced before, and pending at, the adoption by the General Assembly, of the rules of practice and procedure herein provided for, shall be heard and determined, according to the practice now in use, unless otherwise provided for by said rules.

SEC. 24. *Election of Judges and terms of office:* The Justices of the Supreme Court shall be elected by the qualified voters of the State, as is provided for the election of members of the General Assembly. They shall hold their offices for eight years. The Judges of the Superior Courts shall be elected in like manner, and shall hold their offices for eight years; but the Judges of the Superior Courts elected at the first election under this Constitution, shall, after their election, under the superintendence of the Justices of the Supreme Court, be divided by lot into two equal classes, one of which shall hold office for four years, the other for eight years.

SEC. 25. *Judges of the Superior Courts may be elected by Districts:* The General Assembly may provide by law that the Judges of the Superior Courts, instead of being elected by the voters of the whole State, as is herein provided for, shall be elected by the voters of their respective Districts.

SEC. 26. *Superior Courts to be at all times open:* The Superior Courts shall be, at all times, open for the transaction of all business within their jurisdiction, except the trial of issues of fact requiring a jury.

SEC. 27. *Solicitors, election of, and term of office:* A Solicitor shall be elected for each Judicial District by the qualified voters thereof, as is prescribed for members of the General Assembly, who shall hold office for the term of four years, and prosecute on behalf of the State, in all criminal actions in the Superior Courts, and advise the officers of justice in his District.

SEC. 28. *Sheriffs, Coroners, &c., election of, and term of office:* In each County a Sheriff and Coroner shall be elected by the qualified voters thereof as is prescribed for members of the General Assembly, and shall hold their offices for two years. In each township there shall be a Constable, elected in like manner by the voters thereof, who shall hold his office for two years. When there is no Coroner in the County, the Clerk of the Superior Court for the County may appoint one for special cases. In case of a vacancy existing for any cause, in any of the offices created by this section, the Commissioners for the County may appoint to such office for the unexpired term.

SEC. 29. *Vacancies, how filled:* All vacancies occurring in the offices provided for by this Article of this Constitution, shall be filled by the appointment of the Governor, unless otherwise provided for, and the appointees shall hold their places until the next regular election.

SEC. 30. *Terms of office:* The officers elected at the first election held under this Constitution, shall hold their offices for the terms prescribed for them respectively, next ensuing after the next regular election for members of the General Assembly. But their terms shall begin upon the approval of this Constitution by the Congress of the United States.

SEC. 31. *Justices of the Peace, jurisdiction of, &c.:* The several Justices of the Peace shall have exclusive original jurisdiction under such regulations as the General Assembly shall prescribe, of all civil actions, founded on contract, wherein the sum demanded shall not exceed two hundred dollars, and wherein the title to real estate shall not be in controversy; and of all criminal matters arising within their counties, where the punishment cannot exceed a fine of fifty dollars, or imprisonment for one month. When an issue of fact shall be joined before a Justice, on demand of either party thereto, he shall cause a jury of six men to be summoned, who shall try the same. The party against whom judgment shall be rendered in any civil action, may appeal to the Superior Court from the same, and, if the judgment shall exceed twenty-five dollars, there may be a new trial of the whole matter in the appellate court; but if the judgment shall be for twenty-five dollars or less, then the case shall be heard in the appellate court, only upon matters of law. In all cases of a criminal nature, the party against whom judgment is given may appeal to the Superior Court, where the matter shall be heard anew. In all cases brought before a Justice, he shall make a record of the proceedings, and file the same with the Clerk of the Superior Court for his county.

SEC. 32. *Vacancy, how filled:* When the office of Justice of the Peace shall become vacant, otherwise than by expiration of the term, and in case of a failure by the voters of any district, to elect, the Clerk of the Superior Court for the county, shall appoint to fill the vacancy for the unexpired term.

SEC. 33. *Vacancy in office of Clerk of Superior Court, how filled:* In case the office of Clerk of a Superior Court for a County shall become vacant, otherwise than by the expiration of the term, and in case of a failure by the people to elect, the Judge of the Superior Court for the County shall appoint to fill the vacancy until an election can be regularly held.*

ARTICLE V.

REVENUE AND TAXATION.

SECTION 1. *Capitation tax; equation of taxation; exemptions:* The General Assembly shall levy a capitation tax on every male inhabitant of the State over twenty-one and under fifty years of age, which shall be equal on each, to the tax on property valued at three hundred dollars in cash. The Commissioners of the

---

*NOTE.—The amendments to this and other succeeding Articles, make an alteration in the numbers of many of the sections necessary. This should be borne in mind, whenever the number of certain sections do not correspond with those in the original. Such alterations were not provided for in the several Acts proposing the amendments, yet they would seem to follow as a necessary consequence.

several Counties may exempt from taxation tax in a special cases, on account of poverty and infirmity, and the State and County capitation tax combined, shall never exceed two dollars on the head.

SEC. 2. *Poll tax, how applied:* The proceeds of the State and County capitation tax shall be applied to the purposes of education and the support of the poor, but in no one year shall more than twenty-five per cent, thereof, be appropriated to the latter purpose.

SEC. 3. *Taxes to be ad valorem:* Laws shall be passed taxing, by a uniform rule, all moneys, credits, investments in bonds, stocks, joint-stock companies or otherwise; and, also, all real and personal property, according to its true value in money. The General Assembly may also tax trades, professions, franchises, and incomes, provided, that no income shall be taxed when the property from which the income is derived, is taxed.

SEC. 4. *Power to contract new debts, restricted:* Until the bonds of the State shall be at par, the General Assembly shall have no power to contract any new debt or pecuniary obligation in behalf the State, except to supply a casual deficit, or for suppressing invasion or insurrection, unless it shall in the same bill levy a special tax to pay the interest annually. And the General Assembly shall have no power to give or lend the credit of the State in aid of any person, association or corporation, except to aid in the completion of such Railroads as may be unfinished at the time of the adoption of this Constitution, or in which the State has a direct pecuniary interest, unless the subject be submitted, to a direct vote of the people of the State, and be approved by a majority of those who shall vote thereon.

SEC. 5. *Property exempted:* Property belonging to the State, or to municipal corporations, shall be exempt from taxation. The General Assembly may exempt cemeteries, and property held for educational, scientific, literary, charitable, or religious purposes; also, wearing apparel, arms for muster, household and kitchen furniture, the mechanical and agricultural implements of mechanics and farmers, libraries and scientific instruments, or any other personal property, to a value not exceeding three hundred dollars.

SEC. 6. *County taxes:* The taxes levied by the commissioners of the several counties, for county purposes, shall be levied in like manner with the State taxes and shall never exceed the double of the State tax, except for a special purpose, and with the special approval of the General Assembly

SEC. 7. *Acts levying taxes, to state the object:* Every act of the General Assembly, levying a tax, shall state the special object to which it is to be applied, and it shall be applied to no other purpose.

ARTICLE VI.

SUFFRAGE AND ELLIGIBILITY TO OFFICE.

SECTION 1. *Qualifications of electors:* Every male person born in the United States, and every male person who has been naturalized, twenty-one years old or upwards, who shall have resided in this State twelve months next preceding the election, and thirty days in the County in which he offers to vote, shall be deemed an elector.

SEC. 2. *Registration of electors:* It shall be the duty of the General Assembly to provide from time to time, for the registration of all electors, and no person shall be allowed to vote without registration, or to register, without first taking an oath or affirmation to support and maintain the Constitution and laws of the United States and the Constitution and laws of North Carolina, not inconsistent therewith.

SEC. 3. *Elections by the people to be by ballot; by the General Assembly, by viva voce:* All elections by the people shall be by ballot and all elections by the General Assembly shall be *viva voce.*

SEC. 4. *Eligibility to office; oath;* Every voter, except as hereinafter provided, shall be eligible to office; but before entering upon the discharge of the duties of his office, he shall take and subscribe the following oath: "I, ——, do solemnly swear (or affirm) that I will support and maintain the Constitution and laws of the United States and the Constitution and laws of North Carolina, not inconsistent therewith, and that I will faithfully discharge the duties of my office. So help me God."

SEC. 5. *Persons disqualified:* The following classes of persons shall be disqualified for office: First, All persons who shall deny the being of Almighty God. Second, All persons who shall have been convicted of treason, perjury or of any other infamous crime, since becoming citizens of the United States, or of corruption, or mal-practice in office, unless such person shall have been legally restored to the rights of citizenship.

ARTICLE VII.

MUNICIPAL CORPORATIONS.

SECTION 1. *County Officers:* In each county, there shall be elected, biennially, by the qualified voters thereof, as provided for the election of members of the General Assembly, the following officers: A Treasurer, Register of Deeds, Surveyor and five Commissioners.

SEC. 2. *Duty of Commissioners:* It shall be the duty of the Commissioners to exercise a general supervision and control of the penal and charitable institutions, schools, roads, bridges, levying of taxes and finances of the county, as may be prescribed by law. The Register of Deeds shall be, *ex officio*, Clerk of the Board of Commissioners.

SEC. 3. *County to be divided into discricts;* It shall be the duty of the Commissioners, first elected in each county, to divide the same into convenient districts, to determine the boundaries and prescribe the names of the said districts, and to report the same to the General Assembly before the first day of January, 1869.

SEC. 4. *Reports of division to be approved:* Upon the approval of the reports provided for in the foregoing section, by the General Assembly, the said districts shall have corporate powers for the necessary purposes of local government and shall be known as Townships.

SEC. 5. *Officers of townships:* In each township there shall be biennially elected, by the qualified voters thereof, a Clerk and two Justices of the Peace, who shall constitute a Board of Trustees, and shall, under the supervision of the County Commissioners, have control of the taxes and finances, roads and bridges of the Township as may be prescribed by law. The General Assembly may provide for the election of a larger number of Justices of the Peace in cities and towns and in those townships in which cities and towns are situated. In every township there shall also be biennially elected a School Committee consisting of three persons whose duty shall be prescribed by law.

SEC. 6. *Board of Trustees to assess taxable property:* The township Board of Trustees, shall assess the taxable property of their townships and make return to the County Commissioners, for revision as may be prescribed by law. The Clerk shall also be, *ex officio*, Treasurer of the township.

SEC. 7. *Towns, &c., not to contract debts:* No county, city, town or other municipal corporation, shall contract any debt, pledge its faith, or loan its credit, nor shall any tax be levied, or collected by any officers of the same, except for the necessary expenses thereof, unless by a vote of the majority of the qualified voters therein.

SEC. 8. *No money to be drawn except by law:* No money shall be drawn from any County or Township Treasury, except by authority of law.

SEC. 9. *Taxes to be ad valorem:* All taxes levied by any county, city, town or township, shall be uniform, and *ad valorem*, upon all property in the same, except property exempted by this Constitution.

SEC. 10. *Term and commencement of office:* The County officers first elected under the provisions of this Article shall enter upon their duties ten days after the approval of this Constitution by the Congress of the United States.

SEC. 11. *Governor to appoint Justices:* The governor shall appoint a sufficient number of Justices of the Peace, in each County, who shall hold their places until sections four, five and six of this Article shall have been carried into effect.

SEC. 12. *Charters to remain in force, &c.:* All charters, ordinances and provisions relating to municipal corporations, shall remain in force until legally changed, unless inconsistent with the provisions of this Constitution.

SEC. 13. *Not to pay certain debts:* No County, City, Town or other municipal corporation, shall assume or pay, nor shall any tax be levied or collected, for the payment of any debt, or the interest upon any debt, contracted, directly or indirectly, in aid or support of the rebellion.

ARTICLE VIII.

CORPORATIONS OTHER THAN MUNICIPAL.

SECTION 1. *Corporations, how created:* Corporations may be formed under general laws; but shall not be created by special act, except for municipal purposes, and in cases where, in the judgment of the Legislature, the object of the corporation cannot be attained under general laws. All general laws and special acts passed pursuant to this section, may be altered, from time to time or repealed.

SEC. 2. *Debts of, how secured:* Dues from corporations shall be secured by such individual liabilities of the corporations and other means, as may be prescribed by law.

SEC. 3. *Corporation, what:* The term Corporation, as used in this article, shall be construed to include all associations and joint-stock companies, having any of the powers and privileges of corporations, not possessed by individuals or partnerships. And all corporations shall have the right to sue, and shall be subject to be sued, in all courts, in like cases as natural persons.

SEC. 4. *Legislature to provide for organizing cities, &c.:* It shall be the duty of the Legislature to provide for the organization of cities, towns, and incorporated villages, and to restrict their power of taxation, assessments, borrowing money, contracting debts, and loaning their credit, so as to prevent abuses in assessments and in contracting debts, by such municipal corporation.

ARTICLE IX.

EDUCATION.

SECTION 1. *Education to be encouraged:* Religion, morality, and knowledge being necessary to good government and happiness of mankind, schools, and the means of education, shall forever be encouraged.

SEC. 2. *Public Schools provided for:* The General Assembly at its first session under this Constitution, shall provide by taxation and otherwise for a general and uniform system of Public Schools, wherein tuition shall be free of charge to all the children of the State between the ages of six and twenty-one years.

SEC. 3. *School districts:* Each County of the State shall be divided into a convenient number of Districts, in which one or more Public Schools shall be maintained, at least four months in every year; and if the Commissioners of any County shall fail to comply with the aforesaid requirements of this section, they shall be liable to indictment.

SEC. 4. *Property devoted to education:* The proceeds of all lands that have been, or hereafter may be, granted by the United States to this State and not otherwise specially appropriated by the United States or heretofore by this State; also all moneys, stocks, bonds, and other property now belonging to any fund for purposes of education; also the net proceeds that may accrue to the State from sales of estrays, or from fines, penalties and forfeitures; also the proceeds of all sales of the swamp lands belonging to the State: also all money that shall be paid as an equivalent for exemption from military duty; also, all grants, gifts, or devises that may hereafter be made to this State, and not otherwise appropriated by the grant, gift or devise, shall be securely invested, and sacredly preserved as an irreducible educational fund, the annual income of which, together with so much of the ordinary revenue of the State as may be necessary, shall be faithfully appropriated for establishing and perfecting, in this State, a system of free public schools, and for no other purposes or uses whatsoever.

SEC. 5. *University and public schools:* The General Assembly shall have power to provide for the election of trustees of the University of North Carolina, in whom when chosen, shall be vested all the privileges, rights, franchises and endowments heretofore in anywise granted to or conferred upon the trustees of said University; and the General Assembly may make such provisions, laws and regulations from time to time as may be necessary and expedient for the maintenance and management of said Univerity.

SEC. 6. *Benefits of the University to be free:* The General Assembly shall provide that the benefits of the University, as far as practicable, be extended to the youth of the State free of expense for tuition; also, that all the property which has heretofore accrued to the State, or shall hereafter accrue from escheats, unclaimed dividends or distributive shares of the estates of deceased persons, shall be appropriated to the use of the University.

SEC. 7. *Board of Education:* The Governor, Lieutenant Governor, Secretary of State, Treasurer, Auditor, Superintendent of Public Instruction and Attorney General, shall constitute a State Board of Education.

SEC. 8. *Its President and Secretary:* The Governor shall be President, and the Superintendent of Public Instruction shall be Secretary, of the Board of Education.

SEC. 9. *Board succeeds the President and Directors of the Literary Fund; powers of:*

The Board of Education shall succeed to all the powers and trusts of the President and Directors of the Literary Fund of North Carolina, and shall have full power to legislate and make all needful rules and regulations in relation to free public schools, and the educational fund of the State; but all acts, rules and regulations of said Board may be altered, amended, or repealed by the General Assembly, and when so altered, amended or repealed they shall not be re-enacted by the Board.

SEC. 10. *Sessions of the Board:* The first session of the Board of Education shall be held at the Capital of the State, within fifteen days after the organization of the State government under this Constitution; the time of future meetings may be determined by the Board.

SEC. 11. *Quorum:* A majority of the Board shall constitute a quorum for the transaction of business.

SEC. 12. *Expenses of the Board:* The contingent expenses of the Board shall be provided for by the General Assembly.

SEC. 13. *Department of Agriculture, &c.:* As soon as practicable after the adoption of this Constitution, the General Assembly shall establish and maintain, in connection with the University, a Department of Agriculture, of Mechanics, of Mining, and of Normal Instruction.

SEC. 14. *Every child may be compelled to go to school:* The General Assembly is hereby empowered to enact that every child of sufficient mental and physical ability, shall attend the public schools during the period between the ages of six and eighteen years, for a term of not less than sixteen months, unless educated by other means.

ARTICLE X.

HOMESTEADS AND EXEMPTIONS.

SECTION 1. *Exemptions; personal property:* The personal property of any resident of this State, to the value of five hundred dollars, to be selected by such resident, shall be, and is hereby exempted, from sale under execution, or other final process of any Court, issued for the collection of any debt.

SEC. 2. *Homestead:* Every homestead and the dwelling and buildings used therewith, not exceeding in value one thousand dollars, to be selected by the owner thereof, or in lieu thereof, at the option of the owner, any lot in a city, town or village, with the dwelling and buildings used thereon, owned and occupied by any resident of this State, and not exceeding the value of one thousand dollars, shall be exempt from sale under execution, or other final process, obtained on any debt. But no property shall be exempt from sale for taxes or for payment of obligations contracted for the purchase of said premises.

SEC. 3. *Exempt from payment of debts:* The homestead, after the death of the owner thereof, shall be exempt from the payment of any debt, during the minority of his children, or any one of them.

SEC. 4. *Laborer's Lien:* The provisions of section one and two of this Article shall not be so construed as to prevent a laborer's lien for work done and performed for the person claiming such exemption, or a mechanic's lien for work done on the premises.

SEC. 5. *Widow's right to:* If the owner of a homestead die, leaving a widow, but no children the same shall be exempt from the debts of her husband, and the rents and profits thereof shall inure to her benefit, during her widowhood, unless she be the owner of a homestead, in her own right.

SEC. 6. *Property of married women:* The real and personal property of any female in this State, acquired before marriage, and all property, real and personal, to which she may after marriage, become in any manner entitled, shall be and remain, the sole and separate estate and property of such female, and shall not be liable for any debts, obligations or engagements of her husband, and may be devised or bequeathed, and, with the written assent of her husband, conveyed, by her, as if she were unmarried.

SEC. 7. *Husband may insure his life for the benefit of his wife, &c.:* The husband may insure his own life for the sole use and benefit of his wife and children, and in case of the death of the husband, the amount thus insured, shall be paid over to the wife and children, or the guardian, if under age, for her, or their own use, free from all the claims of the representatives of the husband, or any of his creditors.

SEC. 8. *Homestead may be disposed of by deed:* Nothing contained in the foregoing sections of this Article shall operate to prevent the owner of a homestead from disposing of the same by deed; but no deed made by the owner of a homestead shall be valid without the voluntary signature and assent of his wife, signified on her private examination according to law.

ARTICLE XI.

PUNISHMENTS, PENAL INSTITUTIONS AND PUBLIC CHARITIES.

SECTION 1. *Punishments:* The following punishments only, shall be known to the laws of this State, viz: death, imprisonment, with, or without hard labor, fines, removal from office, and disqualification to hold and enjoy any office of honor, trust, or profit, under this State.

SEC. 2. *Object of punishment; death penalty:* The objects of punishments being not only to satisfy justice, but also to reform the offender, and thus to prevent crime, murder, arson, burglary, and rape, and these only, may be punishable with death, if the General Assembly shall so enact.

SEC. 3. *Penitentiary:* The General Assembly shall, at its first meeting make provision for the erection and conduct of a State's Prison or Penitentiary at some central and accessible point within the State.

SEC. 4. *Houses of correction:* The General Assembly may provide for the erection of Houses of Correction, where vagrants and persons guilty of misdemeanors shall be restrained and usefully employed.

SEC. 5. *Houses of refuge:* A House or Houses of Refuge may be established, whenever the public interest may require it, for the correction and instruction of other classes of offenders.

SEC. 6. *Males and females to be separated:* It shall be required by competent legislation, that the structure and superintendence of penal institutions of the State, the County jails, and City police-prisons, secure the health, and comfort of the prisoners, and that male and female prisoners be never confined in the same room or cell.

SEC. 7. *Board of Public Charities;* Beneficent provision for the poor, the unfortunate and orphan, being one of the first duties of a civilized and Christian State, the General Assembly shall, at its first session, appoint and define the duties of a Board of Public Charities, to whom shall be entrusted the supervision of all charitable and penal State institutions, and who shall annually report to the Governor upon their condition, with suggestions for their improvement.

SEC. 8. *Orphan Houses:* There shall also, as soon as practicable, be measures devised by the State for the establishment of one or more Orphan Houses, where destitute orphans may be cared for, educated and taught, some business or trade.

SEC. 9. *Idiots and inebriates education of:* It shall be the duty of the Legislature, as soon as practicable, to devise means for the education of idiots (and reformation of) inebriates.

SEC. 10. *Blind, and Deaf-mutes:* The General Assembly shall provide that all the deaf-mutes, the blind, and the insane of the State, shall be cared for at the charge of the State.

SEC. 11. *Penal and charitable institutions self-supporting:* It shall be steadily kept in view by the Legislature, and the Board of Public Charities that all penal and charitable institutions should be made as nearly self-supporting as is consistent with the purposes of their creation.

ARTICLE XII.

MILITIA.

SECTION 1. *Who liable to militia duty:* All able-bodied male citizens of the State of North Carolina between the ages of twenty-one and forty years who are citizens of the United States, shall be liable to duty in the Militia: *Provided*, That all persons who may be adverse to bearing arms, from religious scruples, shall be exempt therefrom.

SEC. 2. *Organization, &c.:* The General Assembly shall provide for the organizing, arming, equipping and discipline of the Militia and for paying the same when called into active service.

SEC. 3. *Governor, Commander-in-Chief:* The Governor shall be Commander-in-Chief, and have power to call out the Militia to execute the law, suppress riots and insurrection and to repel invasion.

SEC. 4. *Exemptions from militia duty:* The General Assembly shall have power to make such exemptions as may be deemed necessary, and to enact laws that may be expedient for the government of the Militia.

ARTICLE XIII.

AMENDMENTS.

SECTION 1. *Convention, how called:* No Convention of the people shall be called by the General Assembly unless by the concurrence of two-thirds of all the members of each House of the General Assembly.

SEC. 2. *Constitution, how amended:* No part of the Constitution of this State shall be altered, unless a bill to alter the same shall have been read three times in each House of the General Assembly and agreed to by three-fiths of the whole number of members of each House respectively; nor shall any alteration take place until the bill, so agreed to, shall have been published, six months previous to a new election of members to the General Assembly. If after such publication the alteration proposed by the preceding General Assembly shall be agreed to, in the first session thereafter by two-thirds of the whole representation in each House of the General Assembly, after the same shall have been read three times on three several days, in each House, then the said General Assembly shall prescribe a mode by which the amendment or amendments may be submitted to the qualified voters of the House of Representatives throughout the State; and if, upon comparing the votes given in the whole State, it shall appear that a majority of the voters voting thereon, have approved thereof, then, and not otherwise, the same shall become a part of the Constitution.

ARTICLE XIV.

MISCELLANEOUS.

SECTION 1. *Indictments:* All indictments which shall have been found, or may hereafter be found, for any crime or offence committed before this Constitution takes effect may be proceeded upon in the proper Courts, but no punishment shall be inflicted which is forbidden by this Constitution.

SEC. 2. *Penalty for fighting duels;* No person who shall hereafter fight a duel, or assist in the same as a second, or send, accept, or knowingly carry a challenge therefor, or agree to go out of this State to fight a duel, shall hold any office in this State.

SEC. 3. *Drawing money from the Treasury*: No money shall be drawn from the Treasury but in consequence of appropriations made by law, and an accurate account of the receipts and expenditures of the public money shall be annually published.

SEC. 4. *Mechanics' and laborers' lien:* The General Assembly shall provide by proper legislation, for giving to mechanics and laborers an adequate lien on the subject matter of their labor.

SEC. 5. *Officers, terms of office, &c.:* In the absence of any contrary provision, all officers in this State, whether heretofore elected, or appointed by the Governor shall hold their positions only, until other appointments are made by the Governor, or, if the officers are elective, until their successors shall have been chosen and duly qualified, according to the provisions of this Constitution.

SEC. 6. *Seat of government:* The seat of government in this State shall remain at the City of Raleigh.

SEC. 7. *Holding more than one office:* No person who shall hold any office or place of trust or profit under the United States, or any department thereof, or under this State, or under any other State, or government, shall hold or exercise any other office or place of trust or profit under the authority of this State, or be eligible to a seat in either House of the General Assembly: *Provided*, That nothing herein contained shall extend to officers in the militia, Justices of the Peace, Commissioners of Public Charities, or Commissioners for special purposes.

Done in Convention at Raleigh, the sixteenth day of March, in the year of our Lord, one thousend eight hundred and sixty-eight, and of the Independence of the United States, the ninety-second.

No. XII.

STATE OF NORTH CAROLINA.

POPULATION BY COUNTIES FROM 1790 TO 1870.

COUNTIES.	AGGREGATE.								
	1870	1860	1850	1840	1830	1820	1810	1800	1790
Total,........	1071361	992622	869039	753419	737987	638829	555500	478103	393751
	......	......	......	......	......	......	......	......	......
Alamance........	11874	11852	11444	......	......	......	......	......	......
Alexander........	6868	6022	5220	......	......	......	......	......	......
Alleghany........	3691	3590	......	......	......	......	......	......	......
Anson............	12428	13664	13489	15077	14095	12534	8831	8146	5133
Ashe.............	9573	7956	8777	7467	6987	4335	3694	2783	......
Beaufort.........	13011	14766	13816	12225	10969	9850	7203	6242	5462
Bertie...........	12950	14310	12851	12175	12262	10805	11218	11249	12606
Bladen...........	12831	11995	9767	8022	7811	7276	5671	7028	5084
Brunswick........	7754	8406	7272	5265	6516	5480	4778	4110	3071
Buncombe.........	15412	12654	13425	10084	16281	10542	9277	5812	......
Burke............	9777	9237	7772	15799	17888	13411	11007	9929	8118
Cabarrus.........	11954	10546	9747	9259	8810	7248	6158	5094	......
Caldwell.........	8476	7497	6317	......	......	......	......	......	......
Camden...........	5361	5343	6049	5663	6733	6347	5347	4191	4033
Carteret.........	9010	8186	6939	6591	6597	5609	4823	4399	3732
Caswell..........	16081	16215	15269	14693	15185	13253	11757	8701	10096
Catawba..........	10984	10729	8862	......	......	......	......	......	......
Chatham..........	19723	19101	18449	16222	15405	12661	12977	11861	9221
Cherokee.........	8080	9166	6838	3427	......	......	......	......	......
Chowan...........	6450	6842	6721	6690	6697	6464	5297	5132	5011
Clay.............	2461	......	......	......	......	......	......	......	......
Cleaveland.......	12696	12348	10396	......	......	......	......	......	......
Columbus.........	8474	8597	5909	3941	4141	3912	3022	......	......
Craven...........	20516	16268	14709	13438	13734	13394	12676	10245	10469
Cumberland.......	17035	16369	20610	15284	14834	14446	9382	9264	8671
Currituck........	5131	7415	7236	6703	7655	8098	6985	6928	5219
Dare.............	2778	......	......	......	......	......	......	......	......
Davidson.........	17414	16601	15320	14606	13389	......	......	......	......
Davie............	9620	8494	7866	7574	......	......	......	......	......
Duplin...........	15542	15784	13514	11182	11291	9744	7863	6796	5662
Edgecombe........	22970	17376	17189	15708	14935	13276	12423	10421	10255
Forsyth..........	13050	12692	11168	......	......	......	......	......	......
Franklin.........	14134	14107	11713	10980	10665	9741	10166	8529	7559
Gaston...........	12602	9307	8073	......	......	......	......	......	......
Gates............	7724	8443	8426	8161	7866	6837	5965	5881	5392
Granville........	24831	23396	21249	18817	19355	18222	15576	14015	10982
Greene...........	8687	7925	6619	6595	6413	4533	4867	4218	6893
Guilford.........	21736	20056	19754	19175	18737	14511	11420	9442	7191
Halifax..........	20408	19442	16589	16865	17739	17237	13620	13945	13965
Harnett..........	8895	8039	......	......	......	......	......	......	......

POPULATION BY COUNTIES—Continued.

COUNTIES.	AGGREGATE.								
	1870	1860	1850	1840	1830	1820	1810	1800	1790
Haywood	7921	5801	7074	4975	4578	4073	2780	......	......
Henderson	7706	10448	6853	5129	......	......	......	......	......
Hertford	9273	9504	8142	7484	8537	7712	6052	6701	5828
Hyde	6445	7732	7636	6458	6184	4967	6029	4829	4120
Iredell	16931	15347	14719	15685	14918	13071	10972	8856	5435
Jackson	6683	5515	......	......	......	......	......	......	......
Johnston	16897	15656	13726	10599	10938	9607	6867	6301	5634
Jones	5002	5730	5038	4945	5608	5216	4968	4339	4822
Lenoir	10434	10220	7828	7605	7723	6799	5572	4005	......
Lincoln	9573	8195	7746	25160	22455	18147	16359	12660	9224
Macon	6615	6004	6389	4869	5333	......	......	......	......
Madison	8192	5908	......	......	......	......	......	......	......
Martin	9647	10195	8307	7637	8539	6320	5987	5629	6080
McDowell	7592	7120	6246	......	......	......	......	......	......
Mecklenburg	24299	17374	13914	18273	20073	16895	14272	10439	11395
Mitchell	4705	......	......	......	......	......	......	......	......
Montgomery	7487	7649	6872	10780	10919	8693	8430	7677	4725
Moore	12040	11427	9342	7988	7745	7128	6367	4767	3770
Nash	11077	11687	10657	9047	8490	8185	7268	6975	7393
New Hanover	27978	21715	17668	13312	10959	10866	11465	7060	6831
Northampton	14749	13372	13335	13369	13391	13242	13082	12353	9981
Onslow	7569	8856	8283	7527	7814	7016	6669	5623	5387
Orange	17507	16947	17055	24356	23908	23492	20135	16362	12216
Pasquotank	8131	8940	8950	8514	8641	8008	7674	5379	5497
Perquimans	7945	7238	7332	9790	7419	6857	6052	5708	5440
Person	11170	11221	10781	7346	10027	9029	6642	6402	......
Pitt	17276	16080	13397	11806	12093	10001	9169	9084	8275
Polk	4319	4043	......	......	......	......	......	......	......
Randolph	17551	16793	15832	12875	12406	11331	10112	9234	7276
Richmond	12882	11009	9818	8909	9396	7537	6695	5623	5055
Robeson	16262	15489	12826	10370	9433	8204	7528	6839	5326
Rockingham	15708	16746	14495	13442	12935	11474	10316	8277	6187
Rowan	16810	14589	13870	12109	20786	26009	21543	20060	15828
Rutherford	13121	11573	13550	19202	17557	15351	13202	10753	7808
Sampson	16436	16624	14585	12157	11634	8908	6620	6719	6065
Stanly	8315	7801	6922	......	......	......	......	......	......
Stokes	11208	10402	9206	16265	16196	14033	11645	11026	8528
Surry	11252	10380	18443	15079	14504	12330	10366	9505	7191
Transylvania	3536	......	......	......	......	......	......	......	......
Tyrrell	4173	4944	5133	4657	4732	4319	3364	3395	4744
Union	12217	11202	10051	......	......	......	......	......	......
Wake	35617	28627	24888	21118	20398	20102	17086	13437	10192
Warren	17768	15726	13912	12919	11877	11158	11004	11284	9397
Washington	6516	6357	5664	4525	4552	3986	3464	2422	......
Watauga	5287	4957	3400	......	......	......	......	......	......
Wayne	18144	14905	13486	10891	10331	9040	8687	6772	6133
Wilkes	15539	14749	12099	12577	11968	9967	9054	7247	8143
Wilson	12258	9720	......	......	......	......	......	......	......
Yadkin	10697	10714	......	......	......	......	......	......	......
Yancey	5909	8655	8205	5962	......	......	......	......	......

No. XIII.

Executive and State Officers of N. C.

EXECUTIVE AND STATE OFFICERS OF N. C.

GOVERNORS UNDER THE LORD'S PROPRIETORS UNDER CHARTER OF CHARLES II.

DATE.	NAMES.	DATE.	NAMES.
1663	William Drummond.	——	Henderson Walker.
1667	Samuel Stevens.	1704	Robert Daniel.
1674	Sir George Carteret.	——	Sir Nathaniel Johnson.
1677	Sir George Eastchurch.	——	Thomas Carey.
——	—— Miller, Deputy.	1712	Edward Hyde.
——	—— John Culpepper.	1712	Geo. Pollock.
1683	Seth Sothel.	1713	Charles Eden.
1689	Philip Ludwell.	1724	George Burrington.
1693	Thos. Smith.	1725	Sir Richard Everhard.
1694	John Archdale.	1729	The Lord's Proprietors surrendered their charter to the Crown.
1608	Thomas Harvey.		

GOVERNORS UNDER THE CROWN:

DATE.	NAMES.	DATE.	NAMES.
1730	George Burrington.	1753	Matthew Rowan.
1734	Gabriel Johnston.	1765	William Tryon.
1753	Arthur Dobbs.	1771	Josiah Martin.

GOVERNORS UNDER THE CONSTITUTION ELECTED BY THE GENERAL ASSEMBLY:

DATE.	NAMES.	COUNTIES.
1776	Richard Caswell	Lenoir.
1779	Abner Nash	Craven.
1781	Thomas Burke	Orange.
1782	Alexander Martin	Guilford.
1784	Richard Caswell	Lenoir.
1787	Samuel Johnston	Chowan.
1789	Alexander Martin	Guilford.

EXECUTIVE AND STATE OFFICERS.—Continued.

DATE.	NAME.	COUNTIES.
1792	Richard Dobbs Spaight, Sr.	Craven.
1795	Samuel Ashe	New Hanover.
1798	Wm. R. Davie	Halifax.
1799	Benjamin Williams	Moore.
1802	James Turner	Warren.
1805	Nathaniel Alexander	Mecklenburg.
1807	Benjamin Williams	Moore.
1808	David Stone	Bertie.
1810	Benjamin Smith	Brunswick.
1811	William Hawkins	Warren.
1814	William Miller	Warren.
1817	John Branch	Halifax.
1820	Jesse Franklin	Surry.
1821	Gabriel Holmes	Sampson.
1824	Hutchings G. Burton	Halifax.
1827	James Iredell	Chowan.
1828	John Owen	Bladen.
1830	Montford Stokes	Wilkes.
1832	David L. Swain	Buncombe.
1835	Richard Dobbs Spaight, Jr.	Craven.

GOVERNORS ELECTED BY THE PEOPLE.

DATE.	NAMES.	COUNTIES.
1837	Edward B. Dudley	New Hanover.
1841	John M. Morehead	Guilford.
1845	William A. Graham	Orange.
1849	Charles Manly	Wake.
1851	David S. Reid	Rockingham.
1854	Warren Winslow, *ex officio*	Cumberland.
1855	Thomas Bragg	Northampton.
1858	John W. Ellis	Rowan.
1861	Henry T. Clark, ex officio	Edgecombe.
1863	Z. B. Vance	Buncombe.
1866	W. W. Holden, Provisional	Wake.
1866	Jonathan Worth	Randolph.
1868	W. W. Holden	Wake.
1870	Tod R. Caldwell, now (1874) in office	Burke.

LIEUTENANT GOVERNORS.

DATE.	NAMES.	DATE.	NAME.
1869	Tod R. Caldwell.	1871	C. H. Brogden.

EXECUTIVE AND STATE OFFICERS—CONTINUED.

SECRETARIES OF STATE.

DATE.	NAME.	DATE.	NAME.
1777	James Glasgow.	1864	Charles R. Thomas.
1778	William White.	1866	R. W. Best.
1811	William Hill.	1868	Henry J. Menninger.
1859	Rufus H. Page.	1872	Wm. H. Howerton.
1863	J. P. H. Russ.		

TREASURERS:

DATE.	NAME.	DATE.	NAME.
1776	{ Richard Caswell. { Samuel Johnston.	1839	Charles L. Hinton.
		1843	John H. Wheeler.
1777	Memucan Hunt.	1845	Charles L. Hinton.
1787	John Haywood.	1852	Daniel W. Courts.
1827	William S. Robards.	1863	Jonathan Worth.
1830	Robert H. Burton.	1865	Wm. Sloan.
——	William S. Mhoon.	1866	Kemp P. Battle.
1835	Samuel F. Patterson.	1869	David A. Jenkins.
1837	Daniel W. Courts.		

COMPTROLLERS:

DATE.	NAME.	DATE.	NAME.
1783	John Craven.	1836	William F. Collins.
1808	Samuel Goodwin.	1851	William J. Clarke.
1825	Joseph Hawkins.	1855	George W. Brooks.
1827	John L. Henderson.	1857	Curtis H. Brogden.
——	James Grant.	1867	S. W. Burgin.
1834	Nathan Stedman.		

AUDITORS:

DATE.	NAME.	DATE.	NAME.
1868 to 1873	Henderson Adams.	1873 to 1877	John Reilley.

SUPERINTENDENT OF PUBLIC INSTRUCTION.

S. S. ASHLEY,
ALEX. McIVER.

PRESENT EXECUTIVE.

Tod R. Caldwell, Governor, born in Burke County, 19th February, 1818; graduated at University in 1840: admitted to the bar same year; elected member of the House 1842 and 1844, and to the Senate 1850. In 1865 elected to State Convention; in 1868 elected Lieutenant Governor, and in December, 1870, on the deposition of Gov. Holden, succeeded to the Executive Chair. In 1872, elected by the people Governor for four years from 1st January, 1873.

John B. Neathery, Private Secretary, salary $75 and fees.

Curtis H. Brogden, of Wayne, Lieutenant Governor and President of the Senate. Pay same as Speaker of the House of Representatives.

W. H. Howerton, of Rowan, Secretary of State, salary $1,000 and fees.

J. Howerton Bailey, Clerk to Secretary of State.

David A. Jenkins, of Gaston, Treasuerer, salary $3,000.

A. D. Jenkins, Teller, employed and paid by Treasurer.

Donald W. Bain, Chief Clerk, salary $1,500.

John Reilly, of Cumberland, Auditor, salary $1,250.

Wm. B. Wetherell, Chief Clerk, salary $900.

Alexander McIver, Superintendent of Public Instruction, salary $1,500.

John C. Gorman, of Wake, Adjutant General, salary $300.

T. L. Hargrove, of Granville, Attorney General, salary $1,500.

W. C. Kerr, of Mecklenburg, State Geologist, salary $2,500.

Thos. R. Purnell, of New Hanover, Librarian, salary $600.

Henry M. Miller, of Wake, Keeper of Capitol, salary $750.

GOVERNORS COUNCIL.

The Secretery of State, Treasurer, Auditor and Superintendent of Public Instruction.

No. XIV.

Judiciary.

JUDICIARY.

JUSTICES OF SUPREME COURT.

DATE.	NAME.	DATE.	NAME.
1818	John Lewis Taylor, Leonard Henderson, John Hall.	1860	M. E. Manly.
		1868	Edwin G. Reade.†
1829	John D. Toomer, Thomas Ruffin.	1870	Wm. B. Rodman.†
1832	Joseph J. Daniel.	——	Rob't. P. Dick.
1844	Frederick Nash.	——	Thomas Settle.†
1848	Wm. H. Battle.	1871	N. Boyden.
	Richmond M. Pearson.†	1872	Wm. P. Bynum.†

Those marked thus † now in office.

SUPREME COURT.

Richmond M. Pearson, of Yadkin, Chief Justice, salary $2,500.

Edwin G. Reade, of Person, Associate Justice, salary $2,500.

W. P. Bynum, of Mecklenburg, Associate Justice, salary $2,500.

Thomas Settle, of Guilford, Associate Justice, salary $2,500.

William B. Rodman, of Beaufort, Associate Justice, salary $2,500.

Tazewell L. Hargrove, of Granville, Attorney General.

Wm. H. Bagley, of Wake, Clerk, salary $1,000 and fees.

D. A. Wicker, of Wake, Marshall.

Supreme Court meets in Raleigh on the first Monday in January and June.

SUPERIOR COURTS.

The State is divided into twelve Judicial Districts, and for each a Judge and Solicitor are elected, who are required by the Constitution to reside in their respective Districts.

The terms of the several Courts begin in each year, at the times herein stated, and are required by law to continue to be held for two weeks, (Sundays and legal holidays excepted) unless the business be sooner disposed of.

FIRST JUDICIAL DISTRICT.

J. W. Albertson, of Perquimans County, Judge.

Willis Bagley, of Perquimans County, Solicitor.

Currituck—On the second Monday in January and July.

Camden—On the fourth Monday in January and July.

Pasquotank—On the fourth Monday after the second Monday in January and July.

Perquimans—On the sixth Monday after the second Monday in January and July.

Chowan—On the eighth Monday after the second Monday in January and July

Gates—On the tenth Monday after the second Monday in January and July.

Tyrrell—On the twelfth Monday after the second Monday in January and July.

Hyde—On the fourteenth Monday after the second Monday in January and July.

Dare—On the sixteenth Monday after the second Monday in January and July.

SECOND JUDICIAL DISTRICT,

W. A. Moore, of Washington, Judge.

Joseph J. Martin, of Martin County, Solicitor.

Hertford—On the first Monday in September and February.

Washington—On the third Monday in September and February.

Martin—On the fourth Monday after the third Monday in September and February.

Beaufort—On the sixth Monday after the third Monday in September and February.

Bertie—On the eighth Monday after the third Monday in February and September.

Pitt—On the second and twelfth Monday after the third Monday in February and second Monday after the third Monday in September.

Edgecombe—On the tenth Monday after the third Monday in September and February, and on the third Monday in July.

THIRD JUDICIAL DISTRICT.

William J. Clarke, of Craven County, Judge.

John V. Sherard, of Wayne County, Solicitor.

Wilson—On the second Monday in March and September.

Wayne—On the second Monday after the second Monday in March and September.

Craven—On the fourth Monday after the second Monday in March and September.

Lenoir—On the sixth Monday after the second Monday in March and September.

Jones—On the eighth Monday after the second Monday in March and September.

Greene—On the tenth Monday after the second Monday in March and September.

Pamlico—On the twelfth Monday after the second Monday in March and September.

FOURTH JUDICIAL DISTRICT.

Daniel L. Russel, Jr., of Brunswick, Judge.

Edward Cantwell, of New Hanover, Solicitor.

Carteret—On second Monday in February and August.

Brunswick—On second Monday after second Monday in February and August.

Columbus—On the fourth Monday after the second Monday in February and August.

Robseon—On the sixth Monday after the second Monday in February and August.

Bladen—On the eighth Monday after the second Monday in February and August.

New Hanover—On the second Monday in January and tenth Monday after the second Monday in February, and fourth Monday in June, and tenth Monday after the second Monday in August.

Onslow—On the twelfth Monday after the second Monday in February and August.

Duplin—On the fourteenth Monday after the second Monday in February and August.

Sampson—On the sixteenth Monday after the second Monday in February and August.

FIFTH JUDICIAL DISTRICT.

Ralph P. Buxton, of Cumberland, Judge.

Neil McKay, of Harnett, Solicitor.

Harnett—On the second Monday of August and February.

Moore—On the second Monday after the second Monday of August and February.

Montgomery—On the fourth Monday after the second Monday of August and February.

Stanly—On the sixth Monday after the second Monday of August and February.

Union—On the eighth Monday after the second Monday of August and February.

Anson—On the tenth Monday after the second Monday of August and February.

Richmond—On the twelfth Monday after the second Monday of August and February.

Cumberland—On the fourteeth Monday after the second Monday in February and August.

SIXTH JUDICIAL DISTRICT.

Samual W. Watts, of Franklin, Judge.

William R. Cox, of Wake, Solicitor.

Nash—On the second Monday of February and August.

Warren—On the second Monday after the second Monday of August and February.

Franklin—On the fourth Monday after the second Monday of August and February.

Johnston—On the sixth Monday after the second Monday in February and August.

Wake—On the first Monday in January, the eighth Monday after the second Monday in February; the fourth Monday in June, and the eighth Monday after the second Monday in August.

Granville—On the tenth Monday after the second Monday in February and August, two terms in addition to those now held by law, beginning on the third Monday of January and the third Monday of July respectively.

Halifax—On the twelfth Monday after the second Monday in August and February.

Northampton—On the fourteenth Monday after the second Monday in August and February.

SEVENTH JUDICIAL DISTRICT.

Albion W. Tourgee, of Guilford, Judge.

J. R. Bulla, of Randolph, Solicitor.

Alamance—On the second Monday before the first Monday of March and September.

Guilford—On the first Monday in March and September.

Chatham—On the second Monday after the first Monday in March and September.

Caswell—On the fourth Monday after the first Monday of March and September.

Person—On the sixth Monday after the first Monday of March and September.

Orange—On the eighth Monday after the first Monday of March and September.

Rockingham—On the tenth Monday after the first Monday in March and September.

Randolph—On the fourth Monday before the first Monday in March and September.

EIGHTH JUDICIAL DISTRICT.

J. M. Cloud, of Surry, Judge.

A. H. Joyce, of Stokes, Solicitor.

Surry—On the first Monday in March and September.

Davie—On the second Monday after the third Monday of March and September.

Yadkin—On the third Monday of March and September.

Rowan—On the fourth Monday after the third Monday of March and September.

Davidson—On the sixth Monday after the third Monday of March and September.

Forsythe—On the eighth Monday after the third Monday of March and September.

Stokes—On the tenth Monday after the third Monday of March and September.

NINTH JUDICIAL DISTRICT.

Geo. W. Logan, of Rutherford, Judge.

Polk—On the second Monday of March and September.

Rutherford—On the fourth Monday of March and September.

Cleaveland—On the second Monday after the fourth Monday of March and September.

Lincoln—On the fourth Monday after the fourth Monday of March and September.

Gaston—On the sixth Monday after the fourth Monday of March and September.

Mecklenburg—On the eighth Monday after the fourth Monday of March and September.

Cabarrus—On the tenth Monday after the fourth Monday of March and September.

TENTH JUDICIAL DISTRICT.

Anderson Mitchell, of Iredell, Judge.

W. P. Caldwell, of Iredell, Solicitor.

Catawba—On the first Monday in March and September.

Alexander—On the third Monday of March and November.

Caldwell—On the second Monday after the third Monday in March and September.

Alleghany—On the fourth Monday after the third Monday in March and September.

Ashe—On the sixth Monday after the third Monday in March and September.

Wilkes—On the eighth Monday after the third Monday in March and September.

Iredell—On the tenth Monday after the third Monday in March and September.

ELEVENTH JUDICIAL DISTRICT.

James L. Henry, of Buncombe, Judge.

Wm. G. Chandler, of Buncombe, Solicitor.

Watauga—On the second Monday of March and August.

McDowell—On the fourth Monday of March and August.

Henderson—On the second Monday after the fourth Monday of March and August.

Buncombe—On the fourth Monday after the fourth Monday of March and August.

Madison—On the sixth Monday after the fourth Monday of March and August.

Yancey—On the eighth Monday after the fourth Monday of March and August.

Mitchell—On the tenth Monday after the fourth Monday of March and August.

Burke—On the twelfth Monday after the fourth Monday of March and August.

TWELFTH JUDICIAL DISTRICT.

R. H. Cannon, of Jackson, Judge.

R. M. Henry, of Macon, Solicitor.

Graham—On the first Monday of March and August.

Clay—On the second Monday after the third Monday of March and August.

Cherokee—On the third Monday after the third Monday of March and August.

Macon—On the fourth Monday after the third Monday of March and August.

Swain—On the sixth Monday after the third Monday of March and August.

Jackson—On the eighth Monday after the third Monday in March and August.

Haywood—On the tenth Monday after the third Monday of March and August.

Transylvania—On the twelfth Monday after the third Monday of March and August.

UNITED STATES COURTS.

The stated terms of the United States Circuit and District Courts are as follows:

United States Circuit Court—Eastern District North Carolina—Held in Raleigh first Monday in June and last Monday in November.

H. L. Bond, Circuit Court Judge; residence, Baltimore, Md.

Geo. W. Brooks, District Court Judge, Eastern District, N. C.; residence, Elizabeth City.

N. J. Riddick, Circuit Court Clerk; office, Raleigh.

EASTERN DISTRICT COURTS.

Elizabeth City—Third Monday in April and October.

Clerk—M. B. Culpepper; residence, Elizabeth City.

Newbern—Fourth Monday in April and October.

Clerk—Geo. E. Tinker; residence, Newbern.

Wilmington—First Monday after the fourth Monday in April and October.

Clerk—Wm. Larkins; residence, Wilmington.

U. S. Marshal—Robert M. Douglas. Official headquarters, Greensboro, N. C.

District Attorney—R. C. Badger; residence, Raleigh, N. C.

Deputy for Eastern District—J. B. Hill, Raleigh, N. C.

U. S. CIRCUIT COURT—WESTERN DISTRICT N. C.

H. L. Bond, U. S. Circuit Court Judge, Baltimore, Md.

Robt. P. Dick, U. S. District Judge, Western District N. C.; residence, Greensboro', N. C.

Circuit and District Courts in the Western District are held at the same time.

Greensboro'—First Monday in April and October.

Clerk—John W. Payne; residence, Greensboro'.

Statesville—Third Monday in April and October.

Clerk—Henry C. Cowles; residence, Statesville.

Asheville—First Monday after the fourth Monday in April and October.

Clerk—E. R. Hampton; residence, Asheville.

Virgil S. Lusk, U. S. District Attorney; residence, Asheville.

Robert M. Douglas, U. S. Marshal; residence, Greensboro', N. C. Official headquarters, Greensboro', N. C.

JUDGES OF THE SUPERIOR COURTS OF NORTH CAROLINA FROM 1777.

1777 to 1790. John Williams, of Granville county, died October, 1799. Samuel Ashe, of New Hanover, elected Governor in 1795.

Samuel Spencer, of Anson, died 1794.

1790. S. McCay, of Rowan, died 1808.

John Haywood, of Halifax, elected 1794; resigned in 1800.

Alfred Moore, of Brunswick, elected in 1798; appointed Associate Justice of the Supreme Court of the United States, December 10th, 1799.

John Louis Taylor, of Cumberland, elected in 1798; appointed Judge of the Supreme Court of North Carolina, in 1818; died February, 1829.

Samuel Johnston, of Chowan, appointed February 10th, 1800; resigned November 18th, 1803.

John Hall, of Warren, elected in 1800; appointed Judge Supreme Court in 1818; resigned December, 1832; died 1833.

Francis Locke, of Rowan, elected in 1803; resigned February 7th, 1814.

David Stone, of Bertie, elected in 1795, and resigned in 1798, and elected Governor in 1808.

Samuel Lowrie, of Mecklenburg, elected in 1806; died December, 1818.

Blake Baker, of Warren, appointed in 1808; commission expired in December. 1808; died in 1818.

Leonard Henderson, of Granville, elected in 1808; resigned in 1816; elected Judge of the Supreme Court in 1818; died August, 1833.

Joshua Wright, of New Hanover, elected in 1808; died in 1811.

Henry Seawell, of Wake, appointed July 5th, 1811; commission expired in 1811: appointed in 1813; resigned in 1819; elected in 1832; died in 1835.

Edward Harris, of Craven, elected in 1811; died in 1813.

Duncan Cameron, of Orange, appointed February, 1814; resigned November, 1816.

Thomas Ruffin, of Orange, elected 1816; resigned December, 1818; appointed July 15, 1825; resigned 1828; elected Judge of the Supreme Court in 1829; resigned 1859; died 1870.

Joseph J. Daniel, of Halifax, appointed March, 1816; elected Judge of the Supreme Court in 1832; died February, 1848.

Robert H. Burton, of Lincoln, appointed March, 1818; resigned in 1818.

John Paxton, of Rutherford, elected in 1818; died in 1826.

John D. Toomer, of Cumberland, elected in 1818; resigned in 1819; appointed Judge of the Supreme Court in 1829; commission expired December, 1829; elected in 1836; resigned in 1840.

Frederick Nash, of Orange, elected in 1818; resigned in July, 1826; elected in 1836; transferred to the Supreme Court in 1844.

Archibald D. Murphy, of Orange, elected in 1818; resigned in 1820.

James Iredell, of Chowan, appointed March, 1819; resigned May, 1819.

John R. Donnell, of Craven, appointed in 1819; resigned in 1836.

Willie P. Mangum, of Orange, elected in 1819; appointed May 18, 1826; commission expired in 1826; elected in 1828; Senator to Congress in 1830.

William Norwood, of Orange, appointed in 1820; resigned in 1836.

George E. Badger, of Wake, elected in 1820; resigned in 1826.

Robert Strange, of Cumberland, elected in 1826; elected Senator to Congress in 1836.

James Martin, of Rowan, elected in 1826; resigned in 1835.

David L. Swain, of Buncombe, elected in 1830; elected Governor in 1832.

Thomas Settle, of Rockingham, elected in 1832.

Romulus M. Saunders, elected in 1835; resigned in 1840; elected in 1852; died in 1867.

Edward Hall, of Warren, appointed February, 1840; commission expired January, 1841.

John M. Dick, of Guilford, elected in 1835.

John L. Baily, of Pasquotank, elected in 1836.

Richmond M. Pearson, of Davie, elected in 1836; transferred to the Supreme Court in 1848.

David F. Caldwell, of Rowan, appointed in 1844.

Matthias E. Manly, of Craven, elected December, 1840.

Augustus Moore, of Chowan, appointed in 1848; resigned the same year.

Wm. H. Battle, of Edgecombe, appointed in 1840; appointed to the Supreme Court in 1848; resigned in December, 1848; elected to the Superior Court in January, 1849.

John W. Ellis, of Rowan, elected in 1848.

DATE.	NAME OF JUDGES.	DATE.	NAME OF JUDGES.
1854	S. J. Person.		Edward J. Warren.
1859	R. R. Heath.	1868	Alexander Little.
	J. G. Shepherd.		Clinton N. Cilley.
1859	James W. Osborne.	1870	C. C. Pool.
	Geo. Howard, Jr.		C. R. Thomas.
1860	R. S. French.		Daniel L. Russell.
1861	Thomas Ruffin, Jr.		A. W. Tourgee.
1862	John Kerr.		Geo. W. Logan.
	Rob't. B. Gilliam.		E. W. Jones.
1863	Edwin G. Reade.		S. W. Watts.
	Wm. M. Shipp.		John M. Cloud.
1865	David A. Barnes.		James L. Henry.
	R. P. Buxton.		Riley A. Cannon.
	D. G. Fowle.	1871	Wm. A. Moore.
	Anderson Mitchell.		Wm. J. Clarke.
	Augustus S. Merrimon.	1872	Jonathan W. Albertson.

JUDGES OF THE SUPERIOR COURTS NOW IN OFFICE.

DISTRICT.	NAME.	DISTRICT.	NAME.
First	J. W. Albertson.	Seventh	Albion W. Tourgee.
Second	W. A. Moore.	Eighth	J. M, Cloud.
Third	W. J. Clarke.	Ninth	Geo. W. Logan.
Fourth	Daniel L. Russell.	Tenth	Anderson Mitchell.
Fifth	Ralph Bnxton.	Eleventh	John L. Henry.
Sixth	Samuel W. Watts.	Twelfth	R. H. Cannon.

ATTORNEY GENERALS OF NORTH CAROLINA.

Waightstill Avery, of Burke county, elected in 1777; resigned in 1779.

Blake Baker, of Edgecombe, elected in 1794; resigned in 1803.

Hutchins G. Burton, of Halifax, elected in 1810; resigned in November, 1816.

William Drew, of Halifax, elected in 1816; resigned in November, 1825.

John R. J. Daniel, of Halifax, elected in 1834.

William Eaton, Jr., of Warren, in 1851.

Oliver Fitts, of Warren, in 1808,
John Haywood, of Halifax, in 1791.
James Iredell, of Chowan, in 1779.
Robert H. Jones, of Warren, in 1828.
Alfred Moore, of Brunswick, in 1790.
William Miller, of Warren, in 1810.
Hugh McQueen, of Chatham, in 1840.
Bartholomew F. Moore, of Halifax, in 1848.
Romulus M. Saunders, of Caswell, in 1828.
Edward Stanly, of Beaufort, in 1846.
Henry Seawell, of Wake, in 1803.
John L. Taylor, of Cumberland, in 1808.
James F. Taylor, of Wake, in 1825; died in June, 1828.
Spier Whitaker, of Halifax, elected in December, 1842.

DATE.	NAME.	DATE.	NAME.
1852	M. W. Ransom.	1868	William Coleman.
1855	J. B. Batchelor.	1870	L. P. Olds.
1856	W. A. Bailey.	1871	W. M. Shipp.
1856	W. A. Jenkins.	1873	T. L. Hargrove.
1862	Sion H. Rogers.		

7

No. XV.

General Assembly of North Carolina.

GENERAL ASSEMBLY OF NORTH CAROLINA.

SPEAKERS OF THE SENATE.

DATE.	NAME.	DATE.	NAME.
1777	Samuel Ashe.	1823	Bartlett Yancey.
1778	Allen Jones.	1824	“ “
1779	Abner Nash.	1825	“ “
1780	Alexander Martin.	1826	“ “
1781	“ “	1827	“ “
1782	Richard Caswell.	1828	Jesse Speight.
1783	“ “	1829	Bedford Brown.
1784	“ “	1830	David F. Caldwell.
1785	“ “ & Alex Martin.	1831	“ “
1786	James Coor.	1832	Wm. D. Mosely.
1787	Alexander Martin.	1833	“ “
1788	“ “	1834	“ “
1789	Charles Johnson.	1835	“ “
1790	William Lenoir.	1836	Hugh Waddell.
1791	“ “	1837	“ “
7792	“ “	1838	Andrew Joyner.
1793	“ “	1839	“ “
1794	“ “	1840	“ “
1795	Benj. Smith.	1841	“ “
1796	“ “	1842	Louis D. Wilson.
1797	“ “	1843	“ “
1798	“ “	1844	Burgess S. Gaither.
1799	“ “	1845	“ “
1800	Joseph Riddick.	1846	Andrew Joyner.
1801	“ “	1847	“ “
1802	“ “	1848	Calvin Graves.
1803	“ “	1849	“ “
1804	“ “	1850	Weldon N. Edwards.
1805	Alexander Martin.	1851	“ “
1806	Joseph Riddick.	1852	“ “
1807	“ “	1853	“ “
1808	“ “	1854	Warren Winslow.
1809	“ “	1855	“ “
1810	“ “	1856	W. W. Avery.
1811	“ “	1857	“ “
1812	George Outlaw.	1859	H. I. Clark.
1813	“ “	1860	“ “
1814	“ “	1862	Giles Mebane.
1815	John Branch.	1864	“ “
1816	“ “	1866	M. E- Manley.
1817	Bartlett Yancey.	1868	Tod R. Caldwell.
1818	“ “	1870	“ “
1819	“ “	1871	E. J. Warren.
1820	“ “	1872	C. H. Brogden, (Lieut. Governor
1821	“ “		for 4 years from Jan. 1, 1873.)
1822	“ “		

SPEAKERS OF THE HOUSE.

DATE.	NAME.	DATE.	NAME.
1777	Abner Nash.	1823	Alfred Moore.
1778	Thomas Benbury.	1825	John Stanly. James Iredell.
1779	" "	1826	" "
1780	" "	1827	Thomas Settle.
1781	" "	1828	" "
1782	" "	1829	Wm. J. Alexander.
1783	Edward Starkey.	1830	Charles Fisher.
1784	Thomas Benbury.	1831	" "
1785	Wm. Blount, Rich'd D. Spaight.	1832	Louis D. Henry.
1786	John B. Ashe.	1833	Wm. J. Alexander.
1787	John Sitgreave.	1834	" "
1788	Stephen Cabarras,	1835	Wm. H. Haywood.
1789	" "	1836	" "
1790	" "	1837	" "
1791	" "	1838	Wm. A. Graham.
1792	" "	1839	" "
1793	John Leigh.	1840	" "
1794	Timothy Bloodworth.	1841	" "
1795	John Leigh.	1842	Calvin Graves.
1796	Mussendine Matthews.	1843	" "
1797	" "	1844	Edward Stanly.
1798	" "	1845	" "
1799	" "	1846	" "
1800	Stephen Cabarras.	1847	" "
1801	" "	1848	R. B. Gilliam.
1802	" "	1849	" "
1803	" "	1850	Jas. C. Dobbin.
1804	" "	1851	" "
1805	" "	1852	John Baxter.
1806	Joshua G. Wright.	1853	" "
1808	William Gaston.	1854	Samuel P. Hill.
1809	Thomas Davis.	1855	"
1810	William Hawkins.	1856	Jesse G. Shepherd.
1811	John Steele.	1857	" "
1812	William Miller.	1857	Thomas Settle.
1813	" "	1858	" "
1814	Frederick Nash.	1859	Wm. T. Dortch, till Sept. 1861
1815	John Craig.	1862	R. B. Gilliam. N. N. Fleming.
1816	James Iredell.	1864	R. S. Donnell.
1817	" "	1862	M. S. Robbins.
1818	" "	1863	Thomas Settle.
1819	R. M. Saunders.	1865	R. Y. McAden.
1820	" "	1867	S. F. Phillips.
1821	James Mebane.	1868	Jos. W. Holden.
1822	John D. Jones.	1870	T. J. Jarvis.
1823	Alfred Moore.	1872	J. L. Robinson.

GENERAL ASSEMBLY OF NORTH CAROLINA.

SENATE, 1873-'74.

OFFICERS.	POST OFFICES.	COUNTY AND STATE.	
C. H. Brogden, Lt. Gov., Pres't *ex offi.*	Goldsboro'	Wayne,	N. C.
W. L. Saunders, Principal Clerk	Wilmington	New Hanover,	"
W. H. H. Cowles, Assistant Clerk	Wilkesboro'	Wilkes,	"
J. McL. Turner, Engrossing Clerk	Asheville	Buncombe,	"
J. E. Morris, Principal Doorkeeper	Newbern	Craven,	"
Guilford Christmas, Ass't Doorkeeper	Warrenton	Warren,	"
W. J. Wilson, En. Cl'k Gen Assembly	Forks of Pigeon	Haywood,	"

SENATORS.	POST OFFICES.	COUNTY AND STATE.	
Allen, W. A	Kenansville	Duplin,	N. C.
Avera, W. H	Selma	Johnston,	"
Barnhardt, J. C	Pioneer Mills	Cabarrus,	"
Chamberlain, J. L	South Mills	Camden,	"
Cowles, A. C	Hamptonville	Yadkin,	"
Cramer, J. T	Thomasville	Davidson,	"
Cunningham, J. W	Cun'gham's Store	Person,	"
Davis, W. K	Louisburg	Franklin,	"
Dunham, J. W	Wilson	Wilson,	"
Ellis, Dr. J. R	Hickory Tavern	Catawba,	"
Ellis, J. W	Whiteville	Columbus,	"
Epps, Henry	Halifax	Halifax,	"
Flemming, W. W	Marion	McDowell,	"
Grandy, C. W., Jr.	Elizabeth City	Pasquotank,	"
Gudger, J. M	Barnsville	Yancey,	"
Harris, J. H	Raleigh	Wake,	"
Hill, G. N	Robeson,	Brunswick,	"
Holloman, George D	Jackson	Northampton,	"
Horton, P	Elksville	Wilkes,	"
Humphrey, L. W	Goldsboro'	Wayne,	"
Hyman, J. A	Warrenton	Warren,	"
Johnson, S. L	Plymouth	Washington,	"
King, R. W	Kinston	Lenoir,	"
Long, R. T	Rockingham,	Richmond,	"
Love, Dr. W. L	Franklin,	Macon,	"
Mabson, G. L	Wilmington,	New Hanover,	"
McCabe, A	Tarboro'	Edgecombe,	"
McCauley, C. M. T	Monroe	Union,	"
McCotter, J	Johnson's Mills	Pitt,	"
Merrimon, J. H	Asheville	Buncombe,	"
Miller, Dr. W. J. T	Shelby	Cleaveland,	"
Morehead, J. T., Jr	Greensboro'	Guilford,	"
Morehead, J. Turner	Leaksville	Rockingham,	"
Murphy, Dr. C. T	Clinton	Sampson,	"
Murray, W. J	Big Falls	Alamance,	"
Nicholson, T. A	Eagle Mills	Iredell,	"
Norwood, J. W	Hillsboro'	Orange,	"
Powell, Dr. R. J	Pittsboro'	Chatham,	"
Price, Charles	Mocksville	Davie,	"
Ransom, E	Columbia	Tyrrell,	"

SENATE—Continued.

SENATORS.	POST OFFICES.	COUNTY AND STATE.	
Scott, J. G	Jacksonville	Onslow,	N. C.
Seymour, A. S	Newbern	Craven,	"
Smith, B	Oxford	Granville,	"
Stafford, J. M	Salem	Forsythe,	"
Todd, J. W	Jefferson	Ashe,	"
Troy, W. C	Fayetteville	Cumberland,	"
Walker, Martin	Rutherfordton	Rutherford,	"
Waring, R. P	Charlotte	Mecklenburg,	"
Welch, W. P	Waynesville	Haywood,	"
Worth, Dr. J. M	Ashboro'	Randolph,	"

GENERAL ASSEMBLY OF NORTH CAROLINA.

HOUSE OF REPRESENTATIVES, 1873-'74.

OFFICERS.	POST OFFICE.	COUNTIES.
J. L. Robinson, Speaker	Franklin	Macon,
S. D. Pool, Principal Clerk	Newbern	Craven,
W. M. Hardy, Assistant Clerk	Asheville	Buncombe,
A. H. Boyden, Engrossing Clerk	Salisbury	Rowan,
John H. Hill, Doorkeeper	Ashboro'	Randolph,
J. E. Carter, Assistant Doorkeeper	Gold Hill	Rowan.

REPRESENTATIVES.	POST OFFICE.	COUNTIES.
Abbott, I. B	Newbern	Craven,
Anderson, Charles	Calahan	Davie,
Anderson, J. S	Hayesville	Clay,
Ballard, R. H	Gatesville	Gates,
Bean, J. W	Cedar Falls	Randolph,
Bennett, R. T	Wadesboro'	Anson,
Blackwell, D. A	French Broad	Buncombe,
Blythe, James	Blue Ridge	Henderson,
Bowe, Geo. W	Yanceyville	Caswell,
Bowman, J. W	Bakersville	Mitchell,
Brooks, John H	Shallotte	Brunswick,
Brown, J. T	Lexington	Davidson,
Brown, J. E	Charlotte	Mecklenburg,
Bryan, A. M	Cherrylane	Alleghany,
Bryan, W. P	Bethel	Pitt,
Bryan, W. H	Newton Grove	Sampson,
Bryant, John	Halifax	Halifax,
Bryan, A. C	Trap Hill	Wilkes,
Bryson, J. N	Cashin's Valley	Jackson,
Bryson, T. D	Charleston	Swain,
Bullard, G. W	Fayetteville	Cumberland,
Bunn, Willis	Battleboro'	Edgecombe,
Byrd, C. R	Burnsville	Yancey,
Carson, Dr. J. M	Taylorsville	Alexander,
Carter, W. S	Fairfield	Hyde,
Cobb, Joseph	Tarboro'	Edgecombe,
Copeland, E. G	Goldsboro'	Wayne,
Carson, Samuel	Washington	Beaufort,
Costner, A	Lincolnton	Lincoln,
Cox, G. W	Johnson's Mills	Pitt,
Craige, Kerr	Salisbury	Rowan,
Darden, J. R	Belvidere	Perquimans,
Davis, A	Snow Hill	Greene,
Dickey, B. K	Murphy	Cherokee,
Dudley, E. R	Newbern	Craven,
Dula, T. J	Wilkesboro'	Wilkes,
Ellison, Stewart	Raleigh	Wake,
Fletcher, R	Rockingham	Richmond,
Foster, T. J	Yanceyville	Caswell,
Freeman, Dr. G. W	Marion	McDowell,
Gant, Jesse	Big Falls	Alamance,
Gidney, J. W	Shelby	Cleaveland,
Gilbert, M. V'B	Raleigh	Wake,
Gilmer, J. W	Gilmer's Store	Guilford,

GENERAL ASSEMBLY OF NORTH CAROLINA.

HOUSE OF REPRESENTATIVES.—Continued.

REPRESENTATIVES.	POST OFFICE.	COUNTIES.
Godfrey, F. M	Elizabeth City	Pasquotank,
Goodwyn, J. J	Halifax	Halifax,
Gorman, John C	Raleigh	Wake,
Grady, J. R	Harnett C. H	Harnett,
Gray, O. N	Beacon Hill	Dare,
Gudger, H. A	Marshall	Madison,
Guyther, D. C	Plymouth	Washington,
Hampton, N. B	Columbus	Polk,
Hanner, O. A	St. Lawrence	Chatham,
Haynes, H. P	Pigeon Valley	Haywood,
Heaton, J	Wilmington	New Hanover,
Hinnant, Jesse	Earpsboro'	Johnston,
Houston, R. B. B	Catawba Station	Catawba,
Hughes, H. T	Oxford	Granville,
Johns, A. B	Leaksville	Rockingham,
Johnston, T. D	Asheville	Buncombe,
Jones, Edmond	Patterson	Caldwell,
Jones, S. A	Shiloh	Camden,
Jones, B. H	Jackson	Northampton,
Jones, Dr. Pride	Hillsboro'	Orange,
Jones, B	Gum Neck	Tyrrell,
Lloyd, Alfred	Wilmington	New Hanover,
Jordan, Allen	Troy	Montgomery,
Joyner, W. H	Princeton	Johnston,
King, George H	Warrenton	Warren,
Lindsay, J. E	Rocky Mount	Nash,
Luckey, Dr. F. N	China Grove	Rowan,
Lutterloh, T. S	Fayetteville	Cumberland,
Marler, John G	Yadkinville	Yadkin,
Maxwell, J. R	Dismal	Sampson,
McGehee, Montford	Cun'gham's Store	Person,
McLaurin, Wm	Wilmington	New Hanover,
McNeill, Thomas A	Shoe Heel	Robeson,
Michael, John	Lexington	Davidson,
Miller, F. C	Windsor	Bertie,
Mitchell, J. G. H	Red Shoal	Stokes,
Mizell, J. R	Jamesville	Martin,
Moring, John M	Morrisville	Chatham,
Moses, H. C	Wilson	Wilson,
Norment, W. S	Lumberton	Robeson,
Outlaw, J. K	Outlaw's Bridge	Duplin,
Paschall, John W. H	Macon Depot	Warren,
Patrick, John	Hookerton	Greene,
Perry, A. H	Elizabethtown	Bladen,
Perry, R. S	Raleigh	Wake,
Presson, L	Monroe	Union,
Reid, S. W	Charlotte	Mecklenburg,
Reid, John W	Ashboro'	Randolph,
Rhodes, J. C	Dudley	Wayne,
Richardson, V. V	Whiteville	Columbus,
Scott, Jacob F	Trenton	Jones,
Settle, David	Wentworth	Rockingham,
Shackelford, John W	Richlands	Onslow,
Sharp, James	Harrellsville	Hertford,

GENERAL ASSEMBLY OF NORTH CAROLINA.

HOUSE OF REPRESENTATIVES.—Continued.

REPRESENTATIVES.	POST OFFICE.	COUNTIES.
Shaw, John	Carthage	Moore,
Shinn, T. J	Statesville	Cabarrus,
Shinn, C. L	Granite Hill	Iredell,
Sneed, R. G	Townesville	Granville,
Stanford, John D	Kenansville	Duplin,
Stowe, W. A	Wood Lawn	Gaston,
Todd, J. B	Boone	Watauga,
Trivett, Squire	Jefferson	Ashe,
Turner, C. L	Olin	Iredell,
Waddill, Dr. M. T	Norwood	Stanley,
Warlick, P. A	Hickory Tavern	Burke,
Watson, Jones	Chapel Hill	Orange,
Waugh, H. M	Dobson	Surry,
Webb, Silas	Morehead	Carteret,
Wheeler, W. H	Salem	Forsythe,
Whisnant, Eli	First Broad	Rutherford,
Whitmire, F. J	Brevard	Transylvania,
Wiley, Wm	Jamestown	Guilford,
Williamson, John H	Louisburg	Franklin,
Winslow, J. L	Wardville	Chowan,
Woodhouse, J. M	Poplar Branch	Currituck,

No. XVI.

Public Institutions in North Carolina.

PUBLIC INSTITUTIONS IN NORTH CAROLINA.

BRANCH MINT OF THE UNITED STATES.

Located at Charlotte. This establishment was authorized by act of Congress, passed the 3rd of March, 1835. Is now operating as an Assay office only, C. J. Cowles, of Wilkes County, Assayer in charge. Salary $1,500.

UNIVERSITY OF NORTH CAROLINA.

Situated at Chapel Hill, Orange county, 28 miles w. n. w. from Raleigh; Rev. Sol. Pool, President.

THE NORTH CAROLINA INSTITUTION FOR THE DEAF AND DUMB AND THE BLIND.

The North Carolina Institution for the education of the Deaf and Dumb and the Blind, is located at Raleigh.

Officers—John Nichols, Principal; R. B. Ellis, Steward; L. E. Heartt, Treasurer.

Board of Directors—John Nichols, President; R. S. Tucker, C. D. Heartt, Albert Johnson, Handy Lockhart, T. F. Lee, W. W. White.

The Institution has a full corps of teachers in the Deaf Mute and Blind Departments. Can accommodate —— pupils. The course of instruction includes eight years. All applications for the admittance of pupils should be made to the Principal.

INSANE ASYLUM OF NORTH CAROLINA.

Situated in the vicinity of Raleigh. Will accommodate 220 patients.

Dr. Eugene Grissom, Superintendent; Dr. E. T. Fuller, Assistant Physician; Mrs. Bettie Huggins, Steward; Mrs. Mary A. Lawrence, Matron; J. C. L. Harris, Treasurer.

Board of Directors—Wesley Whitaker, President; T. M. Argo, of Wake, G. W. Brodie, of Wake; Dr. J. G. Ramsey, of Rowan; T. George Walton, of Burke; G. W. Stanton, of Wilson; Dr. T. L. Banks, of Wake; J. P. Prairie, of Wake; Rev. J. W. Hood, of Wake; Henry Walser, of Davidson; W. R. Myers, of Mecklenburg; C. L. Harris, of Wake; Dr. E. Burke Haywood, of Wake.

Time of annual meeting of the Board, first Wednesday in November in each year.

STATE PENITENTIARY.

Board of Directors and Executive Committee—John R. Harrison, of Wake, President; W. D. Jones, of Wake; Jacob S. Allen, of Wake; G. W. Welker, of Guilford; John M. Coffin, of Rowan.

Officers—W. J. Hicks, Architect; W. H. Thompson, Warden; M. Grausman, Steward; Dr. W. G. Hill, Physician; —— Dispensator.

STATE BOARD OF EDUCATION.

The Governor, Lieutenant-Governor, Secretary of State, Treasurer, Auditor, Superintendent of Public Instruction and Attorney General, constitute the State Board of Education.

The Governor is President, and the Superintendent of Public Instruction Secretary of the Board.

THE BOARD OF MEDICAL EXAMINERS OF THE STATE OF NORTH CAROLINA.

Created by act of Legislature, session 1858–'59. Elected every six years by N. C. Medical Society. Meets annually at the time and place of meeting of the State Medical Society. No person engaging in the practice of medicine in the State since April 15, 1859, is authorized to collect his bills. without having obtained the license of this Board.

Members—Dr. C. J. O'Hagan, Greenville, President; Dr. Wm. A. B. Norcom, Edenton; Dr. C. Tate Murphy, Clinton; Dr. Geo. L. Foote, Warrenton; Dr. J. W. Jones, Tarboro'; Dr. R. I. Payne, Lexington; Dr. C. Duffy, Jr., Newbern, Secretary and Treasurer.

No. XVII.

Table showing Area of each County, number of Acres listed, value per Acre, County Seat, and distance from Raleigh.

8

TABLE

Showing Area of each County, Number of Acres Listed, Value per Acre, County Seat and Distance from Raleigh.

	COUNTY.	COUNTY TOWN.	Area in Square Miles.‡	No. of Acres Listed.	Average value of Acre.	Distance from Raleigh.
1	Alamance	Graham	500	235,662	$ 6 10	miles 54
2	Alexander	Taylorsville	300	151,154	4 90	150
3	Alleghany	Sparta	200	119,356	2 80	
4	Anson	Wadesboro',	650	312,123	4 80	143
5	Ashe	Jefferson	395	239,137	2 03	202
6	Beaufort	Washington	600	392,078	1 70	127
7	Bertie	Windsor	800	351,251	5 60	157
8	Bladen	Elizabeth Town	800	508,922	2 60	99
9	Bruswick	Smithville	950	540,926	1 50	173
10	Buncombe	Asheville	1,000	346,274	3 42	256
11	Burke	Morganton	400	194,389	3 85	197
12	Cabarrus	Concord	350	221,661	7 80	130
13	Caldwell	Lenoir	450	219,035	3 90	200
14	Camden	Camden C. H.	280	110,883	6 90	219
15	Carteret	Beaufort	400	144,155	2 50	168
16	Caswell	Yanceyville	400	265,338	8 50	66
17	Catawba	Newton	250	251,669	5 90	175
18	Chatham	Pittsboro'	700	494,712	4 40	34
19	Cherokee	Murphy	700	1,205,993	1 40	367
20	Chowan	Edenton	250	80,948	3 30	182
21	Clay	Hayesville		99,060	1 90	
22	Cleaveland	Shelby	650	274,255	3 20	190
23	Columbus	Whiteville	600	303,218	1 80	125

TABLE.—(*Continued.*)

	COUNTY.	COUNTY TOWN.	Area in Square Miles.	No. of Acres Listed.	Average value of Acre.	Distance from Raleigh.
24	Craven	Newbern	1,000	469,640	$ 1 70	miles 120
25	Cumberland	Fayetteville	600	471,666	2 70	60
26	Currituck	Currituck C. H.	[illegible]	142,298	4 20	242
27	Dare					
28	Davidson	Lexington	650	345,861	7 50	117
29	Davie	Mocksville	250	162,535	7 60	120
30	Duplin	Kenansville	670	453,562	2 90	89
31	Edgecombe	Tarboro'	600	322,295	10 60	76
32	Forsythe	Winston	250	208,580	5 50	110
33	Franklin	Louisburg	450	300,132	5 00	36
34	Gaston	Dallas	350	220,556	5 10	175
35	Gates	Gatesville	300	182,882	5 00	167
36	Graham					
37	Granville	Oxford	750	487,927	6 90	45
38	Greene	Snow Hill	280	151,960	5 80	89
39	Guilford	Greensboro'	600	407,214	5 40	82
40	Halifax	Halifax	680	414,708	7 10	87
41	Harnett	Lillington	590	335,921	2 20	
42	Haywood	Waynesville	900	324,526	1 60	294
43	Henderson	Hendersonville	600	188,570	4 80	250
44	Hertford	Winton	320	194,140	5 20	155
45	Hyde	Swanquarter	430	149,915	5 60	203
46	Iredell	Statesville	600	360,670	4 90	145
47	Jackson	Webster	1,308	315,644	6 10	
48	Johnston	Smithfield	670	459,555	3 30	27
49	Jones	Trenton	380	203,496	3 40	120
50	Lenoir	Kinston	450	255,030	5 30	80

51 Lincoln	Lincolnton	420	177,247	4 30	172
52 Macon	Franklin	600	442,266	1 01	331
53 Madison	Marshall	450	207,616	1 20	
54 Martin	Williamston	450	259,931	4 80	140
55 McDowell	Marion	450	260,129	4 10	200
56 Mecklenburg	Charlotte	720	311,006	6 50	158
57 Mitchell	Bakersville		194,307	1 03	
58 Montgomery	Troy	550	278,300	1 90	115
59 Moore	Carthage	650	500,758	2 10	79
60 Nash	Nashville	600	310,075	4 70	44
61 New Hanover	Wilmington	1,000	496,893	2 90	148
62 Northampton	Jackson	350	316,358	6 70	108
63 Onslow	Jacksonville	600	287,497	2 20	145
64 Orange	Hillsboro'	650	267,589	5 50	40
65 Pamlico					
66 Pasquotank	Elizabeth City	250	124,870	10 20	215
67 Perquimans	Hertford	250	145,951	6 40	194
68 Person	Roxboro'	370	234,103	6 40	54
69 Pitt	Greenville	650	366,302	7 30	102
70 Polk	Columbus	300	130,592	1 30	
71 Randolph	Ashboro'	880	497,227	3 90	72
72 Richmond	Rockingham	900	480,915	2 50	135
73 Robeson	Lumberton	900	571,337	2 70	91
74 Rockingham	Wentworth	450	337,547	6 01	116
75 Rowan	Salisbury	600	310,593	7 50	118
76 Rutherford	Rutherfordton	870	302,988	3 50	216
77 Sampson	Clinton	940	507,132	2 90	94
78 Stanly	Albemarle	280	238,341	2 80	110
79 Stokes	Danbury	550	258,462	3 70	110
80 Surry	Dobson	900	284,609	3 70	145
81 Swain					
82 Transylvania	Brevard		155,341	3 04	
83 Tyrrell	Columbia	320	114,153	3 06	200
84 Union	Munroe	350	399,685	8 10	160
85 Wake	Raleigh	950	572,427	5 70	
86 Warren	Warrenton	480	317,976	6 40	62
87 Washington	Plymouth	700	177,039	3 20	162
88 Watauga	Boone	500	190,174	2 10	
89 Wayne	Goldsboro'	450	339,125	6 20	51

TABLE.—(*Continued.*)

	COUNTY.	COUNTY TOWN.	Area in Square Miles.‡	No. of Acres Listed.	Average Value of Acre.	Distance from Raleigh.
90	Wilkes	Wilkesboro'	550	383,574	$ 2 70	miles 172
91	Wilson	Wilson	250	202,036	5 40	
92	Yadkin	Yadkinville	310	209,874	4 30	
93	Yancey	Burnsville	680	147,997	2 30	245
				26,871,860	†3 90	

†Average of the State.
‡The area is approximate.

No. XVIII

Electoral Vote of North Carolina.

ELECTORAL VOTE OF NORTH CAROLINA.

I. In the first election for President (for term from 4th March, 1789, to 3rd March, 1793,) North Carolina did not vote, not having ratified the Constitution at the time of election.

II. At the second election, term from 1791 to 1797, the Electors gave her twelve electoral votes for George Washington and John Adams.

III. For the third term, from 1797 to 1801, the Electors for North Carolina gave one vote for John Adams, eleven votes for Thomas Jefferson, one vote for Thomas Pinckney, six votes for Aaron Burr, three votes for James Iredell, one vote for Geo. Washington and one vote for C. C. Pinckney of South Carolina.

IV. For the fourth term, 1801 to 1805, the Electors for North Carolina gave eight votes for Thomas Jefferson, eight votes for Aaron Burr, four votes for John Adams, and four votes for C. C. Pinckney.

V. For the fifth term, 1805 to 1809, the vote of North Carolina was fourteen votes for Thomas Jefferson for President, and fourteen votes for George Clinton as Vice President.

VI. For the 6th term, from 1809 to 1813, the vote was eleven votes for James Madison, as President, and three votes for C. C. Pinckney, of South Carolina; eleven votes for George Clinton, as Vice President, and three votes for Rufus King.

VII. For the 7th term, 1813 to 1817, fifteen votes for James Madison as President, and fifteen votes for Elbridge Gerry as Vice President.

VIII. For the 8th term, 1817 to 1821, fifteen votes for James Munroe, as President, and fifteen for D. D. Tompkins, as Vice President.

IX. For the 9th term, 1821 to 1825, same as above.

X. From 1825 to 1929, fifteen votes for Jackson as President, and fifteen votes for John C. Calhoun, as Vice President.

XI. From 1829 to 1833, same as above.

XII. From 1833 to 1837, fifteen votes for Jackson, as President, and fifteen votes for Martin Van Buren, as Vice President.

XIII. From 1837 to 1841, Fifteen votes for Van Buren, as President, and fifteen votes for R. M. Johnson, as Vice President.

XIV. Term from 1841 to 1845, fifteen votes for Harrison, as President, and fifteen votes for John Tyler, as Vice President.

XV. Term from 1845 to 1849, eleven votes for Henry Clay, as President, and eleven votes for Theodore Frelinghusen, as Vice President.

XVI. Term 1849 to 1853, eleven votes for Z. Taylor, as President, and eleven votes for M. Fillmore, as Vice President.

XVII. Term from 1853 to 1857, ten votes for Franklin Pierce, as President, and ten votes for William R. King, as Vice President.

XVIII. Term 1857 to 1861, ten votes for Buchanan, as President, and same for Breckenridge, as Vice President.

XIX. Term from 1861 to 1865, ten votes for Breckenridge, as President, and same for Lane as Vice President.

XX. Term no vote.

XXI. 1869 to 1873, Nine votes for Grant as President, and same for Colfax as Vice President.

XXII. 1873 to 1877, Grant for President, and Wilson for Vice President.

No. XIX.

Statistical Tables.

COUNTIES.	No. of Voters by Census of 1870.		Total.	Regist'ed Voters. 1868.		President. 1868.		Attorney Gen'l. 1870.		Convention. 1871.		Governor's Vote. 1872.	
	White.	Color'd.		White.	Color'd.	Rep.	Dem.	Rep.	Dem.	Rep.	Dem.	Cladw'll	Mer'mn
Currituck......	870	261	1,131	1,000	389	416	907	327	846	400	681	349	763
Camden........	784	478	1,262	672	477	590	528	526	623	538	540	554	562
Pasquotank....	946	896	1,842	762	963	1,047	590	920	837	1,051	638	1,053	657
Perquimans....	904	793	1,697	807	796	913	580	795	656	855	584	910	642
Gates.........	915	528	1,443	815	508	452	672	356	744	420	765	512	754
Chowan........	696	695	1,391	624	656	690	520	692	603	722	588	742	576
Hertford......	945	860	1,805	771	743	741	714	273	297	855	772	983	874
Hyde..........	962	451	1,413	923	560	572	791	629	754	542	703	610	816
Beaufort......	1,916	1,048	2,964	1,707	1,098	1,318	1,227	1,398	1,501	1,326	1,205	1,565	1,331
Pitt..........	1,894	1,686	3,580	1,694	1,654	1,752	1,559	1,754	1,732	1,778	1,724	1,775	1,782
Bertie	1,228	1,399	2,627	1,049	1,373	1,517	753	1,346	879	1,443	804	1,514	940
Martin........	1,133	1,027	2,160	1,030	945	1,021	1,027	1,107	1,116	1,243	1,031	1,048	1,035
Washington ...	871	628	1,499	720	721	955	343	561	798	915	458	917	402
Tyrrell.......	662	268	930	429	195	195	339	328	429	367	291	347	391
Dare..........	565	91	656					168	265	236	194	270	232
Pamlico.......												358	440
Total.......	15,291	11,109	26,400	13,003	11,078	12,122	10,555	11,180	11,880	12,691	10,978		

SECOND CONGRESSIONAL DISTRICT.

COUNTIES.	No. of voters by Census of 1870.		Total.	Regist'ed Voters. 1868.		President. 1868.		Attorney General 1870.		Convention. 1871.		Governor's Vote. 1872.	
	White.	Colored		White.	Colored	Rep.	Dem.	Rep.	Dem.	Rep.	Dem.	Caldw'll	Mer'mn
Northampton..	1,315	1,838	3,153	1,264	1,952	1,931	1,045	1,800	959	1,993	888	1,900	1,095
Halifax........	1,469	3,182	4,651	1,402	3,446	3,206	1,593	3,230	1,347	3,584	1,556	3,640	1,673
Warren........	1,123	2,470	3,593	1,038	2,422	2,308	1,053	2,206	873	2,453	988	2,380	1,107
Edgecombe....	1,747	3,541	5,288	1,486	2,868	2,676	1,473	2,878	776	3,321	1,236	3,452	1,474
Wilson	1,423	1,039	2,462	1,153	947	897	1,103	948	1,191	1,117	1,141	1,152	1,319
Greene	875	867	1,742	729	735	756	557	1,006	794	930	686	947	783
Wayne	2,086	1,711	3,797	1,607	1,304	1,421	1,487	1,785	1,764	1,824	1,615	1,949	1,749
Lenoir.........	1,038	1,093	2,131	1,023	1,201	1,215	861	1,224	911	1,178	958	1,270	944
Jones..........	587	569	1,156	487	600	592	422	559	519	575	523	639	559
Craven........	2,028	2,821	4,849	1,873	3,422	3,535	1,493	2,764	1,500	3,173	1,483	2,708	1,140
Totals,	13,691	19.131	32,822	12.062	18,897	18,537	11,087	18,400	10,234	20,148	11,074		

THIRD CONGRESSIONAL DISTRICT.

[illegible]	[illegible] voters [illegible] Census of 187[illegible]		Total.	Regist'ed voters. 1868.		President. 1868.		Attorney Gen'ral 1870.		Convention. 1871.		Governor's vote. 1872.	
	White.	Colored		White.	Colored	Rep.	Dem.	Rep.	Dem.	Rep.	Dem.	Caldw'll	Mer'mn
Onslow........	1,125	475	1,600	954	481	417	879	368	788	412	660	492	892
Duplin	1,837	1,155	2,992	1,712	1,181	1,025	1,580	952	1,505	1,029	1,421	1,035	1,750
Sampson.......	1,962	1,098	3,060	1,839	1,058	1,026	1,447	945	1,397	1,210	1,339	1,464	1,697
Harnett........	1,195	563	1,758	1,022	542	645	789	562	840	590	816	695	795
Cumberland....	1,997	1,463	3,460	1,921	1,560	1,592	1,680	1,671	1,741	1,715	1,484	1,883	1,890
Bladen....	1,466	1,152	2,618	1,239	1,301	1,372	1,079	1,292	1,115	1,429	919	1,448	1,208
Columbus	1,225	617	1,842	1,038	591	503	957	487	937	642	951	693	1,045
Brunswick	968	732	1,700	838	902	879	698	723	720	842	659	708	711
New Hanover..	2,884	3,559	6,443	2,643	4,113	3,968	2,290	2,914	2,027	3,702	2,123	3,614	2,261
Moore	1,905	548	2,453	1,536	589	1,019	884	791	1,113	880	839	881	1,055
Carteret	1,449	623	2,072	1,171	687	823	898	821	881	737	915	730	1,062
	18,013	11,985	29,998	15,913	13,005	13,269	13,181	1 ,526	13,064	13,188	12,126		

FOURTH CONGRESSIONAL DISTRICT.

COUNTIES.	No. of voters by Census of 1870.		Total.	Regist'ed Voters. 1868.		President. 1868.		Attorney General 1870.		Convention. 1871.		Governor's Vote. 1872.	
	White.	Colored		White.	Colored	Rep.	Dem.	Rep.	Dem.	Rep.	Dem.	Caldw'll	Mer'mn
Johnston	2,353	1,077	3,430	1,874	998	1,204	1,348	1,212	1,709	1,325	1,447	1,374	1,481
Wake..........	4,432	3,306	7,738	3,663	3,181	3,433	2,953	3,504	3,117	3,647	3,102	3,843	3,269
Chatham	2,753	1,255	4,008	2,358	1,225	1,765	1,559	1,124	1,861	1,757	1,480	1,683	1,774
Orange	2,339	1,210	3,549	2,272	1,393	1,453	1,907	991	1,708	1,299	1,752	1,321	1,945
Granville	2,506	2,551	5,057	2,246	2,928	2,754	3,148	2,368	2,008	2,826	1,991	2,655	1,976
Franklin.......	1,406	1,382	2,788	1,393	1,529	1,431	1,376	1,437	1,379	1,521	1,414	1,560	1,475
Nash	1,283	886	2,169	1,174	915	837	1,096	788	980	1,184	1,181	1,293	1,284
	17,072	11,667	28,739	14,980	12,169	12,877	12,367	11,424	12,762	13,559	12,367		

FIFTH CONGRESSIONAL DISTRICT.

COUNTIES.	No. of voters by Census of 1870.		Total.	Register'd voters 1868.		President. 1868.		Attorney Gen'ral 1870.		Convention. 1871.		Governor's vote. 1872.	
	White.	Color'd.		White.	Colored	Rep.	Dem.	Rep.	Dem.	Rep.	Dem.	Caldw'll	Mer'mn
Randolph.......	3,039	483	3,522	2,386	472	1,752	877	1,242	1,280	1,310	1,226	1,389	1,364
Davidson.......	2,816	681	3,497	2,328	701	1,843	835	1,150	1,216	1,409	1,262	1,516	1,384
Guilford........	3,313	1,178	4,491	2,783	1,276	2,169	1,496	1,717	1,793	1,741	1,745	1,831	1,849
Alamance.......	1,731	743	2,474	1,502	834	1,102	1,055	1,043	788	902	1,178	1,015	1,270
Person..........	1,270	917	2,187	1,147	975	953	1,054	765	1,092	845	923	810	1,101
Caswell........	1,510	1,892	3,402	1,410	2,128	1,957	1,409	251	637	1,544	1,265	1,456	1,415
Rockingham....	1,891	1,184	3,075	1,810	1,421	1,463	1,513	1,143	1,590	1,322	1,422	1,301	1,653
Stokes..........	1,766	469	2,235	1,328	410	783	744	560	989	747	853	830	905
Totals.......	17,336	7,547	24,883	14,694	8,217	12,022	8,983	7,620	8,748	9,821	9,874		

SIXTH CONGRESSIONAL DISTRICT.

COUNTIES.	No. of Voters by Census of 1870.		Total.	Regist'ed Voters. 1868.		President. 1868.		Attorney General 1870.		Convention. 1871.		Governor's Vote. 1872.	
	White.	Colored		White.	Colored	Rep.	Dem.	Rep.	Dem.	Rep.	Dem.	Caldw'll	Merm'n
Robeson.......	1,962	1,314	3,276	1,613	1,250	1,318	1,337	1,623	1,685	1,561	1,288	1,583	1,631
Montgomery...	1,037	348	1,385	864	346	727	341	545	481	597	469	653	475
Richmond......	1,374	1,248	2,622	1,124	1,187	1,254	808	1,162	863	1,144	790	1,304	1,016
Anson.........	1,299	1,061	2,360	1,162	1,109	1,002	1,050	986	1,052	949	1,031	1,019	1,191
Stanly........	1,225	252	1,477	1,041	242	466	651	452	598	483	627	366	646
Cabarrus	1,608	777	2,385	1,398	790	940	1,112	851	963	808	1,013	811	1,161
Union.....,....	1,731	477	2,208	1,360	456	811	930	634	788	664	773	631	1,022
Gaston	1,512	667	2,179	1,187	511	878	678	696	958	660	860	688	927
Lincoln........	1,292	511	1,803	1,055	453	625	738	510	822	553	843	706	903
Catawba.......	1,749	295	2,044	1,520	289	488	1,131	149	1,043	276	1,220	422	1,261
Mecklenburg ..	2,326	2,298	4,624	2,329	1,981	1,962	2,149	1,936	2,161	2,089	2,026	2,261	2,511
Totals.......	17,815	9,248	27,063	14,653	8,614	10,471	10,925	9,544	11,414	9,784	10,950		

SEVENTH CONGRESSIONAL DISTRICT.

COUNTIES.	No. of Voters by Census of 1870.		Total.	Register'd Votes. 1868.		President. 1868.		Attorney General 1870.		Convention. 1871.		Governor's Vote. 1872.	
	White.	Colored		White.	Colored	Rep.	Dem.	Rep.	Dem.	Rep.	Dem.	Caldw'll	Mer'mn
Forsythe.......	2,141	432	2,573	1,861	430	1,261	787	1,014	954	1,133	936	1,115	1,033
Surry..........	1,975	298	2,273	1,318	244	818	737	502	1,007	929	826	838	989
Yadkin........	1,765	258	2,023	846	49	266	435	245	596	848	627	866	759
Davie..........	1,311	569	1,880	882	463	652	690	683	762	733	704	662	826
Rowan.........	2,391	1,042	3,433	1,977	1,160	1,332	1,530	973	1,459	1,003	1,398	1,118	1,655
Iredell.........	2,494	844	3,338	2,008	756	859	1,412	404	1,263	777	1,467	994	1,738
Alexander.....	1,088	140	1,228	875	125	351	516	247	504	281	530	389	545
Wilkes........	2,544	251	2,795	2,224	261	1,205	820	911	913	1,117	872	1,294	1,034
Alleghany......	644	47	691	543	55	245	284	158	377	177	317	184	339
Ashe...........	1,667	106	1,773	1,308	82	634	644	698	791	720	589	761	752
Watauga,......	952	54	1,006	717	45	303	348	268	500	237	489	353	435
Totals........	18,972	4,041	23,013	14,559	3,670	7,926	8,203	6,103	9,126	7,955	8,755		

EIGHTH CONGRESSIONAL DISTRICT.

COUNTIES.	No. of voters by Census of 1870.		Total.	Register'd voters 1868.		President. 1868.		Attorney Gener'l 1870.		Convention. 1871.		Governor's vote. 1872.	
	White.	Colored		White.	Colored	Rep.	Dem.	Rep.	Dem.	Rep.	Dem.	Cladw'll	Mer'mn
Caldwell	1,272	218	1,490	1,032	203	396	617	251	638	404	651	332	829
Burke	1,383	387	1,770	1,221	556	927	741	693	803	639	768	683	852
Cleveland	1,968	368	2,336	1,528	312	656	1,037	314	1,212	309	1,117	547	1,099
Mitchell	815	36	851	676	49	529	117	471	280	503	84	628	195
Yancey	1,011	56	1,067	1,598	252	840	632	511	879	341	462	382	503
McDowell	1,160	499	1,659	1,077	396	740	607	551	599	488	576	519	700
Rutherford	1,968	441	2,409	1,635	458	1,279	685	1,134	898	1,207	596	1,013	727
Polk	653	162	1,815	524	143	405	195	360	189	335	208	342	224
Henderson	1,202	231	1,433	882	176	640	361	555	403	737	338	716	505
Transylvania	648	56	704	328	53	186	232	149	367	115	293	203	379
Buncombe	2,554	467	3,021	2,007	411	10,35	1,090	981	1,436	1,166	1,308	1,114	1,538
Madison	1,338	64	1,402	1,056	50	529	458	489	510	590	562	641	635
Haywood	1,367	100	1,467	1,061	81	412	660	401	723	390	733	420	749
Jackson	1,050	213	1,263	875	39	220	607	229	587	191	719	166	554
Swain	....	....	....	....	....	....	....	....	....	....	....	29	332
Macon	1,183	83	1,266	957	53	323	572	246	530	176	739	130	655
Clay	480	18	498	400	10	155	234	174	218	215	213	142	252
Graham	....	....	....	....	....	....	....	....	....	....	....	....	....
Cherokee	1,293	151	1,444	916	35	443	423	304	522	410	440	433	486
Totals	21,345	3,550	24,895	17,776	3,277	9,715	9,258	7,913	10,794	8,616	9,907		

No. XX.

State Debt.

FROM ANNUAL REPORT OF THE STATE TREASURER TO THE GOVERNOR OF NORTH CAROLINA, FOR FISCAL YEAR ENDING SEPTEMBER 30, 1873.

STATE OF NORTH CAROLINA,
TREASURY DEPARTMENT,
Raleigh, Nov. 12th, 1873.

I again call the attention of the General Assembly to the necessity of making some provision in regard to the debt. The statements show *in extenso* the amount of the same, when due and for what purpose issued. It is seen that the entire amount, excluding special tax and unconstitutional bonds, is $17,881,045, with past due interest, say $5,506,154.85. For specific information I distribute the same as follows:

1st. Old or ante-war bonds, dated prior to the war, total amount,	$ 8,378,200
Accrued interest,	2,513,460
Total,	$10,891,660

These were sold by the State, or by its agents, on an average at par for gold. There is no charge that their proceeds were not honestly expended, although in some instances the investments were unfortunate. For example, the following enterprises, for which $291,000 bonds are outstanding, are almost, if not quite *total failures*, adding a little, if anything, to the wealth of the State, viz:

Cape Fear and Deep River Navigation Works,	$145,500
Fayetteville and Western Plank Road,	50,500
Neuse and Tar River Improvements,	25,000
Fayetteville and Centre Plank Road,	45,000
Fayetteville and Warsaw Plank Road,	10,000
Tar River,	15,000
	$291,000

The following enterprises, for which $4,210,500 bonds are outstanding, are not failures, *i. e.*, they add something to the prosperity of the country, but the interest of the State in them has little, if any market value:

Atlantic and North Carolina Railroad,	$1,351,500
Albemarle and Chesapeake Canal,	324,000
Western (Coal Fields) Railroad,	386,000
Western North Carolina Railroad,	1,136,000
Wilmington, Charlotte and Rutherford Railroad, (now Carolina Central.)	1,013,000
Total,	$4,210,500

The above companies have never declared a dividend. The Wilmington, Charlotte and Rutherford Railroad Company has gone out of the hands of the State altogether by sale of all its franchise and property.

The following investments, for which bonds now outstanding amount to $2,865,000, have considerable value, viz:

The Insane Asylum,	$ 71,000
North Carolina Railroad,	2,794,000

The bonds issued for the North Carolina Railroad Company are made by the charter of the Company a lien on the State stock in the Company. The bondholders, under a decree of the United States Circuit Court, in the suit of Swazey and others *vs.* the North Carolina Railroad Company and others, are now receiving the dividends and will, no doubt, at least when the bonds become due, obtain the stock itself, if they so desire.

2. The second class of bonds consists of those issued since the war, but under acts passed before, as follows:

Wilmington, Charlotte & Rutherford Railroad,	$ 434,000
Western North Carolina Railroad,	2,294,000
Total principal,	$2,728,000

These bonds were sold for not over about sixty cents in the dollar for currency, when gold was at a large premium, netting to the company considerably less than fifty cents in gold.

I have already stated that the interest of the State has been altogether lost in the Wilmington, Charlotte and Rutherford Railroad Company, and it is probable that the same will sooner or later be the case in regard to the Western North Carolina Railroad Company.

3. There is a third class of bonds issued during the late war, and for that reason not marketable, but having been for internal improvement purposes, should be included in a general settlement of our debt, viz:

Wilmington, Charlotte and Rutherford Railroad Company,	$ 493,000
Western North Carolina Railroad Company,	220,000
Western Railroad Company,	200,000
	$ 913,000

4. A fourth class of bonds consists of those issued to take up past due interest, viz:

Under the Funding Act of 1866,	$ 2,417,400
Under the Funding Act of 1868,	1,711,400
Total principal,	$ 4,128,800

Nearly all the bonds issued under the former act were for old bonds matured, and for coupons of old bonds. Those issued under the Funding Act of 1868 were for old bonds matured, all recognized bonds that had become defaced and mutilated, bonds of the denomination of $100 and $200, coupons of old bonds and coupons of bonds issued since the war to the Wilmington, Charlotte and Rutherford Railroad Company, the Western North Carolina Railroad Company, and under the Funding Act of 1866. But none were for coupons of Convention or special tax bonds.

5. A fifth class of bonds comprises those issued under ordinances or acts passed since the war, viz:

To Chatham Railroad Company, (now Raleigh and Augusta Air Line,) under ordinance of Convention of 1868,	$ 1,200,000
Williamston and Tarboro Railroad Company,	150,000
	$1,350,000

The bonds for the Chatham Railroad were disposed of, it is stated, at about sixty cents in currency. What amount the $150,000 to the Williamston and Tarboro Railroad brought I am not informed; at any rate the investment has been disastrous, and now the interest of the State is entirely lost by sale under bankruptcy proceedings.

Lastly, are the "special tax bonds," in the aggregate $11,407,000, detailed as follows:

Wilmington, Charlotte and Rutherford Railroad,	$ 3,000,000
Western N. C. Railroad (Eastern Division,)	273,000
Western N. C. Railroad (Western Division,)	6,367,000
Western (Coal Fields) Railroad,	1,320,000
Williamston and Tarboro Railroad,	300,000
Atlantic, Tennessee and Ohio Railroad (outstanding,)	147,000
	$11,407,000

Of the above, the first million of dollars of bonds issued to the Wilmington, Charlotte and Rutherford Railroad Company, were sold, it is said, at about fifty cents in the dollar and the proceeds were used in paying the debts of the company contracted on construction account, but the residue, about $2,000,000, was sold at a heavy sacrifice at almost nominal prices, and the company derived little benefit from them. The same may be said of those issued for the Western North Carolina Railroad Company. At any rate, but little work was done on the road from their proceeds. The bonds for the Williamston and Tarboro Railroad Company were sold at better rates, but as said above, the State has lost its entire investment. The Western (Coal Fields) Railroad Company derived no benefit worthy of mention from the $1,320,000 issued for that Company.

The foregoing statements show that the experience of the State in railroad and navigation enterprises has been unfortunate, with one exception, the North Carolina Railroad Company. Even this was for many years non-dividend paying. Practically, as to the rest of the debt, except that contracted on account of the Insane Asylum, the State has nothing whatever to show, except whatever general in- case of property has been made by the partial construction of the works.

Such general improvement in the value of property in the State does not exist. The valuation of the real estate of North Carolina, in 1860, was in round numbers $97,670,000. In 1872, it was in round numbers, $82,100,000. I am unable to give a comparison as to personal property, because it was not taxed according to its value until 1868, but I think as the total valuation of real and personal estate, in 1872, was $123,500,000, there has been a similar retrogade as to both.

I have gone into this matter in such detail because those who sneer at our not paying interest on the public debt ignore the facts of our situation.

Omitting special tax bonds altogether, the interest on the rest of our debt, supposing our accrued interest to be funded, would be $1,406,663.99 per annum. To this add the expense of supporting the State government and it will be necessary to raise $1,900,000 per annum, or 1 and 3-5 per cent. of the real and personal property. Add an amount for county taxation equal to that for State government expenses, and we have, outside the towns and cities, 2 and 1-10 per cent. of our property. And in many of the cities and towns the levies for municipal purposes are as large, if not larger. Now add, as the holders of special tax bonds propose, a tax of $855,000, or ¾ of 1 per cent. on the property, and we have a grand total of 2 and 8-10 per cent.

It is manifest that our people cannot and will not pay such enormous levies. Any attempt to enforce it would result in total repudiation. Even if any General Assembly should vote a levy at present, even omitting special tax bonds, the people would reverse their action at the next election. But I am strongly of opinion that good policy requires a speedy adjustment of the public debt. Delay is dangerous. The interest is accumulating The popular mind is becoming accustomed to the alternative of repudiation. Our good fame is stigmatized. Our bond-holders are a class of influential men, and their increasing ill-humor and consequent denunciation of our State, not only affect the credit of the citizens, but operate to drive off immigration and capital from our limits.

The re-establishment of the public credit will besides tend to nerve our people to greater energy in adherence to their own contracts. Nothing so much tends to impair morality in the citizen as the spectacle of laxity of principle in the commonwealth.

And then the restoration of credit is essential to any future negotiations for borrowing money. The bonds of the State, if allowed to remain outstanding, will be a perpetual reminder of our breach of faith. In all financial circles they will be exhibited as proofs that any new ventures in our securities will be as disastrous as the investments in the repudiated securities. If, however, we can compromise the debt, any sacrifices the creditors submit to will be charged where they justly belong, to the terrible losses of the war.

I have already stated those losses are demonstrated by the present condition of the investments entered into by the State. It is not necessary to add to the list the enormous destruction of our property by the war, the annihilation of our system of labor, the ruin of our wealthiest people by the abolition of slavery, the death or disabling of multitudes of our young men in battle or by disease, the sweeping away of our personal property, our horses, our cattle, our farming implements, the deterioration of our lands. It is not necessary to call to mind the effects on a half ruined people of the financial troubles of 1867 and of the present year. Every fair-minded man will admit that if ever a State can be justified in demanding that creditors should abate part of their demands proportioned to losses by causes unforeseen by both parties at the time of the creation of the debt, that State is North Carolina.

It is said by some that the General Assembly ought to surrender to the creditors all the State property acquired by the creation of the debt, and refuse to pay any more. I have shown that in several instances the interest of the State has been sacrificed. For example, I state its lien on the Wilmington, Charlotte and Rutherford Railroad Company has been subordinated to another mortgage, by the foreclosure of which the road has passed into other hands. Its stock in the Western North Carolina Railroad Company is threatened by foreclosure of a like mortgage. It would have been lost a year ago if the General Assembly had not authorized an appeal to the Supreme Court of the United States. The surrender of interests whose value has been impaired or destroyed by voluntary action of the State will not have any appearance of fairness.

In one case a considerable portion of the bonds might be exchanged for stock of the State. I mean the North Carolina Railroad Company. The holders of bonds issued for that company have already obtained a decree for sequestration of the dividends. It is threatened to apply to the court for a further decree to sell the stock to pay deficiencies of past due interest unpaid. Whether this be done or not, certainly at the maturity of the bonds in 1883,-'84 and '85, the bondholders can claim such sale. I respectfully suggest whether it might not be advisable to authorize the exchange at once. This would reduce the debt much more than it would be on a sale of the stock under decree of the court.

The most feasible plan for settling the question of the public debt is to authorize the issue of new bonds, with a tax levied in the act for the payment of the interest, holders of bonds of the State to be allowed to surrender the same and receive the new bonds at such rate by way of compromise as might be prescribed by the General Assembly. I would respectfully suggest that one of the new bonds be offered for two of the old or ante-war bonds and those issued to fund the interest of the same, of like denominations, for three of all other bonds issued since the war, except special tax bonds. As to the latter, let a commission be appointed, whose duty it shall be to estimate what portion of the proceeds went into our public works, and report to the General Assembly. Then the Assembly can declare valid a part of the special tax bonds proportioned to such amount realized.

Of course if any creditor should prefer to decline the proposal indicated and take his chances for better terms hereafter, he could do so. But I am inclined to think that after a full explanation of the poverty of the State, most, if not all, would enter into the arrangement.

I earnestly hope some plan will be carried into effect. I greatly fear that longer delay will result in entire repudiation by inaction at least. Already such a policy is advocated by men of influence, and there is danger that it will become popular. Prompt action only will defeat it.

I learn by the public prints that the Auditor and myself are threatened with a suit by the holders of special tax bonds. This would be in effect a suit against a sovereign State, prohibited by the Constitution of the United States. It will be resisted, of course, to the last extremity. I am informed that the Governor and Attorney General have full power to employ counsel in such defence—if not, I recommend that such power be granted by the General Assembly.

That the State shall pay these bonds in full—many of which were fraudulently sold by State agents, nearly *all* under circumstances which amounted to notice to prudent men not to buy—cannot be entertained, in my opinion, for a moment.

No. XXI.

Railroads of North Caralina.

REMARKS.
A. S. Benton, President.
R. W. King, President.
J. B. Palmer, (Augusta,) President.
Purchased in 1872, by E. Matthews.
W. A. Smith, Pres't, leased in 1871 to Richmond & Danville.
W. J. Hawkins, President.
W. J. Hawkins, President.
A. S. Buford, President.
J. M. Robinson, President.
R. R. Bridgers, President.
R. R. Bridgers, President.
R. R. Bridgers, President.
A. S. Buford, President.
L. C. Jones, President.

y, but requires correction, which another edition will give.

NO. XXII.

Press of North Carolina.

THE PRESS OF NORTH CAROLINA.

PLACE OF PUBLICATION.	NAME OF PRESS.	EDITORS.	POLITICS.
Asheville..........	Citizen..............	R. M. Furman......	Democrat.
Asheville..........	Pioneer............	....	
Asheville,..........	Western Expositor..	W. H. Malone......	Democrat.
Battleboro	Advance............	....	
Charlotte..........	Democrat...........	Wm. J. Yates.......	Democrat.
Charlotte..........	Observer (daily)	C. R. Jones.........	Democrat.
Charlotte	Southern Home.....	D. H. Hill...........	Democrat.
Charlotte..........	Tobacco Leaf.......	J. R. Morris........	Democrat.
Clinton	Reporter............	E. W. Kerr.........	Democrat.
Concord	Sun	C. H. Harris........	Democrat.
Danbury	Register............	W. R. Pepper	Democrat.
Durham...........	Tobacco Plant......	J. B. Green.........	Democrat.
Edenton	Record..............	....	Democrat.
Elizabeth City.....	Carolinian..........	P. John.............	Republican.
Enfield............	Times...............	David Bond.........	Democrat.
Fayetteville........	Eagle...............	M. J. McSween.....	Democrat.
Fayetteville........	Gazette.............	M. Myrover.........	Democrat.
Fayetteville........	Presbyterian........	....	Religious.
Fayetteville........	Statesman..........	O. H. Blocker	Democrat.
Goldsboro	Messenger..........	J. A. Bonitz........	Democrat
Greensboro.........	Patriot..............	P. F. Duffy.........	Democrat.
Greensboro.........	New North State ...	A. H. Ball..........	Republican
Greenville.........	Register............	Blow & Lyon.......	Democrat.
Henderson.........	Register............	S. J. Skinner.......	Democrat.
Hickory...........	Piedmont Press.....	Avery & Hussey....	Democrat.
Hillsboro..........	Recorder............	J. D. Cameron......	Democrat.
Kinston,...........	Gazette.............	E. A. Wilson.......	Democrat.
La Grange.........	Review	Samuel S. Nash.....	Democrat.
Louisburg.........	Courier.............	Geo. S. Baker.......	Democrat.
Lumberton........	Robesonian.........	J. S. McDiarmid....	Democrat.
Madison...........	Enterprise..........	....	Democrat.
Magnolia..........	Monitor	W. S. Hannaford ...	Democrat.
Milton............	Chronicle...........	C. N. B. Evans......	Democrat.
Mt. Airy..........	News...............	J. T. Brown	Democrat.
Monroe	Enquirer............	Boylen & Wolfe	Democrat.
Newbern	Journal of Commerce	S. D. Pool, Jr.......	Democrat.
Newbern	Newbernian.........	S. M. Carpenter.....	Democrat.
Newbern	Our Living and Dead	S. D. Pool..........	Neutral.
Newbern	Republic Courier....	George W? Nason,Jr	Republican.
Newbern	Times, (daily).......	J. S. Mannix........	Republican.
Oxford............	Carolina Herald.....	Wm. Biggs..........	Democrat.
Oxford............	Torch Light........	Davis & Robinson ..	Democrat.
Polkton...........	Ansonian...........	L. L. Polk..........	Democrat.
Raleigh............	Biblical Recorder ...	A. F. Redd..........	Religious, Baptist
Raleigh............	Christian Advocate..	J. B. Bobbitt........	Religious, Meth.
Raleigh............	Crescent, (daily)....	John S. Hampton...	Democrat.
Raleigh............	Era................	M. V'B. Gilbert.....	Republican.
Raleigh............	Friend of Temp'ance	R. H. Whitaker.....	Temperance
Raleigh............	News, (daily).......	Jordan Stone........	Democrat.
Raleigh............	Republican, (daily)..	J. D. Uzzell	Republican.
Raleigh............	Sentinel, (daily).....	Josiah Turner, Jr. ..	Democrat.

THE PRESS OF NORTH CAROLINA.—*Continued.*

PLACE OF PUBLICATION.	NAME OF PRESS.	EDITORS.	POLITICS.
Raleigh............	Spirit of the Age ...	S. J. Falls..........	Temperance.
Raleigh............	State Ag. Journal...	R. T. Fulghum......	Agricultural.
Reidsville..........	Record.............	....	Democrat.
Rocky Mount......	Mail................	W. L. Thorpe.......	Democrat.
Rutherfordton.....	Star................	....	Republican.
Rutherfordton.....	Western Record.....	....	
Salem..............	Press................	Blum & E. T. Levi..	Democrat.
Salisbury..........	Watchman..........	Bruner & Stewart...	Democrat.
Shelby.............	Cleaveland Banner..	M. Durham.........	Democrat.
Statesville	American	Drake & Son........	Republican.
Statesville	Intelligencer.........	A. K. Murchison....	Democrat.
Tarboro............	Enquirer South.....	E. R. Stamps........	Democrat.
Wadesboro.........	Argus...............	L. L. Knight & Son.	Democrat.
Wadesboro.........	Pee Dee Herald.....	....	
Warrenton.........	Gazette......	H. A. Foote.........	Democrat.
Washington........	Express............	D. M. Bogart........	Democrat.
Weldon............	Roanoke News......	H. E. T. Manning...	Democrat.
Wilmington........	Daily Journal.......	Englehard, Saunders	Democrat.
Wilmington........	Morning Star, (daily)	W. H. Bernard......	Democrat.
Wilmington........	Post, (daily)........	J. C. Saunders......	Republican.
Wilson	Advance...........	Williams & Williams	Democrat.
Wilson	Plain Dealer........	R. W. Singletary....	Democrat.
Winston...........	Nat. Republican....	....	Republican.
Winston...........	Sentinel............	Geo. Matthews......	Democrat.

NO. XXIII

Counties.

ALAMANCE COUNTY.

Alamance County was erected in 1848, out of Orange County. It is bounded on the north by Caswell, east by Orange, south by Chatham, and west by Guilford. It derives its name from Alamance Creek, famous in early history for a battle fought on its banks, between the Royal Governor of the colony, William Tryon, and the people under Herman Husbands, Rednap Howell, and others.

Its capital is Graham, named in compliment to Hon. William A. Graham, 54 miles from Raleigh.

COUNTY OFFICERS.

Offices.	Names.
Superior Court Clerk	William A. Albright.
Register of Deeds	Thomas G. McLean.
Sheriff	James T. Hunter.
Coroner	John A. Moore.
Surveyor	John R. Pugh.
Treasurer	John L. Scott.
Commissioners	Thomas M. Holt. David W. Kerr. J. G. Pinnix. Wm. J. Stockard. Berry Davidson.

JUSTICES OF THE PEACE.

Names.	Date of Qualification.	Post Office Address.
William Patterson	August 19th, 1873.	Rock Creek.
R. C. Kimory	" "	Patterson's Store.
J. R. Garret	August 9th, 1873.	Curtis' Mills.
E. S. Euliss		Hartshorn.
R. L. Mebane	August 19th, 1873.	Gibsonville.
Peter Michael	" "	Gibsonville.
Asa Isely	" "	Company Shops.
H. H. Morton	" "	Morton's Store.
J. G. Pinnix	August 9th, 1873.	Big Falls.
P. R. Harden	August 19th, 1873.	Graham.
Joseph McAdams	" "	Company Shops.
Green Andrews		Graham.
P. L. Sellars		Company Shops.
S. P. Holt	August 19th, 1873.	Graham.
W. H. Lay	" "	Graham.
Johnson Gurwood	" "	Graham.
Wm. Stafford		Saxapahaw.
T. A. Marrow	" "	Oaks.
Henry Thompson	" "	Graham.
J. C. Patton	" "	Mebanesville.
S. A. White	" "	Mebanesville.
W. P. Barnwell	August 9th, 1873.	Pleasant Grove.
John S. Shaw	August 19th, 1873.	Pleasant Grove.
A. Murray		Big Falls.

ALAMANCE COUNTY—Continued.

MEMBERS OF GENERAL ASSEMBLY.

Years.	Senate.	House.
1854	With Randolph county. William B. Lane..........	Giles Mebane. J. W. Lancaster.
1856	M. W. Holt................	D. A. Montgomery. George Patterson.
1858	Jonathan Worth............	J. I. Scales. B. F. Roney.
1860	Jonathan Worth............	Giles Mebane. John Tapscott.
1862	Giles Mebane..............	R. Y. McAden. E. F. Watson.
1864	Giles Mebane..............	R. Y. McAden. C. F. Faucett.
1866	M. S. Robbins.............	R. Y. McAden. A. H. Boyd.
1868	Emanuel Shoffner...... G. W. Welker..........	John A. Moore.
1870	With Guilf'd Co., form'd 26th Senatorial District. John A. Gilmer......... Wm. A. Smith*..........	Stephen White.
1872	With Guilf'd Co., form'd 24th Senatorial District. James T. Morehead, jr.. W. J. Murray	Jesse Grant.

*Seat vacated and James A. Graham elected.

ALEXANDER COUNTY.

Was erected in 1846, formed from Iredell, Caldwell and Wilkes Counties.

It is bounded on the north by Wilkes, on the east by Iredell, and on the south by Catawba, and the west by Caldwell county.

Capital Taylorsville; its distance from Raleigh, 150 miles, in compliment to Chief Justice Taylor, or Gen. Z. Taylor, then in the zenith of his fame, having just conquered at battles of Reseca del Palma and Buena Vista, Mexico.

COUNTY OFFICERS.

Offices.	Names.
Superior Court Clerk..................	E. M. Stevenson.
Register of Deeds.....................	J. B. Pool.
Sheriff...............................	H. W. Mays.
Coroner...............................	
Surveyor..............................	J. F. Sharpe.
Treasurer.............................	J. T. Perry.

ALEXANDER COUNTY—Continued.

Offices.	Names.
Commissioners	A. C. McIntosh. D. W. Moose. J. L. Davis. D. S. Miller. D. A. Daniel.

The Coroner has not made his bond.

JUSTICES OF THE PEACE.

Names.	Date of qualification.	Post Office Address.
H. H. Drum	Sept. 1st, 1873.	Elk Shoal.
Ezekiel McLelland	" "	Stony Point.
T. F. Murdah	" "	York Institute.
Jacob Lentz	" "	Stony Point.
George J. Allen	" "	York Institute.
Wm. F. Patterson	" "	York Institute.
J. H. Childers	" "	Taylorsville.
Wesley Laws	" "	Taylorsville.
Reuben Watts	" "	Taylorsville.
W. W. Chapman	" "	Taylorsville.
F. B. Rees	" "	Taylorsville.
John Brown	" "	Little River.
Z. T. Morets	" "	Wittenburgs.
E. M. Moore	" "	Wittenburgs.
D. McMatheson	" "	Taylorsville.
E. C. Harrington	" "	Taylorsville.
Davolt Little	" "	Taylorsville.

MEMBERS OF GENERAL ASSEMBLY.

Years.	Senate.	House.
1854	With Iredell and Wilkes, formed 45th Senatorial District. Anderson Mitchell	A. M. Bogle.
1856	R. Parks	A. C. McIntosh.
1858	L. B. Carmichael	——— Burke.
1860	L. Q. Sharp	J. M. Carson.
1862	L. Q. Sharp	J. M. Carson.
1864	A. M. Bogle	J. M. Carson.
1866	J. H. Hill	J. M. Carson.
1868	J. H. McLaughlin	B. P. Matheson.
1870	With Iredell county, formed 36th Senatorial District. Romulus Z. Linney	J. M. Carson.
1872	Thomas A. Nicholson. Phineas Horton	J. M. Carson.

ALLEGHANY COUNTY.

Created by act ratified February, 1859, from a portion of Ashe County. It is bounded on the north by the Virginia line, south by Wilkes, on the east by Surry county, and west by Ashe. It derives its name from the range of mountains in which it is located. Its capital is Gap Civil, about 175 miles from Raleigh.

COUNTY OFFICERS.

Offices.	Names.
Superior Court Clerk	J. J. Gambill.
Register of Deeds	F. M. Michael.
Sheriff	John R. Wyatt.
Coroner	J. T. Hawthorn.
Surveyor	M. F. Joines.
Treasurer	A. J. Carson.
Commissioners	C. H. Doughten. J. H. Doughten. David Holbrook. A. M. Smith. A. J. Rector.

JUSTICES OF THE PEACE.

Names.	Date of Qualification.	Post Office Address.
C. J. Edwards	Sept. 1st, 1873.	Gap Civil.
George McReevs	" "	Gap Civil.
Daniel Whitehead	" "	Gap Civil.
P. C. Huggins	" "	Gap Civil.
Wm. H. Joines	" "	Gap Civil.
G. W. Thompson	" "	Cherry Lane.
C. J. Roberts	" "	Cherry Lane.
Josiah Caudill	" "	Gap Civil.
G. W. Prewitt	" "	Gap Civil.
D. C. Jones	" "	Gap Civil.
M. F. Joines	" "	Gap Civil.
J. L. Pugh	" "	Gap Civil.
John S. Parsons	" "	Gap Civil.

MEMBERS OF GENERAL ASSEMBLY.

Years.	Senate.	House.
1860		
1862		
1864	Jonathan Horton	F. A. McMillan.
1868	S. P. Smith	John L. Smith.
1870	With Ashe and Wilkes, formed 39th Senatorial District. C. L. Cook	Robert Gambrel.
1872	With Ashe and Watauga, formed 35th Senatorial District. J. W. Todd	A. M. Bryan.

ANSON COUNTY.

Anson County was erected as early as 1749; from Bladen County, and comprehended all the western portion of the State, from New Hanover and Bladen on the east, as far as the limits of the State extended on the west, more than one-half of the State.

It derives its name from Admiral Anson, the celebrated Circumnavigator, who at the time (1749) was in the zenith of his fame, having only a short time previous obtained a victory over the French fleet off Cape Finisterre.

Wadesboro', its capital town, derives its name from Thomas Wade, who was Colonel of the minute men of Salisbury District, in 1775. Distance from Raleigh 143 miles.

COUNTY OFFICERS.

Offices.	Names.
Superior Court Clerk	J. M. Covington.
Register of Deeds	John Stacy.
Sheriff	J. M. Wall.
Coroner	T. J. Lockhart.
Surveyor	W. H. Cox.
Treasurer	F. C. Allen.
Commissioners,	T. Redfearn, Chairman. G. C. Jones. J. J. Dunlap. H. W. Ledbetter. T. J. Hardison.

JUSTICES OF THE PEACE.

Names.	Date of Qualification.	Post Office Address.
Benj. Chears	Aug. 9th, 1873.	White's Store.
Edmond D. Gaddy	" "	Wadesboro.
James W. Henly	Sept. 1st, 1873.	Cedar Hill.
Moody H. Allen	" "	Beverly.
C. C. Braswell	" "	Ansonville.
J. M. Broadaway	" "	Ansonville.
Isaac M. Williams	" "	Polkton.
Hawey T. Knotts	" "	Wadesboro.
Jno. C. McLaucklen	" "	Wadesboro.
Henry Powell	" "	Wadesboro.
J. P. McRae	Sept. 15th, 1873.	Wadesboro.
J. M. Little, (Mayor)	June 2nd, 1873.	Wadesboro.
A. M. Boggan	Sept. 1st, 1873.	Lilesville.
Vincent Parsons	" "	Morven.
Thos, J. Hardison	" "	Wadesboro.
Wm. Webb	" "	Wadesboro.
W. T. Williams	" "	Lilesville.
J. W. McGregor	" "	

ANSON COUNTY.—Continued.

MEMBERS OF GENERAL ASSEMBLY.

Years.	Senate.	House.
1777	John Childs	George Davidson, Wm. Pickett.
1778	John Childs	George Davidson, Stephen Miller.
1779	John Childs	Stephen Miller, Charles Medlock.
1780	John Childs	Stephen Miller, Richard Farr.
1782	Thomas Wade	Stephen Miller, John Jackson.
1783	Thomas Wade	John Jackson, John Auld.
1784	Stephen Miller	James Terry, John Dejarnell.
1785	Stephen Miller	James Terry, John Dejarnell.
1785	Stephen Miller	James Terry, Wm. Wood.
1786	Stephen Miller	William Wood, Wm. Lanier.
1787	Stephen Miller	Lewis Lanier, Pleasant May.
1788	John Auld	Lewis Lanier, Pleasant May.
1789	Lewis Lanier	Wm. Wood, Pleasant May.
1791	Thomas Wade	Wm. Wood, James Pickett.
1792	James Marshall	Wm. Wood, Pleasant May.
1793	James Marshall	Wm. Wood, Pleasant May.
1794	James Pickett	Pleasant May, Daniel Young.
1795	James Pickett	Pleasant May, Daniel Young.
1796	Wm. May	Isaac Jackson, Daniel Young.
1797	James Marshall	Isaac Jackson, Daniel Ross.
1798	John Auld	Lewis Lanier, Pleasant May.
1799	Thomas Wade	Wm. Wood, Pleasant May.
1800	James Marshall	Daniel Ross, Clement Lanier.
1801	James Marshall	Clement Lanier, John Culpepper.
1802	James Marshall	Wm. Lanier, Robert Troy.
1803	James Marshall	Wm. Lanier, James Hough.
1804	James Marshall	Adam Lockhart, William Lanier.
1805	James Marshall	Joseph Pickett, Wm. Lanier.
1806	James Marshall	William Lanier, Robert Troy.
1807	James Marshall	Lawrence Moore, Wm. Johnston.
1808	Thos. Threadgill	Wm. Johnston, Lawrence Moore.
1809	Thos. Threadgill	Joseph Pickett, Lawrence Moore.
1810	James Marshall	Wm. Johnston, David Cuthbertson.
1811	James Marshall	D. Cuthbertson, Wm. R. Pickett.
1812	James Marshall	Wm. Johnston, Wm. R. Pickett.
1813	Wm. Johnson	D. Cuthbertson, Joseph Pickett.
1814	Lawrence Moore	Joseph Pickett, Wm. Dismukes.
1815	Lawrence Moore	Wm. Dismukes, Joseph Pickett.
1816	Lawrence Moore	Wm. Dismukes, Joseph Pickett.
1817	Joseph Pickett	James Colman, Boggan Cash.
1818	Wm. Marshall	Jonathan Taylor, Boggan Cash.
1819	Wm. Marshall	Boggan Cash, Geo. Dismukes.
1820	Wm. Marshall	Joseph White, Jeremiah Benton.
1821	Wm. Marshall	Joseph White, John Smith.
1822	Wm. Marshall	Joseph White, John Smith.
1823	Wm. Marshall	Joseph White, James Gordon.
1824	Wm. Marshall	Joseph White, James Gordon.
1825	Joseph Pickett	John Smith, Clement Marshall.
1826	Joseph Pickett	John Smith, Clement Marshall.
1827	Joseph Pickett	Alex. Little, Clement Marshall.
1828	Clement Marshall	Wm. A. Morris, John Smith.
1829	Clement Marshall	Wm. A. Morris, Jos. White.
1830	Clement Marshall	Wm. A. Morris, Joseph White.
1831	Clement Marshall	Wm. A. Morris, Alex, Little.

ANSON COUNTY.—Continued.

Years.	Senate.	House.
1832	Wm. A. Morris	M. W. Cuthbertson, T. D. Parks.
1833	Wm. A. Morris	P. W. Kittrell, A. W. Brandon.
1834	Alex. Little	Pleasant W. Kittrell, A. W. Brandon.
1835	Alex. Little	John A. McRae, Jere. Benton.
1836	Absalom Myers	John A. McRae, John Grady.
1838	J. White	George Dunlap, P. H. Winston.
1840	Abs. Myers	P. H. Winston, John McCollum.
1842	Abs. Myers	Thomas S. Ashe, John McCollum.
1844	P. G. Smith	Jno. Trull, J. M. Waddill.
1846	D. D. Daniel	J. R. Hargrave, Jon. Trull.
1848	D. D. Daniel	J. R. Hargrave, Jon. Trull.
1850	Purdie Richardson	Atlas Jones Dargan, Benj. I. Dunlap.
1852	Purdie Richardson	Atlas J. Dargan, Carey Tolson.
1854	Thos. S. Ashe	Atlas J. Dargan, W. W. Welkens.
1856	Dr. Myers	Atlas J. Dargan, Wm. M. Pickett.
1858	S. W. Walkup	J. A. Leak, A. J. Dargan.
1860	S. W. Walkup	L. L. Polk, E. R. Liles.
1862	Wm. C. Smith	Purdie Richardson R. H. Burns,
1864	Wm. C. Smith	A. J. Dargan, L. L. Polk.
1866	D. A. Covington	A. J. Dargan, W. P. Kendall.
1868	P. T. Beaman	D. Ingram.
1870	A. J. Dargan	W. E. Smith.
1872	C. M. T. McCauley*	R. T. Bennett.

*Anson and Union form the 27th Senatorial District.

ASHE COUNTY.

Ashe County was formed in 1799 from "that portion of Wilkes lying west of the extreme height of the Appalachian Mountains." It is the extreme northwest corner of the State; bounded on the north by the Virginia line, east by the Appalachian Mountains, which separate it from Wilkes and Alleghany, and south by Watauga, Wilkes and Caldwell Counties.

It was called in honor of Samuel Ashe, who was but a short time before the erection of this county, Governor of the State.

The character of Governor Ashe is one of which North Carolina may be well proud.

Its capital town preserves in North Carolina the name of Thomas Jefferson, the third President of the United States. Its distance from Raleigh 202 miles.

COUNTY OFFICERS.

Offices.	Names.
Superior Court Clerk	Robert Parson.
Register of Deeds	George W. Ray.
Sheriff	Wm. Latham.
Coroner	Robert Goss.
Surveyor	James Sapp.

ASHE COUNTY—CONTINUED.

Offices.	Name.
Treasurer	John H. Vannoy.
Commissioners	John H. Carson. David Worth. Amos Michael. Wilborn Shepard. E. C. Bartlett.

JUSTICES OF THE PEACE.

Names.	Date of Qualification.	Post Office Address.
John Brown	Sept. 1st, 1873.	
A. Roark	" "	Solatude.
John Pennington	" "	
J. W. Calhoun	" "	North Fork.
Gideon Poe	" "	
Gideon Weaver	" "	Stagg's Creek.
Patterson Grayburn	" "	
James Ellen	" "	
Stephen Pennington	" "	Hilton.
David Dickson	" "	
John Eldridth	" "	
A. Clark	" "	House Creek.
Ahart Phipps	" "	
John C. Plummer	" "	Chestnut Hill.
Wm. Carson	" "	
G. W. Woody	" "	Flint Hill.
Elihue Phillips	" "	
Sepair Yeates	" "	Gap Creek.
Thomas Ray	" "	Elk X Roads.
R. T. Hardin	" "	Jefferson.
W. H. Gentry and H. H. Ray, and A. P. Caldinon	" "	Jefferson.

MEMBERS OF GENERAL ASSEMBLY.

Years.	Senate.	House.
1800	George Koontz	John Calloway, Nathan Horton.
1801	George Koontz	Rich'd Williams, William Horton.
1802	George Koontz	Nathan Horton, John Calloway.
1803	John Calloway	Rich'd Williams, Jonathan Bake.
1804	James M. Caleb	Rich'd Williams, Joseph Calloway.
1805	Nathan Horton	Rich'd Williams, John Koontz.
1806	Nathan Horton	Joseph Calloway, Rich'd Williams.

ASHE COUNTY—CONTINUED.

Years.	Senate.	House.
1807	John Calloway	Rich'd Williams, T. McGimpsey.
1808	John Calloway	Rich'd Williams, Bedent Baird.
1809	John Calloway	T. McGimpsey, Rich'd Williams.
1810	Richard Williams	Martin Gambill, David Miller.
1811	Richard Williams	David Miller, Martin Gambill.
1812	George Bower	David Edwards, E. Calloway.
1813	George Bower	E. Calloway, David Miller.
1814	George Bower	E. Calloway, Wm. Horton.
1815	George Bower	E. Calloway, Wm. Horton.
1816	George Bower	E. Calloway, Wm. Horton.
1817	George Bower	E. Calloway, Joseph Doughton.
1818	E. Calloway	Francis Bryan, Miles Allen.
1819	E. Calloway	Bedent Baird, Richard Gentry.
1820	R. Gentry	John Harden, A. B. McMillan.
1821	E. Calloway	A. B. McMillan, Abner Smith.
1821	Richard Gentry	Rich'd Gentry, John Harden.
1823	E. Calloway	A. B. McMillan, J. Weaver.
1824	E. Calloway	Joshua Weaver, A. B. McMillan.
1825	Abner Smith	Wm. Herbert, Reuben Hartley.
1826	A. B. McMillan	J. Blevins, Zachariah Baker.
1827	A. B. McMillan	Zach. Baker, Anderson Mitchell.
1828	John Harden	A. Mitchell, James Calloway.
1829	A. Mitchell	J. Calloway, Zachariah Baker.
1830	John Ray	James Horton, J. Calloway.
1831	John Ray	J. Calloway, Taliaferro Witcher.
1832	John Ray	T. Witcher, Jonathan Horton.
1833	G. Phillips	T. Witcher, Jonathan Horton.
1834	Noah Mast	J. Horton, Taliaferro Witcher.
1835	John Gambill	T. Witcher, Jonathan Horton.
1836	Edmund Jones	James M. Nye.
1838	Edmund Jones	James M. Nye.
1840	A. Mitchell	A. B. McMillan.
1842	Edmund W. Jones	George Bower.
1844	A. B. McMillan	Benjamin Calloway.
1846	A. B. McMillan	Benjamin Calloway.
1848	George Bower	Reuben Mast.
1850	George Bower	A. B. McMillan.
1852	George Bower	B. C. Calloway.
1854	George Bower	Allen Gentry.
1856	A. Brant	Allen Gentry.
1858	Joseph Dobson	Allen Gentry.
1860	Joseph Dobson	T. N. Crumpler.
1862	Isaac Jarrett	J. M. Gentry.
1864	Jonathan Horton	F. A. McMillan.
1866	A. C. Cowles	Robert Gambrill.
1868	Samuel P. Smith	Matthew Carson.
1870	C. L. Cook*	S. O. Wilcox.
1872	J. W. Todd	Squire Trivett.

*With Alleghany and Watauga form the 35th Senatorial District.

BEAUFORT COUNTY.

Beaufort County was formed in 1741, from Bath County, now abolished, and derives its name from Henry, Duke of Beaufort, in whom was vested the proprietary rights of George, Duke of Albemarle, and who, with the other proprietors (except Lord Granville,) surrendered in 1729 their rights to the English Crown. (George II.)

It is bounded on the north by the counties Martin and Washington, east by Hyde and Pamlico, south by Craven County, and West by Pitt County.

Washington is its capital, 127 miles from Raleigh.

COUNTY OFFICERS.

Offices.	Names.
Superior Court Clerk	George L. Windley.
Register of Deeds	James H. Cordon.
Sheriff	Fenner J. Satchwell.
Coroner	William Baynor.
Surveyor	Daniel Cutler.
Treasurer	George E. Buckman.
Commissioners	Samuel Windley, Chairman. James E. Merriam. George C. Respess. John D. Watson. Henry Hodges.

JUSTICES OF THE PEACE.

Names.	Date of Qualification.	Post Office Address.
William B. Campbell	Sept. 1st, 1873.	Washington.
William M. Cherry	" "	Washington.
C. C. Rountree	" "	Washington.
C. H. Moore	" "	Washington.
Henry Duff	" "	Washington.
Essex Staten	Sept. 6th, 1873.	Washington.
John B. Respess	Sept. 1st, 1873.	Washington.
H. N. Warters	" "	Washington.
James F. Crawley	" "	Bath.
Joseph Y. Bonner	" "	Bath.
P. H. Johnson	" "	Pantego.
J. H. Topping	" "	Pantego.
W. H. Von Eberstine	" "	Chocowinety.
William Stilley	" "	Chocowinety
George A. Spain	" "	Goose Creek.
E. B. Hopkins	" "	Goose Creek.
W. A. Thompson	October 28th, 1873.	Aurora.
J. M. Hubbard	Jan. 5th, 1874.	Aurora.
One vacancy		Bath.

BEAUFORT COUNTYC

MEMBERS OF GENERAL ASSEMBLY.

Years.	Senate.	House.
1777	Thomas Respess	Nathan Keas, William Brown.
1778	Thomas Respess	Andrew Ellison, William Brown.
1779	Thomas Respess	Robert Trippe, John Kennedy.
1780	Thomas Respess	William Brown, Samuel Willis.
1781	Wm. Brown	Charles Crawford, Thomas A. Grist.
1782	Wm. Brown	Richard N. Stevens, John Gray Blount.
1783	Wm. Brown	Thomas Anderson, John G. Blount.
1784	John Smaw	Thomas Anderson, John G. Blount.
1785	John Smaw	Thomas Anderson, John G. Blount.
1786	John Bonner	John G. Blount, Henry Smaw.
1787	John Bonner	Henry Smaw, John G. Blount.
1788	William Brown	John G. Blount, Henry Smaw.
1789	William Brown	John G. Blount, Richard Grice.
1791	John Kennedy,	Richard Blackledge, John Lanier.
1792	Richard Blackledge	John Lanier, James Bonner.
1793	Richard Blackledge	Charles Crawford, Frederic Grist.
1795	Richard Blackledge.	C. Crawford, F. Grist.
1796	John G. Blount	John Kennedy, jr., T. Ellison.
1797	Hans Patton	F. Grist, Thomas Ellison.
1800	H. S. Bonner	John Kennedy, Frederic Grist.
1801	H. S. Bonner	F. Grist, J. Kennedy.
1802	H. S. Bonner	F. Grist, Thomas Ellison.
1803	H. S. Bonner	F. Grist, Thomas Ellison.
1804	N. W. Bonner	F. Grist, Thomas Ellison.
1805	Thomas Smaw	Stephen Owens, F. Grist.
1806	Thomas Smaw	F. Grist, S. Owens.
1807	Thomas Smaw	James Williams, F. Grist.
1808	Frederic Grist	J. Williams, Jonathan Marsh.
1809	Frederic Grist	J. Williams, Thomas Boyd.
1810	Frederic Grist	J. Williams, T. Boyd.
1811	Frederic Grist	James Latham, Everard Hall.
1812	Thomas Bowen	George Boyd, J. Latham.
1813	Stephen Owens	William Worsley, Slade Pearce.
1814	Reading Grist	J. O. K. Williams, George Boyd.
1815	Reading Grist	J. O. K. Williams, Thomas Latham.
1816	Reading Grist	J. O. K. Williams, Wm. Vines.
1817	Reading Grist	T. Latham, Wm. Vines.
1818	Reading Grist	T. Latham, Jesse Robeson.
1819	Richard Hines	J. Robeson, John S. Smallwood.
1820	Jesse Robeson	Thomas W. Blackledge, John Adams.
1821	Jesse Robeson	Thomas W. Blackledge, J. Adams.
1822	J. O. K. Williams	T. W. Blackledge, W. Ormond.
1823	J. O. K. Williams	W. Ormond, T. W. Blackledge.
1824	J. O. K. Williams	T. W. Blackledge, James Satchwell.
1825	J. O. K. Williams	Thomas Ellison, Wm. A. Blount.
1826	J. O. K. Williams	W. A. Blount, T. Ellison.
1827	J. O. K. Williams	W. A. Blount, T. W. Blackledge.
1828	J. O. K. Williams	T. Latham, T. W. Blackledge.
1829	Joseph B. Hinton	S. Smallwood, J. W. Williams.
1830	Joseph B. Hinton	S. Smallwood, J. W. Williams.
1831	W. S. Rowland	Richard H. Bonner, David O. Freeman.
1832	Joseph B. Hinton	Richard Bonner, Henry S. Clark.
1833	Wm. E. Smaw	Wm. L. Kennedy. S. Smallwood.

BEAUFORT COUNTY.—Continued.

Years.	Senate.	House.
1834	J. McWilliams	Henry S. Clark, S. Smallwood.
1835	J. O. K. Williams	H. S. Clark, S. Smallwood.
1836	J. O. K. Williams	F. C. Satterthwaite, S. Smallwood.
1838	J. O. K. Williams	W. A. Blount, John McWilliams.
1840	William Selby	J. O. K. Williams, S. P. Allen.
1842	W. B. Hodges	S. P. Allen, J. W. Williams.
1844	Joshua Taylor	Edward Stanly, Frederic Grist.
1846	David Carter	Edward Stanly, Thomas D. Smaw.
1848	Thomas D. Smaw	Edward Stanly, W. W. Hayman.
1850	A. Grist	Jesse R. Stubbs, Wm. H. Tripp.
1852	R. Murray	Wm. H. Tripp, Jesse R. Stubbs.
1854	Allen Grist	Jesse R. Stubbs.
1856	Allen Grist	Jesse R. Stubbs, J. Eborn.
1858	Richard S. Donnells	—— Sparrow, —— Windley.
1860	Frederick Grist	R. S. Donnell, W. T. Marsh.
1862	*E. J. Warren	R. S. Donnell, W. T. Marsh.
1864	E. J. Warren	R. S. Donnell, D. M. Carter.
1866	Isaiah Respess	Henry Harding, C. M. Gorham.
1868	J. B. Respess	Hiram E. Stilley.
1870	E. J. Warren	Thomas Sparrow.
1872	†J. B. Respess H. E. Stilley	Samuel Carson.

*With Hyde formed 3d District.

†With Dare, Hyde, Martin and Washington form 2d Senatorial District.

BERTIE COUNTY.

Bertie was formed as early as 1722, from Albemarle county, (now abolished,) and derives its name from James and John Bertie, in whom the proprietary rights of the Earl of Clarendon was vested. Their names appear in the deed of surrender in 1729 of their rights to the crown.

It is situated in the eastern part of the State, and bounded on the north by the county of Hertford, east by the Chowan river, which separates it from Chowan county, south by the Roanoke river, which separates it from the county of Martin, and west by a part of Northampton county and the Roanoke river, which separate it from Halifax county.

Windsor is its capital town, beautifully situated on the Cashier river, and navigable for vessels.

COUNTY OFFICERS.

Offices.	Name.
Superior Court Clerk	W. P. Gurley.
Register of Deeds	B. F. King.
Sheriff	F. W. Bell
Coroner	Bryant Lee.

BERTIE COUNTY.—Continued.

COUNTY OFFICERS—Continued.

Offices.	Name.
Surveyor..............................	
Treasurer..............................	John G. Mitchell.
Commissioners..............................	Wm. T. Ward, Chairman. D. L. Cole. John W. Heckstall. Wright Cherry. Cato Mountain.

JUSTICES OF THE PEACE.

Names.	Date of Qualification.	Post Office Address.
Henry C. Fager....................	Aug. 15th, 1873.	Windsor.
John G. Mitchell..................	Aug. 16th, 1873.	Windsor.
....	" "	Windsor.
Henry C. Cooper.,................	Aug. 30th, 1873.	Windsor.
James W. Smith...................	Nov. 8th, 1873.	Merry Hill.
Simon T. Hughes..................	Aug. 9th, 1873.	Windsor or Colerain.
Jos. Leary........................	Sept. 6th, 1873.	Colerain.
John W. Sessoms,.................	Aug. 13th, 1873.	Colerain.
David Watford....................	Aug. 19th, 1873.	Colerain.
Abram Jenkins....................	Aug. 12th, 1873.	Windsor.
Asa Williford.....................	Aug. 29th, 1873.	
Henry Parker.....................	Aug. 16th, 1873.	Roxobel.
Watson Lewis.....................	Aug. 18th, 1873.	Lewiston.
H. P. Harrell.....................	" "	Lewiston.

MEMBERS OF GENERAL ASSEMBLY.

Years.	Senate.	House.
1777	Zed. Stone..................	William Jordan, Simon Turner.
1778	Zed. Stone..................	William Jordan, James Campbell.
1779	Zed. Stone..................	John Pugh Williams, Jonathan Jacocks.
1780	Jon. Jacocks................	William Horn, David Turner.
1781	Jon. Jacocks................	William Horn, David Turner.
1782	Jon. Jacocks................	William Horn, David Turner.
1783	Jon. Jacocks................	William Horn, David Turner.
1784	Jon. Jacocks................	Zed Stone, Andrew Oliver.
1785	Jon. Jacocks................	Thomas Collins, Andrew Oliver.
1786	Zed, Stone..................	Thomas Collins, Andrew Oliver.
1787	John Johnston..............	Andrew Oliver, William Horn.
1788	John Johnston..............	William Horn, Francis Pugh.
1789	John Johnston..............	William Horn, Francis Pugh.

BERTIE COUNTY—Continued.

MEMBERS OF GENERAL ASSEMBLY.

Years.	Senate.	House.
1790	Francis Pugh..............	David Stone, David Turner.
1791	Jasper Charlton............	David Stone, William J. Dawson.
1792	Jasper Charlton........ ...	David Stone, Tristam Lowther.
1793	Jasper Charlton............	David Stone, John Wolfendon.
1794	John Wolfendon............	Jonathan Jacocks, David Stone.
1795	John Wolfendon............	Jonathan Jacocks, John Johnston.
1796	Timothy Walton............	George Outlaw, John Johnston.
1797	Francis Pugh..............	George Outlaw, J. B. Jordan.
1800	John Johnston.............	Joseph Jordan, Thomas Fitts.
1801	Jona. Jacocks..............	Henry K. Peterson, Joseph Eason.
1802	George Outlaw.............	James W. Clark, Henry Peterson.
1803	Henry Peterson............	James W. Clark, James Tunstall.
1804	Joseph Jordan.............	William Cherry, Joseph H. Bryan.
1805	Joseph Jordan.............	William Cherry, Joseph H. Bryan.
1806	George Outlaw.............	Prentis Law, Joseph Eason.
1807	George Outlaw.............	Joseph H. Bryan, Joseph Eason.
1808	George Outlaw.............	Joseph H. Bryan, Joseph Eason.
1809	Joseph Jordan.............	Joseph H. Bryan, Geo. L. Ryan.
1810	George Outlaw.............	George L. Ryan, Thomas Speller.
1811	George Outlaw.............	David Stone, William Sparkman.
1812	George Outlaw.............	David Stone, William Sparkman.
1813	George Outlaw.............	Timothy Walton, Whit. H. Pugh.
1814	George Outlaw.............	William Sparkman, Whit. H. Pugh.
1815	Wm. Sparkman	Wm. H. Pugh, Jonathan Jacocks.
1816	Wm. Sparkman	Simon A. Bryan, J. H. Jacocks.
1817	George Outlaw.............	Thos. L. West, J. H. Jacocks.
1818	Thos. L. West..............	William Hinton, Joseph Jordan.
1819	Wm. Hinton...............	George B. Outlaw, Simon A. Bryan.
1820	Joshua Taylor.............	George B. Outlaw, Thos. Brickell.
1821	George Outlaw.............	Robert C. Watson, Thos. Brickell.
1822	George Outlaw.............	Thomas Brickell, Simon A. Bryan.
1823	George B. Outlaw..........	James G. Mhoon, S. A. Bryan.
1824	George B. Outlaw..........	Wm. H. Roscoe, J. G. Mhoon.
1825	John Nicholls	William H. Roscoe, J. G. Mhoon.
1826	Wm. Gilliam...............	J. G. Mhoon, Joseph D. White.
1827	George O. Askew..........	Thomas H. Speller, J. D. White.
1828	George O. Askew..........	Joseph Watford, Wm. S. Mhoon.
1829	George O. Askew..........	Wm. S. Mhoon, Alexander W. Mebane.
1830	George O. Askew..........	Wm. S. Mhoon, A. W. Mebane.
1831	George O. Askew..........	Lewis Thompson, David Outlaw.
1832	George O. Askew..........	David Outlaw, Thomas J. Pugh.
1833	A. W. Mebane..............	David Outlaw, Thomas J. Pugh.
1834	A. W. Mebane..............	David Outlaw, Thomas J. Pugh.
1835	A. W. Mebane..............	John F. Lee, Thomas H. Speller.
1836	A. W. Mebane..............	John F. Lee, Thomas H. Speller.
1838	Wm. W. Cherry............	Lewis Bond; James R. Rayner.
1840	Lewis Bond	Lewis Thompson, John R. Gilliam.
1842	Jas. S. Mitchell............	James R. Rayner, John F. Lee.
1844	Lewis Thompson...........	W. W. Cherry, Lewis Bond.
1846	J. R. Gilliam...............	John Bond, Richard O. Britton.
1848	Lewis Thompson...........	J. B. Cherry, K. Biggs.
1850	Lewis Bond	J. B. Cherry, P. H. Winston.
1852	Lewis Thompson...........	J. B. Cherry, S. B. Spruill.
1854	Jos. B. Cherry.............	P. H. Winston, David Outlaw.

BERTIE COUNTY.—Continued.

MEMBERS OF GENERAL ASSEMBLY.—Continued.

Years.	Senate.	House.
1856	Jos. B. Cherry.............	David Outlaw, John Wilson.
1858	Jos. B. Cherry..............	David Outlaw, P. T. Henry.
1860	David Outlaw...............	P. T. Henry, J. R. Ferguson.
1862	Thos. M. Garrett............	P. T. Henry, James Bond.
1864	John Pool..................	P. T. Henry, James Bond.
1865	....	Lewis Thompson, P. T. Henry.
1866	David Outlaw...............	P. T. Henry, J. W. Beasely.
1868	Jas. W. Beasely............	Parker D Robbins.
1870	With Hertford forms 5th District................. Jas. W. Beasley	Parker D. Robbins, (colored.)
1872	With North'mpt'n forms 2nd District............ Geo. D. Holloman......	F. C. Miller.

BLADEN COUNTY.

Bladen County was formed as early as 1734, from New Hanover County, and comprehended at the time the whole western portion of the State as far as the limits of North Carolina extended.

It was so called in honor of Martin Bladen, one of the Lords Commissioners of Trade and Plantations.

It is situated in the south-eastern part of North Carolina, and is bounded on the north by the county of Cumberland, and South River, which separates it from Sampson county; on the east by the same river, which separates it from New Hanover County; on the south by the counties of Brunswick and Columbus; and on the west by the county of Robeson.

Elizabethtown, its capital, is situated on the Cape Fear River, and distant from Raleigh 99 miles.

COUNTY OFFICERS.

Offices.	Names.
Superior Court Clerk....................	Evander Singletary.
Register of Deeds.......................	Alexander Pone.
Sheriff..................................	W. H. Sikes.
Coroner..................................	E. D. Bizzell.
Surveyor.................................	R. M. Croom.
Treasurer................................	Howard Wilkeson.
Commissioners...........................	W. McHorrell, Chairman. John Newell. A. J. Shaw. D. Kelly. James Daniel.

BLADEN COUNTY—Continued.

JUSTICES OF THE PEACE.

Names.	Date of Qualification.	Post Office Address.
W. A. Atkinson	Sept. 1st, 1873.	Elizabethtown.
James Daniel	" "	Elizabethtown.
B. L. Jones	" "	Bladenboro.
John A. Gupton	" "	Bladenboro.
Alexander McDonald	" "	Tar Heel.
E. W. Esters	" "	Tar Heel.
John T. Council	" "	Prospect Hall.
Amos Martin	" "	Prospect Hall.
John W. Wallace	" "	Abbottsburg.
J. W. Buie	" "	Abbottsburg.
A. K. Cromartie	" "	Dalton.
Fred Harrison	" "	Dalton.
N. S. McLaughlin	" "	Vicksburg.
Rufus Register	" "	Vicksburg.
E. G. Grimsley	" "	West Brooks.
J. J. Bright	" "	West Brooks.
A. J. Blizzard	" "	French's Creek.
William Devane	" "	French's Creek.
Thomas S. Lewis	" "	Little Sugar Loaf.
Luther Cromartie	" "	Little Sugar Loaf.
D. D. Beard	" "	Melvinsville.
Samuel Vinson	" "	Melvinsville.
R. W. Tatom	" "	Melvinsville.
O. J. Gardner	" "	Melvinsville.

MEMBERS OF GENERAL ASSEMBLY.

Years.	Senate.	House.
1774		William Salter, Walter Gibson.
1775		William Salter, James White.
1778	Thomas Owen	Benjamin Clark.
1783	Thomas Owen	Samuel Cain, Francis Lucas.
1784	Thomas Owen	Peter Robeson, Samuel Cain.
1785	Thomas Brown	James Richardson.
1786	Thomas Brown	Peter Robertson, J. Richardson.
1787	Thomas Owen	Samuel Cain, John Brown.
1788	Thomas Brown	J. Brown, S. Cain.
1791	Jos. R. Gautier	Duncan Stewart, Josiah Lewis.
1792	Duncan Stewart	Josiah Lewis, John Hall.
1793	D. Stewart	Josiah Lewis, James Bradley.
1794	D. Stewart	James Bradley, Josiah Lewis.
1795	D. Stewart	James Bradley, Hugh Waddell.
1796	Josiah Lewis	H. Waddell, J. Bradley.
1797	J. Lewis	James Morehead, J. Bradley.
1800	J. Lewis	Street Ashford, J. Bradley.
1801	T. W. Harvey	Sam'l N. Richardson, Richard Holmes.
1802	S. N. Richardson	Richard Holmes, Amos Richardson.

BLADEN COUNTY—Continued.

MEMBERS OF GENERAL ASSEMBLY—Continued.

Years.	Senate.	House.
1803	S. N. Richardson	Amos Richardson, Street Ashford.
1804	Richard Holmes	A. Richardson, Michael Molton.
1805	Richard Holmes	A. Richardson; M. Molton.
1806	Richard Holmes	James B. White, A. Richardson.
1807	Richard Holmes	J. B. White, David Gillaspie.
1808	Samuel Andres	Thomas Brown, James Owen.
1809	Samuel Andres	T. Brown, J. Owen.
1810	Samuel Andres	T. Brown, J. Owen.
1811	Isaac Wright	T. Brown, J. Owen.
1812	Isaac Wright	David Gillaspie, John Owen.
1813	Isaac Wright	D. Gillaspie, John Owen.
1814	Richard Parish	James J. Cummings, John Sellers.
1815	James J. McKay	John Sellers, J. J. Cummings.
1816	Jas. J. McKay	Wm. J. Cowan, John Sellers.
1817	Jas. J. McKay	Wm. J. Cowan, John Sellers.
1818	Jas. J. McKay	Thos. White, Wm. G. Beatty.
1819	John Owen	T. White, Joseph Wilson.
1820	John Owen	Jos. Wilson, J. J. McKay.
1821	Simon Green	Sam'l B. Andres, Wm. J. Cowan.
1822	Jas. J. McKay	R. Melvin, John J. McMillan.
1823	Daniel Shipman	R. Melvin, William Davis.
1824	Daniel Shipman	J. J. McMillan, John T. Gilmore.
1825	Robert Melvin	Isaac Wright, John J. McMillan.
1826	Jas. J. McKay	J. J. McMillan, John T. Gilmore.
1827	John Owen	J. J. McMillan, John T. Gilmore.
1828	Mal. McInnis	J. J. McMillan, Robert Melvin.
1829	Mal. McInnis	Robert Melvin, J. J. McMillan.
1830	Jas. J. McKay	John W. McMillan, Salter Loyd.
1831	John T. Gilmore	J. J. McMillan, Robert Lyon.
1832	Robert Melvin	Robert Lyon, William Jones.
1834	J. J. McMillan	Robert Lyon, George Cromartie.
1835	George Cromartie	R. Lyon, B. Fitzrandolph.
1836	James Burney	Joseph M. Gillespie.
1838	Robert Melvin	George T. Barksdale.
1840	Robert Melvin	George W. Bannerman.
1842	Robert Melvin	George W. Bannerman.
1844	Robert Melvin	H. H. Robinson.
1846	Richard Wooten	T. S. D. McDowell.
1848	Richard Wooten	T. S. D. McDowell.
1850	Richard Wooten	T. S. D. McDowell.
1854	T. D. McDowell	George M. White.
1856	A. J. Jones	George M. White.
1858	T. D. McDowell	J. H. Stephens.
1860	John D. Taylor	C. F. Davis.
1862	J. W. Ellis	J. W. Russ.
1864	J. W. Ellis	J. W. Russ.
1866	Salter Loyd	J. A. Richardson.
1868	John W. Purdie	F. W. Forster.
1870	With Columbus forms 14th Senatorial District. J. C. Currie	A. W. Fisher.
1872	With Brunswick forms 13th Senatorial District. G. N. Hill	A. H. Perry.

BRUNSWICK COUNTY.

BRUNSWICK COUNTY was formed in 1764, from the counties of Bladen and New Hanover.

It derives its name from the Prince of Brunswick, who married this year (1764), the King's eldest sister.

It is situated in the extreme south-eastern portion of North Carolina, and is bounded on the north by the Cape Fear River, which separates it from New Hanover and Bladen; on the east, by the Cape Fear River, which separates it from New Hanover; on the south, by the Atlantic Ocean and the South Carolina line; on the west, by Waccamaw River, which separates it from Columbus County.

Its capital is SMITHVILLE, distance from Raleigh one hundred and seventy-three miles.

COUNTY OFFICERS.

Offices.	Names.
Superior Court Clerk	Samuel P. Swain,
Register of Deeds	Lewis A. Galloway.
Sheriff	Edward W. Taylor.
Coroner	Julius W. Taylor.
Surveyor	George W. Grissett.
Treasurer	John L. Wescott.
Commissioners	Ezra Thomas. Chairman. Geo. K. Andrews. A. J. Swinson. Wallace Styron. Benj. L. Butler.

JUSTICES OF THE PEACE.

Names.	Date of Qualification.	Post Office Address.
John L. Wescott	Aug. 11th, 1873.	Smithville.
Lewis A. Galloway	" " "	Smithville.
Limas Mimbs	" 14th "	Supply Post Office.
Franklin Galloway	" 11th, "	Supply Post Office.
Wallace Styron	" 11th, "	Supply Post Office.
S. J. G. Milliken	" 16th, "	Shallotte Post Office.
Christopher Evans	" 25th, "	Shallotte Post Office.
Benjamin Locke	" 18th, "	Easy Hill Post Office.
Ezra Thomas	" 26th, "	Easy Hill Post Office.
A. J. Swinson	" 26th, "	Robeson Post Office.
J. C. Lawton	" 26th, "	Bolton.
John H. Ments	" 26th, "	Shallotte Post Office.
F. M. Hughes	" 25th, "	Shallotte Post Office.

BRUNSWICK COUNTY—Continued.

MEMBERS OF GENERAL ASSEMBLY.

Years.	Senate.	House.
1776	Maurice Moore	Cornelius Harnett, A. McClaine.
1777	Archibald McClaine	Wm. Lord, Richard Quince.
1778	Archibald McClaine	Lewis Dupre, William Gause.
1782	Archibald McClaine	Wm. Waters, Dennis Hawkins.
1783	Benjamin Smith	Wm. Waters, Dennis Hawkins.
1784	William Walters	Jacob Leonard, David Flowers.
1785	William Walters	Jacob Leonard, Robert Howe.
1787	A. M. Forster	Lewis Dupre, Jacob Leonard.
1788	Lewis Dupre	Jacob Leonard, John Cains.
1791	Lewis Dupre	Benjamin Smith, Wm. E. Lord.
1792	Benjamin Smith	Alfred Moore, W. E. Lord.
1793	B. Smith	Wm. Wingate, Wm. E. Lord.
1794	B. Smith	Wm. Wingate, Abraham Bissant.
1795	B. Smith	Wm. Wingate, Ab. Bissant.
1796	B. Smith	Wm. E. Lord, Absalom Bissant.
1797	B. Smith	A. Bissant, George Davis.
1800	B. Smith	Benjamin Mills, A. Bissant.
1801	Wm. Wingate	John G. Scull, Benj. Mills.
1802	Wm. Wingate	John G. Scull, Benj. Mills.
1803	Wm. Wingate	John G. Scull, Thomas Leonard.
1804	Benjamin Smith	Thomas Leonard, Maurice Moore.
1805	B. Smith	Thomas Leonard, Richard Parrish
1806	B. Smith	Richard Parrish, Thomas Leonard.
1807	B. Smith	Thomas Leonard, Thomas Russ.
1808	B. Smith	Thomas Leonard, Thomas Russ.
1809	B. Smith	Thomas Leonard, George Davis.
1810	B. Smith	Thomas Leonard, Thomas Russ.
1811	Thos. Leonard	Jacob W. Leonard, Maurice Moore.
1812	Wm. Wingate	Maurice Moore, Robert Potter.
1813	Wm. Wingate	Maurice Moore, Thomas Russ.
1814	Jacob Leonard	Alfred Moore, Thomas Russ.
1815	J. W. Leonard	Uriah Sullivan, John C. Baker.
1816	Benjamin Smith	Edward Mills, Wm. Simmons.
1817	Jacob Leonard	Alfred Moore, John C. Baker.
1818	Jacob Leonard	J. C. Baker, Alfred Moore.
1819	John C. Baker	Alfred Moore, John Neele.
1821	J. W. Leonard	Francis N. Waddell, A. Moore.
1822	John C. Baker	Samuel Frink, Alfred Moore.
1823	John C. Baker	Alfred Moore, J. W. Leonard.
1824	John C. Baker	Alfred Moore, Jacob W. Leonard.
1825	John C. Baker	John J. Gause, Alfred Moore.
1826	Benj. R. Locke	Alfred Moore, Jacob Leonard, Jr.
1827	B. R. Locke	A. Moore, Jacob Leonard, Jr.
1828	Jacob Leonard	Thomas B. Smith, Wm. L. Hall.
1829	J. Leonard	John P. Gause, Marsden Campbell.
1830	Wm. R. Hall	Benj. S. Leonard, John P. Gause.
1831	Wm. R. Hall	J. P. Gause, Samuel Laspeyre.
1832	Wm. R. Hall	S. A. Laspeyre, John Waddell.
1833	Wm. R. Hall	S. A. Laspeyre, Benj. S. Leonard.
1834	Maurice Moore	Rt. C. McCracken, Abram Baker.
1835	Frederic J. Hill	Wm. R. Hall, Abram Baker.
1836	James Burney	Frederic J. Hill.
1838	Robert Melvin	F. J. Hill.
1840	R. Melvin	F. J. Hill.
1842	R. Melvin	Armeline Bryan.

BRUNSWICK COUNTY—Continued.

MEMBERS OF GENERAL ASSEMBLY—Continued.

Years.	Senate.	House.
1844	R. Melvin	H. H. Waters.
1846	R. Wooten	H. H. Waters.
1848	Richard Wooten	H. H. Waters.
1850	Richard Wooten	John H. Hill.
1852	T. D. McDowell	H. H. Waters.
1854	T. D. McDowell	Gaston Mears.
1856	A. J. Jones	T. D. Meares.
1858	T. D. McDowell	T. D. Meares.
1860	John D. Taylor	T. D. Meares.
1862	John W. Ellis	Dan'l L. Russell.
1864	John W. Ellis	Dan'l. L. Russell.
1866	Salter Lloyd With New Hanover forms 13th District.	D. C. Allen.
1868	Exum Legg A. H. Galloway	B. T. Morrell.
1870	Charles McClammy A. H. Galloway With Brunswick and Bladen forms 13th District.	John A. Brooks.
1872	G. N. Hill	J. A. Brooks.

BUNCOMBE COUNTY.

Buncombe County was formed in 1791, from Burke and Rutherford counties, and derives its name from Col. Edward Buncombe, of that part of Tyrrell which is now Washington county; he was Colonel of the 5th regiment raised by North Carolina for the Continental army.

Colonel Buncombe was a native of St. Kitts, one of the West India islands. He inherited land in Tyrrell county and built a house, now in the possession of his descendants.

Buncombe county is situated in the western portion of the State; bounded on the north and west by the Appalachian Mountains and the new county of Madison, east by Rutherford and McDowell counties, south by Henderson county and Transylvania, and west by Haywood county and the Tennessee line.

Its capital is Asheville, named in compliment to Governor Samuel Ashe, of New Hanover county. It was originally called Morristown, and is a most flourishing village, not far from the French Broad River. 256 miles from Raleigh.

BUNCOMBE COUNTY.—Continued.

COUNTY OFFICERS.

Offices.	Names.
Superior Court Clerk	James E. Reed.
Register of Deeds	James R. Patterson.
Sheriff	James M. Young.
Coroner	Dr. D. F. Summey.
Surveyor	R. V. Blackstock.
Treasurer	J. H. Courtney.
Commissioners	E. J. Asten, Chairman. W. R. Murray. S. F. Williams. G. W. Hampton. W. F. Davidson.

MEMBERS OF GENERAL ASSEMBLY.

Years.	Senate.	House.
1792	Wm. Davidson	Gabriel Ragsdale, Wm. Brittain.
1793	Robert Love	William Brittain, Gabriel Ragsdale.
1794	Robert Love	Wm. Brittain, Gabriel Ragsdale.
1795	Robert Love	Wm. Brittain, Gabriel Ragsdale.
1796	James Brittain	Wm. Brittain, Philip Hoodenpye.
1797	James Brittain	Wm. Brittain, Thomas Love.
1800	Josh. Williams	Thomas Love, Zebulon Baird.
1801	Josh. Williams	Thomas Love, Zebulon Baird.
1802	James Brittain	Thomas Love, Zebulon Baird.
1803	Josh. Williams	Thomas Love, Zebulon Baird.
1804	James Brittain	Thomas Love, Jacob Boyler.
1805	James Brittain	Thomas Love, Jacob Boyler.
1806	Zebulon Baird	Thomas Love, Joseph Pickens.
1807	James Brittain	Thomas Love, Joseph Pickens.
1808	Jno. McFarland	Thomas Love, Malcolm Henry.
1809	Zebulon Baird	Thomas Foster, Joseph Pickens.
1810	Rt. Williamson	Philip Brittain, Zephaniah Horton.
1811	Rt. Williamson	Philip Brittain, Samuel Davidson.
1812	John Longmire	Zephaniah Horton, Thomas Foster.
1813	J. Longmire	Hamilton Hyde, Thomas Foster.
1814	J. Longmire	Hamilton Hyde, Thomas Foster.
1815	Ep. Hightower	Zeph. Horton, James Lowrie.
1816	John Longmire	Philip Brittain, James Lowrie.
1817	Thomas Foster	Philip Brittain, Charles Moore.
1818	Zebulon Baird	Charles Moore, James Whitaker.
1819	Thomas Foster	James Whitaker, J. M. Cathey.
1821	Zebulon Baird	Wm. D. Smith, Wm. Brittain, Sr.
1822	Zebulon Baird	Wm. D. Smith, John Anderson.
1823	Philip Brittain	James Lowrie, James Whitaker.
1824	P. Brittain	David L. Swain, Benoni Sams.
1825	A. A. McDowell	David L. Swain, James Weaver.
1826	A. A. McDowell	D. L. Swain, James Allen.

BUNCOMBE COUNTY.—Continued.

MEMBERS OF GENERAL ASSEMBLY.—Continued.

Years.	Senate.	House.
1827	A. A. McDowell	John Clayton, James Allen.
1828	A. A. McDowell	John Clayton, David L. Swain.
1829	James Allen	David L. Swain, Wm. Orr.
1830	James Gudger	James Weaver, Wm. Orr.
1831	James Allen	James Brevard, John Clayton.
1832	James Allen	James Weaver, John Clayton.
1833	John Clayton	James Weaver, Joseph Henry.
1834	James Lowry	Joseph Henry, James Weaver.
1835	Hodge Rabun	Nath'l Harrison, Joseph Pickett.
1836	James Gudger	Montreville Patton, John Clayton.
1838	Hodge Rabun	M. Patton, Philip Brittain.
1840	T. L. Clingman	M. Patton, Thomas Morris.
1842	J. Cathey	John Burgin, Geo. W. Candler.
1844	N. W. Woodfin	John A. Fagg, John Thrash.
1846	N. W. Woodfin	John A. Fagg, A. B. Chunn,
1848	N. W. Woodfin	Newton Coleman, T. W. Atkin.
1850	N. W. Woodfin	Marcus Erwin, James Sharpe.
1852	N. W. Woodfin	Jas. Lowrie, J. A. Fagg.
1854	David Coleman	Z. B. Vance.
1856		Marcus Erwin.
1858	With Madison Co. form'd 40th District. B. M. Edney.	J. S. F. Baird.
1860	Marcus Erwin	A. S. Merrimon.
1862	Wm. M. Shipp	——— Burgin.
1864	M. Patton	J. M. Gudger.
1866	L. S. Gash	M. Patton.
1868	James Blythe	G. W. Candler.
1870	James H. Merrimon	T. D. Johnston.
1872	James H. Merrimon	T. D. Johnston, D. Blackwell.

BURKE COUNTY.

Burke County was formed in 1777, from Rowan county, and named in compliment to the celebrated English Statesman and Orator, Edmund Burke. It is located in the north-western portion of the State, and bounded on the north by the counties of Yancey and Caldwell, on the east by Catawba, on the south by Cleveland and Rutherford, and on the west by McDowell.

Morganton, the capital of Burke County, is called in compliment of General Daniel Morgan, and is 197 miles from Raleigh.

BURKE COUNTY—CONTINUED.

COUNTY OFFICERS.

Offices.	Names.
Superior Court Clerk	D. C. Pearson.
Register of Deeds	W. T. Harbison.
Sheriff	E. P. Moore.
Coroner	M. D. Brittain.
Surveyor	J. P. Beck.
Treasurer	J. L. Laxton.
Commissioners	G. P. Erwin, Chairman. E. A. Perkins. J. A. Puett. Thomas Parkes. Frank Warlick.

JUSTICES OF THE PEACE.

Names.	Date of Qualification.	Post Office Address.
F. D. Irvin	Sept. 1873.	Morganton.
J. C. McNeely	" "	Morganton.
W. A. Ross	" "	Morganton.
J. H. Howard	" "	Morganton.
J. W. Berry	" "	Icard, Burke Co.
J. H. Huffman	" "	Icard, Burke Co.
Arnold Wilson	" "	Icard, Burke Co.
L. F. Warlick	" "	Icard, Burke Co.
Nathan Chapman	" "	Warlick's Mill.
Amos Huffman	" "	Warlick's Mill.
J. H. Ramsey	" "	Morganton.
A. C. Cartwell	" "	Morganton.
W. E. Powe	" "	Morganton.
John Eppley	" "	Brindletown.
J. P. Beck	" "	Morganton.
L. F. Walker	" "	Morganton.
W. E. Corpeny	" "	Morganton.
Jim. D. Kincaide	" "	Morganton.

MEMBERS OF GENERAL ASSEMBLY.

Years.	Senate.	House.
1778	Charles McDowell	E. McClain, Jas. Wilson.
1779	Ephraim McClain	Thomas Wilson, William Morrison.
1780	Ephraim McClain	Hugh Brevard, Jos. McDowell.

BURKE COUNTY—Continued.

MEMBERS OF GENERAL ASSEMBLY—Continued.

Years.	Senate.	House.
1781	Andrew Woods	Hugh Brevard, Jos. McDowell.
1782	Charles McDowell	Waightstill Avery, Jos. McDowell.
1783	Charles McDowell	J. McDowell, Waightstill Avery.
1784	Charles McDowell	W. Avery, J. McDowell.
1785	Charles McDowell	J. McDowell, W. Avery.
1786	Charles McDowell	J. McDowell, David Vance.
1787	Charles McDowell	J. McDowell, Jos. McDowell, jr.
1788	Charles McDowell	J. McDowell, Jos. McDowell, jr.
1791	Joseph McDowell	J. McDowell, jr. David Vance.
1792	Joseph McDowell	J. M. McDowell, Jos. McDowell, jr.
1793	Joseph McDowell	W. Avery, Alex. Erwin.
1794	Joseph McDowell	Alex. Erwin, John McDowell.
1795	Joseph McDowell	A. Erwin, Conrad Heldebrand.
1796	W. Avery	Wm. White, Alexander Erwin.
1797	James Murphy	A. Erwin, Conrad Heldebrand.
1800	Andrew Beard	Wm. Davenport, Wm. Walton.
1801	A. Beard	B. Smith, David Tate.
1802	Wm. Davenport	David Tate, Thomas McEntire.
1803	Andrew Beard	David Tate, Thomas Coleman.
1804	John H. Stevely	A. Erwin, Hodge Rabourn.
1805	J. H. Stevely	John Carson, Brice Collins.
1806	J. H. Stevely	John Carson, Brice Collins.
1807	William Tate	Brice Collins, David Tate.
1808	Israel Pickens	Abraham Fleming, Thos. Brevard.
1809	I. Pickens	Charles McDowell, I. T. Avery.
1810	David Tate	I. T. Avery, Charles McDowell.
1811	David Tate	Charles McDowell, I. T. Avery.
1812	Hodge Rabourn	Wm. Dickson, John M. Greenlee.
1813	Hodge Rabourn	Wm. Dickson, Brice Collins.
1814	David Tate	Brice Collins, Wm. Dickson.
1815	A. A. McDowell	Brice Collins, Joel Coffee.
1816	Alex. Perkins	Brice Collins, John Phagan.
1817	A. Perkins	Brice Collins, J. R. McDowell.
1818	David Tate	J. R. McDowell, Matthew Beard.
1819	A. Perkins	Brice Collins, J. R. McDowell.
1821	David Tate	Brice Collins, Wm. Dickson.
1822	Samuel P. Carson	Matthew Baird, Merritt Burgin.
1823	J. R. McDowell	Wm. Roane, Brice Collins.
1824	Samuel P. Carson	Alney Burgin. Peter Ballew.
1825	J. R. McDowell	Peter Ballew, Edwin Poor.
1826	Matthew Baird	David Newland, Edwin Poor.
1827	Merritt Burgin	David Newland, David Neill.
1828	M. Burgin	David Newland, Mark Brittain.
1829	M. Burgin	Joseph Neill, David Newland.
1830	David Newland	E. A. Hooper, Alney Burgin.
1831	Mark Brittain	Alney Burgin, F. P. Glass.
1832	Jas. McDowell	A. Burgin, F. P. Glass.
1833	Mark Brittain	A. Burgin, David Corpening.
1834	Samuel P. Carson	Jas. H. Perkins, Samuel Fleming.
1835	Peter Ballew	E. J. Erwin, Jas. H. Perkins.
1836	Thomas Baker	E. J. Erwin, James H. Perkins, and E. P. Miller.
1838	Thomas Baker	Edward J. Erwin, Wm. M. Carson, and E. P. Miller.

BURKE COUNTY—Continued.

MEMBERS OF GENERAL ASSEMBLY—Continued.

Years.	Senate.	House.
1840	B. S. Gaither...............	William M. Carson, E. P. Miller, and Jos. Neal.
1842	A. Burgin..................	Samuel J. Neal, Tod R. Caldwell, and W. W. Avery.
1844	B. S. Gaither...............	T. R. Caldwell, Benj. Burgin.
1846	S. F. Patterson.....	Wm. F. McKesson, J. J. Erwin.
1848	S. F. Patterson.............	Tod R. Caldwell, John S. Erwin.
1850	Tod R. Caldwell............	W. W. Avery, T. G. Walton.
1852	*Anderson Mitchell........	W. W. Avery, J. S. Erwin.
1854	C. T. M. Davis..............	W. F. McKesson.
1856	W. W. Avery...............	
1858	E. P. Miller................	Tod R. Caldwell.
1860	W. W. Avery................	J. H. Pearson.
1862	S. J. Neal..................	John Parks.
1864	A. C. Avery................	John Sudderth.
1866	Edmund W. Jones..........	Samuel C. Wilson.
1868	Edmund W. Jones..........	Samuel C. Wilson.
1870	W. B. Council..............	J. C. Mills.
1872	W. W. Fleming .... / J. M. Gudger...........	P. A. Warlick.

*Burke county, with Caldwell, McDowell, Mitchell and Yancey forms 36th District.

CABARRUS COUNTY.

Cabarrus County was formed in 1792, from Mecklenburg County, and was so named in compliment to Stephen Cabarrus, member from Chowan County, and Speaker of the House of Commons. Mr. Cabarrus lived in Edenton, or near at a place called Pembroke. He was a native of France, a man of great vivacity and talent, a useful and honorable man.

It is situated in the south-western part of the State, and is bounded on the north by Rowan and Iredell, east by Stanly county, south by Union and west by Mecklenburg.

Concord is its capitol, 139 miles from Raleigh.

COUNTY OFFICERS.

Offices.	Names.
Superior Court Clerk....................	John A. McDonald.
Register of Deeds.......................	Joseph Young.
Sheriff..................................	R. S. Harris.
Coroner..................................	....
Surveyor.................................	....

CABARRUS COUNTY—Continued.

COUNTY OFFICERS—Continued.

Offices.	Names.
Treasurer	J. S. Fisher.
Commissioners	L. G. Heilig. D. S. Caldwell. John Hileman. A. M. Wilhelm.

JUSTICES OF THE PEACE.

Names.	Date of Qualification.	Post Office Address.
J. M. W. Alexander	Sept. 1st, 1873.	Harrisburg.
N. A. Kirkpatrick	" "	Harrisburg.
P. M. Morris	" "	Concord.
John H. Morrison	" "	Concord.
E. G. Irvin	" "	Tulin.
S. A. Grier	" "	Concord.
C. M. B. Goodnight	" "	Mill Hill.
C. W. Alexander	" "	Concord.
J. A. Barnhardt	" "	Concord.
Solomon Fisher	" "	Concord.
Edmond Foil	" "	Concord.
D. W. Honeycutt	" "	Gold Hill.
John F. Miller	" "	Gold Hill.
H. C. McAllister	" "	Mount Pleasant.
Wm. H. Orchard	" "	Concord.
Solomon Farr	" "	Concord.
J. M. McCurdy	" "	Pioneer Mills.
R. P. Isenhour	" "	Concord.
J. S. Fisher	" "	Concord.
W. J. Hill	" "	Concord.
James Wallace	Nov. 12th, 1873.	Tulin.
Daniel Bangle	" 2nd, "	Mount Pleasant.

MEMBERS OF GENERAL ASSEMBLY.

Years.	Senate.	House.
1793	Caleb Phifer	Paul Barringer, James Bradshaw.
1794	Caleb Phifer	Robert Smith, James Bradshaw.
1795	Caleb Phifer	Robert Smith, James Bradshaw.
1796	Caleb Phifer	Jas. Bradshaw, Archi'd McKurdy.
1797	Caleb Phifer	Jas. Bradshaw, Archi'd McKurdy.
1800	Caleb Phifer	Jas. Bradshaw, John Allison.
1801	Caleb Phifer	Robert Smith, James Bradshaw.
1802	James Bradshaw	John Allison, A. McKurdy.
1803	Wm. L. Alexander	John Allison, John Phifer.
1804	Wm. L. Alexander	John Allison, John Phifer.
1805	Wm. L. Alexander	John Allison, John Phifer.
1806	George Harris	Paul Barringer, A. Houston.

CABARRUS COUNTY—Continued.

MEMBERS OF GENERAL ASSEMBLY—Continued.

Years.	Senate.	House.
1807	George Harris	Paul Barringer, A. Houston.
1808	George Harris	Paul Barringer, A. Houston.
1809	Robert W. Smith	Paul Barringer, A. Houston.
1810	Robert W. Smith	Paul Barringer, John Phifer.
1811	Robert W. Smith	Paul Barringer, John Phifer.
1812	Robert W. Smith	Paul Barringer, John Phifer.
1813	Robert W. Smith	Paul Barringer, John Phifer.
1814	Robert W. Smith	Paul Barringer, John Phifer.
1815	Robert W. Smith	Paul Barringer, John Phifer.
1816	Abraham C. McKee	Samuel Morrison, John F. Phifer.
1817	Abraham C. McKee	John F. Phifer, George Klutts.
1818	John N. Phifer	John F. Phifer.
1819	William R. Pharr	William McLean, C. Melchor.
1821	William R. Pharr	William McLean, C. Melchor.
1822	Paul Barringer	William McLean, C. Melchor.
1823	John Phifer	William McLean, C. Melchor.
1824	L. H. Alexander	Robert Pickens, C. Melchor.
1825	L. H. Alexander	J. C. Barnhardt, Robert Pickens.
1826	L. H. Alexander	J. C. Barnhart, Robert Pickens.
1827	L. H. Alexander	Wm. McLean, J. C. Barnhardt.
1828	L. H. Alexander	William McLean, J. C. Barnhardt.
1829	Ch. Melchor	Daniel M. Barringer, Wm. McLean
1830	Ch. Melchor	D. M. Barringer, J. C. Barnhart.
1831	Ch. Melchor	D. M. Barringer, Wm. McLean.
1832	A. Houston	D. M. Barringer, George Ury.
1833	George Kluts	D. M. Barringer, William McLean.
1834	George Klutts	D. M. Barringer, Jacob Williams.
1835	David Long	Levi Hope, George Barnhardt.
1836	Christophor Melchor	William S. Harris.
1838	Christophor Melchor	Daniel Boger.
1840	Christophor Melchor	Daniel M. Barringer.
1842	W. F. Pharr	Daniel M. Barringer.
1844	W. F. Pharr	Caleb Phifer, H. Robinson.
1846	Christophor Melchor	Jos. W. Scott, L. B. Krimminger.
1848	R. Kendall	Rufus Barringer, J. W. Scott.
1850	Rufus Barringer	Jos. W. Scott, John Shimpock.
1852	D. A. G. Palmer	W. S. Harris, John Shimpock.
	Cabarrus with Stanly forms 28th District.	
1854	A. C. Freeman	D. M. Barringer.
1856	E. R. Gibson	C. N. White.
1858	—— Davis	E. B. Burns.
1860	Victor C. Barringer	Wm. S. Harris.
1862	J. W. Smith	Wm. S. Harris.
1864	J. E. McEachin	P. B. C. Smith.
1866	——Palmer	J. M. Long.
1868	Christophor Melchor	John P. Gibson,
1870	Valentine Mauney	J. L. Henderson.
1872	J. C. Barnhardt	Thos. J. Shinn.

CALDWELL COUNTY.

FORMED IN 1841, out of the counties of Burke and Wilkes. Derives its name from Dr. Joseph Caldwell, President of the University.

It is situated in the north-western portion of the State, and is bounded on the north by Watauga and Ashe, east by Wilkes and Alexander, south by Catawba and Burke, and west by Burke, Wautaga and Mitchell.

Its capital is Lenoir, named in compliment of Gen. Lenoir. 200 miles from Raleigh.

COUNTY OFFICERS.

Offices.	Names.
Superior Court Clerk	R. B. Wakefield.
Register of Deeds	S. M. Clarke.
Sheriff	R. R. McCall.
Coroner	H. A. Steel.
Surveyor	John M. Houk.
Treasurer	M. A. Barnhardt.
Commissioners	Isaac Oxford, Chairman.
	J. M. Conly.
	Carroll Moore.
	S. G. H. Jones.
	T. S. Hoover.

JUSTICES OF THE PEACE.

Names.	Date of Qualification.	Post Office Address.
W. A. Tuttle	Aug. 7th, 1873.	Lenoir.
James Hood	" "	Lenoir.
Leander Houk	" "	Lenoir.
John G. Ballew	" "	Lenoir.
Israel P. Conly	" "	Lovelady.
Joseph Sherrill	" "	Lovelady.
Elkanah Flowers	" "	Cedar Valley.
Sion H. Oxford	" "	Cedar Valley.
Thomas Livingston	" "	King's Creek.
William R. Saunders	" "	King's Creek.
Calvin C. Jones	" "	Fort Defiance.
Calvin Carlton	" "	Fort Defiance.
Robert Holloway	" "	Patterson.
Thomas J. Austin	" "	Patterson.
Judson Moore	" "	Globe.
Madison Estes	" "	Globe.
J. N. Harshaw	" "	Collettsville.
John H. Setzer	" "	Collettsville.

CALDWELL COUNTY.—CONTINUED.

MEMBERS OF GENERAL ASSEMBLY.—CONTINUED.

Years.	Senate.	House.
1842	A. Burgin	William Dickson.
1844	B. S. Gaither	William Dickson.
1846	S. F. Patterson	E. P. Miller.
1848	S. F. Patterson	E. P. Miller.
1850	Tod R. Caldwell	John Hayes.
1852	A. Mitchell	E. P. Miller.
1854	C. N. T. Davis	S. F. Patterson.
1856	W. W. Avery	C. W. Clark.
1858	E. P. Miller	T. J. Dula.
1860	W. W. Avery	W. W. Dickson.
1862	S. J. Neal	—— Barnhardt.
1864	S. F. Patterson	J. M. Isbell.
1866	A. C. Avery	Jas. C. Harper.
1868	E. W. Jones	Jas. C. Harper.
1870	W. B. Council	Ed. Jones.
1872	W. W. Flemming J. M. Gudger*	Ed. Jones.

*With Burke, McDowell, Mitchell and Yancey, the 36th District.

CAMDEN COUNTY.

CAMDEN COUNTY was formed in 1777, from Pasquotank county, and derives its name from the Earl of Camden, who was a distinguished English Statesman, Judge, and friend of popular rights. In Parliament he strongly opposed the taxation of America, and for his liberal principles was removed from his elevated position as Lord High Chancellor of England, 1770, by Lord North's ministry.

The name of this county in the original act, is spelt Cambden.

It is situated in the north-eastern portion of the State, and bounded on the north by the Virginia line, south by Albemarle Sound, east by Currituck county, and west by Pasquotank River, which separates it from Pasquotank county.

COUNTY OFFICERS.

Offices.	Name.
Superior Court Clerk	P. G. Morrisette.
Register of Deeds	W. W. Morrisette.
Sheriff	D. D. Ferebee.
Coroner	J. W. Etheridge.
Surveyor	John K. Abbott*.
Treasuer	R. H. Berry.
Commissioners	John D. Buford, Chairman. T. C. Ferebee. John W. Starke. C. C. Williams. Dr. F. N. Mullen.

*Not qualified.

CAMDEN COUNTY—Continued.

JUSTICES OF THE PEACE.

Names.	Date of Qualification.	Post Office Address.
John W. Halstead	Sept. 1st, 1873.	South Mills.
Nelson Proctor	" "	South Mills.
T. B. Boushall	" "	Camden C. H.
Thomas Palmer	" "	Camden C. H.
S. B. Forbes	" "	Shiloh.
M. S. Morrisett	" "	Shiloh.

MEMBERS OF GENERAL ASSEMBLY.

Years.	Senate.	House.
1778	Isaac Gregory	John Gray, Caleb Grandy.
1779	Isaac Gregory	Willis Butt, Caleb Grandy.
1780	Isaac Gregory	William Burgess, D. Sawyer.
1782	Isaac Gregory	Dempsey Sawyer, Benjamin Jones.
1786	Isaac Gregory	Lemuel Sawyer, Peter Dauge.
1787	Isaac Gregory	Enoch Sawyer, Peter Dauge.
1788	Isaac Gregory	Enoch Sawyer, Peter Dauge.
1789	Isaac Gregory	Enoch Sawyer. Peter Dauge.
1790	Peter Dauge	Charles Grandy, William Burgess.
1791	Peter Dauge	Charles Grandy, William Burgess.
1792	Peter Dauge	Charles Grandy, William Burgess.
1793	Peter Dauge	William Neavill, Nathan Snowden.
1795	Isaac Gregory	Nathan Snowden, Caleb Grandy.
1796	Isaac Gregory	Enoch Daily, Josiah Morgan.
1797	Joseph Forksey	Enoch Daily, Z. Burgess.
1800	Joseph Forksey	Thomas Mercer, Lemuel Sawyer.
1801	Joseph Forksey	Thomas Mercer, Lemuel Sawyer.
1802	Thomas Burgess	Thomas Mercer, Caleb Perkins.
1803	Nathan Snowden	Joseph Morgan, Caleb Perkins.
1804	Arthur Old	Joseph Morgan, David Duncan.
1805	Arthur Old	Joseph Morgan, Caleb Perkins.
1806	Arthur Old	Joseph Morgan, Caleb Perkins.
1807	Arthur Old	Caleb Perkins, Thomas Bell.
1808	Nathan Snowden	Caleb Perkins. Thomas Bell.
1809	Caleb Perkins	Thomas Bell, Dempsey Sawyer.
1810	Gideon Lamb	Thomas Bell, Dempsey Sawyer.
1811	Caleb Perkins	Dempsey Sawyer, William Mercer.
1812	Joseph Dozier	Dempsey Sawyer, John Kelly.
1813	Thomas Bell	Dempsey Sawyer, Thomas Etheridge.
1814	Thomas Bell	John Kellar, Baily Parker.
1815	Caleb Perkins	Baily Barco, John H. Brocket.
1816	Caleb Perkins	Willis Wilson, Ezekiel Trotman.
1817	Caleb Perkins	Baily Barco, Willis Wilson.
1818	John Kelly	William Hearing, William Mercer.
1819	Caleb Perkins	William Mercer, John Jones.
1820	Caleb Perkins	William Mercer, John Jones.
1821	Luke J. Lamb	W. B. Webster, Samuel Mercer.

CAMDEN COUNTY.—Continued.

MEMBERS OF GENERAL ASSEMBLY—Continued.

Years.	Senate.	House.
1822	Mason Culpepper	W. B. Webster, John Jones.
1823	Caleb Perkins	W. B. Webster, Thomas Tillett.
1824	Caleb Perkins	W. B. Webster, Thomas Tillett.
1825	Willis Wilson	Thomas Tillett, Thomas Dozier.
1826	Willis Wilson	Thomas Dozier, Simeon Jones.
1827	Willis Wilson	Thomas Tillett, Thomas Dozier.
1828	Haywood S. Bell	Thomas Dozier, W. B. Webster.
1829	Haywood S. Bell	Thomas Dozier, A. H. Grandy.
1830	Caleb Perkins	A. H. Grandy, Thomas Dozier.
1831	Haywood S. Bell	A. H. Grandy, Thomas Dozier.
1832	Haywood S. Bell	B. D. Hardison, Thomas Tillett.
1833	Enoch Nash	Thomas Tillett, Caleb Barco.
1834	Edmund I. Barco	Thomas Tillett, Jas. N. McPherson.
1835	Thomas Tillett	Jas. N. McPherson, J. S. Burgess.
1836	Daniel Lindsay	D. Pritchard.
1838	Caleb Etheridge	J. S. Burgess.
1840	Caleb Etheridge	A. H. Grandy.
1842	Caleb Etheridge	Cornelius G. Lamb.
1844	Caleb Etheridge	Cornelius G. Lamb.
1846	John Barnard	D. D. Ferebee.
1848	John Barnard	D. D. Ferebee.
1850	John Barnard	Caleb Barco.
1852	H. M. Shaw	Caleb Barco.
1854	J. B. Jones	Wilson Harrison.
1856	J. B. Jones	D. D. Ferebee.
1858	C. C. Wilkers	D. D. Ferebee.
1860	B. F. Simmonds	D. D. Ferebee.
1862	D. McD. Lindsay	John Forbes.
1864	D. McD. Lindsay	W. A. Duke.
1866		
1868	Elihu White Jos. W. Etheridge	
1870	Rufus K. Speed James C. Skinner	John L. Chamberlain.
1872	John L. Chamberlain C. W. Grandy	S. A. Jones.

Camden, Currituck, Chowan, Gates, Hertford, Pasquotank and Perquimans form the 1st Senatorial District.

CARTERET COUNTY.

CARTERET was one of the original precincts of the Lords Proprietors, and was called in honor of one of them, who is styled in the charter of Charles II. as "our right truly and well beloved counsellor, Sir George Carteret, Knight and Baronet, Vice-Chancellor of our Household." He is described by a cotemporary writer, as "the passionate and ignorant, and not too honest Sir George Carteret."

Its situation is in the extreme eastern portion of the State, and is bounded on the north by the Pamlico Sound and county of Craven, south and east by the Atlantic Ocean, and west by the counties of Jones and Onslow.

Its capital is Beaufort, which possesses a fine harbor, great depth of water, and is destined to become the marine depot of North Carolina. Its distance from Raleigh is 168 miles.

COUNTY OFFICERS.

Offices.	Name.
Superior Court Clerk	James Rumley.
Register of Deeds	John Rumley.
Sheriff	John D. Davis.
Coroner	Thomas W. Lindsey.
Surveyor	Willie L. Arendell.
Treasurer	James C. Davis.
Commissioners	Wm. J. Doughty. George Dennis. John T. Willis. Jesse Fulcher. J. Finley Wade.

JUSTICES OF THE PEACE.

Names.	Date of qualification.	Post Office Address.
John W. Sanders	October 6th, 1873.	Sanders' Store.
Jeremiah Watson	" "	Sanders' Store.
Joshua T. Dennis	" "	Newport.
David W. Morton	" "	Newport.
David S. Quinn	" "	Newport.
W. L. Arendell	" "	Morehead City.
Wm. S. Bell, Sr	" "	Newport.
Thaddeus C. Davis	" "	Newport.
William J. Bushal	" "	Beaufort.
A. C. Davis	" "	Beaufort.
A. C. Thompson	" "	Beaufort.
George W. Wade	" "	Beaufort.
John L. Guthrie	" "	Beaufort.
George W. Jerkins	" "	Beaufort.

CARTERET COUNTY.—Continued.

JUSTICES OF THE PEACE.—Continued.

Names.	Date of Qualification.	Post Office Address.
John Leffers	Oct. 6th, 1873.	Beaufort.
Thomas Chadwick	" "	Beaufort.
P. D. Murphy	" "	Beaufort.
M. B. Smith	" "	Beaufort.
John L. Goodwin	" "	Hunting Quarter.
John W. Lupton	" "	Hunting Quarter.
Samuel Dudley	" "	Portsmouth.
Wallis Styron	" "	Portsmouth.

MEMBERS OF GENERAL ASSEMBLY.

Years.	Senate.	House.
1778		Sol. Shepard.
1783		Enoch Ward, Eli West.
1785		Enoch Ward, Eli West.
1786	John Easton	Eli West, John Fulford.
1787	John Easton	Eli West, John Fulford.
1788	Joseph Hill	John Fulford, Wm. Shepard.
1791	Malachi Bell	John Fulford, A. Jones.
1792	David Ward	Adam Gaskins, William Russell.
1793	D. Ward	A. Gaskins, Wm. Russell.
1794	D. Ward	A. Gaskins, Wm. Russell.
1795	D. Ward	James Wallace, Wm. Russell.
1796	John Fulford	James Wallace, Aden Jones.
1797	John Fulford	Asa Bishop, Newell Bell.
1800	Newell Bell,	Elijah Piggot, John McKairn.
1801	Asa Bishop	Elijah Piggot, John McKairn.
1802	William Fisher	Elijah Piggot, Samuel Easton.
1803	W. Fisher	Samuel Easton, Thomas Harriss.
1804	Asa Bishop	Samuel Easton, John Robards.
1805	Nathaniel Pinkham	Thomas Russell, John Robards.
1806	N. Pinkham	T. Russell, J. Robards.
1807	N. Pinkham	T. Russell, J. Robards.
1808	Elijah Piggot	Jacob Henry, John Robards.
1809	Belcher Fuller	Jacob Henry, John Robards.
1810	B. Fuller	John Robards, N. Pinkham.
1811	B. Fuller	J. Robards, Abraham Piggot.
1812	B. Fuller	J. Robards, Nathaniel Pinkham.
1813	B. Fuller	J. Robards, Nathaniel Pinkham.
1814	A. Wilson	J. Robards, H. Hill.
1815	Lebbeus Hunter	Hatch Hill, John Robards.
1816	John Robards	Whittington Davis, Elijah Piggot.
1817	George H. Dudley	John Mayo, N. Pinkham.
1818	Whittington Davis	Nat. Pinkham, Isaac Hellen.
1819	Andrew Wilson, Jr.,	Isaac Hellen, N. Pinkham.
1821	Whittington Davis	W. D. Styron, Otway Burns.
1822	W. Davis	Otway Burns, Isaac Hellen.

CARTERET COUNTY—Continued.

MEMBERS OF GENERAL ASSEMBLY—Continued.

Years.	Senate.	House.
1823	W. Davis	Isaac Hellen, Edward H. Bell.
1824	W. Davis	Otway Burns, Wm. H. Borden.
1825	W. Davis	Otway Burns, Wm. H. Borden.
1826	W. Davis	Edward H. Bell, Otway Burns.
1827	Nathan Fuller	David W. Borden, Otway Burns.
1828	Otway Burns	J. S. W. Hellen, David W. Borden.
1829	Otway Burns	J. S. W. Hellen, David W. Borden.
1830	David W. Borden	Thomas Marshall, John F. Jones.
1831	Otway Burns	John F. Jones, J. W. Hunt.
1832	Thomas Marshall	Otway Burns, D. W. Borden.
1833	Otway Burns	Samuel Leffers, David Whitehurst.
1834	Otway Burns	James Manny, Elijah S. Bell.
1835	James W. Bryan	James W. Hunt, Thos. Marshall.
1836	Jas. W. Bryan	Thomas Marshall.
1838	Enoch Foy	Elijah S. Bell.
1840	Isaac Hellen	Elijah Whitehurst.
1842	Jas. W. Howard	Thomas Marshall.
1844	Isaac Hellen	E. Whitehurst.
1846	James W. Howard	Jennings Piggot.
1848	E. S. Bell	Jennings Piggot.
1850	M. F. Arendell	Jennings Piggot.
1852	M. F. Arendell	E. Whitehurst.
1854	Richard Oldfield	L. T. Oglesby.
1856	Wm. P. Ward	
1858	Wm. P. Ward	S. Lefforts.
1860	M. F. Arendell	D. W. Whitehurst.
1862	Calvin Koonce	
1864	M. F. Arendell	S. D. Pool.
1866	Calvin Koonce	J. M. Perry.
1868	W. A. Moore	J. H. Davis.
1870	Wm. J. Clarke	L. W. Martin.
1872	J. G. Scott	Silas Webb.

*Carteret, Jones and Onslow form the 9th Senatorial District.

CASWELL COUNTY.

Caswell County was erected in 1777, out of Orange County.

It derives its name from Richard Caswell, the first Governor under the Constitution.

Caswell County is situated in the north-western part of North Carolina, and forms a beautiful compact square, having the Virginia line on the north; Person County on the east; Alamance and Orange on the south; and Rockingham County on the west.

It capital is Yanceyville, named in compliment to Bartlett Yancey, and distant from Raleigh 66 miles.

CASWELL COUNTY.—Continued.

COUNTY OFFICERS.

Offices.	Names.
Superior Court Clerk	H. F. Brandon.
Register of Deeds	Geo. W. Pinnix.
Sheriff	J. C. Griffith.
Coroner	Levi C. Page.
Surveyor	Jno. R. Winston.
Treasurer	Thos. D. Johnston.
Commissioners	Phillip Hodnett, Chairman. Yancey Jones. W. W. Adams. Wilson Carey. H. J. Phelps.

JUSTICE OF THE PEACE.

Names.	Date of Qualification.	Post Office Address.
Thomas J. Brown	August, 1873.	Yanceyville.
Joseph C. Pinnix	" "	Yanceyville.
N. M. Lewis	Sept. 5th, 1873.	Milton.
John L. Staton	August, 1873.	Milton.
J. E. Jordon	" "	Milton.
Thos. S. Harrison	" "	Purley.
Thos. J. Dailey	" "	Purley.
John D. Keesee	" "	Pelham.
James M. Hodges	" "	Pelham.
Jos. C. Allison	" "	Blackwell's.
John S. Blackwell	" "	Blackwell's.
John W. Williamson	" "	Locust Hill.
Abner Miles	" "	Anderson's Store.
John S. Miles	" "	Anderson's Store.
James M. Simpson	" "	Anderson's Store.
Jerry Smith	" "	Prospect Hill.
F. L. Warren	" "	Prospect Hill.
A. B. Newman	Sept. 6th, 1873.	Leasburg.
Jno. B. Smith	" 13th, "	Leasburg.

MEMBERS OF GENERAL ASSEMBLY.

Years.	Senate.	House.
1778	Dempsey Moore	John Atkinson, Richard Moore.
1782	Dempsey Moore	David Shelton, Robert Dickens.
1785	Dempsey Moore	Robert Dickens, Adam Sanders.
1786	Dempsey Moore	Adam Sanders, Robert Dickens.
1788	Robert Payne	Benjamin Douglass, John Graves.
1791	Robert Dickens	James Williamson, John Graves.

CASWELL COUNTY.—Continued.

MEMBERS OF GENERAL ASSEMBLY—Continued.

Years.	Senate.	House.
1792	James Williamson	John Graves, David Shelton.
1793	John Williams	John Graves, David Shelton.
1794	John Williams	Gabriel Lea, William Parks.
1795	John Williams	Solomon Graves, David Burfort.
1796	Wynn Dickson	Robert Blackwell, Solomon Graves.
1797	Wynn Dickson	Robert Blackwell, Solomon Graves.
1800	Samuel Morton	James Yancey, Richard Simpson.
1801	Samuel Morton	James Yancey, John McAden.
1802	Marmaduke Williams	John McAden, James Yancey.
1803	Samuel Morton	James Yancey, Young McAden.
1804	Samuel Morton	Richard Hornbuckle, Laurence Lea.
1805	Azariah Graves	Richard Hornbuckle, John McMullen.
1806	A. Graves	James Burton, John McMullen.
1807	A. Graves	J. Burton, James Yancey.
1808	A. Graves	J. Yancey, James Burton.
1809	A. Graves	Isaac Rainey, Nathaniel Williams.
1810	A. Graves	Isaac Rainey, Nathaniel Williams.
1811	A. Graves	James Yancey, Isaac Rainey.
1812	Nathaniel Williams	Samuel Dabney, James Rainey.
1813	N. Williams	Quinten Anderson, B. Graves.
1814	B. Graves	Isaac Rainey, John P. Harrison.
1815	B. Graves	Romulus M. Saunders, Bedford Brown.
1816	R. M. Saunders	W. Watkins, Bedford Brown.
1817	Bartlett Yancey	B. Brown, R. M. Saunders.
1818	B. Yancey	R. M. Saunders, B. Graves.
1819	B. Yancey	R. M. Saunders, B. Graves.
1821	B. Yancey	Quinten Anderson, B. Graves.
1822	B. Yancey	James Yancey, B. Graves.
1823	B. Yancey	Bedford Brown, James Rainey.
1824	B. Yancey	John E. Lewis, Chas. D. Donoho.
1825	B. Yancey	John E. Lewis, Charles D. Donoho.
1826	B. Yancey	John E. Lewis, C. D. Donoho.
1827	B. Yancey	John E. Lewis, C. D. Donoho.
1828	Bedford Brown	James H. Ruffin, James Kerr.
1829	B. Brown	John Wilson, James Kerr.
1830	James Kerr	Littleton A. Gwinn, Stephen Dodson.
1831	J. Kerr	L. A. Gwinn, John F. Garland.
1832	J. Kerr	Barzillai Graves, L. A. Gwinn.
1833	J. Kerr	John E. Brown, Stephen Dodson.
1834	J. Kerr	J. E. Brown, L. A. Gwinn.
1835	J. Kerr	L. A. Gwinn, Stephen Dodson.
1836	J. Kerr	L. A. Gwynn, William A. Lea.
1838	James Kerr	Levi Walker, L. A. Gwinn.
1840	James Kerr	Calvin Graves, Levi Walker.
1842	Bedford Brown	Calvin Graves, Levi Walker.
1844	L. A. Gwynn	Calvin Graves, J. K. Lea.
1846	Calvin Graves	John B. McMullen, Richard Jones.
1848	Calvin Graves	John B. McMullen, Richard Jones.
1850	George Williamson	Samuel P. Hill, D. S. Johnson.
1852	Elija K. Withers	Samuel P. Hill, W. Long.
1854	J. A. Graves	Samuel P. Hill, W. Long.
1856	S. P. Hill	Wm. Long, E. K. Withers.
1858	Bedford Brown	John Kerr, S. E. Williams.
1860	Bedford Brown	John Kerr, S. P. Hill.
1862	Bedford Brown	S. S. Harrison, Wm. Long.

CASWELL COUNTY—Continued.

MEMBERS OF GENERAL ASSEMBLY—Continued.

Years.	Senate.	House.
1864	William Long	M. McGehee, S. S. Harrison.
1866	Livingston Brown	P. Hodnet, Wm. Long.
1868	Bedford Brown	P. Hodnet, Wm. Long.
1870	Wilson Carey	P. Hodnet, Wm. Long.
1872	John W. Norwood John W. Cunningham	Thomas J. Foster, Geo. Bowe.

(The delegates to the Convention to amend the Constitution, in June, 1835, were William A. Lea and Calvin Graves.)

Caswell, Orange and Person form 20th Senatorial District.

CATAWBA COUNTY.

Catawba County was formed in 1842 from Lincoln county, and derives its name from the river which forms its northern and eastern boundaries.

It is located in the western portion of the State, and bounded on the north by the Catawba River which separates it from Caldwell county, on the east by the Catawba river, which separates it from Iredell county, on the south by Lincoln, and on the west by Burke.

Its county seat is Newton, which has a commodious Court House, and other Public Buildings, many stores and handsome private residences, 175 miles from Raleigh. Its inhabitants are distinguished for their industry and integrity.

COUNTY OFFICERS.

Offices.	Names.
Superior Court Clerk	Miles O. Sherrill.
Register of Deeds	James M. Brown.
Sheriff	Jonas Cline.
Coroner	Reuben Yoder.
Surveyor	Drury Hamilton.
Treasurer	George A. Ikerd.
Commissioners	Franklin L. Herman. Peter W. Whitener. George M. Wilfong. Andrew Fry. Daniel Deal.

CATAWBA COUNTY—Continued.

JUSTICES OF THE PEACE.

Names.	Date of Qualification.	Post Office Address.
C. W. Hermon	Sept. 1873.	Newton.
P. F. Smith	" "	Newton.
M. A. Thornburg	" "	Newton.
A. G. Corpening	" "	Newton.
J. W. Williams	" "	Newton.
J. L. Hewitt	" "	Newton.
J. K. P. Little	" "	Newton.
N. E. Sigman	" "	Newton.
N. D. Lutes	" "	Newton.
Jacob Mosteller	" "	Jacob's Fork.
J. W. Bandy	" "	Mill Grove.
J. W. Gabriel	" "	Mountain Creek.
L. A. Lockman	" "	Sherrill's Ford.
Abel Whitner	" "	Hickory Tavern.
Marcus Barger	" "	Hickory Tavern.
J. H. Bruns	January 14, 1874.	Hickory Tavern.
G. W. Cansler	Sept. 1st, 1873.	Catawba Station.
S. C. Brown	" "	Sherrill's Ford.

MEMBERS OF GENERAL ASSEMBLY.

Years.	Senate.	House.
1843 } 1852 }	(See Lincoln County.)	
1854	John F. Hoke	A. Sherrill.
1856		G. P. Rowe.
1858	F. D. Reinhardt	H. Sherrill.
1860	Jasper Stowe	Jonas Cline.
1862	J. H. White	George S. Hooper.
1864	M. L. McCorkle	W. P. Reinhardt.
1866	M. L. McCorkle	W. P. Reinhardt.
1868	Lawson A. Mason	W. P. Reinhardt.
1870	E. Crowell	R. R. B. Houston.
1872	James R. Ellis	R. R. B. Houston.

With Lincoln forms the 37th District.

CHATHAM COUNTY.

Chatham County was formed in 1770, and called in compliment of that distinguished English statesman and orator William Pitt, Earl of Chatham.

Chatham County, situated near the centre of the State, is bounded on the north by Alamance and Orange, on the east by Wake and a small portion of Cumberland, on the south by Moore, and west by Randolph.

Its capital is Pittsboro', 34 miles west of Raleigh.

CHATHAM COUNTY.—Continued.

COUNTY OFFICERS.

Offices.	Names.
Superior Court Clerk	S. T. Petty.
Register of Deeds	W. H. Hatch.
Sheriff	G. J. Williams.
Coroner	William Haithcock.
Surveyor	P. J. Snipes.
Treasurer	J. M. Woody.
Commissioners	W. S. Gunter. A. J. Riggsbee. J. D. Brasington. Oliver Vestal. B. F. Snipes.

JUSTICES OF THE PEACE.

Names.	Date of Qualification.	Post Office Address.
J. A. Womack	Sept. 1st, 1873.	Pittsboro'.
H. P. Straughn	" "	Pittsboro'.
B. G. Womble	" "	Pittsboro'.
T. H. Burgess	" "	Grove.
W. P. Holt	" "	Grove.
C. R. Scott	" "	Rialto.
Y. A. Oldham	" "	Rialto.
W. B. Carter	" "	Mud Lick.
J. P. M. Picket	" "	Mud Lick.
Ira Braxton	" "	Cane Creek.
Oliver Clark	" "	Cane Creek.
L. W. Gorrell	" "	St. Lawrence.
O. A. Hanner	" "	St. Lawrence.
H. O. Dunlap	" 22, 1873.	Pedler's Hill.
B. N. Watson	" 1 "	Pedler's Hill.
H. H. Fike	" "	Beaumont.
N. M. Alston	" "	Beaumont.
R. N. Buie	" "	Egypt.
J. P. Badders	" "	Egypt.
J. H. Farrar	" 9 "	Lockville.
B. W. Brown	" 25 "	Lockville.
J. E. Bryan	" 8 "	Lockville.
O. P. Hamlet	" 1 "	Bellevoir.
J. B. West	" 1 "	Bellevoir.
James J. Lane	" 6 "	Harper's X Roads.
John W. Calder	Nov. 25th, 1873.	Harper's X Roads.

CHATHAM COUNTY—CONTINUED.

MEMBERS OF GENERAL ASSEMBLY.

Years.	Senate.	House.
1777	Ambrose Ramsay	Alexander Clark, John Birdson.
1778	Ambrose Ramsay	Alexander Clark, James Williams.
1779	Ambrose Ramsay	Jeduthan Harper, John Lutrell.
1780	Ambrose Ramsay	Mial Scurlock, James Williams.
1781	Ambrose Ramsay	Jas. Williams, John Ledhill.
1782	William B. Smith	Jas. Williams, John Ledhill.
1783	Ambrose Ramsay	Matthew Jones, Richard Hennon.
1784	Ambrose Ramsay	Elisha Cain, Joseph Stewart.
1785	Ambrose Ramsay	Joseph Stewart, Roger Griffith.
1786	Ambrose Ramsay	James Anderson, Joseph Stewart.
1787	Ambrose Ramsay	James Anderson, Joseph Stewart.
1788	Ambrose Ramsay	James Anderson, Joseph Stewart.
1789	George Lucas	James Anderson, Joseph Stewart.
1790	Joseph Stewart	James Anderson, John Mebane.
1791	Joseph Stewart	John Mebane, James Anderson.
1792	Joseph Stewart	James Anderson, John Mebane.
1793	Joseph Stewart	George Lucas, John Mebane.
1794	Joseph Stewart	George Lucas, John Dabney.
1795	Joseph Stewart	John Mebane, Mial Scurlock.
1796	Lemuel Smith	John Dabney, Thomas Stokes.
1797	George Lucas	Thomas Stokes, John Dabney.
1798	Joseph Stewart	George Lucas, John Mebane.
1799	James Gaines	John Dabney, John Mebane.
1800	James Gaines	James Alston, John Mebane.
1801	Lemuel Smith	John Dabney, John Mebane.
1802	Joseph J. Alston	George Dismukes, John Dabney.
1803	Joseph J. Alston	John Mebane, John Dabney.
1804	William Brantley	John Farrar, Andrew Headen.
1805	William Brantley	John Farrar, William O'Kelly.
1806	Winship Stedman	Andrew Headen, John Farrar.
1807	John Farrar	John Mebane, Andrew Headen.
1808	John Farrar	John Mebane, Andrew Headen.
1809	Roderick Cotten	John Mebane, Charles Kennon.
1810	Micajah McGee	Mark Bynum, Nathan Stedman.
1811	Roderick Cotten	Andrew Headen, John Mebane.
1812	Micajah McGee	Mark Bynum, William O'Kelly.
1813	John Farrar	Bartholomew Lightfoot, John B. Mebane.
1814	Andrew Headen	John A. Ramsay, William O'Kelly.
1815	John Farrar	John A. Ramsay, William O'Kelly.
1816	John Farrar	William O'Kelly, Richard C. Cotten.
1817	John Farrar	Richard C. Cotten, John J. Alston.
1818	William O'Kelly	Richard C. Cotten, John A. Ramsay.
1819	John Farrar	Thomas Hill, John A. Ramsay.
1820	Jesse Bray	Richard Freeman, James C. Barbee.
1822	Jesse Bray	R. C. Cotten, W. Underwood.
1823	Robert Marsh	William Underwood, A. Ramsay.
1824	Robert Marsh	Ambrose K. Ramsay, Wm. Underwood.
1825	Robert Marsh	William Underwood, J. J. Brooks.
1826	Robert Marsh	Ambrose K. Ramsay, Thomas Hill.
1827	Joseph Ramsay	Nathaniel G. Smith, Nathan A. Stedman.
1828	Joseph Ramsay	Nathaniel G. Smith, Joseph J. Brooks.
1829	Joseph Ramsay	Joseph J. Brooks, Hugh McQueen.
1830	Joseph Ramsay	Nathaniel G. Smith, Joseph J. Brooks.
1831	William Rencher	Joseph J. Brooks, Hugh McQueen.
1832	Nathan A. Steadman	John S. Guthrie, Hugh McQueen.

CHATHAM COUNTY—Continued.

MEMBERS OF GENERAL ASSEMBLY.—Continued.

Years.	Senate.	House.
1833	Nathan A. Steadman........	R. C. Cotten, John S. Guthrie.
1834	Hugh McQueen	R. C. Cotten, William Foushee.
1835	Hugh McQueen	R. C. Cotten, John S. Guthrie.
1836	William Albright............	Spencer McClennahan, John S. Guthrie, R. C. Cotten.
1838	William Albright	Spencer McClennahan, John S. Guthrie, R. C. Cotten.
1840	William Albright	Spencer McClennahan, John S. Guthrie, I. Clegg.
1842	William Albright	John S. Guthrie, Thomas Lassiter, John J. Jackson.
1844	William Albright	D. Hackney, J. H. Haughton, J. S. Guthrie.
1846	William Albright	Daniel Hackny, Thomas Lassiter, Maurice Q. Waddell.
1848	William Albright	D. Hackney, S. McClennahan, J. H. Headen.
1850	J. H. Haughton............	R. C. Cotten, D. Hackny, G. M. Brazier.
1852	Wm. Albright..............	J. F. Reeves, Richard C. Cotten, Turner Bynum.
1854	John H. Haughton..........	J. H. Headen, R. C. Cotten.
1856	R. E. Rives.................	R. C. Cotten, Daniel Hackny, Turner Bynum.
1858	E. B. Straughn..............	J. A. Moore, R. Green, W. P. Taylor.
1860	W. S. Harris.................	W. P. Taylor, N. Green, Turner Bynum.
1862	Wm. P. Taylor.............	T. B. Harris, W. J. Herndon, M. Q. Waddell,
1864	E. H. Straughan............	J. H. Headen, W. J. Headen, W. P. Hadley.
1866	R. B. Paschal...............	G. Moore, J. May, Thos. W. Womble.
1868	Silas Burns.................	W. T. Gunter, J. H. Long.
1870	Gaston Albright............	R. J. Powell, J. A. Womack.
1872	R. J. Powell................	John M. Moring, O. H. Hanner.

Chatham is 22d Senatorial District.

CHEROKEE COUNTY.

Cherokee County was formed in 1839, from Macon county. Its name is derived from the tribe of Indians who once owned a part of this county.

It is situated in the extreme south-western part of the State, and bounded on the north by White Mountain, which separates it from Tennessee and the county of Clay, on the east by Graham and Clay counties, south by the Georgia line, and west by Tennessee.

Its capital is Murphy, named in compliment to the Hon. Archibald D. Murphy, once a Judge of our Superior Court. 367 miles from Raleigh.

CHEROKEE COUNTY—Continued.

COUNTY OFFICERS.

Offices.	Names.
Superior Court Clerk	James C. Axley.
Register of Deeds	J. H. Hennesa.
Sheriff	A. S. Hill.
Coroner	P. M. G. Rhea.
Surveyor	Wm. Beal.
Treasurer	A. H. Mauney.
Tax Collector	J. B. Fain.
Commissioners	R. D. McCombs, Chairman. P. V. Brittain. James Whitaker. Spencer Coleman. Ansel Rogers.

JUSTICES OF THE PEACE.

Names.	Date of Qualification.	Post Office Address.
Luis Hubbard	Sept. 1st, 1873.	Murphy.
W. G. Payne	" "	Wolf Creek.
Elisha Craig	" "	Shoal Creek.
Henry Moss	" "	Marble Spring.
Silas Rose, (P. N.)	" "	Beaver.
Joel Simons	" "	Wolf Creek.
D. S. Suddeth	" "	Murphy.
J. P. Burnett	Sept. 3rd, 1873.	Murphy.
Robert Bruce	Sept. 6th, 1873.	Murphy.
A. E. Eovans	Sept. 9th, 1873.	Murphy.
Drury Weeks	Sept. 26th, 1873.	Murphy.
Thomas C. Tatham	Dec. 1st, 1873.	Valley Town.
Curtis Radford	Feb. 7th, 1874.	Beaver.

MEMBERS OF GENERAL ASSEMBLY.

Years.	Senate.	House.
1840		Geo. W. Hays.
1842	Wm. H. Thomas	Geo. W. Hays.
1844	Michael Francis	Geo. W. Hays.
1846	Michael Frances	Geo. W. Hays.
1848	Wm. H. Thomas	Geo. W. Hays.
1850	Wm. H. Thomas	Geo. W. Hays.

CHEROKEE COUNTY—Continued.

MEMBERS OF GENERAL ASSEMBLY—Continued.

Years.	Senate.	House.
1852	Wm. H. Thomas	Geo. W. Hays.
1854	Wm. H. Thomas	John Roland.
1856	Wm. H. Thomas	C. M. Stiles.
1858	Wm. H. Thomas	W. Walker.
1860	Wm. H. Thomas	Geo. W. Hays.
1862	C. D. Smith	J. H. Bryson.
1864	J. C. Bryson	W. H. Herberg.
1866	R. M. Henry	
1868	W. Levi Love	J. R. Simons.
1870	W. Levi Love	B. K. Dickey.
1872	W. Levi Love	B. K. Dickey.

Cherokee, Graham, Jackson, Macon and Swain Counties compose the 42nd Senatorial District.

CHOWAN COUNTY.

Chowan County was one of the original precincts of the Lords Proprietors. under charter of King Charles II., and derives its name from the tribe of Indians, Chowanokes, who once owned and inhabited this territory.

It is situated in the north-eastern part of the State; bounded on the north by Gates County, on the east by Perquimans, on the south by the Albemarle Sound, and on the west by the Chowan River, which separates it from Gates and Hertford Conntics.

Its capital is Edenton, named in compliment after Charles Eden, the royal Governor of the Provice in 1720. He died in 1722, and lies buried in Bertie County.

This ancient borough was settled in 1716, which was originally called Queen-Anne's Creek.

COUNTY OFFICERS.

Offices.	Names.
Superior Court Clerk	Wm. R. Skinner.
Register of Deeds	Oliver F. Gilbert.
Sheriff	Miles C. Brinkley.
Coroner	Vacant.
Surveyor	Vacant.
Treasurer	Charles Blair.
Commissioners,	Augustus M. Moore. John S. Chapple. Townsend E. Ward. Edward Mayo. Peter K. Jones.

CHOWAN COUNTY—Continued.

JUSTICES OF THE PEACE.

Names.	Date of Qualification.	Post Office Address.
P. F. White	September 1873.	Edenton.
C. E. Robinson	" 20th, "	Edenton.
T. C. Spruill	" 21st, "	Edenton.
Jos. T. Waff	Dec. 13th, "	Edenton.
R. D. Simpson	Sept. 1st, "	Edenton.
John A. Bunch	" " "	Edenton.
Allen C. Ward	" " "	Wardsville.
Wm. D. Welch	" " "	Wardsville.

MEMBERS OF GENERAL ASSEMBLY.

Years.	House of Commons.	Years.	House of Commons.
1774	Joseph Hewes.	1806	William Slade,
1775	Joseph Hewes,	1807	Jos. B. Skinner,
1776	Joseph Hewes,	1808	Wm. A. Littlejohn,
1777	John Green,	1809	John Beasley,
1778	Joseph Hewes,	1810	Mathias E. Sawyer,
1779	Joseph Hewes,	1811	Mathias E. Sawyer,
1780	Robert Smith,	1812	Henry Flury.
1781	Robert Smith,	1813	James Iredell,
1782	Hugh Williamson,	1814	Jos. B. Skinner,
1783	William Cumming,	1815	Jos. B. Skinner,
1784	Stephen Cabarrus,	1816	James Iredell,
1785	Stephen Cabarrus,	1817	James Iredell,
1786	Stephen Cabarrus,	1818	James Iredell,
1787	Stephen Cabarrus,	1819	James Iredell,
1788	William Cumming,	1820	James Iredell,
1790	John Hamilton,	1821	George Blair, Jr.
1791	John Hamilton,	1822	George Blair, Jr.
1792	John Hamilton,	1823	James Iredell,
1793	William Cumming,	1824	James Iredell,
1794	Robert Hardy,	1825	James Iredell,
1795	Stephen Cabarrus,	1826	James Iredell,
1796	Thomas Johnson,	1827	James Iredell,
1797	Thomas Johnson,	1828	James Bozman.
1798	James Greenbury,	1829	Samuel T. Sawyer,
1799	John B. Blount,	1830	Samuel T. Sawyer,
1800	William Slade,	1831	Samuel T. Sawyer,
1801	Josiah Collins,	1832	Samuel T. Sawyer,
1802	Nathaniel Allen,	1833	J. Malachi Haughton.
1803	Jos. B. Littlejohn,	1834	Frederick Noscum,
1804	Thomas Johnson,	1835	Hugh W. Collins.
1805	Allen Gilchrist,		

CHOWAN COUNTY.—CONTINUED.

MEMBERS OF GENERAL ASSEMBLY.

Years.	Senate.	House.
1774	....	Thomas Benbury, Thomas Hunter.
1775	....	Thomas Oldham, Thomas Benbury.
1777	Luke Sumner..............	Thomas Benbury, Jacob Hunter.
1778	Luke Sumner..............	Wm. Boyd, Thomas Benbury.
1779	Luke Sumner..............	Wm. Boyd, Thomas Benbury.
1780	Luke Sumner..............	Wm. Boyd, Thomas Benbury.
1781	Charles Johnson...........	Michael Payne, Thomas Benbury.
1782	Charles Johnson...........	Michael Payne, Thomas Benbury.
1783	Charles Johnson...........	Stephen Chambers, Richard Benbury.
1784	Charles Johnson...........	Clement Hall, Michael Payne.
1785	Michael Payne.............	Hugh Williamson, Clement Hall.
1786	Jacob Jordan..............	Josiah Copeland, Lemuel Creecy.
1787	Jacob Jordan..............	Josiah Copeland, Lemuel Creecy.
1788	Charles Johnson...........	Stephen Cabarrus, Lemuel Creecy.
1790	Charles Johnson...........	Stephen Cabarrus, Lemuel Creecy.
1791	Charles Johnson...........	Stephen Cabarrus, Richard Benbury.
1792	Charles Johnson...........	Stephen Cabarrus, Lemuel Creecy.
1793	Lemuel Creecy.............	Stephen Cabarrus, Benjamin Coffield.
1794	Lemuel Creecy.............	Benjamin Coffield, Richard Benbury.
1795	Lemuel Creecy.............	Benjamin Coffield, Richard Benbury.
1796	Lemuel Creecy.............	Richard Benbury, Benjamin Coffield.
1797	Lemuel Creecy.............	Richard Benbury, Benjamin Coffield.
1798	Lemuel Creecy.............	Richard Benbury, Shadenck Felton.
1799	Frederick Lutan...........	John Bennet, Stephen Cabarrus.
1800	Richard Benbury...........	Stephen Cabarrus, Reuben Small.
1801	John Bond.................	Stephen Cabarrus, Reuben Small.
1802	John Bond.................	Stephen Cabarrus, Reuben Small.
1803	John Bond.................	Stephen Cabarrus, Samuel McGuire.
1804	John Bond.................	Stephen Cabarrus, Reuben Small.
1805	Thomas Brownrigg.........	Stephen Cabarrus, Benjamin Coffield.
1806	Thomas Brownrigg.........	Samuel McGuire, Baker Hoskins.
1807	Thomas Brownrigg.........	Frederick Norcum, Baker Hoskins.
1808	Thomas Brownrigg.........	Samuel McGuire, Baker Hoskins.
1809	Frederick Norcum..........	Samuel McGuire, Miles Welch.
1810	Richard Hoskins...........	Samuel McGuire, Micajah Bunch.
1811	Richard Hoskins...........	Thomas Coffield, Samuel McGuire.
1812	Richard Hoskins...........	Micajah Bunch, Thomas Coffield.
1813	Thomas Coffield...........	John Goodwin, Henry Skinner.
1814	Richard Hoskins...........	John Goodwin, Henry Skinner.
1815	Richard Hoskins...........	Wm. Saunders, Henry Skinner.
1816	Henry Skinner.............	Richard T. Brownrigg, Jeremiah Mixson
1817	Charles E. Johnson.........	Jeremiah Mixson, James Skinner.
1818	Richard T. Brownrigg......	Samuel McGuire, Samuel Gregory.
1819	Charles E. Johnson.........	James Skinner, Samuel Gregory.
1820	Charles E. Johnson.........	James Skinner, Samuel Gregory.
1821	Richard Hoskins...........	James Skinner, Samuel Gregory.
1822	Richard T. Brownrigg......	Henry Elliot, James Skinner.
1823	William Bullock...........	Joshua Mewborn.
1824	William Bullock...........	Wm. Walton, J. N. Hoskins.
1825	William Bullock...........	Wm. Walton, Joshua Mewborn.
1826	William Bullock...........	Josiah McKiel, William Jackson.
1827	William Walton............	William Beyrum, Wm. Jackson.
1828	William Walton............	Josiah McKiel, Wm. Beyrum.
1829	William Walton............	Wm. Beyrum, George Blair

CHOWAN COUNTY.—Continued.

MEMBERS OF GENERAL ASSEMBLY—Continued.

Years.	Senate.	House.
1830	William Walton	Wm. Jackson, George Blair.
1831	Richard T. Brownrigg	Josiah H. Skinner, Wm. Jackson.
1832	William Bullock	Josiah H. Skinner, Baker F. Welch.
1833	Jos. B. Skinner	Baker F. Welch, Chas. W. Nixon.
1834	Samuel T. Sawyer	Baker F. Welch, Wm. Beyrum.
1835	William Bullock	Wm. Beyrum, Thomas S. Hoskins.
1836	William W. Cowper	Thomas S. Hoskins.
1838	Rufus R. Speed	Robert T. Paine.
1840	Rufus R. Speed	Robert T. Paine.
1842	Whitmel J. Stallings	Wm. R. Skinner.
1844	Whitmel J. Stallings	Robert T. Paine.
1846	Whitmel J. Stallings	Robert T. Paine.
1848	Henry Willey	Robert T. Paine.
1850	Henry Willey	Wm. E. Bond.
1852	Henry Willey	Hugh W. Collins.
1854	Henry Willey	J. C. Badham.
1856	R. Dillard	J. C. Badham.
1858	R. Dillard	J. C. Badham.
1860	M. L. Eure	R. H. Small.
1862	M. L. Eure	Lemuel C. Benbury.
1864	M. L. Eure	Lemuel C. Benbury.
1866	H. Willey	R. D. Simpson.
1868	E. White Jos. W. Etheridge	Richard Clayton.
1870	Rufus K. Speed James C. Skinner	John Page.
1872	John L. Chamberlain C. W. Grandy	John L. Winslow.

Chowan, Camden, Currituck, Gates, Hertford, Pasquotank, and Perquimans Counties form the first Senatorial District.

CLAY COUNTY.

WAS formed in 1861, from the eastern portion of Cherokee county. Bounded on the north by Graham county, east by Swain county, south by Clay county, and west by Cherokee. Called in compliment of Henry Clay, of Kentucky.

Its capital is Hayesvile or Fort Hembrie. Distance from Raleigh about 350 miles.

COUNTY OFFICERS.

Offices.	Names.
Superior Court Clerk	E. G. Smith.
Register of Deeds	Wm. McConnell.
Sheriff	James P. Cherry.
Coroner	None.
Surveyor	None.
Treasurer	Watson Curlis.
Commissioners	J. M. Crawford, Chairman.
	J. H. Alexander.
	C. L. Truett.
	John Patterson.
	G. W. Sanderson.

JUSTICES OF THE PEACE.

Names.	Date of Qualification.	Post Office Address.
W. H. McClure	Sept. 1st, 1873.	Hayesville.
A. J. Curtis	" "	Hayesville.
W. J. R. McConnell	" "	Hayesville.
H. K. Martin	" "	
M. G. Pendergrass	" "	
John Patterson	" "	Hayesville.
L. Anderson	" "	Hayesville.
H. G. Green	" "	Hayesville.
W. P. Crawford	" "	Hayesville.
J. M. Bell	" "	
W. F. Plott	Oct. 6th, 1873.	

MEMBERS OF GENERAL ASSEMBLY.

Years.	Senate.	House.
1868	W. L. Love	J. O. Hicks.
1870	W. L. Love	J. F. Anderson.
1872	W. L. Love	J. F. Anderson.

Cherokee, Clay, Graham, Jackson, Macon and Swain form the 42nd Senatorial District.

CLEAVELAND COUNTY.

CLEAVELAND COUNTY was formed in 1841, out of Rutherford and Lincoln counties, and derives its name from Colonel Benjamin Cleaveland, of Wilkes county, who with a detachment of men from Wilkes and Surry under his and the command of Major Joseph Winston, engaged in the battle of King's Mountain.

It is situated in the south-western part of the State, and is bounded on the north by Burke county, on the east by Lincoln and Gaston, on the south by the South Carolina line, and on the west by Rutherford and McDowell counties.

Its capital is Shelby, which town preserves the name of Isaac Shelby, a distinguished revolutionary officer. Its distance from Raleigh is 190 miles.

COUNTY OFFICERS.

Offices.	Names.
Superior Court Clerk	J. Jenkins.
Register of Deeds	R. J. Durham.
Sheriff	B. F. Logan.
Coroner	Albert Green.
Surveyor	Rufus Roberts.
Treasurer	G. M. Green.
Commissioners	Allen Bettis, Chairman.
	D. D. Lattimore.
	W. B. Stroud.
	E. D. Dickson.
	J. R. Oates.

JUSTICES OF THE PEACE.

Names.	Date of Qualification.	Post Office Address.
L. C. Lommoms	Aug. 19th. 1873.	Grassy Pond, S. C.
Jas. F. Ray	" "	Grassy Pond, S. C.
O. W. Holland	" "	Nicholsonville.
L. L. Smith	" "	Nicholsonville.
N. N. Thomasson	" "	Shelby.
D. D. Hordim	" "	Shelby.
J. W. Inoin	Aug. 9th, 1873.	Shelby.
A. F. Ware	Oct. 6th, 1873.	Shelby.
P. B. Harmon	Aug. 19th, 1873.	Shelby.
W. O. Worl	" "	Shelby.
F. L. Hoke	Aug. 9th, 1873.	Shelby.
C. G. Love	Aug. 19th. 1873.	Shelby.
D. Froneborger	" "	Shelby.
Albert Blanton	" "	Shelby.
S. Maggness	" "	Shelby.
F. Y. Hicks	Aug. 9th, 1873.	Shelby.
R. G. Wells	Aug. 19th, 1873.	Shelby.

CLEAVELAND COUNTY—Continued.

JUSTICES OF THE PEACE.—Continued.

Names.	Date of Qualification.	Post Office Address.
G. W. Blanton	Aug. 9th, 1873.	Shelby.
R. W. Falls	Aug. 19th, 1873.	Shelby.
J. Cook	Aug. 9th, 1873.	Shelby.
Wm. Swafford	" "	Shelby.
Henny Hoyle	" "	Shelby.
Andrew Parker	" "	Shelby.

MEMBERS OF GENERAL ASSEMBLY.

Years.	Senate.	House.
1844	Thos. Jefferson	J. S. Hamrick.
1846	Columbus Mills	Joshua Beam.
1848	Dr. W. J. T. Miller	J. Y. Hamrick.
1850	John G. Bynum	G. G. Holland.
1852	John G. Bynum	A. W. Burton.
1854	Columbus Mills	J. J. Holland, W. W. Wright.
1856	Columbus Mills	W. M. Blanton, F. S. Ramsour.
1858	L. A. Mills	A. G. Waters, G. Dickson.
1860	A. W. Burton	A. G. Waters, J. R. Logan.
1862	M. O. Dickerson	David Beam, J. R. Logan.
1864	W. J. T. Miller	J. W. Gidney, David Beam.
1866	C. L. Harris	Geo. W. Whitfield.
1868	J. B. Eaves	Plato Durham.
1870	G. M. Whitesides	Lee M. McAfee.
1872	W. J. T. Miller	John W. Gidney.

Cleaveland and Gaston form the 38th Senatorial District.

COLUMBUS COUNTY.

Columbus County was formed in 1808, from Bladen and Brunswick. Its name is derived from Christopher Columbus, a native of Genoa, who in the year 1492 discovered America.

It is situated in the south-eastern portion of North Carolina, and bounded on the north by Bladen, on the east by Brunswick and Bladen, on the south by the South Carolina line, and west by Robeson county.

Its capital is Whitesville, derived from James B. White, one of the first members in the General Assembly. 125 miles distant from Raleigh.

COLUMBUS COUNTY.—Continued.

COUNTY OFFICERS.

Offices.	Name.
Superior Court Clerk	Isaac Jackson.
Register of Deeds	J. W. Council.
Sheriff	W. Q. Maultsby.
Coroner	Robert D. Sessions.
Surveyor	James A. Thompson.
Treasurer	Thomas S. Memory.
Commissioners	W. M. Baldwin. Samuel B. Jennings. Caleb Spivey. Milton Campbell. Caswell Porter.

JUSTICES OF THE PEACE.

Names.	Date of Qualification.	Post Office Address.
A. G. Smith	Sept. 1st, 1873.	Flemington.
Thomas Barefoot	" "	Bogue Swamp.
S. W. Smith	" "	Whiteville.
Elijah Creech	" "	Whiteville.
W. M. Baldwin	" "	Whiteville.
W. S. Frink	" "	Peacock's Store.
J. C. Lennon	" "	Whiteville.
M. W. Pridgen		Whiteville.
Burgwine Brown	" "	Whiteville.
Cassady Bullard	" "	Cerro Gordo.
W. K. Williamson	" "	Cerro Gordo.
Samuel Stricklin	" "	Fair Bluff.
E. W. Fowler	" "	Bug Hill.
J. J. C. Gore	" "	Bug Hill.
J. J. Long	" "	Whiteville.
J. W. Gore	" "	Whiteville.
M. M. Harrelson	" "	Whiteville.
Manuel Wright	" "	Whiteville.

MEMBERS OF GENERAL ASSEMBLY.

Years.	Senate.	House.
1809	James B. White	Wynn Nance, Thomas Frink.
1810	James B. White	Thomas Frink, Wynn Nance.
1811	Wyan Nance	Jonathan Pierce, Thomas Frink.

COLUMBUS COUNTY.—Continued.

MEMBERS OF GENERAL ASSEMBLY—Continued.

Years.	Senate.	House.
1812	Wynn Nance	Thomas Frink, Jonathan Pierce.
1813	Wynn Nance	Golborough Flower, Jacob Guiton.
1814	Thomas Frink	Absalom Powell, P. Coleman.
1815	Thomas Frink	John Gore, David Guiton,
1816	Thomas Frink	Caleb Stephens, Jacob Guiton.
1817	Thomas Frink	Caleb Stephens, Jacob Guiton.
1818	Jonathan Pierce	Caleb Stephens, Jacob Guiton.
1819	Thomas Frink	J. H. White, R. Wooten.
1820	Jacob Guiton	L. R. Simmons, R. Wooten.
1821	Thomas Frink	L. R. Simmons, Levi Stephens.
1822	Alexander Troy	Caleb Stephens, Richard Wooten.
1823	Thomas Frink	J. H. White, Caleb Stephens.
1824	Thomas Frink	Richard Wooten, Luke R. Simmons.
1825	Alex. Formyduval	L. R. Simmons, Caleb Stephens.
1826	James Burney	Caleb Stephens, L. R. Simmons.
1827	James Burney	Caleb Stephens, L. R. Simmons.
1828	James Burney	Caleb Stephens, L. R. Simmons.
1829	James Burney	L. R. Simmons, Richard Wooten.
1830	Luke R. Simmons	Marmaduke Powell, Caleb Stephens.
1831	Luke R. Simmons	Caleb Stephens, Marmaduke Powell.
1832	Luke R. Simmons	Joseph Maultsby, Caleb Stephens.
1833	Luke R. Simmons	Caleb Stephens, Marmaduke Powell.
1834	Caleb Stephens	Marmaduke Powell, Thomas Frink.
1835	Caleb Stephens	Thomas Frink, Marmaduke Powell.
1836	James Burney	J. Maultsby.
1838	Robert Melvin	Augustus Smith.
1840	Robert Melvin	Absalom Powell.
1842	Robert Melvin	Nathan L. Williamson.
1844	Robert Melvin	N. L. Williamson.
1846	Richard Wooten	N. L. Williamson.
1848	Richard Wooten	N. L. Williamson.
1850	Richard Wooten	John A. Maultsby.
1852	T. S. D. McDowell	Forney George.
1854	T. S. D. McDowell	A. J. Jones.
1856	A. J. Jones	D. T. Williamson.
1858	T. S. D. McDowell	J. H. Stephens.
1860	John D. Taylor	N. L. Williamson.
1862	J. W. Ellis	W. M. Baldwin.
1864	J. W. Ellis	Forney George.
1866	Salter Lloyd	J. M. McGoughan.
1868	John W. Purdie	D. P. High.
1870	J. C. Currie	C. C. Gore.
1872	J. W. Ellis	V. V. Richardson.

Columbus and Robeson form the 16th Senatorial District.

CRAVEN COUNTY.

CRAVEN COUNTY was one of the original precincts of the Lords Proprietors, and derives its name from William, Earl of Craven, to whom with others the charter from Charles the Second was granted. He was a brave cavalier, and old soldier of the German discipline, and supposed husband to the Queen of Bohemia.

It is situated in the eastern part of the State, bounded on the north by Pitt and Beaufort and Pamlico counties, on the east by the Pamlico Sound, on the south by Carteret and Jones, and on the west by Pitt and Lenoir counties.

Its capital is Newbern, one of the largest and oldest towns in the State; beautifully located at the confluence of the Neuse and Trent rivers. It derives its name from Bern, the place of nativity of Christopher Baron de Graaffenreidt, who, in 1709, emigrated to this State and settled near this place.

COUNTY OFFICERS.

Offices.	Names.
Superior Court Clerk	I. Edwin West.
Register of Deeds	James C. Harrison.
Sheriff	Orlando Hubbs.
Coroner	Vacant.
Surveyor	Vacant.
Treasurer	David N. Kilburn.
Commissioners	Edward R. Stanly, Chairman.
	John Patterson.
	Robert C. Kehoe.
	Edward H. Hill.
	Jesse Brooks.

JUSTICES OF THE PEACE.

Names.	Date of Qualification.	Post Office Address.
W. H. Ellison	August 10th 1873.	Swift Creek.
Charles M. Roach	" "	Swift Creek.
Samuel W. Latham	" "	Newbern.
Jas. A. Askins	" "	Newbern.
George H. Grover	August 9th, 1873.	Newbern.
Edmund W. Fisher	August 27th, 1873.	Newbern.
Jos. Williams	" 16th, "	Woodbridge.
Edward Bull	" 21st, "	Woodbridge.
Phillip J. Lee	" "	Woodbridge.
Simon Leach	" "	Woodbridge.
R. T. Berry	" "	Woodbridge.
E. R. Dudley	" "	Woodbridge.
C. L. Wetherington	" 16 "	Dover Station.
Enoch Luton	" 20 "	Dover Station.

CRAVEN COUNTY—Continued.

JUSTICES OF THE PEACE—Continued.

Names.	Date of Qalification.	Post Office Address.
W. L. Palmer	Aug. 22 1873.	Newbern.
David N. Kilburn	" 16 "	Newbern.
Richard Tucker	" 16 "	Newbern.
Edward A. Richardson	" 18 "	Newbern.
Henry P. Hickman	" 16 "	Newbern.
John R. Good	" 16 "	Newbern.
Joseph Mumford	" 16 "	Newbern.

LIST OF MEMBERS TO THE HOUSE OF COMMONS FROM NEWBERN.

Years.	House of Commons.	Years.	House of Commons.
1777	Abner Nash,	1807	Francis X. Martin,
1778	Richard Cogdell,	1808	William Gaston,
1779	Richard Cogdell,	1809	William Gaston,
1780	James Green, jr.	1810	Daniel Carthy,
1781	Richard D. Spaight, sr.,	1811	Daniel Carthy,
1782	Richard D. Spaight, sr.,	1812	John Stanly,
1783	Richard D. Spaight, sr.,	1813	John Stanly,
1784	Spyers Singleton,	1814	John Stanly,
1785	William Lisdale,	1815	John Stanly,
1786	John Sitgreaves,	1816	George E. Badger,
1787	John Sitgreaves,	1818	John Stanly,
1788	John Sitgreaves,	1819	John Stanly.
1789	John Sitgreaves,	1820	Edward E. Graham,
1791	James Coor,	1821	Francis L. Hawks,
1792	Richard D. Spaight, sr.,	1822	E. E. Graham,
1793	Isaac Guion,	1823	John Stanly,
1794	Daniel Carthy,	1824	William Gaston,
1795	Isaac Guion,	1825	John Stanly,
1796	Thomas Badger,	1826	John Stanly,
1797	Edward Graham,	1827	William Gaston,
1798	John Stanly,	1828	William Gaston,
1799	John Stanly,	1829	Charles B. Spaight,
1800	George Ellis,	1830	Charles B. Spaight,
1801	George Ellis,	1831	William Gaston,
1802	Edward Harris,	1832	Charles B. Shepard,
1803	Edward Harris,	1833	Charles B. Shepard,
1804	Frederick Nash,	1834	Matthias E. Manly,
1805	Frederick Nash,	1835	Mathias E. Manly,
1806	Francis X. Martin,		

In 1835 the representation from the Borough was abolished.

CRAVEN COUNTY.—Continued.

MEMBERS OF GENERAL ASSEMBLY—Continued.

Years.	Senate.	House.
1777	James Coor	John Tillman, Nathan Bryan.
1778	James Coor	Nathan Bryan, Abner Nash.
1779	James Coor	Hardy Bryan, Benj. Williams.
1780	James Coor	Wm. Bryan, Wm. Blount.
1781	James Coor	Wm. Bryan, John Tillman.
1782	James Coor	Wm. Bryan, John Tillman.
1783	James Coor	Wm. Blount, William Bryan.
1784	James Coor	William Blount, William Bryan.
1785	James Coor	Richard D. Spaight, sr., Abner Neale.
1786	James Coor	Richard D. Spaight, sr., Abner Neale.
1787	James Coor	Richard Nixon, Richard D. Spaight, sr.
1788	Benjamin Williams	Richard Nixon, John Allen.
1789	James Coor	Richard Nixon, John Allen.
1790	John Bryan	Levi Dawson, John Allen.
1791	John Carney	Levi Dawson, John Allen.
1792	John Carney	John Tillman, John Allen.
1793	John Carney	John Tillman, John Allen.
1794	John C. Bryan	John Tillman, John Allen.
1795	John C. Bryan	John S. West, Wm. Bryan.
1796	Wm. McClure	John S. West, Wm. Bryan.
1797	Wm. McClure	Henry Tillman, Wm. Blackledge.
1798	John Bryan	Phillip Neale, Wm. Blackledge.
1799	John Bryan	Phillip Neale, Wm. Blackledge.
1800	William Gaston	James Gatling, John S. Nelson.
1801	Richard D. Spaight, sr.	Lewis Fonville, Henry Tillman.
1802	John Bryan	Lewis Fonville, Wm. Bryan.
1803	Stephen Harris	Lewis Fonville, Wm. Bryan.
1804	Wm. Bryan	John S. Richardson, Lewis Fonville.
1805	Wm. Bryan	John S. Nelson, Charles Hatch.
1806	Wm. Bryan	Lewis Fenville, John S. Nelson.
1807	Wm. Bryan	Edward Harris, John S. Nelson.
1808	Henry Tillman	Stephen Harris, John S. Nelson.
1809	Wm. Bryan	Wm. Blackledge, John S. Nelson.
1810	John S. West	Vine Allen, John S. Nelson.
1811	John S. West	Vine Allen, John S. Nelson.
1812	William Gaston	Henry Tillman, Fred J. Cox.
1813	Vine Allen	Fred. J. Cox, Benners Vail.
1814	Wright Stanly	Henry Carroway, James Ray.
1815	Reuben P. Jones	Joseph Nelson.
1816	John S. Smith	John S. Nelson, Thos. O'Bryan.
1817	John S. Smith	John S. Nelson, Thos. O'Bryan.
1818	William Gaston	Abner Neale, Vine Allen.
1819	William Gaston	Richard D. Speight, Abner Neale.
1820	Richard D. Spaight	Amos Rowe, Wm. S. Blackledge.
1821	Richard D. Spaight	John M. Bryan.
1822	Richard D. Spaight	John M. Bryan, James C. Cole.
1823	John H. Bryan	Jonn M. Bryan, S. Whitehurst.
1824	John H. Bryan	S. Whitehurst, T. C. Bryan.
1825	Richard D. Spaight	S. Whitehurst, A. H. Richardson.
1826	Richard D. Spaight	A. H. Richardson, S. Whitehurst.
1827	Richard D. Spaight	Charles J. Nelson, Lucas Benners.
1828	Richard D. Spaight	Charles J. Nelson, John M. Bryan.
1829	Richard D. Spaight	Nathaniel Smith, John M. Bryan.
1830	Richard D. Spaight	John M. Bryan, A. F. Gaston.
1831	Richard D. Spaight	Abner Hartley, Wm. M. Nelson.

CRAVEN COUNTY—Continued.

MEMBERS OF GENERAL ASSEMBLY.—Continued.

Years.	Senate.	House.
1832	Richard D. Spaight.........	Abner Hartley, Wm. M. Nelson.
1833	Richard D. Spaight.........	John B. Dawson, F. P. Latham.
1834	Richard D. Spaight.........	Abner Hartley, F. P. Latham.
1835	Thomas J. Pasteur..........	John M. Bryan, Abner Neale.
1836	John M. Bryan	Abner Hartley, Abner Neale.
1838	Samuel J. Biddle...........	Samuel Hyman, W. C. Wadsworth.
1840	Thomas J. Pasteur..........	Samuel Hyman, W. C. Wadsworth.
1842	Thomas J. Pasteur..........	O. S. Dewey, N. H. Street.
1844	Thomas J. Pasteur..........	Wm. H. Washington, F. J. Prentiss.
1846	N. H. Street................	Wm. H. Washington, H. T. Guion.
1848	Wm. H. Washington........	W. B. Wadsworth, George S. Stevenson.
1850	Wm. H. Washington........	Geo. S. Stevenson, A. T. Jerkins.
1852	Wm. H. Washington........	R. A. Russell, C. B. Wood.
1854	C. B. Wood	S. W. Chadwick, George Green.
1856	J. Craven	C. Kilby, H. C. Jones.
1858	J. D. Flanner................	J. Bryan, H. C. Jones.
1860	N. H. Street.................	C. C. Clark, F. E. Alford.
1862	W. B. Wadsworth..........	J. B. J. Barrow, B. M. Coit.
1864	Nathaniel Whitfield........	J. J. Gaskins, Wm. Lane.
1866	M. E. Manly	S. W. Chadwick, A. C. Latham.
1868	W. H. Sweet................	A. S. Seymour, A. W. Stevens, B. W. Morris.
1870	W. J. Clarke............ R. F. Lehman...........	R. Tucker,* E. R. Dudley,* G. B. Willis.*
1872	A. S. Seymour..............	E. R. Dudley, J. B. Abbott.

*Colored.

CUMBERLAND COUNTY.

Cumberland County was formed in 1754, from the upper part of Bladen; derives it name from the Duke of Cumberland.

It is situated in nearly the centre of the State, having Harnett county on the north, Sampson on the east, Bladen and Robeson on the south, Richmond and Moore counties on the west.

Its capital town is Fayetteville. This flourishing and ancient town was settled in 1762. It was first called Campbelltown, then Cross Creek, and in 1784, its name was changed to Fayetteville, in honor of General Lafayette, who was a native of France, and who perilled his life and fortune in the cause of liberty. He was a Major-General in the American army, fought in her battles, was wounded at Brandywine, and having aided in the freedom of this country, he returned to his native land.

Fayetteville is distant from Raleigh sixty miles. It is located on the Cape Fear River, which is navigable to this place for steam and other boats.

On the 29th of May, 1831, Fayetteville was almost wholly destroyed by fire.

CUMBERLAND COUNTY—CONTINUED.

COUNTY OFFICERS.

Offices.	Names.
Superior Court Clerk	Alex McPherson, Jr.
Register of Deeds	William F. Campbell.
Sheriff	Robert W. Hardie.
Coroner	None.
Surveyor	Foster Mason.
Treasurer	James D. Nott.
Commissioners	Alfred A. McKethan. Cader Parker. Hector McNeill. Arthur Horn. Walter J. Smith.

JUSTICES OF THE PEACE.

Names.	Date of Qualification.	Post Office Address.
S. A. Baldwin	Aug. 18th, 1873.	Fayetteville.
A. F. Hobbs	" "	Fayetteville.
M. E. Wade	" "	Fayetteville.
C. C. Bell	" "	Fayetteville.
Duncan G. McRae	" "	Fayetteville.
William H. Porter	" "	Fayetteville.
John J. Minor	" "	Fayetteville.
Alvin G. Thornton	" "	Fayetteville.
Matthew N. Leary, Sr.	" "	Fayetteville.
John A. McKay	" "	Fayetteville.
John A. McFarland	" "	Fayetteville.
Isaac W. Goodwin	" "	Fayetteville.
H. L. Hall	" "	Fayetteville.
A. K. McDiarmid	" "	Fayetteville.
Duncan B. Gillis	" "	Fayetteville.
W. M. Fort	" "	Fayetteville.
J. B. Carver	" "	Fayetteville.
John C. Blocker	" "	Fayetteville.
G. A. Downing	" "	Fayetteville.
George W. Graham	" "	Fayetteville.
Archibald A. Johnson	" "	Fayetteville.
John W. McLaurin	" "	Fayetteville.
George L. McKay	" "	Fayetteville.

CUMBERLAND COUNTY—Continued.

LIST OF MEMBERS TO THE HOUSE OF COMMONS FROM FAYETTEVILLE.

Years.	House of Commons.	Years.	House of Commons.
1791	James Porterfield.	1816	John Winslow.
1792	John L. Taylor.	1817	John Winslow.
1793	John L. Taylor.	1818	John Winslow.
1794	John L. Taylor.	1819	John Winslow.
1796	Robert Cochran.	1820	John A. Cameron.
1797	James Dick.	1821	Robert Strange.
1801	Wm. W. Jones.	1822	Robert Strange.
1802	Robert Cochran.	1823	Robert Strange.
1803	Thomas Davis.	1824	John Matthews.
1804	Robert Cochran.	1825	John Matthews.
1805	John Hay.	1826	Robert Strange.
1806	William Duffy.	1827	John D. Eccles.
1807	Samuel Goodwin.	1828	John D. Eccles.
1808	Samuel Goodwin.	1829	John D. Eccles.
1809	Thomas Davis.	1830	Louis D. Henry.
1810	John A. Cameron.	1831	Louis D. Henry.
1811	John A. Cameron.	1832	Louis D. Henry.
1812	John A. Cameron.	1833	James Seawell.
1813	Larkin Newley.	1834	James Seawell.
1814	Thomas Davis.	1835	Thomas L. Hybart.
1815	John Winslow.		

Borough representation ceased.

MEMBERS OF GENERAL ASSEMBLY.

Years.	Senate.	House.
1778		Robert Rowan, Peter Mallet.
1779		Robert Cochran, Robert Rowan.
1780		Robert Cochran, Edward Winslow.
1781		David Smith. Thomas Anthony.
1782		Edward Winslow, Patrick Travis.
1783		Patrick Travis, Edward Winslow.
1784	Thomas Armstrong	Patrick Travis, Edward Winslow.
1785	Thomas Armstrong	Robert Rowan, David Smith.
1786	Thomas Armstrong	John Hay, Edward Winslow.
1787	Alexander McAllister	Wm. B. Grove, James Thackston.
1788	Alexander McAllister	John McKay, Wm. B. Grove.
1789	Alexander McAllister	John McKay, Wm. B. Grove.
1791	Farquhar Campbell	John McKay, Joseph Kearnes.
1792	Farquhar Campbell	Joseph Kearnes, Neill Smith.
1793	Farquhar Campbell	Neill Smith.
1794	John McNeill	Hector McAllister, Neill Smith.
1795	John McNeill	Hector McAllister.
1796	John McNeill	Neill Smith, Samuel Northington.
1797	Hector McAllister	Daniel McLean, Neill Smith.
1798	Alexander McAllister	Samuel Northington, Sam'l D. Purviance.
1799	Daniel McLean	Neill Smith, Samuel D. Purviance.

CUMBERLAND COUNTY.—Continued.

MEMBERS OF GENERAL ASSEMBLY—Continued.

Years.	Senate.	House.
1800	Hector McAllister	John Dickson, Wm. Lord.
1801	Samuel D. Purviance	John Dickson, Wm. Lord.
1802	William Lord	John Dickson, Daniel Smith.
1803	John Dickson	Daniel Smith, Samuel Northington.
1804	Hector McAllister	Archibald McNeill.
1805	John McKay	Stephen Gilmore, John Kearnes.
1806	John McKay	Colin Shaw, John Kearnes.
1807	John McKay	John Kearnes, Colin Shaw.
1808	John Dickson	James Campbell.
1809	William Lord	John Kay, James Campbell.
1810	Colin Shaw	Isaac Folsome, John S. Nelson.
1811	John Dickson	Thomas Gilmore, Farq. McKay.
1812	John Smith	Robert Campbell, Richard Huckabee.
1813	John Smith	Richard Huckabee, Robert Campbell.
1814	John Smith	Richard Huckabee, Mark Christian.
1815	John Dickson	Richard Huckabee, Neill McNeill.
1816	Richard Huckabee	Neill McNeill, John C. Williams.
1817	Lauch. Bathune	John C. Williams, Neill McNeill.
1818	Lauch. Bathune	Jona. Evans, Neill McNeill.
1819	Richard Huckabee	Jona. Evans, Neill McNeill.
1820	John Black	Neill McNeill, Alexander McAllister.
1821	Richard Huckabee	Neill McNeill, Louis D. Henry.
1822	Lauch. Bethune	Neill McNeill, Louis D. Henry.
1823	Lauch. Bethune	Neill McNeill, Samuel P. Ashe.
1824	Lauch. Bethune	Neill McNeill, Alexander Elliott.
1825	Lauch. Bethune	Alexander Elliott, Samuel P. Ashe.
1826	Alexander Elliott	Joseph Hodges, A. McDearmid.
1827	Lauch. Bethune	Joseph Hodges, A. McDearmid.
1828	Arch'd. McDearmid	Alexander McNeill, Joseph Hodges.
1829	Arch'd. McDearmid	Alexander McNeill, Alexander Buie.
1830	Wm. Murchison	Alexander McNeill, Alexander Buie.
1831	John D. Toomar	David McNeill, John Barclay.
1832	John D. Toomar	David McNeill, John D. Eccles.
1833	Duncan McCormick	David McNeill, Dillon Jordan.
1834	Duncan McCormick	Dillon Jordan, David McNeill.
1835	Duncan McCormick	Dillon Jordan, David McNeill.
1836	Duncan McCormick	Stephen Hollingsworth, Dillon Jordan.
1838	Arch'd. McDearmid	Stephen Hollingsworth, David Reid.
1840	Arch'd McDearmid	David Reid, John Monroe.
1842	David Reid	John Monroe, Duncan K. McRae.
1844	Thomas N. Cameron	Duncan Shaw. B. F. Atkins.
1846	Thomas N. Cameron	Geo. W. Pegram, Duncan Shaw.
1848	Alexander Murchison	James C. Dobbin, Geo. W. Pegram.
1850	Thomas N. Cameron	James C. Dobbin, Geo. W. Pegram.
1852	A Murchison	James C. Dobbin, Geo. W. Pegram.
1854	Warren Winslow	Jesse G. Shepherd, Malcom J. McDearmid. C. H. Coffin.
1856	D. McDiarmid	J. G. Shepherd, J. Stewart, L. Bethel.
1858	J. T. Gilmore	Wm. L. McKay, C. C. Barbee, J. S. Harrington.
1860	Duncan Shaw	C. G. Wright, J. S. Harrington, J. C. Williams.
1862	W. B. Wright	J. G. Shepherd, John McCormick, Neill McKay.

CUMBERLAND COUNTY.—Continued.

MEMBERS OF GENERAL ASSEMBLY—Continued.

Years.	Senate.	House.
1864	W. B. Wright...............	J. G. Shepherd, A. D. McLane, J. McCormick.
1866	A. McLean..................	W. L. McKay, T. S. Lutterloh.
1868	J. S. Harrington, L. D. Hall.	John S. Leary, Isham Sweat.
1870	W. C. Troy, C. T. Murphy...	C. W. Broadfoot, G. H. Currie.
1872	W. C. Troy..................	G. W. Bullard, T. S. Lutterloh.

Cumberland and Harnett counties form the 16th Senatorial District.

CURRITUCK COUNTY.

Currituck County was one of the early precincts of the State in 1729, when the Lords Proprietors surrendered their rights to the English Crown. It derives its name from a tribe of Indians who once inhabited and owned the country.

Its location is the extreme north-eastern portion of North Carolina: bounded on the north by the Virginia line, east by the Atlantic Ocean, south by the Albemarle Sound, and west by Camden County.

Its court house, on Currituck Sound, is beautifully located, and is distant from Raleigh 242 miles.

COUNTY OFFICERS.

Offices.	Names.
Superior Court Clerk.....................	A. O. Dey.
Register of Deeds........................	H. E. Baxter.
Sheriff..................................	Jno. F. Frost.
Coroner..................................	Vacant, (dead.)
Surveyor.................................	H. B. Ansell.
Treasurer................................	C. T. Sears.
Commissioners............................	T. L. Sanderson, Chairman. P. H. Morgan. W. H. Bray. W. D. Tate. T. J. Poyner.

CURRITUCK COUNTY—Continued.

JUSTICES OF THE PEACE.

Names.	Date of qualification.	Post Office Address.
H. H. Simmons	Sept. 1st, 1873.	Gibbs Woods.
E. W. Holt	" 5th, "	Shingle Landing.
W. H. Cowell	" 1st, "	Indian Ridge.
V. L. Pitts	" "	Currituck C. H.
Elias Williams	" "	Knott's Island.
S. J. Waterfield	" "	Knott's Island.
James M. Woodhouse	" "	Poplar Branch.
Graham G. Gallop	" "	Powell's Point.
J. D. Wicker	" "	North Banks.
Benjamin D. Pillett	" "	North Banks.

MEMBERS OF GENERAL ASSEMBLY.

Years.	Senate.	House.
1777	Samuel Jarvis	James White, James Ryan.
1778	Col. Perkins	William Ferebee, Howell Williams.
1779	Col. Perkins	Thomas Younghusband, John Humphries
1780	Samuel Jarvis	James Phillips, John Humphries.
1781	Samuel Jarvis	James Phillips, John Humphries.
1782	William Ferebee	Thomas Jarvis, Joseph Ferebee.
1783	William Ferebee	James Phillips, Joseph Ferebee.
1784	James Phillips	James White, Joseph Ferebee.
1785	Willis Etheridge	Joseph Ferebee, James White.
1786	Willis Etheridge	Joseph Ferebee, John Humphries.
1787	Howell Williams	Joseph Ferebee, John Humphries.
1788	Howell Williams	Thos. P. Williams, Griffith Dauge.
1789	Howell Williams	Thos. P. Williams, Andrew Duke.
1790	John Humphries	Joseph Ferebee, Andrew Duke.
1791	John Humphries	Spence Hall, Joseph Ferebee.
1792	John Humphries	Spence Hall, Alex. L. Whitehall.
1793	Spence Hall	Alex. L. Whitehall, Andrew Duke.
1794	Spence Hall	Andrew Duke, Saml. Ferebee.
1795	Joseph Ferebee	Thomas Williams, Jesse Simmons.
1796	Joseph Ferebee	Thomas Williams, Jesse Simmons.
1797	James Phillips	Thos. Martin, Malachi Jones.
1798	Saml. Salyear	Malachi Jones, T. Williams.
1799	Saml. Salyear	Malachi Jones, T. Williams.
1800	Saml. Salyear	Thomas Williams, Thos. C. Ferebee.
1801	Jonathan Lindsay	Thomas Garrett, Thos. C. Ferebee.
1802	Jonathan Lindsay	Thos. C. Ferebee, Thomas Garrett.
1803	Samuel Ferebee	Jacob Perkins, Thos. Anderson.
1804	Samuel Ferebee	Aaron Bright, William Simmons.
1805	Samuel Ferebee	Willoughby Dozier, Willis Simmons.
1806	Samuel Ferebee	Willoughby Dozier, Danl. Lindsay.
1807	Thomas Williams	Willis Simmons, Jonathan Lindsay.
1808	Thomas Williams	Willis Sommons, Willoughby Dozier.
1809	Jonathan Lindsay	Brickhouse Bell, Jesse Barnard.

CURRITUCK COUNTY.—Continued.

MEMBERS OF GENERAL ASSEMBLY—Continued.

Years.	Senate.	House.
1810	Thomas Williams	Jesse Barnard, Brickhouse Bell.
1811	Jonathan Lindsay	Brickhouse Bell, Thomas Garrett.
1812	Jonathan Lindsay	Brickhouse Bell, Thomas Garrett.
1813	Thomas Sanderson	Simeon Sawyer, Willis Simmons.
1814	Thomas Sanderson	Brickhouse Bell, Sam. Salyer.
1815	Thomas Williams	Brickhouse Bell, John T. Hampton.
1816	Thomas Williams	Brickhouse Bell, John T. Hampton.
1817	Spence Hall	John T. Hampton, C. Etheridge.
1818	Spench Hall	J. T. Hampton, C. Etheridge.
1819	Edmund S. Lindsay	J. T. Hampton, Enoch Ball.
1820	Edmund S. Lindsay	Enoch Ball, John T. Hampton.
1821	Edmund S. Lindsay	John Forbes, John Shipp.
1822	Edmund S. Lindsay	Cartwright Bell, Jesse Barnard.
1823	Thos. C. Ferebee	W. D. Barnard, John Forbes.
1824	Saml. Salyear	Enoch Ball, Willoughby D. Barnard.
1825	Saml. Salyear	W. D. Barnard, Enoch Ball.
1826	Saml. Salyear	W. D. Barnard, Enoch Ball.
1827	Saml. Salyear	W. D. Barnard, Enoch Ball.
1828	Saml. Salyear	Enoch Ball, Benj. T. Simmons.
1829	Caleb Etheridge	W. D. Barnard, Benj. T. Simmons.
1830	Jona. J. Lindsay	W. D. Barnard, Benj. T. Simmons.
1831	Jona. J. Lindsay	John B. Jones, Benj. T. Simmons.
1832	Jona. J. Lindsay	John B. Jones, Benj. T. Simmons.
1833	Daniel Lindsay	John B. Jones, James M. Sanderson.
1834	Dan. Lindsay, jun	Joshua Harrison, Wallace Bray.
1835	Daniel Lindsay	Joshua Harrison, Alfred Perkins.
1836	Daniel Lindsay	Alfred Perkins.
1838	Caleb Etheridge	Alfred Perkins.
1840	Caleb Etheridge	John B. Jones.
1842	Caleb Etheridge	John B. Jones.
1844	Caleb Etheridge	John B. Jones.
1846	John Barnard	John B. Jones.
1848	John Barnard	Thomas Grigg.
1850	John Barnard	Samuel B. Jarvis.
1852	H. M. Shaw	Samuel B. Jarvis.
1854	J. B. Jones	Samuel B. Jarvis.
1856	J. B. Jones	Samuel B. Jarvis.
1858	C. C. Williams	B. M. Baxter.
1860	B. T. Simmons	B. M. Baxter.
1862	D. McD. Lindsay	B. M. Baxter.
1864	D. McD. Lindsay	Jos. J. Baxter.
1866	W. D. Ferebee	W. G. Grandberry.
1868	Elisha A. White Jos. W. Etheridge	Thos. Sanderlin.
1870	Rufus K. Speed James C. Skinner	J. M. Woodhouse.
1872	John L. Chamberlain C. W. Grandy	J. M. Woodhouse.

Camden, Currituck, Chowan, Gates, Hertford, Pasquotank and Perquimans form the first Senatorial District.

DARE COUNTY.

DARE COUNTY was formed from Hyde and Currituck counties, in 1870, bounded on the north by the Albemarle Sound, east by the Atlantic Ocean, south by Hyde. Its capital is Manteo, about 250 miles from Raleigh.

"As early as 13th day of August, 1584, at Ralegh's colony on Roanoke Island, North Carolina, the native chieftain, Manteo, was admitted into fellowship of Christ's flock by Holy baptism, and five days afterwards Eleanor, daughter of the Governor and wife of Ananias Dare, was delivered of a daughter in Roanoke, and ye same was christened there the Sunday following, and because this childe was the first christian born in Virginia shee was named Virginia Dare."—*Hakluyte, III*, 314.

COUNTY OFFICERS.

Offices.	Names.
Superior Court Clerk	W. D. Chaddic.
Register of Deeds	G. B. Blien.
Sheriff	W. T. Brinkley.
Coroner	Sheriff Acting.
Surveyor	W. R. Sutton.
Treasurer	Sheriff acting.
Commissioners	J. W. Etheridge. Cornelius Parrie. G. W. Creef. Abraham Owens. A. J. Austin.

JUSTICES OF THE PEACE.

Names.	Date of Qualification.	Post Office Address.
Thos. R. Mann	Dec. 29th, 1873.	Manteo.
R. R. Quidley	Aug. 11th, 1873.	The Cape.
A. J. Austin	" "	Manteo.
Geo. R. Midgett, col	Nov. 1st, 1873.	Manteo.
A. N. Holmes	Jan. 22d, 1873.	Manteo.
John A. Scarborough	" 27th, "	Kinnekeet.
E. Williams	" 24th, "	Kinnekeet.

MEMBERS OF GENERAL ASSEMBLY.

Years.	Senate.	House.
1872	J. B. Respess H. E. Stilley	O. N. Gray.

Beaufort, Dare, Hyde, Martin, Washington and Tyrrell form the 2d Senatorial District.

DAVIDSON COUNTY.

DAVIDSON COUNTY was formed in 1822, from Rowan, named in compliment of Gen. William Davidson, who fell at the passage of the Catawba at Cowan's Ford, during the Revolutionary War, 1781.

It is in the western part of the State; it is bounded on the north by Forsythe, east by Guilford and Randolph, south by the Yadkin River, which separates it from Stanly and Rowan, and on the west by the same river, which separates it from Rowan.

LEXINGTON is its capital, a most flourishing and beautiful village, and distant 117 miles from Raleigh.

COUNTY OFFICERS.

Offices.	Names.
Superior Court Clerk	Levi E. Johnson.
Register of Deeds	W. H. Moffit.
Sheriff	Jacob. A. Sowers.
Coroner	T. C. Ford, (special.)
Surveyor	Peter E. Yink.
Treasurer	David W. Pickett.
Commissioners,	W. L. Cecil. Abram Cross. T. W. Hartley. D. C. Kinnell. James Smith.

JUSTICES OF THE PEACE.

Names.	Date of Qualification.	Post Office Address.
S. S. Jones	Sept. 1st, 1873.	Clemmonsville.
David Smith	" "	Jackson Hill.
Peter Cross	" "	Silver Hill.
E. S. Koonce	" "	Lexington.
Andrew Young	" "	Lexington.
John Q. Burton	" "	Thomasville.
S. J. Huffman	" "	Lexington.
F. Raper	" "	Arcadia.
H. H. Hartley	" "	Tyro.
M. L. Hedrick	" "	Silver Hill.
Levi Hedrick	" "	Silver Hill.
E. Hedgecock	" "	Browntown.
J. A. Heitman	" "	Lexington.
H. Clay Thomas	" "	Thomasville.
James Smith	" "	Lexington.
H. B. Dusenberry	" "	Lexington.
Levi Beck	" "	Lexington.
Jno. G. Surratt	" "	Jackson Hill.
G. W. Morris	" "	Jackson Hill

DAVIDSON COUNTY.—Continued.

JUSTICES OF THE PEACE—Continued.

Names.	Date of Qalification.	Post Office Address.
	Sept. 1, 1873.	
Geo. Smith	" "	Jackson Hill.
Wm. Hedrick	" "	Thomasville.
Jacob Yise	" "	Midway.
A. G. Morris	" "	Jackson Hill.
H. C. Hedrick	" "	Lexington.
A. W. Jarrett	" "	Cotton Grove.
E. P. May	" "	Lexington.
W. H. Badgett	" "	Jackson Hill.
S. A. Mock	" "	Midway.
Joseph Roach	" "	Cotton Grove.

MEMBERS OF GENERAL ASSEMBLY.

Years.	Senate.	House.
1823	Alex. R. Cladeleugh	J. Hargrave, W. Bodenhamer.
1824	Jesse Hargrave	W. Bodenhamer, J. Clemons.
1825	Jesse Hargrave	John M. Smith, Joseph Spurgen.
1826	John M. Smith	Thomas Hampton, John Ward.
1827	John M. Smith	Thomas Hampton, Absalom Williams.
1828	John M, Smith	Thomas Hampton, Absalom Williams.
1829	Ransom Harris	W. W. Wiseman, Lewis Snyder.
1830	Ransom Harris	Joseph Spurgen, Wm. W. Wiseman.
1831	Charles Hoover	John A. Hogan, John W. Thomas.
1832	John A. Hogan	W. W. Wiseman, Henry Ledford.
1833	John A. Hogan	W. W. Wiseman, Henry Ledford.
1834	John A. Hogan	George Smith, Charles Brummell.
1835	John A. Hogan	George Smith, Charles Brummell.
1836	John L. Hargrove	Charles Brummell, Meshack Pinckston.
1838	Wm. R. Holt	Burgess S. Beal, Charles Brummell.
1840	Alfred Hargrave	Charles Brummell, Burgess S. Beal.
1842	John W. Thomas	Charles Brummell, Henry Walser.
1844	Alfred Hargrave	B. S. Douthitt, C. L. Payne.
1846	Saml. Hargrave	Hoover and H. Walser.
1848	John W. Thomas	J. M. Leach, H. Walser.
1850	Saml. Hargrave	J. M. Leach, Alfred Forster.
1852	Saml. Hargrave	J. M. Leach, W. Harris.
1854	J. W. Thomas	J. M. Leach, J. P. Mabry.
1858	B. C. Douthitt	H. Walser, —— Brummell.
1860	John W. Thomas	Lewis Haynes, E. B. Clark.
1862	H. Adams	R. L. Beall, H. Walser.
1864	H. Adams	C. F. Low, Lewis Haynes.
1866	J. M. Leach	C. F. Low, J. H. Shelton.
1868	P. A. Long	Jabez Mendenhall, Geo. Kinny.
1870	F. C. Robbins	Jacob Clinard, J. T. Brown.
1872	John T. Cramer	J. T. Brown, John Michael.

DAVIE COUNTY.

DAVIE COUNTY was formed in 1836 from Rowan, and named in honor of Gen. William R. Davie.

It is located in the north-west part of North Carolina, and bounded on the north by Yadkin county, east by the Yadkin River, which separates it from Davidson county, south by Rowan county, and west by Iredell.

Its capital is Mocksville, and distant 120 miles west of Raleigh.

COUNTY OFFICERS.

Offices.	Name.
Superior Court Clerk	H. B. Howard.
Register of Deeds	Epraim Gaither.
Sheriff	Wilborn Stonestreet.
Coroner	Beal Ijames.
Surveyor	W. K. Gibbs.
Treasuer	Mathew Fulford.
Commissioners	P. H. Cain, Chairman. John Lunn. Denton Ijames. Thomas T. Maxwell. N. A. Peebles.

JUSTICES OF THE PEACE.

Names.	Date of Qualification.	Post Office Address.
Cheshier Sain	Aug. 9th, 1873.	Mocksville.
C. U. Rich	Sept. 1st, "	Mocksville.
Braxton Bailey	" "	Mocksville.
J. A. McCubbins	Aug. 15th, 1873.	Jerusalem.
A. T. Grant	Sept. 1st, 1873.	Jerusalem.
G. W. Baity	Aug. 19th, 1873.	Clarksville.
A. M. Richardson	Sept. 1st, "	Clarksville.
W. K. Gibbs	Aug. 27th, "	Smith Grove.
James N. Brock	Sept. 1st, "	Farmington.
Charles Anderson	" "	Calahaln.
W. A. Williams	" "	Calahaln.
A. H. Stewart	" "	Fulton.
H. E. Robertson	" "	Fulton.

DAVIE COUNTY—Continued.

MEMBERS OF GENERAL ASSEMBLY.

Years.	Senate.	House.
1842	Samuel Rebelin.............	G. A. Miller.
1844	Nathaniel Boyden...........	G. A. Miller.
1846	Dr. Samuel E. Kerr.........	G. A. Miller.
1848	John A. Lillington..........	M. Clement.
1850	John A. Lillington..........	Stephen Douthitt
1852	John A. Lillington..........	B. Gaither.
1854	C. F. Fisher................	W. B. Marsh.
1856	J. G. Ramsay...............	W. B. Marsh.
1858	J. G. Ramsay...............	B. Gaither.
1860	J. G. Ramsay...............	H. B. Howard.
1862	J. G. Ramsay...............	H. B. Howard.
1864	W. B. Marsh	R. F. Johnston.
1866	Robert F. Johnston.........	J. H. Clement.
1868	Wm. M. Robbins...........	James A. Kelley.
1870	W. M. Robbins.............	James A. Kelley.
1872	Charles Price...............	Charles Anderson.

DUPLIN COUNTY.

Duplin County was formed as early as 1749, from upper part of New Hanover county. Its early settlers were Irish, and the name reminded them of Dublin, their ancient capital.

It is located in the south-eastern part of North Carolina, and is bounded on the north by Wayne and Lenoir counties, on the east by Lenoir, Jones and Onslow, on the south by New Hanover, and west by Sampson county.

Its capital is Kenansville, distant eighty-nine miles east of Raleigh.

COUNTY OFFICERS.

Offices.	Names.
Superior Court Clerk....................	John D. Southerland.
Register of Deeds.........................	James M. Sprunt.
Sheriff..	Bland Wallace.
Coroner..	E. B. Herring.
Surveyor......................................	Joseph J. Ward.
Treasurer	John A. McArthur.
Commissioners.............................	D. T. McMillan, Chairman. D. J. Middleton. Joel Loftin. George W. Lamb. Jacob Smith.

DUPLIN COUNTY.—CONTINUED.

JUSTICES OF THE PEACE.

Names.	Date of Qualification.	Post Office Address.
Rhaford Lanier	Sept. 1st, 1873.	Cypress Creek.
Nicanor James, Jr	" "	Chinquepin.
D. G. Morisey	" "	Warsaw.
Daniel Bowden	" "	Warsaw.
W. H. Winders	" "	Warsaw.
C. D. Hill	" "	Faison's.
M. Moore	" "	Warsaw.
H. Broadhurst	" "	Mount Olive.
Kinsey Jones	" "	Branch's Store.
Henry Dail	" "	Branch's Store.
Lewis Herring	" "	Branch's Store.
Jas. G. Branch	" "	Branch's Store.
W. H. Grady	" "	Albretson's.
Jos. E. Hornegay	" "	Outlaw's Bridge.
John R. Miller	" "	Sarecta.
John G. Smith	" "	Sarecta.
Wm. Sandlin	" "	Hallsville.
Edward Armstrong	" "	Hallsville.
W. J. Boney	" "	Wallace.
G. J. McMillan	" "	Teacheys.
O. W. Murray	" "	Teacheys.
Jo. J. Ward	" "	Teacheys.
R. C. Johnson	" "	Warsaw.
O. J. Carroll	" "	Magnolia.
Jas. Usher	" "	Magnolia.
W. A. Moore	" "	Magnolia.
G. W. Carroll	" "	Kenansville.
W. D. Pearsall	" "	Kenansville.
Jno. A. Bryan	Jan. 5th, 1874.	Kenansville.

MEMBERS OF GENERAL ASSEMBLY.

Years.	Senate.	House.
1777	James Kenan	Richard Clinton, Robert Dickson.
1778	James Kenan	Richard Clinton, Thos. Hicks.
1779	James Kenan	Richard Clinton, James Gillaspie.
1780	James Kenan	Joseph Dickson, James Gillaspie.
1782	Jamss Kenan	Richard Clinton, James Gillaspie.
1783	James Kenan	James Gillaspie, Richard Clinton.
1784	James Gillaspie	Robert Dickson, Richard Clinton.
1785	James Gillaspie	Robert Dickson, Jos. T. Rhodes.
1786	James Gillaspie	Jos. T. Rhodes, Robert Dickson.
1787	James Kenan	Robert Dickson, Charles Ward.
1788	James Kenan	Robert Dickson, Charles Ward.
1791	James Kenan	Jos. T. Rhodes, James Pearsall.

DUPLIN COUNTY—Continued.

MEMBERS OF GENERAL ASSEMBLY—Continued.

Years.	Senate.	House.
1792	James Gillaspie	Shadrach Stallings, William Beck.
1793	James Kenan	Jos. T. Rhodes, Jas. Pearsall.
1794	Levin Watkins	Daniel Glisson, Jos. T. Rhodes.
1795	Levin Watkins	Wm. Dickson, James Middleton.
1796	Jos. T. Rhodes	Daniel Glisson, James Middleton.
1797	Jos. T. Rhodes	Joseph Dixon, Daniel Glisson.
1798	Levin Watkins	Shadrach Stallings, Thos. Kenan.
1799	Levin Watkins	Thomas Kenan, Daniel Glisson.
1800	Levin Watkins	Charles Hooks, Thos. Kenan.
1801	Levin Watkins	Shadrach Stallings, Charles Hooks.
1802	Levin Watkins	Charles Hooks, Daniel Glisson.
1803	Levin Watkins	Charles Hooks, Daniel Glisson.
1804	Thomas Kenan	Charles Hooks, Hugh McCanne.
1805	Joseph T. Rhodes	Daniel Glisson, Hugh McCanne.
1806	Joseph T. Rhodes	Daniel Glisson, Andrew McIntire.
1807	Joseph T. Rhodes	Daniel Glisson, Andrew McIntyre.
1808	Joseph T. Rhodes	Daniel Glisson, Andrew McIntyre.
1809	oseph T. Rhodes	Daniel Glisson, David Wright.
1810	Charles Hooks	Daniel Glisson, David Wright.
1811	Charles Hooks	David Wright, Daniel Glisson.
1812	Stephen Miller	David Wright, John Beck.
1813	Joseph Gillaspie	David Wright, John Beck.
1814	Joseph Gillaspie	David Wright, —— Kornegay.
1815	Joseph Gillaspie	David Wright, John E. Hussey.
1816	Daniel Glisson	John Pearsall, John E. Hussey.
1817	Daniel Glisson	John Pearsall, John E. Hussey.
1818	Daniel Glisson	John Pearsall, John E. Hussey.
1819	Daniel Glisson	John Pearsall, Stephen Graham.
1820	Daniel Glisson	Stephen Graham, James Nixon.
1821	Daniel L. Kenan	John Waitkins, Andrew Hurst.
1822	Daniel Glisson	Jas. M. Nixon, Archd. Maxwell.
1823	Jeremiah Pearsall	Stephen Miller, Wm. H. Frederick.
1824	Jeremiah Pearsall	James M. Nixon, Stephen Miller.
1825	John E. Hussey	Benjamin Best, Stephen Miller.
1826	Stephen Miller	Benjamin Best, Wm. K. Frederick.
1827	Andrew Hurst	Daniel Glisson, Jos. Gillaspie.
1828	Stephen Miller	Wm. Wright, Jos. Gillaspie.
1829	Stephen Miller	Wm. Wright, John Farrier.
1830	Stephen Miller	Wm. Wright, Wm. K. Frederick.
1831	Stephen Miller	Wm. Wright, Jos. Gillaspie.
1832	John E. Hussey	Jos. Gillaspie, Alex. O. Grady.
1833	John E. Hussey	Alex. O. Grady, Jos. Gillaspie.
1834	John E. Hussey,	Jas. K. Hill, Owen R. Kenan.
1835	John E. Hussey	Jas. K. Hill, Owen R. Kenan.
1836	John E. Hussey	Owen R. Kenan, Jas. H. Jarman.
1838	Jas. K. Hill	Jas. H. Jarman, Hampton Sullivan.
1840	Jas. K. Hill	Jas. G. Dickson, Hampton Sullivan.
1842	Austin Levinson	Isaac B. Kelly, Jas. G. Dickson.
1844	James K. Hill	I. B. Kelly, J. G. Dickson.
1846	James K. Hill	I. B. Kelly, I. P. Davis.
1848	Stephen Traham	I. B. Kelly, J. G. Dickson.
1850	B. W. Hening	I. B. Kelly, N. P. Matthis.
1852	B. W. Hening	David Reid, W. A. Hill.
1854	B. W. Hening	N. B. Whitford, W. J. Houston.

DUPLIN COUNTY.—Continued.

MEMBERS OF GENERAL ASSEMBLY.—Continued.

Years.	Senate.	House.
1856	W. J. Houston	B. Southerland, W. R. Ward.
1858	W. J. Houston	J. D. Stanford, W. P. Ward.
1860	Jas. Dickson	J. D. Stanford, J. J. Branch.
1862	Jas. Dickson	J. D. Stanford, L. W. Hodges.
1864	R. W. Ward	H. M. Faison, Z. Smith.
1866	Isaac B. Kelly	T. S. Kenan, Z. Smith.
1868	Wm. A. Allen	Isaac B. Kelly, N. E. Armstrong.
1870	Wm. A. Allen	John D. Stanford, N. E. Armstrong.
1872	Wm. A. Allen L. W. Humphrey	John D. Stanford, J. K. Outlaw.

Duplin and Wayne form the 10th Senatorial District.

EDGECOMBE COUNTY.

Edgecombe County was formed from Craven county in 1733, by the Governor (Burrington) and Council, and confirmed by the Legislature, which met at Edenton in 1741.

Its name is Saxon, and signifies "a valley environed with hills," and is derived from the Earl of Mount Edgecombe, who, as Capt. Edgecombe, of the navy, had served with reputation under Admiral Byng, in 1756, in Minorca.

It is located in the eastern part of North Carolina, and is bounded on the north by Halifax county, east by Martin county, south by Pitt, Wilson and Wayne counties, and west by Nash county.

Tarborough is the capital, on the Tar River, distant from Raleigh 76 miles. The original name of Tar River was *Tau*, which, in the native Indian tongue, means "River of Health."

COUNTY OFFICERS.

Offices.	Names.
Superior Court Clerk	John Norfleet.
Register of Deeds	B. J. Keech.
Sheriff	Battle Bryan.
Coroner	None.
Surveyor	None.
Treasurer	Robert H. Austin.
Commissioners	Micajah P. Edwards, Chairman. Napoleon B. Bellamy. McD. Mathewson. Wm. T. Godwin. ———

EDGECOMBE COUNTY—Continued.

JUSTICES OF THE PEACE.

Names.	Date of Qualification.	Post Office Address.
C. S. Cowper	Sept. 1st, 1873.	Tarboro.
R. S. Taylor	" "	Tarboro.
McDonald Mathewson	" "	Tarboro.
F. U. Whitted	" "	Tarboro.
Isaac J. Hargiss	" "	Tarboro.
George W. Howard	" "	Tarboro.
H. E. Barfield	" "	Tarboro.
N. B. Bellamy	" "	Tarboro.
Dempsey Batts	" "	Tarboro.
Almus Hart	" 3rd, 1873.	Tarboro.
Benj. Johnson	" 1st, "	Tarboro.
L. G. Estes	" "	Enfield.
Jas. W. Draughan	" "	Whitaker's.
E. W. Wilcox	" "	Whitaker's.
Willis Bunn	" "	Battleboro'.
K. C. Pope	" "	Battleboro'.
Theophilus Thomas	" "	Rocky Mount.
Wm. T. Gay	" "	Rocky Mount.
John N. Taylor	" "	Rocky Mount.
Wm. A. Duggan	" "	Tarboro.
Dempsey Thorn	" "	Tarboro.
R. S. Williams	" "	Tarboro.
William R. Cobb	" "	Sparta.
Richard Johnson	" "	Sparta.
Elisha Harrell	" "	Sparta.
Robert Walston	" "	Sparta.
Isaac C. Mann	" "	Sparta.
David Lane	" "	Tarboro.
John Lancaster	" "	Tarboro.
Wells Dawes	" "	Sharpsburg.
John J. Proctor	" "	Sharpsburg.

MEMBERS OF GENERAL ASSEMBLY.

Years.	Senate.	House.
1777	Elisha Battle	Jonas Johnston, Nathan Boddie.
1778	Elisha Battle	Jonas Johnston, Isaac Sessums.
1779	Elisha Battle	William Haywood, Etheldred Exum.
1780	Elisha Battle	Etheldred Gray, Henry Horn, jr.
1781	Elisha Battle	Robert Diggs. James Wilson.
1782	Isaac Sessums	Robert Diggs, James Wilson.
1783	Elisha Battle	Robert Diggs, James Wilson.
1784	Isaac Sessums	Robert Diggs, John Dobien.
1785	Elisha Battle	Etheldred Phillips, Robert Diggs.
1786	Elisha Battle	Etheldred Phillips, Robert Diggs.
1787	Elisha Battle	Robert Diggs, John Dobien.
1788	Etheldred Gray	Wm. Fort, Joshua Killibrew.
1789	Etheldred Gray	John Leigh, Bythel Bell.
1790	Etheldred Philips	John Leigh, Bythel Bell.

EDGECOMBE COUNTY—Continued.

MEMBERS OF GENERAL ASSEMBLY—Continued.

Years.	Senate.	House.
1791	Etheldred Phillips	John Leigh, Bythel Bell.
1792	Etheldred Phillips	John Leigh, Thomas Blount.
1793	Etheldred Phillips	John Leigh, Jeremiah Hilliard.
1794	William Gray	John Leigh, Jeremiah Hilliard.
1795	William Gray	John Leigh, David Coffield.
1796	Nathan Mayo	Bythel Bell, John Leigh.
1797	Nathan Mayo	Nathan Gilbert, Frederic Phillips.
1798	Thomas Blount	Adam J. Haywood, Jeremiah Haywood.
1799	Thomas Blount	Lawrence O'Bryen, Jeremiah Hilliard.
1800	Bythell Bell	Jeremiah Hilliard, Wm. Hyman.
1801	Richard Harrison	Jeremiah Hilliard, George Brownrigg.
1802	Richard Harrison	George Brownrigg, Jeremiah Hilliard.
1803	Richard Harrison	Jeremiah Hilliard, George Brownrigg.
1804	Richard Harrison	George Brownrigg, Henry Haywood.
1805	Richard Harrison	Joseph Farmer, L. W. Sumner.
1806	Richard Harrison	L. W. Sumner, Henry I. Toole.
1807	Richard Harrison	Henry I. Toole, John Cotton.
1808	Henry I. Toole	Nathan Stancie, Hardy Flowers.
1809	Henry I. Toole	Hardy Flowers, Wm. Balfour.
1810	Henry I. Toole	Jas. W. Clarke, Hardy Flowers.
1811	Henry I. Toole	Wm. Balfour, Jas. W. Clarke.
1812	James W. Clark	Joseph Farmer, James Benton.
1813	James W. Clark	Joseph Farmer, James Benton.
1814	James W. Clark	Joseph Farmer, James Benton.
1815	Joseph Bell	James Benton, Louis D. Wilson.
1816	Joseph Bell	James Benton, Louis D. Wilson.
1817	James Benton	Louis D. Wilson, John Horn.
1818	James Benton	Louis D. Wilson, John Horn.
1819	James Benton	L. D. Wilson, Moses Baker.
1820	Louis D. Wilson	William Wilkins, Moses Baker.
1821	Hardy Flowers	Jos. R. Lloyd, William Wilkins.
1822	Hardy Flowers	William Wilkins, Moses Baker.
1823	Hardy Flowers	illiam Wilkins, Moses Baker.
1824	Louis D. Wilson	Henry Bryan, Richard Hines.
1825	Louis D. Wilson	Henry Bryan, Moses Baker.
1826	Louis D. Wilson	Benj. Sharpe, Hardy Flowers.
1827	Louis D. Wilson	Benj. Sharpe, Benj. Wilkinson.
1828	Louis D. Wilson	Benj. Sharpe, Benj. Wilkinson.
1829	Louis D. Wilson	Moses Baker, Gray Little.
1830	Louis D. Wilson	Hardy Flowers, Gray Little.
1831	Louis D. Wilson	Redding Pittman, Hardy Flowers.
1832	Louis D. Wilson	Gray Little, John W. Potts.
1833	Hardy Flowers	John W. Potts, Turner Bynum.
1834	Hardy Flowers	John W. Potts, Turner Bynum.
1835	Benjamin Sharpe	S. Deberry, Jos. J. Pipkin.
1836	Thomas H. Hall	Jos. . Daniel, James George.
1838	Louis D. Wilson	Robert Bryan, W. S. Baker.
1840	Louis D. Wilson	W. S. Baker, Joshua Barnes.
1842	Louis D. Wilson	Joshua Barnes, R. E. McNair.
1844	Louis D. Wilson	Joshua Barnes, R. R. Bridgers.
1846	Louis D. Wilson	Wyatt Moye, m. F. Dancy.
1848	Wyatt Moye	Wm. F. Dancy, Wm. Thigpen.
1850	Henry T. Clark	oshua Barnes, Kenneth Thigpen.
1852	Henry T. Clark	m. Norfleet, W. Ellis.
1854	Henry T. Clark	Joshua Barnes, David Williams.

EDGECOMBE COUNTY.—CONTINUED.

MEMBERS OF GENERAL ASSEMBLY—CONTINUED.

Years.	Senate.	House.
1856	Henry T. Clark	R. R. Bridgers, J. S. Dancey.
1858	Henry T. Clark	R. R. Bridgers, J. S. Dancey.
1860	Henry T. Clark	R. R. Bridgers, J. H. Woodard.
1862	Jesse H. Powell	David Cobb, Robert Bynum.
1864	Jesse H. Powell	D. Cobb, L. D. Farmer.
1866	Henry T. Clark	J. H. Baker, J. H. Woodard.
1868	N. B. Bellamy	George Peck, J. H. Woodard.
1870	N. B. Bellamy	R. M. Johnson, Willis Bunn.
1872	Henry Eppes	Willis Bunn, David Cobb.

Edgecombe is the 5th Senatorial District.

FORSYTHE COUNTY.

FORSYTHE COUNTY was formed in 1848, from Stokes County.

Forsythe County derives its name from Col. Benjamin Forsythe, of Stokes County, who resided in Germantown. In 1807 he represented Stokes County in the House of Commons.

In the war of 1812 he was appointed a Captain of a Rifle Company, and marched to Canada, where, in a skirmish in 1814, he was killed.

It is located in the north-western part of the State, and is bounded on the north by Stokes County, east by Guilford County, south by Davidson County, and west by Yadkin County.

Its capital is WINSTON, and is distant from Raleigh one hundred and ten miles. This village preserves the name of Joseph Winston, who rendered important military services in the revolution, and civil service since.

COUNTY OFFICERS.

Offices.	Names.
Superior Court Clerk	John Blackburn.
Register of Deeds	C. S. Hauser.
Sheriff	J. G. Hill.
Coroner	Aug. Fogle.
Surveyor	John W. Jones.
Treasurer	R. F. Linville
Commissioners	Sam'l. B. Stauber. A. E. Conrad. David Smith. Anderson Nicholson. Philip Kerner.

FORSYTHE COUNTY—Continued.

JUSTICES OF THE PEACE.

Names.	Date of Qualification.	Post Office Address.
Thomas T. Best	August 9th, 1873.	Winston.
John M. Stafford	" "	Salem.
Romulus S. Linville	" "	Kernersville.
Thomas M. Marshall	" "	Salem Chapel.
Jesse F. Grubbs	" "	Salem Chapel.
John H. Cox	" "	Old Town.
John H. Chamelin	" 11th, "	Abbott's Creek.
Lorenzo F. Weavil	" "	Abbott's Creek.
John H. Morris	" 15th, "	Walkertown.
Wm. A. Harper	" "	Lewisville.
John Masten	" 12th, "	Winston.
Joseph B. Bodenhamer	" 15th, "	Winston.
Henry W. Fries	" "	Salem.
Charles T. Pope	" "	Salem.
Fewel Fulton	" "	Salem Chapel.
Phillip Mock	" "	Vienna.
Nath'l. F. Sullivan	" "	Sedge Garden.
Abraham P. Styers	" "	Bethania.
V. W. Perry	" "	Kernersville.
M. V. B. Warner	" "	Lewisville.
Thomas Spaugh	" "	Salem.
H. R. Lehman	" "	Vienna.
Philip Billeter	" "	Old Town.
Augustus Fogle	" "	Salem.
William Spainhour	Dec. 15th, "	Bethania.

MEMBERS OF GENERAL ASSEMBLY.

Years.	Senate.	House.
1854	J. J. Martin	J. A. Waugh, Allen Flynt.
1856	J. J. Martin	J. A. Waugh, J. Mastin.
1858	J. J. Martin	F. Fries, J. Masten.
1860	Jesse A. Waugh	John F. Poindexter, Philip Barrow.
1862	Jas. E. Matthews	John P. Nissen, E. Kerner.
1864	Jas. E. Matthews	W. H. Wheeler, W. P. Stike.
1866	Jas. E. Matthews	P. A. Wilson, E. B. Teague.
1868	Peter A. Wilson	John P. Vest.
1870	—— Adams	John. P. Nisson.
1872	John M. Stafford	Wm. H. Wheeler.

Forsythe and Stokes form the thirty-second District.

FRANKLIN COUNTY.

FRANKLIN COUNTY was founded in 1779. The General Assembly in that year obliterated the name of Bute, and divided its territory into the counties of Franklin and Warren. It derives its name from Benjamin Franklin, the Philosopher and Sage, who rendered such signal services to his country in the Revolution in a civil capacity. He was born January 1706, in Boston, and died in Philadelphia, April, 1790, where he lies buried.

It is located near the centre of the State, joining Wake County, in which is the seat of Government. Bounded on the north by Warren, east by Nash, south and west by Wake.

Its capital is LOUISBURG, and is distant 36 miles north-east of Raleigh.

COUNTY OFFICERS.

Offices.	Name.
Superior Court Clerk	Dr. R. H. Timberlake.
Register of Deeds	Jno. B. Tucker.
Sheriff	James C. Wynne.
Coroner	None, special appointments made.
Surveyor	None, special appointments made.
Treasurer	B. P. Clifton.
Commissioners	Gen. P. B. Hawkins, Chairman. Thos. K. Thomas. Joshua Perry. B. F. Bullock, jr. Henry W. Fuller, (col.)

JUSTICES OF THE PEACE.

Names.	Date of Qualification.	Post Office Address.
M. T. Hawkins	Sept. 17th, 1873.	Kittrell.
N. H. Woodliff	" "	Kittrell.
W. K. Phillips	" "	Youngsville.
F. P. Pearce	" "	Youngsville.
N. Davis	" 1st, "	Louisburg.
A. Thomas	" "	Louisburg.
Joshua Perry	" "	Louisburg.
Archibald Taylor	" "	Louisburg.
W. H. Mitchell	" "	Franklinton.
L. L. Long	" "	Franklinton.
John Perry	" "	Franklinton.
Ned Alston	" "	Louisburg.
H. B. Webb	" "	Louisburg.
Thos. K. Thomas	Jan. 1st, 1874.	Louisburg.
Calvin Pippin	Oct. 6th, 1873.	Louisburg.
W. A. Moore	" "	Louisburg.

FRANKLIN COUNTY.—CONTINUED.

JUSTICES OF THE PEACE—CONTINUED.

Names.	Date of Qualification.	Post Office Address.
J. J. Jones........................	Sept. 17th, 1873.	Louisburg.
J. B. Littlejohn..................	" "	Louisburg.
M. N. Young......................	Nov. 21st, "	Louisburg.
A. S. P. Harris..................	" "	Youngsville.
Wm. Mitchell.....................	Sept. 17th, "	Franklinton.
W. K. Martin, jr.................	" "	Youngsville.

MEMBERS OF GENERAL ASSEMBLY.

Years.	Senate.	House.
1780	Henry Hill.................	Joseph Bryant, William Brickell.
1781	Henry Hill.................	William Brickell, William Green.
1782	Henry Hill.................	William Brickell, William Green.
1783	A. M. Foster...............	Simon Jeffreys, Harrison Macon.
1784	Henry Hill.................	Durham Hall, Thomas Sherrod.
1785	Henry Hill	Durham Hall, Thomas Sherrod.
1786	Henry Hill.................	Durham Hall, Richard Ranjoin.
1787	Henry Hill.................	Thomas Sherrod, Jordan Hill.
1788	Thomas Brickell............	Jordan Hill, Brittain Harris.
1789	Henry Hill.................	Thomas Sherrod, Durham Hall.
1790	Henry Hill.................	Thomas Sherrod, Jordan Hill.
1791	Henry Hill.................	Archibald Davis, John Foster.
1792	William Christmas..........	John Foster, Thomas K. Wynn.
1793	William Christmas..........	John Foster, Brittain Harris.
1794	Henry Hill.................	John Foster, Brittain Harris.
1795	Henry Hill.................	Brittain Harris, Archibald Davis.
1796	James Gray.................	Brittain Harris, Archibald Davis.
1797	Henry Hill.................	John Foster, Brittain Harris.
1798	Henry Hill.................	John Foster, Archibald Davis.
1799	Jordan Hill................	Brittain Harris, Archibald Davis.
1800	Jordan Hill................	Brittain Harris, Thomas Lanier.
1801	Jordan Hill................	Eppes Moody, James Seawell.
1802	Jordan Hill................	Eppes Moody, James Seawell.
1803	Jordan Hill................	Brittain Harris, James Seawell.
1804	John Foster................	Eppes Moody, Brittain Harris.
1805	John Foster................	Eppes Moody, James J. Hill.
1806	John Foster................	Eppes Moody, Thomas Lanier.
1807	John Foster................	Eppes Moody, Thomas Lanier.
1808	John Foster................	James J. Hill, Thomas J. Alston.
1809	Benjamin Brickell..........	James J. Hill, Thomas Lanier.
1810	Benjamin Brickell..........	Eppes Moody, Thomas Lanier.
1811	Benjamin Brickell..........	Benjamin F. Hawkins, Eppes Moody.
1812	James J. Hill..............	Thomas Lanier, Benjamin F. Hawkins.
1813	James J. Hill..............	Benjamin F. Hawkins, Thomas Lanier.
1814	Benjamin F. Hawkins.......	Thomas Lanier, Nathaniel Hunt.
1815	Thomas Lanier..............	Nathaniel Hunt, Marma. D. Jeffreys.
1816	Benjamin F. Hawkins.......	Nathaniel Hunt, Marma. D. Jeffreys.
1817	James J. Hill..............	James Houze, William Harrison.

FRANKLIN COUNTY—Continued.

MEMBERS OF GENERAL ASSEMBLY—Continued.

Years.	Senate.	House.
1818	James J. Hill	William Harrison, James Houze.
1819	Benjamin F. Hawkins	M. N. Jeffreys, T. Terrell.
1820	James Houze	William Moore, Jas. Hill.
1821	James Houze	Wm. Moore, M. W. Jeffries.
1822	James Houze	Lark Fox, Guilford Lewis.
1823	Charles A. Hill	Lark Fox, Guilford Lewis.
1824	Charles A. Hill	Lark Fox, Guilford Lewis.
1825	Charles A. Hill	William J. Williams, James Houze.
1826	Charles A. Hill	James Houze, Joel King.
1827	James Houze	Joel King, Henry J. G. Ruffin.
1828	Henry J. G. Ruffin	Richard Ward, William J. Branch.
1829	William P. Williams	William J. Branch, Thomas J. Russell.
1830	William P. Williams	William J. Branch, Gideon Glenn.
1831	William P. Williams	Gideon Glenn, James Davis.
1832	William P. Williams	Alfred A. Lancaster, Nath. R. Tunstall.
1833	Thomas G. Stone	William H. Battle, Jos. J. Maclin.
1834	John D. Hawkins	William H. Battle, Jos. J. Maclin.
1835	Henry G. Williams	Thomas Howerton, Simon G. Jeffreys.
1836	John D. Hawkins	Thomas Howerton, Jos. J. Maclin.
1838	John D. Hawkins	Thomas Howerton, William P. Williams.
1840	John D. Hawkins	Young Patterson, Thomas Howerton.
1842	William P. Williams	Young Patterson, John E. Thomas.
1844	William A. Jeffreys	William K. Martin, James Collins.
1846	John E. Thomas	William K. Martin, James Collins.
1848	James Collins	William K. Martin, D. W. Spring.
1850	James Collins	William K. Martin, Josiah Bridges.
1852	James Collins	William K. Martin, J. Hawkins.
1854	James Collins	William K. Martin.
1856	P. B. Hawkins	L. A. Jeffries.
1858	M. Lankford	W. F. Greene.
1860	W. Harris	W. F. Greene.
1862	W. Harris	A. W. Pierce.
1864	W. Harris	W. K. Davis.
1866	W. Harris	Jos. J. Davis.
1868	W. D. Jones R. I. Wynne	Jas. T. Harris, J. A. Williamson.
1870	L. P. Olds P. B. Hawkins	Jas. T. Harris, J. A. Williamson.
1872	John W. Dunham Wm. K. Davis	Jas. T. Harris, J. A. Williamson.

Franklin, Nash and Wilson form the seventh Senatorial District.

GASTON COUNTY.

GASTON COUNTY was formed in 1846, from Lincoln county, and derives its name from William Gaston, late one of the Judges of the Supreme Court.

It is situated in the south-western part of the State, and is bounded on the north by Lincoln county, east by the Catawba river, which separates it from Mecklenburg county, south by the South Carolina line, and west by Cleaveland county.

Its capital is Dallas, named in compliment to the Hon. George M. Dallas, of Philadelphia, who was Vice-President of the United States in 1844. Distance 175 miles from Raleigh. For many years Gaston county voted with Lincoln and Catawba.

COUNTY OFFICERS.

Offices.	Names.
Superior Court Clerk	Eli. H. Withers.
Register of Deeds	J. G. Lewis.
Sheriff	Robert D. Rhyne.
Coroner	James Q. Holland.
Surveyor	John B. White.
Treasurer	Thomas Wilson.
Commissioners	Richard Rankin, Chairman.
	William D. Glenn.
	Abram B. Titman.
	Ephraim Black.
	Marion D. Friday.

JUSTICES OF THE PEACE.

Names.	Date of Qualification.	Post Office Address.
E. A. Rudisell	Sept. 1st, 1873.	Cherryville.
H. B. Huffsteller	" "	Cherryville.
B. G. Bradley	" "	Dallas.
J. M. Whitesides	" "	Pleasant Ridge.
Wm. G. Warren	" "	South Point.
L. B. Gaston	" "	Pin Hook.
John Farrar	" "	Woodlawn.
W. G. Rutledge	" "	Stanley's Creek.
Miles Withers	" "	Dallas.
Caleb Pasour	" "	Dallas.
F. W. Thompson	" "	Dallas.

GASTON COUNTY—Continued.

MEMBERS OF GENERAL ASSEMBLY.

Years.	Senate.	House.
1856	Jas. H. White	Richard Rankin.
1858	F. D. Reinhart	—— Reagan.
1860	Jasper Stowe	Jas. H. White.
1862	James H. White	A. W. Davenport.
1864	M. L. McCorkle	W. T. Shipp.
1865	Wm. P. Bynum	D. A. Jenkins.
1866	M. L. McCorkle	D. A. Jenkins.
1868	Lawson A. Mason	Jonas Hoffman.
1870	E. Crowell	J. G. Gulick.
1872	W. J. T. Miller	W. A. Stowe.

Gaston and Cleaveland form the 38th District.

GATES COUNTY.

Gates County was formed in 1779, from Hertford, Chowan and Perquimans counties. It derives its name from Gen. Horatio Gates, who at this time was in the zenith of his popularity, having acquired a brilliant victory in 1777 at Saratoga, over General Burgoyne and the English army, but whose laurels were destined to fade on the unfortunate field of Camden.

It is situated in the north-eastern part of the State, and is bounded on the north by the Virginia line, east by Pasquotank, south by Perquimans and Chowan, and west by Hertford county.

Its capital is Gatesville, and is distant from Raleigh 167 miles.

COUNTY OFFICERS.

Offices.	Names.
Superior Court Clerk	R. B. G. Cowper.
Register of Deeds	L. P. Hayes.
Sheriff	B. F. Willey.
Coroner	Hance Hofler.
Surveyor	John Williams.
Treasurer	J. F. Cross.
Commissioners	H. A. Morgan, Chairman. W. P. Roberts. H. H. Hunter. R. H. Riddick. Riddick Gatling.

GATES COUNTY.—Continued.

JUSTICES OF THE PEACE.

Names.	Date of Qualification.	Post Office Address.
John Brady	Sept. 1st, 1873.	Gatesville.
John R. Walton	" "	Gatesville.
Mills H. Eure	" "	Gatesville.
Wm. P. Hayes	" "	Gatesville.
James Duke	" "	Gatesville.
Wm. H. Cross	" "	Gatesville.
John Willey	October, 1873.	Gatesville.
John F. Haslett	Sept. 1st, 1873.	Buckland.
Willie Wiggins	" "	Buckland.
Thomas Parker	" "	Sunsbury.
John R. Hill	" "	Sunsbury.
Joseph T. [illegible]orris	" "	Sunsbury.
John W. Hoiler	" "	Sunsbury.
James A. Roberts	" "	Gatesville.
Nathan O. Ward	" "	Gatesville.

MEMBERS OF GENERAL ASSEMBLY.

Years.	Senate.	House.
1780	James Gregory	Jethro Sumner, James Garrett.
1781	James Gregory	Jethro Sumner, Joseph Reddick.
1782	William Baker	Jethro Sumner, Joseph Reddick.
1783	Jacob Hunter	Joseph Reddick, David Rice.
1784	William Baker	Seth Reddick, Joseph Reddick.
1785	Joseph Reddick	Seth Reddick, David Rice.
1786	Joseph Reddick	Seth Eason, Seth Reddick.
1787	Joseph Reddick	Wm. Baker, John Baker.
1788	Joseph Reddick	Seth Eason, David Rice.
1789	Joseph Reddick	David Rice, Jas. B. Sumner,
1790	Joseph Reddick	David Rice, Jas. B. Sumner.
1791	Joseph Reddick	Thos. Granberry, Jas. B. Sumner
1792	Joseph Reddick	James Baker, Isaac Miller.
1793	Joseph Reddick	Henry Goodman, Miles Benton.
1794	Joseph Reddick	Wm. Lewis, Miles Benton.
1795	Joseph Reddick	Wm. Lewis, Humphrey Hudgins.
1796	Joseph Reddick	James Gatling, John C. Walton.
1797	Joseph Reddick	Humphrey Hudgins, James Gatling.
1798	Joseph Reddick	Humphrey Hudgins, Jas. Gatling.
1799	Joseph Reddick	Humphrey Hudgins, Jas. Gatling.
1800	Joseph Reddick	James Gatling, Humphrey Hudgins.
1801	Joseph Reddick	Humphrey Hudgins, Jas. Gatling.
1802	Joseph Reddick	Humphrey Hudgings, Elisha Hunter.
1803	Joseph Reddick	Humphrey Hudgings, Jas. Gatling.
1804	Joseph Reddick	Humphrey Hudgins, Willis Hoodley.
1805	Joseph Reddick	Humphrey Hudgins, J. D. Goodman.
1806	Joseph Reddick	Humphrey Hudgins, J. D. Goodman.
1807	Joseph Reddick	Humphrey Hudgins, Kedar Ballard.
1808	Joseph Reddick	Humphrey Hudgins, Kedar Ballard.

GATES COUNTY—Continued.

MEMBERS OF GENERAL ASSEMBLY—Continued.

Years.	Senate.	House.
1809	Joseph Reddick	Humphrey Hudgins, Kedar Ballard.
1810	Joseph Reddick	Humphrey Hudgins, Kedar Ballard.
1811	Joseph Reddick	John B. Baker, Humphrey Hudgins.
1812	Kedar Ballard	Robert Reddick, Humphrey Hudgins.
1813	Kedar Ballard	Robert Reddick, Richard Barnes.
1814	Kedar Ballard	Robert Reddick, Richard Barnes.
1815	Joseph Reddick	Robert Reddick, Humphrey Hudgins.
1816	Kedar Ballard	Humphrey Hudgins, Joseph Gordon.
1817	Joseph Reddick	Humphrey Hudgins, I. R. Hunter.
1818	John B. Baker	I. R. Hunter, John Mitchell.
1819	Humphrey Hudgins	David E. Sumner, Abraham Harrell.
1820	John B. Baker	W. W. Riddick, Wm. Barnes.
1821	John C. Gordon	W. W. Riddick, A. Harrell.
1822	John B. Baker	John Walton, A. Harrell.
1823	Abraham Harrell	W. W. Stedman, J. Walton.
1824	Abraham Harrell	John Walton, W. W. Stedman.
1825	Abraham Harrell	John Walton, W. W. Stedman.
1826	Edward R. Hunter	John Walton, W. W. Stedman.
1827	Abraham Harrell	W. W. Stedman, Lemuel Reddick.
1828	Abraham Harrell	W. W. Stedman, Lemuel Reddick.
1829	Wm. W. Cowper	W. W. Stedman, Riseup Rawls.
1830	Wm. W. Cowper	W. W. Stedman, John Willey.
1831	Wm. W. Cowper	Whitmell Stallings, Lemuel Reddick.
1832	Wm. W. Cowper	Whitmell Stallings, John Willey.
1833	John Walton	Lemuel Reddick, John Willey.
1834	W. W. Cowper	Lemuel Reddick, John Willey.
1835	W. W. Cowper	Whitmell Stallings, Lemuel Reddick.
1836	W. W. Cowper	Whitmell Stallings.
1838	Rufus K. Speed	Whitmell Stallings.
1840	Rufus K. Speed	Whitmell Stallings.
1842	Whitmell Stallings	John Willey.
1844	Whitmell Stallings	Reddick Gatlin.
1846	Whitmell Stallings	Reddick Gatlin.
1848	Henry Willey	Charles E. Ballard.
1850	Henry Willey	Mills H. Eure.
1852	Henry Willey	Mills H. Eure.
1854	Henry Willey	Mills H. Eure.
1856	R. Dillard	Hardy Parker.
1858	R. Dillard	Reddick Gatlin.
1860	M. L. Eure	John Boothe.
1862	M. L. Eure	Wm. H. Manning.
1864	M. L. Eure	R. H. Bond.
1866	H. Willey	W. H. Lee.
1868	Jos. W. Etheridge	John Gatlin.
1870	Rufus K. Speed; James C. Skinner	Reddick Gatlin.
1872	John L. Chamberlain; C. W. Grandy	R. H. Ballard.

Camden, Chowan, Currituck, Gates, Hertford, Pasquotank and Perquimans form the 1st Senatorial District.

GRAHAM COUNTY.

Graham County was formed in 1871-'72, from northern portion of Cherokee county, so called in compliment to Hon. William A. Graham.

It is bounded on the north by the Tennessee line, south by Clay county, east by Swain county, and west by Cherokee county.

Its capital is Robbinsville, about 350 miles from Raleigh.

With Jackson, Swain, Macon and Cherokee it forms the 42nd Senatorial District.

COUNTY OFFICERS.

Offices.	Names.
Superior Court Clerk	John G. Tatham.
Register of Deeds	William Carpenter.
Sheriff	William Holloway.
Coroner	Jacob W. Slaughter.
Surveyor	Reuben Carver.
Treasurer	John Barker.
Commissioners	Joseph J. Colvard, Chairman. N. F. Cooper. John Ghorley. George W. Hooper. David E. Hyde.

JUSTICES OF THE PEACE.

Names.	Date of Qualification.	Post Office Address.
Samuel P. Sherrill	Oct. 21st, 1872.	Robinsville.
Calvin Colvard	" "	Robinsville.
L. M. Medlin	" "	Robinsville.
J. T. Rose	" "	Robinsville.
M. B. Crisp	March 3rd, 1873.	Robinsville.
J. B. Caringer	June 14th, 1873.	Robinsville.
John Grant	" "	Robinsville.

GRANVILLE COUNTY.

GRANVILLE COUNTY was formed in 1746, from Edgecombe county, and was so called in honor of the owner of the soil.

The King of England (Charles the II.) granted to Sir George Carteret, and seven other English noblemen, in 1663, a charter for this region, with much more, and it was called Carolina from him. In 1729 these proprietors surrendered to the English crown all their franchises, except John (son of Sir George Carteret, who died in 1696.) He was afterwards created Earl of Granville. He retained his eighth part of the soil. The line was run in 1743. Lord Granville's territory was from 35 deg., 34 min. south, to the Virginia line on the north, and from the Atlantic Ocean on the east, to the Pacific Ocean on the west. A most princely domain.

Its situation is in the northern part of the State, and is bounded on the north by the Virginia line, east by Warren and Franklin counties, south by Wake, and west by Person and Orange counties.

Its capital is Oxford, 36 miles north of Raleigh.

COUNTY OFFICERS.

Offices.	Names.
Superior Court Clerk	Calvin Betts.
Register of Deeds	Augustus H. Cooke.
Sheriff	Jas. I. Moore.
Coroner	None.
Surveyor	Richard D. Jones.
Treasurer	Manly B. Jones.
Commissioners	Wm. H. Puryear, Chairman.
	Jas. A. Bullock.
	Wm. P. Hayes.
	B. B. Royster.
	Joseph C. Coley.

JUSTICES OF THE PEACE.

Names.	Date of Qualification.	Post Office Address.
Wyatt A. Belvin	Aug. 7th, 1873.	Henderson.
Jno. W. Ragland	" "	Henderson.
Wm. H. Hughes	" "	Henderson.
Willis Ragland	" "	Henderson.
B. L. Parrish	" "	Kittrell.
Braxton Hunt	" "	Kittrell.
Jno. S. Burwell	" "	Kittrell.
Wm. M. Blackwell	" "	Oxford.

GRANVILLE COUNTY—Continued.

JUSTICES OF THE PEACE—Continued.

Names.	Date of Qalifica-tion.	Post Office Address.
Wm. E. Bullock	Aug. 7th, 1863.	Tally Ho.
Jno. B. Green	" "	Dutchville.
Frank I. Tilley	" "	Dutchville.
B. D. Howard	" "	Tally Ho.
A. S. Carrington	" "	Tally Ho.
James M. Satterwhite	" "	Oxford.
S. H. Duncan	" "	Oxford.
Richard D. Jones	" "	Oak Hill.
M. S. Daniel	" "	Oak Hill.
Wilkins Stovall	" "	Sassafras Fork.
W. D. Marrow	" "	Sassafras Fork.
R. G. Sneed	" "	Townsville.
James W. Hart	" "	Townsville.
Bourbon Smith	" "	Oxford.
J. K. Wood	" "	Oxford.
H. T. Hughes	" "	Oxford.
Wm. H. Crews	" "	Oxford.
Wm. P. White	Sept. 11th, 1873.	Oxford.

MEMBERS OF GENERAL ASSEMBLY.

Years.	Senate.	House.
1777	Robert Harris	Thomas Person, John Penn.
1778	Robert Harris	Thornton Yancey, Thomas Person.
1779	Robert Harris	Thomas Person, Philemon Hawkins.
1780	Robert Harris	Thomas Person, Philemon Hawkins.
1781	Joseph Taylor	Thomas Person, Richard Henderson.
1782	William Gill	Thomas Person, Philemon Hawkins.
1783	Robert Harris	Thomas Person, Philemon Hawkins.
1784	John Taylor	Thomas Person, Thornton Yancey.
1785	Howell Lewis	Thomas Person, Philemon Hawkins.
1786	Howell Lewis	Thornton Yancey, Philemon Hawkins.
1787	Thomas Person	Thornton Yancey, Philemon Hawkins.
1788	Memucan Hunt	Thomas Person, Elijah Mitchell.
1789	Samuel Clay	Thornton Yancey, Philemon Hawkins.
1790	Samuel Clay	Thornton Yancey, Thomas Person.
1791	Samuel Clay	Elijah Mitchell, Thornton Yancey.
1792	William P. Little	Elijah Mitchell, Thornton Yancey.
1793	William P. Little	Thomas Person, Elijah Mitchell.
1794	William P. Little	James Vaughan, Thomas Person.
1795	William P. Little	Thomas Person, Thomas Taylor.
1796	William P. Little	Thomas Taylor, Elijah Mitchell.
1797	William P. Little	Thomas Taylor, Thomas Person.
1798	William P. Little	Thomas Taylor, Sterling Yancey.
1799	Washington Salter	Thomas Taylor, Sterling Yoncey.
1800	Thomas Taylor	Sterling Yancey, Benjamin E. Person.
1801	Thomas Taylor	John R. Eaton, Samuel Parker.

GRANVILLE COUNTY—Continued.

MEMBERS OF GENERAL ASSEMBLY—Continued.

Years.	Senate.	House.
1802	Thomas Taylor	John R. Eaton, Samuel Parker.
1803	Joseph Taylor	John Washington, Samuel Parker.
1804	Thomas Person	Barnett Pulliam, Henry Yancey.
1805	Thomas Person	John Washington, Henry Yancey.
1806	Thomas Person	Henry Yancey, William Robards.
1807	Thomas Person	Henry Yancey, John Washington.
1808	Thomas Taylor	Samuel Parker, William Robards.
1809	Thomas Taylor	William Hawkins, Henry Yancey.
1810	Thomas Taylor	Daniel Jones, William Hawkins.
1811	Thomas Taylor	William Hawkins, Daniel Jones.
1812	Thomas Person	Woodson Daniel, John R. Eaton.
1813	Thomas Falconer	John Hare, Woodson Daniel.
1814	Thomas Person	Benjamin Bullock, Daniel Jones.
1815	James Young	Daniel Jones, John J. Judge.
1816	Willis Lewis	Daniel Jones, John J. Judge.
1817	Willis Lewis	William Hawkins.
1818	Daniel Jones	Nath. M. Taylor, Benjamin M. Hester.
1819	Daniel Jones	Richard Sneed, Samuel Hillman.
1820	Thomas Person	Richard Sneed, Samuel Hillman.
1821	Jos. H. Bryan	Richard Sneed, Samuel Hillman.
1822	William M. Sneed	Robert Jeter, Thomas Hunt.
1823	William M. Sneed	Robert Jeter, William G. Bowers.
1824	James Nuttall	J. C. Taylor, William G. Bowers.
1825	William M. Sneed	John Glasgow, Nicholas Jones.
1826	William M. Sneed	Nicholas Jones, Willis Lewis.
1827	James Nuttall	John C. Taylor, John Glasgow.
1828	Thomas T. Hunt	James Wyche, Robert Potter.
1829	William M. Sneed	James Wyche, Spencer O'Brien.
1830	William M. Sneed	James Wyche, Spencer O'Brien.
1831	William M. Sneed	Spencer O'Brien, James Wyche.
1832	Thomas W. Norman	Spencer O'Brien, John C. Ridley.
1833	Thomas W. Norman	William R. Hargrove, James Wyche.
1834	James Wyche	Sandy Harris, Robert Potter.
1835	James Wyche	Chas. R. Eaton, Elijah Hester.
1836	John C. Taylor	Robert B. Gilliam, Chas. R. Eaton, William Flemming.
1838	John C. Taylor	Robt. B. Gilliam, Chas. R. Eaton, E. Hester.
1840	William A. Johnson	Robt. B. Gilliam, H. L. Robards, James A. Russell.
1842	Elijah Hester	J. M. Stone, Wm. Russell, Kemp P. Hill.
1844	George C. Eaton	J. M. Stone, J. M. Bullock, J. T. Littlejohn.
1846	James A. Russell	R. B. Gilliam, J. M. Bullock, J. M. Stone.
1848	John Hargrove	R. B. Gilliam, Geo. Green, N. E. Cannady.
1850	Nath. E. Cannady	Jas. S. Amis, Wm. R. Wiggins, L. Parham.
1852	Nath. E. Cannady	Wm. H. Lyon, W. Perry, J. S. Amis.
1854	C. H. K. Taylor	J. M. Bullock, W. H. Lyon, J. S. Amis.
1856	C. H. K. Taylor	T. L. Hayron, J. M. Bullock, T. B. Lyon.
1858	C. H. K. Taylor	T. L. Hayron, J. M. Bullock, T. B. Lyon.
1860	C. H. K. Taylor	J. M. Bullock, W. P. P. Jenkins, S. H. Cannady.

GRANVILLE COUNTY.—Continued.

MEMBERS OF GENERAL ASSEMBLY—Continued.

Years.	Senate.	House.
1862	R. W. Lassiter..............	R. B. Gilliam, J. S. Amis, Eugene Grissom.
1864	R. W. Lassiter..............	J. S. Amis, Eugene Grissom, P. P. Peace.
1866	John D. Bullock.......	E. B. Lyon. W. H. Jenkins, H. Freeman.
1868	R. W. Lassiter..............	J. W. Ragland, A. A. Crawford, Cuffee Mayo.
1870	R. W. Lassiter.......... J. Barnett..............	E. B. Lyon. T. L. Hargrove, W. H. Reavis
1872	Bourbon Smith..............	R. G. Sneed, H. T. Hughes.

Granville forms 21st Senatorial District.

GREENE COUNTY.

Until 1791, there was in North Carolina a county called Dobbs, in compliment to Arthur Dobbs, Royal Governor of the State in 1754. In 1791, Dobbs was divided into Lenoir and Glasgow, and in 1799, the name of Greene was substituted for that of Glasgow.

It was named in compliment to General Nathaniel Greene, who was one of the bravest, most sagacious, and most successful officers of the revolution, and the saviour of the south from the invasions of the British.

Greene county is situated in the south-eastern part of the State. Bounded on the north by Wilson, east by Pitt, south by Lenoir, and west by Wayne.

Its capital is Snow Hill, 89 miles east of Raleigh.

COUNTY OFFICERS.

Offices.	Names.
Superior Court Clerk....................	John D. Grimsley.
Register of Deeds........................	John C. Dixon.
Sheriff..	Wm. J. Taylor.
Coroner.......................................	Joseph G. Witherington.
Surveyor......................................	Samuel H. Edwards.
Treasurer.....................................	John Murphrey.
Commissioners........................	T. E. Hooker, Chairman. R. C. D. Beaman. Charles Best, (col.) W. T. Dixon. Ellis Dixon, (col.)

GREENE COUNTY.—CONTINUED.

JUSTICES OF THE PEACE.

Names.	Date of Qualification.	Post Office Address.
W. F. Dail	Sept. 1st, 1873.	Snow Hill.
John W. Taylor	" "	Snow Hill.
Marcus Sheppard	" "	Snow Hill.
W. P. Ormond	" "	Snow Hill.
Wm. A. Darden, jr	" "	Speight's Bridge.
W. T. Dixon	" "	Hookerton.
Blany Speight	" "	Hookerton.
Josiah Sugg	" "	Hookerton.
Jas. S. Smith	" "	Hookerton.

MEMBERS OF GENERAL ASSEMBLY.

Years.	Senators.	House.
1800	Robert White	Jonas Williams, Wm. Taylor.
1801	Hymrick Hooker	William Taylor, Jonas Williams.
1802	Hymrick Hooker	William Taylor, Jonas Williams.
1803	Hymrick Hooker	Jonas Williams, Henry Best.
1804	Hymrick Hooker	Jonas Williams, Alex. Kilpatrick.
1805	Hymrick Hooker	Jonas Williams, Alex. Kilpatrick.
1806	Hymrick Hooker	Jonas Williams, Kenchen Garland.
1807	Hymrick Hooker	Jonas Williams, H. J. G. Ruffin.
1808	W. V. Speight	H. J. G. Ruffin, Jonas Williams.
1809	W. V. Speight	H. J. G. Ruffin, Jonas Williams.
1810	W. V. Speight	Jonas Williams, Benj. Evans.
1811	W. V. Speight	Abraham Darden, Jonas Williams.
1812	W. V. Speight	Wm. Holliday, Abraham Darden.
1813	W. V. Speight	Wm. Pope, Wm. Holliday.
1814	W. V. Speight	J. C. Shepard, Wm. Pope.
1815	W. V. Speight	Wm. Pope, Jas. Eastwood.
1816	W. V. Speight	Jas. Eastwood, Wm. Pope.
1817	W. V. Speight	R. G. Bright, Wm. Pope.
1818	W. V. Speight	Reuben Wilcox, Wm. Pope.
1819	W. V. Speight	A. Darden, Wm. Pope.
1820	W. V. Speight	Abraham Darden, Wm. Pope.
1821	W. V. Speight	Hymrick Hooker, A. Darden.
1822	W. V. Speight	Chas. Edwards, Jesse Speight.
1823	Jesse Speight	R. G. Bright, Charles Edwards.
1824	Jesse Speight	Charles Edwards, R. H. F. Harper.
1825	Jesse Speight	Charles Edwards, R. H. F. Harper.
1826	Jesse Speight	Charles Edwards, Joseph Ellis.
1827	Jesse Speight	James Harper, Joseph Ellis.
1828	Jesse Speight	James Harper, Joseph Ellis.
1829	Wyatt Moye	James Harper, Arthur Speight.
1830	Wyatt Moye	James Harper, Elisha Uzzell.
1831	Wyatt Moye	Arthur Speight, James Harper.
1832	Wyatt Moye	James Harper, John Beamond.
1833	Wyatt Moye	James Harper, R. L. Allen.
1834	Wyatt Moye	James Harper, James Williams.
1835	Wyatt Moye	James Harper, Thomas Hooker.

GREENE COUNTY—CONTINUED.

MEMBERS OF GENERAL ASSEMBLY—CONTINUED.

Years.	Senate.	House.
1836	Wm. D. Moseley	Thomas Hooker.
1838	Wm. D. Moseley	James Williams.
1840	Jas. B. Whitfield	John W. Taylor.
1842	E. G. Speight	John W. Taylor.
1844	E. G. Speight	James Harper.
1846	E. G. Speight	James G. Edwards.
1848	E. G. Speight	James G. Edwards.
1850	E. G. Speight	B. F. Williams.
1852	J. P. Speight	B. F. Williams.
1854	J. P. Speight	B. F. Williams.
1856	J. P. Speight	A. D. Speight.
1858	J. P. Speight	A. D. Speight.
1860	J. P. Speight	A. D. Speight.
1862	Ed. Patrick	H. B. Best.
1864	J. P. Speight	H. B. Best.
1866	J. [illegible] Coward	F. [illegible] Roundtree.
1868	C. H. Brogden	Joseph Dixon.
1870	C. H. Brogden	— [illegible]ardy.
1872	R. [illegible]. King	Joseph Patrick.

Greene with Lenoir forms the 11th Senatorial District.

GUILFORD COUNTY.

GUILFORD COUNTY was erected in the year 1770, from Rowan and [illegible]range. It was called in compliment of Lord North, who in 1770, succeeded the Duke of Grafton as First Lord of the Treasury and Prime Minister. He was heir to the title of Guilford, and eventually succeeded to it as Earl of Guilford.

Its situation is west of Raleigh, and the county presents on the map a beautiful compact square; bounded on the north by Rockingham, east by Alamance, south by Randolph, and west by Forsythe and Davidson Counties.

Its capital is GREENSBORO', a most flourishing town, named in compliment of General Nathaniel Greene, 82 miles from Raleigh.

COUNTY OFFICERS.

Offices.	Names.
Superior Court Clerk	Abram Clapp.
Register of Deeds	Will. U. Steiner.
Sheriff	R. M. Stafford.
Coroner	James W. Albright.
Surveyor	John W. Freeman.

GUILFORD COUNTY.—Continued.

COUNTY OFFICERS—Continued.

Offices.	Names.
Treasurer	Wyatt W. Ragsdale.
Commissioners	Emsley Armfield, Chairman. James A. Stewart. R. K. Denny. L. C. Winchester. R. F. Sechrest.

JUSTICES OF THE PEACE.

Names.	Date of Qualification.	Post Office Address.
Arington Dillworth	Aug. 16th, 1773.	Greensboro'.
A. P. Eckle	" "	Greensboro',
A. M. Kirkman	" "	Greensboro'.
Wm. E. Edwards	" 15th "	Greensboro'.
Geo. H. Parker	" 20th, "	Greensboro'.
Justin Bothwell	Oct. 8th, "	Greensboro'.
S. S. Gant	Sept. 2nd, "	Alamance.
D. P. Foust	Aug. 20th, "	Deep River.
L. F. Davis	" 15th, "	Deep River.
J. A. Davis	" "	New Garden.
John V. Lindley	" "	Hillsdale.
Obed McMichael	" 19th, "	Hillsdale.
J. J. Busick	" "	Company Mills.
Mebane Apple	" 22nd, "	Long's Mills.
A. G. Amick	" 26th, "	Gibsonville.
A. G. Clapp	" 30th, "	Brown's Summit.
B. G. Chilcut	Sept. 2nd, "	Summerfield.
Archibald Wilson	" "	Brick Church.
John J. Clapp	" 1st, "	Colfax.
F. S. Davis	Aug. 27th, "	Hillsdale.
Austin Reid	Sept. 1st, "	Gilmer's Store.
John C. Hunter	Nov. 3rd, "	Morehead.
James Gant	" "	Center.
T. C. Lamb	Oct. 1st, "	Deep River.
W. W. Wheeler	" 23d, "	Oak Ridge.
Charles Case	Sept. 13th, "	Greensboro'.
W. P. Whorton	Aug. 19th, "	Gibsonville.
W. P. Heath	" 16th, "	Jamestown.
Ithamer Armfield	" "	Friendship.
A. H. Lindsay	" "	Greensboro'.
A. H. Scott	Sept. 1st, "	Jamestown.
P. H. Hodson	" "	Gilmer's Store.
W. F. Thom	" "	Fentress.
W. D. Harden	" "	Gibsonville.
N. P. Rankin	" "	Oak Ridge.
T. J. Benbow	" "	Hillsdale.
Thomas Case	" "	Gilmer's Store.
Paul Coble		Greensboro'.
Henry Clapp	Sept. 1st, "	High Point.
Joseph Worth	" 2d, "	High Point.

GUILFORD COUNTY.—CONTINUED.

MEMBERS OF GENERAL ASSEMBLY.

Years.	Senate.	House.
1777	Ralph Gorrell	John Collier, Robert Lindsay.
1778	Ralph Gorrell	James Hunter, Robert Lindsay.
1779	Alexander Martin	James Hunter, Daniel Gillespie.
1780	Alexander Martin	James Hunter, William Gowdy.
1781	Alexander Martin	William Gowdy, James Hunter.
1782	Alexander Martin	William Gowdy, James Hunter.
1783	Charles Bruce	James Galloway, John Leak.
1784	James Galloway	John Hamilton, John Leak.
1785	Alexander Martin	John Hamilton, Barzellai Gardner.
1786	William Gowdy	John Hamilton, B. Gardner.
1787	Alexander Martin	B. Gardner, William Gowdy.
1788	Alexander Martin	John Hamilton, William Gowdy.
1789	William Gowdy	John Hamilton, Daniel Gillespie.
1790	Daniel Gillespie	Hance Hamilton, Robert Hannah.
1791	Daniel Gillespie	Robert Hannah, B. Gardner.
1792	Daniel Gillespie	Robert Hannah, B. Gardner.
1793	Daniel Gillespie	R. Hannah, B. Gardner.
1794	Daniel Gillespie	B. Gardner, Robert Hannah.
1795	Daniel Gillespie	Hance Hamilton, Hance McCain.
1796	Ralph Gorrell	B. Gardner, Hance Hamilton.
1797	Hance McCain	Hance Hamilton, Samuel Lindsay.
1798	Hance McCain	Samuel Lindsay, George Bruce.
1799	Hance Hamilton	Samuel Lindsay, George Bruce.
1800	Hance Hamilton	Samuel Lindsay, Jonathan Parker.
1801	Samuel Lindsay	George Bruce, Jonathan Parker.
1802	George Bruce	Zaza Brashier, Jonathan Parker.
1803	Samuel Lindsay	John Moore, Jonathan Parker.
1804	Samuel Lindsay	Jonathan Parker, Zaza Brashier.
1805	Hance McCain	Z. Brashier, Richard Mendenhall.
1806	Hance McCain	Z. Brashier, Richard Mendenhall.
1807	Jonathan Parker	Robert Hannah, John Howell.
1808	Jonathan Parker	Robert Hannah, John Howell.
1809	Jonathan Parker	Robert Hannah, John Howell.
1810	Samuel Lindsay	Robert Hannah, William Armfield.
1811	Jonathan Parker	Robert Hannah, John Howell.
1812	Jonathan Parker	John Howell, Robert Lindsay.
1813	Jonathan Parker	Obed Macey, James Gibson.
1814	Jonathan Parker	James Gibson, James McNairy.
1815	Jonathan Parker	John Howell, James McNairy.
1816	John Caldwell	James McNairy, William Ryan.
1817	John Caldwell	William Ryan, Robert Donnell.
1818	John Caldwell	James McNairy, William Ryan.
1819	John M. Dick	R. Donnell, William Dickey.
1820	John W. Caldwell	John Rankin, David Worth.
1821	Jonathan Parker	John Gordon, William Adams.
1822	Jonathan Parker	Samuel Hunter, David Worth.
1823	Jonathan Parker	Samuel Hunter, David Worth.
1824	Jonathan Parker	William Unthank, James Neally.
1825	Jonathan Parker	F. L. Simpson, William Unthank.
1826	Jonathan Parker	F. L. Simpson, John M. Morehead.
1827	Jonathan Parker	F. L. Simpson, John M. Morehead.
1828	Jonathan Parker	F. L. Simpson, Geo. C. Mendenhall.
1829	John M. Dick	Geo. C. Mendenhall, F. L. Simpson.
1830	John M. Dick	Allen Peoples, Geo. C. Mendenhall.

GUILFORD COUNTY.—Continued.

MEMBERS OF GENERAL ASSEMBLY—Continued.

Years.	Senate.	House.
1831	John M. Dick	Amos Weaver, Allen Peeples.
1832	Jonathan Parker	Allen Peeples, David Thomas.
1833	Geo. C. Mendenhall	David Thomas, Allen Peeples.
1834	Jonathan Parker	Ralph Gorrell, Jesse H. Lindsay.
1835	Jas. T. Morehead	Jesse H. Lindsay, Ralph Gorrell.
1836	Jas. T. Morehead	Jesse H. Lindsay, Peter Adams, F. L. Simpson.
1838	Jas T. Morehead	Jesse H. Lindsay, William Doak, David Thomas.
1840	Jas. T. Morehead	George C. Mendenhall, William Doak, Jas. Brannock.
1842	Jas. T. Morehead	Geo. C. Mendenhall, William Doak, Joel McLean.
1844	Jesse H. Lindsay	William Doak, Joel McLean, John A. Smith.
1846	John A. Gilmer	Nathan Hunt, E. W. Ogburn, Peter Adams.
1848	John A. Gilmer	David F. Caldwell, Calvin Johnson, Jas. W. Doak.
1850	John A. Gilmer	David F. Caldwell, Calvin Henderson Wiley, Peter Adams.
1852	John A. Gilmer	C. Johnston, David F. Caldwell, C. H. Wiley.
1854	John A. Gilmer	David F. Caldwell, Ralph Gorrell, C. Johnston.
1856	Ralph Gorrell	D. F. Caldwell, L. M. Scott, E. W. Ogburn.
1858	Ralph Gorrell	John M. Morehead, D. F. Caldwell, A. Clapp.
1860	John M. Morehead	C. P. Mendenhall C. E. Shober, J. L. Gorrell.
1862	Peter Adams	M. S. Sherwood, L. W. Glenn, R. W. Smith.
1864	R. P. Dick	D. F. Caldwell, A. Clapp, A. S. Holton.
1866	Peter Adams	J. T. Morehead, jr., J. S. Houston, W. R. Smith.
1868	E. Shoffner J. W. Walker	Stephen G. Forney, David Hodgin.
1870	John A. Gilmer W. A. Smith	Jonathan Harris, S. C. Rankin.
1872	James T. Morehead Wm. J. Murray	Joseph Gilmer, William Wiley.

Alamance and Guilford form the twenty-fourth Senatorial District

HALIFAX COUNTY.

HALIFAX COUNTY was formed in 1758 from Edgecombe county, and in this year the court house for the counties of Edgecombe, Granville and Northampton was moved from Enfield to the town of Halifax.

It derives its name from the Earl of Halifax, who, in 1758, was the first Lord of the Board of Trade. "It is a name of Saxon origin, and means 'holy hair,' from the sacred hair of a certain virgin, whom a clerk beheaded, because she resisted his passion. She was canonized." It is situated in the north-eastern part of the State, and bounded on the north and east by the Roanoke River, which separates it from Northampton county, on the south by Martin, Edgecombe and Nash counties, and the west by the county of Warren. Its capital town is Halifax, which is beautifully located on the west bank of the Roanoke River, navigable for steam and other boats, and distant from Raleigh 87 miles.

COUNTY OFFICERS.

Offices.	Names.
Superior Court Clerk	John T. Gregory.
Register of Deeds	Ben. H. Franklin.
Sheriff	John A. Reid.
Coroner	W. T. J. Hayes.
Surveyor	One elected but did not qualify.
Treasurer	Edwin T. Clarke.
Commissioners	J. M. Grizzard. John A. White. George W. Daniel. George A. Browne. W. F. Young.

JUSTICES OF THE PEACE.

Names.	Date of Qualification.	Post Office Address.
W. T. J. Hayes	Sept. 1, 1873.	Halifax.
Robert Knight	" "	Halifax.
James H. Reynolds	" "	alifax.
L. F. Larkin	" "	Weldon.
Wm. C. ill	" "	Weldon.
Jas. H. McGee	" "	Weldon.
W. F. Young	" "	Littleton.
Joshua E. Rue, jr	" "	Littleton.
H. J. Hewlin	" "	Brinkleyville.
F. M. Garrett	October, 1873.	Ringwood.
George W. Daniel	" "	alifax.
John W. Johnston		Weldon.

HALIFAX COUNTY—Continued.

JUSTICES OF THE PEACE.

Names.	Date of Qualification.	Post Office Address.
Warren Hartman	Sept. 1st, 1873.	Enfield.
John A. Jones	" "	Enfield.
James T. Dawson	" "	Enfield.
John A. White	" "	Scotland Neck.
R. H. Smith, jr	" "	Scotland Neck.
John [illegible]. Collins	" "	Scotland Neck.
S. R. Spruill	Dec. 16th, 1873.	Palmyra.
Stuart Hardie	Sept. 1st, 1873.	Palmyra.

LIST OF MEMBERS TO THE HOUSE OF COMMONS FROM HALIFAX.

Years.	House of Commons.	Years.	House of Commons.
1774	John Geddy,	1805	Allen Gilchrist,
1775	John Webb,	1806	Allen J. Davie,
1776	Willie Jones,	1807	Joseph J. Daniel,
1777	Willie Jones,	1808	Wm. P. Hall,
1778	Willie Jones,	1809	William Drew,
1779	Henry Montfort,	1810	Halcott J. Pride,
1780	Henry Montfort,	1811	Jeptha Dupree,
1781	Henry Montfort,	1812	Peter Brown,
1782	Henry Montfort,	1813	William Drew,
1783	Henry Montfort,	1814	William Drew,
1784	Henry Montfort,	1815	Joseph J. Daniel,
1785	Charles Pasteur,	1816	William Drew,
1786	Wm. R. Davie,	1817	H. G. Burton,
1787	Wm. R. Davie,	1819	Thomas Burgess,
1788	Goodrum Davis,	1820	Robert A. Jones,
1789	Wm. R. Davie,	1821	Thomas Burgess,
1791	Wm. R. Davie,	1822	Thomas Burgess,
1792	Richard [illegible]. Long,	1823	Jesse A. Bynum,
1793	Wm. R. Davie,	1824	Jesse A. Bynum,
1794	Wm. R. Davie,	*	
1795	John B. Ashe,	1826	Robert Potter,
1796	Wm. R. Davie,	1827	Jesse A. Bynum,
1797	Thaddeus Barnes,	1828	Jesse A. Bynum,
1798	Wm. R. Davie,	1829	Wm. L. Long,
1799	Richard H. Long,	1830	Wm. L. Long,
1800	Richard H. Long,	1831	Wm. L. Long,
1801	Isaac Hilliard,	1832	Wm. L. Long,
1802	Basset Stith,	1833	Wm. L. Long,
1803	William Drew,	1834	Thomas Ousby,
1804	Thomas Hall,	1835	Robert C. Bond.

*No member was elected this year, in consequence of the election having been broken up by a brawl between the contending candidates, Potter and Bynum, and their friends.

HALIFAX COUNTY—Continued.

MEMBERS OF GENERAL ASSEMBLY.

Years.	Senate.	House.
1777	John Bradford	J. John Williams, Egbert Haywood.
1778	Oroondates Davis	Egbert Haywood, John Whitaker.
1779	Oroondates Davis	Wilie Jones, Augustine Willis.
1780	Oroondates Davis	Wilie Jones, William Weldon.
1781	Oroondates Davis	John Branch, Benj. McCulloch.
1782	Wilie Jones	John Branch, Benj. McCulloch.
1783	Benj. McCullock	John Whitaker, John Geddy.
1784	Nicholas Long	Benj. McCulloch, John B. Ashe.
1785	Nicholas Long	John Whitaker, John B. Ashe.
1786	Benj. McCullock	John B. Ashe, Augustine Willis.
1787	Nicholas Long	John Dawson, John Branch.
1788	Wilie Jones	John Jones, John Branch.
1789	John B. Ashe	Peter Quails, Marmaduke Norfleet.
1790	Peter Quails	John Dawson, Willis Alston.
1791	Peter Quails	Willis Alston, Stephen W. Carney.
1792	Peter Quails	Willis Alston, Eaton Pugh.
1793	Peter Quails	James A. Tabb, S. W. Carney.
1794	Willis Alston	Eaton Pugh, John A. Tabb.
1795	Willis Alston	Eaton Pugh, S. W. Carney.
1796	Willis Alston	John A. Tabb, Eaton Pugh.
1797	Stephen W. Carney	Wood J. Hamblin, James A. Tabb.
1798	Stephen W. Carney	Sterling Harwell, M. C. Whitaker.
1799	Stephen W. Carney	Sterling Harwell, W. J. Hamlin.
1800	Stephen W. Carney	M. C. Whitaker, Sterling Harwell.
1801	Stephen W. Carney	M. C. Whitaker, Sterling Harwell.
1802	Stephen W. Carney	Sterling Harwell, M. C. Whitaker.
1803	Jos. John Alston	Sterling Harwell, M. C. Whitaker.
1804	John Alston	William Williams, M. C. Whitaker.
1805	Gideon Alston	William Williams, M. C. Whitaker.
1806	Gideon Alston	William Williams, M. C. Whitaker.
1807	Matthew C. Whitaker	William Williams, Daniel Mason.
1808	M. C. Whitaker	Lewis Daniel, Wm. Williams.
1809	M. C. Whitaker	Wm. E. Webb, Joseph Bryant.
1810	M. C. Whitaker	Wm. E. Webb, Benjamin Edmonds.
1811	John Branch	Wm. E. Webb, J. J. Daniel.
1812	M. C. Whitaker	J. J. Daniel, Wm. E. Webb.
1813	John Branch	James Barnes, W. J. Hamlin.
1814	John Branch	J. Grant, R. Jones.
1815	John Branch	Richard Jones, W. W. Carter.
1816	John Branch	Jesse A. Dawson, Richard Jones.
1817	John Branch	Richard Jones, Jesse A. Dawson.
1818	John Alston	Jesse A. Dawson, Nevill Gee.
1819	John Alston	Richard Jones, Willis Alston.
1820	John Alston	Willis Alston, Jesse A. Dawson.
1821	John Alston	Willis Alson, Jesse A. Dawson.
1822	John Branch	R. A. Jones, Isham Matthews.
1823	Thomas Burgess	Willis Alston, R. A. Jones.
1824	Isham Matthews	Willis Alston, R. B. Daniel.
1825	Isham Matthews	Geo. E. Spruill, R. B. Daniel.
1826	Isham Matthews	A. A. Wyche, George E. Spruill.
1827	Isham Matthews	George E. Spruill, Wm. E. Shine.
1828	Isham Matthews	R. B. Pierce, George E. Spruill.
1829	Isham Matthews	Jesse A. Bynum, Thomas Nicholson.
1830	Isham Matthews	Jesse A. Bynum, Thomas Nicholson.

HALIFAX COUNTY.—Continued.

MEMBERS OF GENERAL ASSEMBLY—Continued.

Years.	Senate.	House.
1831	Isham Matthews	Thomas Nicholson, J. R. J. Daniel.
1832	Isham Matthews	Charles Gee, J. R. J. Daniel.
1833	Isham Matthews	Wm. M. West, J. R. J. Daniel.
1834	John Branch	Wm. L. Long, J. R. J. Daniel.
1835	Andrew Joyner	Sterling H. Gee, Wm. M. West.
1836	Andrew Joyner	I. Matthews, S. H. Gee, B. F. Moore.
1838	Andrew Joyner	Wm. W. Daniel, Major A. Wilcox, Spier Whitaker.
1840	Andrew Joyner	S. H. Gee, B. A. Pope, B. F. Moore.
1842	Andrew Joyner	B. A. Pope, S. H. Gee, B. F. Moore.
1844	Andrew Joyner	S. H. Gee, B. F. Moore.
1846	Andrew Joyner	L. M. Long, M. C. Whitaker.
1848	Andrew Joyner	Wm. L. Long, R. Smith.
1850	Andrew Joyner	W. B. Pope, R. Clinton.
1852	Andrew Joyner	R. H. Smith, J. D. Perkins.
1854	M. L. Wiggins	R. H. Smith, J. D. Perkins.
1856	M. L. Wiggins	Wm. Hill, J. W. Johnson.
1858	M. C. Whitaker	Wm. Hill, W. L. Long.
1860	M. C. Whitaker	A. H. Davis, W. B. Pope.
1862	M. L. Wiggins	Henry Joyner, A. H. Davis.
1864	M. L. Wiggins	Henry Joyner, A. H. Davis.
1866	M. L. Wiggins	D. C. Clarke, W. A. Daniel.
1868	Henry Epps	J. H. Renfrow, W. T. J. Hayes, J. Hutchins.
1870	Henry Epps	Chas. Smith, Jno. Bryant, John Renfrew.
1872	Henry Epps	J. J. Goodwyn, John Bryant.

Halifax forms the 4th Senatorial District.

HARNETT COUNTY.

Was created by act of 7th February, 1855, out of a portion of Cumberland county, called for honor of Cornelius Harnett, a statesman of the Revolution.

Its county seat is Lillington, in respect to Col. Alexander Lillington, of the Revolution army. Distant from Raleigh about 25 miles.

It is bounded on the north by Wake, east by Johnston, south by Cumberland, west by Moore.

For its representatives see Cumberland with which it voted till 1868.

COUNTY OFFICERS.

Offices.	Names.
Superior Court Clerk	Benjamin F. Shaw.
Register of Deeds	D. H. McLean.
Sheriff	K. M. McNeill.

HARNETT COUNTY—Continued.

COUNTY OFFICERS—Continued.

Offices.	Names.
Coroner	W. L. Williams.
Surveyor	John W. Pipkin.
Treasurer	Rora Barnes.
Commissioners	John Maxwell, Chairman. C. S. Barbee. M. V. Prince. James Turnage. Kenneth Murchison.

JUSTICES OF THE PEACE.

Names.	Date of Qualification.	Post Office Address.
A. C. Buie	Sept. 1st, 1873.	Johnsonville.
D. S. Byrd	" "	Harnett C. H.
Neill Clark	" "	Norval.
C. H. Coffield	" "	Harnett C. H.
J. McL. Harrington	" "	Harrington P. O.
J. S. Holt	" "	Chalk Level.
A. J. Kivett	" "	Harnett C. H.
W. J. Long	" "	Harnett C. H
Wm. McLean, (col.)	" "	Harnett C. H.
L. McN. McDonald	" "	Johnsonville.
Neill McLeod	" "	Swann Station.
J. A. Norden	" "	Bunn's Level.
R. A. Norden	" "	Harnett C. H.
J. D. Ryals	" "	Averasboro.
N. S. Steward	" "	Averasboro.
Angus Shaw	" "	Bunn's Level.
J. F. Shaw	" "	Bunn's Level.

MEMBERS OF GENERAL ASSEMBLY.

Years.	Senate.	House.
1868	J. S. Harrington. L. D. Hall.	Neil S. Stewart.
1870	W. C. Troy. C. T. Murphy.	Neil S. Stewart.
1872	W. C. Troy.	J. Gra

Cumberland and Harnett form the 16th Senatorial District.

HAYWOOD COUNTY.

HAYWOOD COUNTY was formed in 1808, from Buncombe county, and named in compliment to John Haywood, who from 1787 to 1827, was Treasurer of North Carolina.

It is situated in the south-west portion of North Carolina; bounded on the north by the Tennessee line, east by Madison and Buncombe, south by Transylvania, and on the west by Swain and Jackson.

Its capital is Waynesville, and is distant from Raleigh 294 miles.

COUNTY OFFICERS.

Offices.	Names.
Superior Court Clerk	J. Ratcliff, Jr.
Register of Deeds	W. H. Leatherwood.
Sheriff	S. J. Shelton.
Coroner	None.
Surveyor	P. W. Edwards.
Treasurer	J. N. Benners.
Commissioners	R. H. Penland, Chairman.
	John Burnett.
	S. Walker.
	W. M. Rhea.
	R. V. Welch.

JUSTICES OF THE PEACE.

Names.	Date of Qualification.	Post Office Address.
J. F. Murry	Sept. 1st, 1873.	Waynesville.
Joseph Liner	" "	Waynesville.
W. W. Medford	" "	Waynesville.
Morgan Mease	" "	Forks of Pigeon.
W. S. Evans	" "	Forks of Pigeon.
T. M. Green	" "	Pigeon River.
Joseph Christopher	" "	Pigeon River.
G. W. McCracken	" "	Crab Tree.
J. M. Queen	" "	Crab Tree.
R. W. Noland	" "	Fines Creek.
A. J. Ferguson	" "	Fines Creek.
E. H. Harvell	" "	Jonathan's Creek.
J. C. Leatherwood	" "	Jonathan's Creek.
J. F. Owen	" "	Mount Starlin.
D. J. Cook	" "	Mount Starlin.
James Cady	" "	Forks of Pigeon.
Fidilia Howell	" "	Forks of Pigeon.

HAYWOOD COUNTY—Continued.

MEMBERS OF GENERAL ASSEMBLY.

Years.	Senate.	House.
1809	John Welch	Thomas Love, Thomas Lenoir.
1810	John Welch	Thomas Love, Thomas Lenoir.
1811	John McFarland	Thomas Love, Thomas Lenoir.
1812	John McFarland	Thomas Lenoir, John Dobson.
1813	John McFarland	Thomas Lenoir, Joseph Chambers.
1814	John McFarland	Thomas Love, Thomas Lenoir.
1815	James Welch	Thomas Love, Joseph Chambers.
1816	Hodge Rabourne	John Stephenson, William Welch.
1817	Thomas Tatham	Thomas Love, Daniel McDowell.
1818	Hodge Rabourne	Thomas Love, Wm. Welch.
1819	Hodge Rabourne	Thomas Love, J. Chambers.
1820	Hodge Rabourne	Thomas Love, J. Chambers.
1821	Hodge Rabourne	James R. Love, Ninian Edmondston.
1822	Hodge Rabourne	James R. Love, Benjamin Clark.
1823	Thomas Love	James R. Love, Ninian Edmondston.
1824	Thomas Love	James R. Love, Ninian Edmondston.
1825	Thomas Love	James R. Love, Ninian Edmondston.
1826	Thomas Love	James R. Love, Ninian Edmondston.
1827	Thomas Love	James R. Love, Benjamin S. Brittain.
1828	Thomas Love	Benj. S. Brittain, Ninian Edmondston.
1829	Wm. Welch	James R. Love, Ninian Edmondston.
1830	Wm. Welch	Ninian Edmondston, James R. Love.
1831	Wm. Parham	Ninian Edmondston, John L. Smith.
1832	Wm. Parham	John L. Smith, Ninian Edmondston.
1833	Wm. Sitton	Ninian Edmondston, John L. Smith.
1834	Ninian Edmondston	John L. Smith, Joseph H. Walker.
1835	Ninian Edmondston	Joseph H. Walker, John L. Smith.
1836	James Gudger	John L. Smith.
1838	Hodge Rabourne	Joseph Keener.
1840	Thos. L. Clingman	Joseph Keener.
1842	J. Cathy	Michael Francis.
1844	Michael Francis	J. Keener.
1846	Michael Francis	Andrew Ferguson.
1848	Michael Francis	Robert G. A. Love.
1850	Michael Francis	Robert G. A. Love.
1852	Michael Francis	Robert G. A. Love.
1854	Michael Francis	Robert G. A. Love.
1856	Michael Francis	S. L. Love.
1860	Michael Francis	S. L. Love.
1862	C. D. Smith	S. L. Love.
1864	S. C. Bryson	S. L. Love.
1866	R. M. Henry	Greene Garrett.
1868	Wm. L. Love	Walter Brown.
1870	Wm. L. Love	W. P. Welch.
1872	Wm. L. Love	H. P. Haynes.

Haywood, Henderson and Transylvania form the 41st Senatorial District.

HENDERSON COUNTY.

HENDERSON COUNTY was formed in 1838, from Buncombe, and named in compliment to Leonard Henderson, late Chief Justice of the Supreme Court. It is situated in the south-western part of North Carolina, and is bounded on the north by Buncombe, east by Polk, south by the South Carolina line, and west by Transylvania.

Its capital is HENDERSONVILLE, two hundred and fifty miles west of Raleigh.

COUNTY OFFICERS.

Offices.	Names.
Superior Court Clerk	C. M. Pace.
Register of Deeds	J. R. Gash.
Sheriff	T. W. Taylor.
Coroner	None.
Surveyor	J. T. Paterson.
Treasurer	J. L. Hood.
Commissioners	Alexander Henry, Chairman. James J. Osborne. B. W. Allen. Benjamin Williams. Samuel Sentell.

JUSTICES OF THE PEACE.

Names.	Date of Qualification.	Post Office Address.
M. M. Patten	Sept. 1st, 1873.	Hendersonville.
A. Shepherd	" "	Hendersonville.
A. M. McCarson	" "	Hendersonville.
H. K. Pace	Jan. 24th, 1874.	Hendersonville.
Samuel Sentell	Oct. 6th, 1873.	Hendersonville.
Thomas Osteen	Jan. 5th, 1874.	Hendersonville.
N. J. Lance	Sept. 1st, 1873.	Shufordsville.
J. R. Baldwin	" "	Shufordsville.
Rufus Edney	" "	Edneyville.
J. J. Lungter	" "	Edneyville.
Thomas Blackwell	" "	Blue Ridge.
S. B. O. McCall	" 20th, "	Blue Ridge.
A. Q. Moore	" 1st, "	Mill's River.
T. R. Murray	" "	Boilstone.
Levi Jones	" "	Flat Rock.

HENDERSON COUNTY.—Continued.

MEMBERS OF GENERAL ASSEMBLY.

Years.	Senate.	House.
1844	Nicholas W. Woodfin.......	John Clayton.
1846	Nicholas W. Woodfin.......	John Baxter.
1848	Nicholas W. Woodfin.......	Henry T. Farmer.
1850	Nicholas W. Woodfin.......	Henry T. Farmer.
1852	Nicholas W. Woodfin.......	John Baxter.
1854	David Coleman.............	John Baxter.
1856	David Coleman.............	John Baxter.
1858	B. M. Edney................	S. Ripley.
1860	Marcus Erwin..............	Jos. P. Jordan.
1862	Wm. M. Shipp..............	Alex. Henry.
1864	M. Patton..................	M. M. Patton.
1866	L. S. Gash..................	James Blythe.
1868	James Blythe...............	W. D. Justus.
1870	James Merrimon............	Brownlow Morris.
1872	W. P. Welch.................	James Blythe.

Haywood, Henderson and Transylvania form the 41st Senatorial District.

HERTFORD COUNTY.

Hertford County was formed as early as 1759, from Chowan, Bertie, and Northampton counties. It was named in compliment to the Marquis of Hertford, an English nobleman, a friend of liberty, and elder brother of Lord Conway, who in 1766, moved in the House of Lords, the repeal of the Stamp Act.

It is situated in the north-eastern part of the State ; bounded on the north by the Virginia line, east by the Chowan river, which separates it from Gates county, south by Bertie, and west by Northampton county.

Its capital is Winton, and is so named in compliment to the Wynns family, for many years a wealthy, patriotic, and distinguished family in this couty. Distant from Raleigh 155 miles. It is beautifully situated on the Chowan river, which is navigable for any shipping that can enter Ocracocke Inlet.

COUNTY OFFICERS.

Offices.	Names.
Superior Court Clerk..................	W. J. Gatling.
Register of Deeds......................	Jas. M. Trader.
Sheriff.................................	Isaac Pipkin.
Coroner................................	B. W. Barham.
Surveyor...............................	John F. Newsome.

HERTFORD COUNTY—Continued.

COUNTY OFFICERS.—Continued.

Offices.	Names.
Treasurer	John A. Vann.
Commissioners,	E. T. Snipes. S. D. Winborn. L. S. Davis. W. B. Alexander. William Reed.

JUSTICES OF THE PEACE.

Names.	Date of Qualification.	Post Office Address.
Samuel M. Aumack	Nov. 2nd, 1873.	Harrellsville.
William B. Alexander	Sept., 1873.	Pitch Landing.
Jno. A. Vann	Sept. 1st, 1871.	Winton.
Levi S. Davis	" "	inton.
Albert G. Vann	" "	Winton.
George H. Mitchell	" 1873.	Winton.
James P. Furnan	" "	Winton.
R. R. Parker	" "	Murfreesboro.
Ely Carter	" "	Murfreesboro.
H. C. Maddrey	" "	Murfreesboro.
S. D. Winborn	" "	Riddickville.
James Everett	" "	Murfreesboro.

MEMBERS OF GENERAL ASSEMBLY.

Years.	Senate.	House.
1777	Robert Sumner	Joseph Dickenson, James Garrett.
1778	Robert Sumner	William Baker, James Manney.
1779	Robert Sumner	illiam Wynns, Nathan Cotten.
1780	Pleasant Jordan	John Baker, Wm. Wynns.
1781	John Baker	Lewis Brown, Thomas Brickell.
1782	John Brickell	Wm. Wynns, Thomas Brickell.
1783	John Baker	Lewis Brown, Thos. Brickell.
1784	John Baker	Wm. Hill, Thos. Brickell.
1785	Robert Sumner	James Manney, Robert Montgomery.
1786	Robert Sumner	Wm. Hill, Thomas Brickell.
1787	Robert Sumner	Thomas Wynns, Robert Montgomery.
1788	Robert Montgomery	Henry Baker, Henry Hill.
1790	Thomas Wynns	Robert Montgomery, Henry Hill.
1791	Thomas Wynns	Robert Montgomery, Henry Hill.

HERTFORD COUNTY.—Continued.

MEMBERS OF GENERAL ASSEMBLY—Continued.

Years.	Senate.	House.
1792	Thomas Wynns............	Henry Hill, James Jones.
1793	Thomas Wynns............	Jethro Darden, Henry Hill.
1794	Thomas Wynns............	Robert Montgomery, Jethro Darden.
1795	Thomas Wynns............	Robert Montgomery, Henry Hill.
1796	Thomas Wynns............	Jethro Darden, James Jones.
1797	Thomas Wynns............	James Jones, Jethro Darden.
1798	Thomas Wynns............	Robert Montgomery, Jas. Jones.
1799	Thomas Wynns............	Robert Montgomery. James Jones.
1800	Thomas Wynns............	Robert Montgomery, James Jones.
1801	Robert Montgomery........	Jamas Jones, Abner Perry.
1802	Robert Montgomery........	James Jones, Abner Perry.
1803	Robert Montgomery........	James Jones, Abner Perry.
1804	Robert Montgomery........	Abner Perry, James Jones.
1805	Robert Montgomery........	James Jones, William H. Murfree.
1806	Robert Montgomery........	James Jones, Abner Perry.
1807	Robert Montgomery........	Lewis Walters, Abner Perry.
1808	Thomas Wynns............	Lewis Walters. Abner Perry.
1809	Thomas Wynns............	Boon Felton, Abner Perry.
1810	Thomas Wynns............	Boon Felton, Lewis Walters.
1811	Thomas Wynns............	Boon Felton, William Jones.
1812	Thomas Wynns............	Wm. H. Murfree, Jethro Darden.
1813	Thomas Wynns............	William Jones, Boon Felton.
1814	Thomas Wynns............	William Jones. Boon Felton.
1815	Thomas Wynns............	Thomas Deans, William Jones.
1816	Thomas Wynns............	William Jones, Thomas Deans.
1817	Thomas Wynns............	Boon Felton, Thomas Manney.
1818	Boon Felton................	John H. Fraser, B. J. Montgomery.
1819	John H. Fraser............	B. J Montgomery, I Carter.
1821	Thomas Deans..............	Jas. Copeland, Jas. D. Wynns.
1822	David E. Sumner..........	Isaac Carter, Lewis M. Jeggitts.
1823	David E. Sumner..........	James Copeland, John Vann.
1824	James Copeland............	John Vann. Isaac Carter.
1825	James Copeland............	John Vann, Isaac Carter.
1826	Elisha H. Sharp	B. J. Montgomery, Leonard Martin.
1827	David O. Askew............	B. J. Montgomery, John H. Wheeler.
1828	David O. Askew............	B. J. Montgomery, John H. Wheeler.
1829	B. J. Montgomery..........	John H. Wheeler, Elisha A. Chamlee.
1830	Jacob Hare..................	John H. Wheeler, Isaac Carter.
1831	B. J. Montgomery..........	Elisha A. Chamlee, Godwin C. Moore.
1832	B. J. Montgomery..........	Isaac Carter, Thomas V. Roberts.
1833	John Vann..................	Isaac Carter, Sipha Smith.
1834	Geo. W. Montgomery........	Isaac Carter, Sipha Smith.
1835	John Vann..................	R. C. Borland, Kenneth Rayner.
1836	Geo. W. Montgomery........	Kenneth Rayner.
1838	Thomas B. Sharp...........	Kenneth Rayner.
1840	B. T. Spiers................	Wm. N. H. Smith.
1842	Godwin C. Moore...........	Starkey Sharp.
1844	Richard G. Cowper.........	Jacob Sharp.
1846	Richard G. Cowper.........	Kenneth Rayner.
1848	Wm. N. H. Smith...........	Kenneth Rayner.
1850	D. V. Sessoms..............	Kenneth Rayner.
1852	Richard G. Cowper.........	W. L. Daniel.
1854	Kenneth Rayner............	W. L. Daniel.
1856	R. G. Cowper...............	Jos. B. Slaughter.

HERTFORD COUNTY.—CONTINUED.

MEMBERS OF GENERAL ASSEMBLY—CONTINUED.

Years.	Senate.	House.
1858	R. G. Cowper	W. N. H. Smith.
1860	J. B. Slaughter	J. J. Yeates.
1862	J. B. Slaughter	John Vann.
1864	J. M. Wynns	John Vann.
1866	J. B. Slaughter	G. C. Moore.
1868	J. W. Beasely	E. T. Snipes.
1870	Rufus K. Speed James C. Skinner	J. R. Jernagan.
1872	John L. Chamberlain C. W. Grandy	James Sharp.

Camden, Chowan, Currituck, Hertford, Gates, Pasquotank and Perquimans form the 1st Senatorial District.

HYDE COUNTY.

HYDE COUNTY was one of the original precincts of North Carolina, and existed previous to 1729, when the Lords Proprietors (except Lord Granville) surrendered their rights to the crown. It was called in honor of Edward Hyde, who was Governor of the colony in 1711.

It is situated in the extreme eastern part of the State, and bounded on the north by Washington and Tyrrell, east by Pamlico Sound, south by Pamlico Sound and Pamlico River, and west by Beaufort county.

Its Court House, Swan Quarter, is 203 miles east of Raleigh.

COUNTY OFFICERS.

Offices.	Names.
Superior Court Clerk	Samuel R. Sadler.
Register of Deeds	Bryan G. Credle.
Sheriff	Henry S. Gibbs.
Coroner	
Surveyor	
Treasurer	Walter P. Burrus.
Commissioners	Jonas Spencer. A. B. Tunnell. R. W. Howard. Thos. R. Jarvis. W. T. Farrow.

HYDE COUNTY—Continued.

JUSTICES OF THE PEACE.

Names.	Date of Qualification.	Post Office Address.
Samuel L. Snell	Sept. 1st, 1873.	Sladesville.
Asa J. Smith	" "	Sladesville.
Thomas M. Jones	" "	Lake Comfort.
N. C. Williams	" "	Swan Quarter.
Wm. S. Cox	" "	Middleton.
R. F. Watson	" "	Middleton.
J. S. Carter	" "	Fairfield.
T. H. B. Gibbs	" "	Eairfield.

MEMBERS OF GENERAL ASSEMBLY.

Years.	Senate.	House.
1777	William Russell	John Jordan, Benj. Parmele.
1778	William Russell	Abram Jones, Jos. Hancock.
1779	William Russell	Joseph Hancock, Benjamin Parmele.
1780	William Russell	Rotheas Latham, George Barrow.
1781	William Russell	Rotheas Latham, Robert Jennett.
1782	William Russell	Robert Jennett, John Eborne.
1783	William Russell	John Eborne, Benjamin Parmele.
1784	Abram Jones	John Eborne, Wm. Russell.
1785	Abram Jones	John Eborne, Thomas Jordan, jr.
1786	Abraham Jones	John Eborne, Southey Rew.
1787	Abraham Jones	John Eborne, Southey Rew.
1788	Abram Jones	John Eborne, Southey Rew.
1789	John Eborne	Michael Peters, James Jasper.
1790	John Eborne	James Jasper, Michael Peters.
1791	John Eborne	James Jasper, Michael Peters.
1792	Benjamin Russell	James Jasper, James Watson.
1793	James Jasper	James Watson, Simon Alderson.
1794	James Jasper	James Watson, Hutchins Selby.
1795	James Jasper	James Watson, Simon Alderson.
1796	Henry Selby	James Watson, Thomas Jordan.
1797	Henry Selby	Simon Alderson, James Watson.
1798	Henry Selby	Seldon Jasper, William Clarke.
1799	Henry Selby	John Jordan, William Clarke.
1800	Joseph Masters	John Jordan, Adam Gaskins.
1801	Henry Selby	John Satchwell, John Jordan.
1802	Henry Selby	John Satchwell, David Carter.
1803	Henry Selby	John Jordan, David Carter.
1804	Henry Selby	David Carter, Thomas Spencer.
1805	John Jordan	David Carter, Zach. Jarvis.
1806	Henry Selby	David Carter, Zach. Jarvis.
1807	Henry Selby	David Carter, James Credle.
1808	Henry Selby	David Carter, James Watson.
1809	John B. Jasper	James Watson, David Carter.
1810	John B. Jasper	John Adams, David Carter.

HYDE COUNTY.—Continued.

MEMBERS OF GENERAL ASSEMBLY—Continued.

Years.	Senate.	House.
1811	Benj. Sanderson	Thomas Spencer, Zachary Eborn.
1812	Benj. Sanderson	Thomas Spencer, John Adams.
1813	Benj. Sanderson	John Adams, Thomas Spencer.
1814	Samuel Clarke	Thomas Spencer, William Jordan.
1815	Samuel Clarke	William Jordan, Thomas Spencer.
1816	David Carter	William Jordan, Thomas Spencer.
1817	B. F. Eborn	Thomas Spencer, William Jordan.
1818	B. F. Eborn	Marvel Wilkinson, Matthias Credle.
1819	B. F. Eborn	Littlejohn Pugh, Matthias Credle.
1820	Thomas Singleton	Littlejohn Pugh, Thomas Spencer.
1821	George W. Jordan	Littlejohn Pugh, Thomas Spencer.
1822	George W. Jordan	Littlejohn Pugh, William Watson.
1823	David Gibbs	Littlejohn Pugh, William Watson.
1824	David Gibbs	William Watson, Tillman Farrow.
1825	David Gibbs	Littlejohn Pugh, John J. Bonner.
1826	Benj. Foreman	Tillman Farrow, John J. Bonner.
1827	Benj. Sanderson	W. D. Styron, John B. Jasper.
1828	Littlejohn Pugh	Wallace D. Tyron, John B. Jasper.
1829	Benj. Sanderson	Foster Jarvis, Marshal Dickinson.
1830	Wm. Selby, sr	Thomas S. Singleton, Foster Jarvis.
1831	William Selby	Thomas S. Singleton, Foster Jarvis.
1832	Caleb Spencer	Daniel Murray, Foster Jarvis.
1833	Dameron Pugh	Daniel Murray, John B. Jasper.
1834	Caleb Spencer	Benj. Watson, John L. Swindell.
1835	William Selby	John L. Swindell, R. M. G. Moore.
1836	J. O. K. Williams	Tillman Farrow.
1838	J. O. K. Williams	Tillman Farrow.
1840	William Selby	Tillman Farrow.
1842	W. B. Hodges	Andrew Shanklin.
1844	Joshua Taylor	Wilson Creedle.
1846	David Carter	Wilson Creedle.
1848	Thomas D. Smaw	Tilghman Farrow.
1850	Allen Grist	E. D. Sanderson.
1852	R. Murray	R. J. Wynne.
1854	Charles McCleese	M. Selby.
1856	F. M. Burgess	Joseph J. Jennett.
1858	——— Bosnight	Tillman Farrow.
1860	Jones Spencer	Tillman Farrow.
1863	Charles McCleese	E. L. Mann.
1864	E. L. Mann	H. S. Gibbs.
1866	Jones Spencer	Tillman Farrow.
1868	John B. Respess	Tillman Farrow.
1870	E. J. Warren	—— Lucas.
1872	John B. Respess H. E. Stilley	W. S. Carter.

Beaufort, Dare, Hyde, Martin, Tyrrell and Washington form the 2d Senatorial District.

IREDELL COUNTY.

IREDELL COUNTY was formed from Rowan, in 1788, and called in honor of James Iredell, Sr., (late Associate Justice of the Supreme Court of the United States), on motion of General John Steele, of Rowan.

It is located in the western part of the State, and bounded on the north by Wilkes and Yadkin, east by Rowan and Davie, south by Mecklenburg, and west by the Catawba River, which separates it from Catawba, Lincoln and Alexander Counties.

Its capital is STATESVILLE, one hundred and forty-five miles west of Raleigh.

COUNTY OFFICERS.

Offices.	Names.
Superior Court Clerk	C. L. Summers.
Register of Deeds	W. D. Summers.
Sheriff	W. F. Wasson.
Coroner	None.
Surveyor	George W. Clegg.
Treasurer	C. A. Carlton.
Commissioners	John Davidson, Chairman. J. M. Turner. R. W. P. Feimster. Isaac Harris. Perry Tomlin.

JUSTICES OF THE PEACE.

Names.	Date of Qualification.	Post Office Address.
Wm. J. Colvert	Sept. 1st, 1873.	Eagle Mills.
Thos. N. Cooper	" "	Eagle Mills.
L. V. Campbell	" "	Eagle Mills.
Thos. L. Jennings	" "	Jenning's Mill.
H. H. Weatherman	" "	New Hope.
L. D. Wilborn	" "	New Hope.
W. Turner, (appointed.)	Oct. 30th, "	Turnersburg.
R. L. [illegible]eaver, (appointed.)	Sept. 13th, "	Olive.
H. H. Mowbray	" 1st, "	Olive.
R. T. Campbell	" "	Snow Creek.
Henry Turner	" "	Cool Springs.
C. W. Kestler	" "	Cool Springs.
A. P. Murdock, (appointed.)	Dec. 19th, "	Statesville.
J. C. Turner, (appointed.)	" "	Statesville.
A. Morrison	Sept. 1st, "	Fancy Hill.
R. A. Stone	" "	Liberty Hill.
J. F. Datson	" "	Cool Springs.
J. A. White	" "	Amity [illegible]ill.
M. F. Freeland	" "	Statesville.
Jacob Boston	" "	Statesville.
W. W. White	" "	Statesville.

IREDELL COUNTY.—Continued.

JUSTICES OF THE PEACE—Continued.

Names.	Date of Qualification.	Post Office Address.
J. B. Powell	Sept. 1st, 1873.	Statesville.
Thos. A. Watts	" "	Statesville.
J. A. Johnson	" "	New Sterling.
R. H. Brown	" "	Troutman's Depot.
W. J. Lippard	" "	Troutman's Depot.
E. M. McNeely	" "	Mooresville.
J. C. Neall, (appointed.)	" 16th, "	Mooresville.
J. B. Cornelius	" 1st, "	Mount Mourne.
E. W. Putman	" "	Mount Mourne.

Two vacancies to be filled when application is made.

MEMBERS OF GENERAL ASSEMBLY.

Years.	Senate.	House.
1789	John Nesbet	Adam Brevard, Musentine Matthews.
1790	John Nesbet	David Caldwell, M. Matthews.
1791	David Caldwell	Musentine Matthews, Alexander Work.
1792	David Caldwell	Musentine Matthews, Burgess Gaither.
1793	John Huggins	James Crawford, Musentine Matthews.
1794	John Huggins	Musentine Matthews, Alexander Work.
795	John Huggins	Musentine Matthews, Burgess Gaither.
1796	David White	Burgess Gaither, Musentine Matthews.
1797	David Caldwell	Musentine Matthews, Burgess Gaither.
1800	Ephraim Davidson	Archibald Sloan, Burgess Gaither.
1801	Ephraim Davidson	M. Matthews, Burgess Gaither.
1802	Ephraim Davidson	Archibald Sloan, M. Matthews.
1803	Ephraim Davidson	Archibald Sloan, George L. Davidson.
1804	David Caldwell	William Young, George L. Davidson.
1805	John Huggins	George L. Davidson, William Young.
1806	John Huggins	George L. Davidson, Andrew Caldwell.
1807	John Huggins	George L. Davidson, Andrew Caldwell.
1808	James Hart	George L. Davidson, Andrew Caldwell.
1809	James Hart	George L. Davidson, Samuel King.
1810	James Hart	Andrew Caldwell, George L. Davidson.
1811	Joseph Guy	George L. Davidson, Samuel King.
1812	Andrew Caldwell	Samuel King, James Stewart.
1813	Andrew Caldwell	Samuel King, James Stewart.
1814	Myles Nesbitt	Jamuel King, James Stewart.
1815	John Huggins	James Stewart, Samuel King.
1816	James Campbell	Samuel King, David F. Caldwell.
1817	Charles D. Conner	David F. Caldwell, Samuel King.
1818	Charles D. Conner	Samuel King, David F. Caldwell.
1819	Charles D. Conner	Samuel King, David F. Caldwell.
1820	Charles D. Conner	Azariah Beall, Theophilus Falls.
1821	James Campbell	Asa Beall, James Hill.
1822	Alexander Torrence	William Harbin, Asa Beall.
1823	Alexander Torrence	James Hill, Asa Beall.
1824	George L. Davidson	A. Beall, James Hill.
1825	George L. Davidson	James J. Hill, Alexander Torrence.

IREDELL COUNTY—CONTINUED.

MEMBERS OF GENERAL ASSEMBLY—CONTINUED.

Years.	Senate.	House.
1826	Samuel King	Richard Allison, Alexander Torrence.
1827	Abner Franklin	William Falls, William J. Summers.
1828	Abner Franklin	Richard Allison, Joseph M. Bogle.
1829	Thomas A. Allison	Joseph M. Bogle, William King.
1830	Pinckney Caldwell	Joseph M. Bogle, Richard Allison.
1831	Pinckney Caldwell	George F. Davidson, Joseph M. Bogle.
1832	Thomas A. Allison	Solomon Lowdermilk, George F. Davidson.
1833	Joseph P. Caldwell	James A. King, William Potts.
1834	Joseph P. Caldwell	Solomon Lowdermilk, James A. King.
1835	John M. Young	James A. King, Solomon Lowdermilk.
1836	George F. Davidson	James A. King, Solomon Lowdermilk, Theo. H. Campbell.
1838	George F. Davidson	Joseph P. Caldwell, John A. Young, J. H. McLaughlin.
1840	R. H. Parks	Joseph P. Caldwell, John A. Young, J. H. McLaughlin.
1842	Thomas Allison	Joseph P. Caldwell, John A. Young, J. H. McLaughlin.
1844	Joseph M. Bogle	Rufus Reed, William Emmerson, W. W. George.
1846	Joseph M. Bogle	Rufus Reed, W. W. George, William H. Haynes.
1848	George F. Davidson	Robert J. McDowell, A. Campbell McIntosh, E. M. Campbell.
1850	George F. Davidson	Joseph M. Bogle, G. G. McKay, E. M. Campbell.
1852	R. H. Parks	
1854	Anderson Mitchell	J. R. B. Adams, Wm. Turner, V. Teague.
1856	R. H. Parks	L. Q. Sharpe, R. H. Parks.
1858	S. B. Carmichael	L. Q. Sharpe, A. B. F. Gaither.
1860	L. Q. Shrape	A. B. Simonton, A. B. F. Gaither.
1862	L. Q. Sharpe	A. B. Simonton, A. B. F. Gaither.
1864	A. M. Bogle	T. A. Allison, John Young.
1866	J. H. Hill	T. A. Allison, L. Q. Sharpe.
1868	John B. McLaughlin	J. H. Rosebore, J. H. Stevenson.
1870	Romulus Z. Lenney	T. A. Nicholson, Geo. F. Davidson.
1872	Thos. A. Nicholson, Phineas Horton	J. H. Hill, Thos. A. Nicholson. C. L. Shinn, C. L. Turner.

Alexander, Iredell and Wilkes form the 34th Senatorial District.

JACKSON COUNTY.

JACKSON COUNTY was created in 1850, but not organized until 1852. It was taken from Haywood and Macon. Bounded on the north by Swain, east by Haywood and Transylvania, south by the State Line, and west by Macon. It preserves the memory of Andrew Jackson. Its county seat is called Webster, from the great Statesman of Massachusetts.

Distant about 300 miles from Raleigh.

JACKSON COUNTY—Continued.

COUNTY OFFICERS.

Offices.	Names.
Superior Court Clerk	E. D. Davis.
Register of Deeds	A. J. Long.
Sheriff	William Bumgarner.
Coroner	
Surveyor	M. M. Brown.
Treasurer	B. H. Cathey.
Commissioners	E. D. Brendle, Chairman. Wilson Ensley. B. N. Queen. Oliver Painter. Woodford Zachary.

JUSTICES OF THE PEACE.

Names.	Date of Qualification.	Post Office Address.
G. W. Hawkins	Aug. 8th, 1873.	East Laport.
H. F. Gibbs	" "	Qualla Town.
Thomas Wilson	" "	Webster.
S. H. Bryson	" "	Webster.
John H. Alley	" 9th, "	Cashier's Valley.
J. L. Corbin	" 13th, "	Cashier's Valley.
M. W. Bryson	" 9th, "	Webster.
J. A. Moore	" 11th, "	East Laport.
S. P. C. Shelton	" 15th, "	East Laport.
R. L. Watson	" 22d, "	Webster.
J. H. Mathis	Sept. 11th, "	East Laport.
T. H. Galloway	Aug. 13th, "	East Laport.
Thomas K. Welch	" 11th, "	Qualla Town.
R. H. Stephens	" 20th, "	East Laport.
E. C. Ashe	" 15th, "	Webster.
Wm. Estice	" 20th, "	Webster.
J. E. McClain	" 30th, "	Big Springs.
F. M. Nations	Dec. 1st, "	Big Springs.
Alfred Wilson	Oct. 12th, "	Cashier's Valley.
John C. Watkins	Feb. 9th, 1874.	Webster.

MEMBERS OF GENERAL ASSEMBLY.

Years.	Senate.	House.
1854	Wm. H. Thomas	T. D. Bryan.
1856	Wm. H. Thomas	John R. Dills.
1858	Wm. H. Thomas	T. D. Bryson.
1860	Wm. H. Thomas	J. R. Love.

JACKSON COUNTY—CONTINUED.

MEMBERS OF GENERAL ASSEMBLY—CONTINUED.

Years.	Senate.	House.
1862	C. D. Smith................	J. Keener.
1864	S. C. Bryson................	W. A. Enloe.
1866	R. M. Henry................	T. D. Bryson.
1868	W. L. Love................	Joseph Keeper.
1870	W. L. Love................	T. D. Bryson.
1872	W. L. Love................	J. N. Bryson.

Cherokee, Graham, Jackson, Macon and Swain form the 42d Senatorial District.

JOHNSTON COUNTY.

JOHNSTON COUNTY was formed in 1746, from Craven county, and named in honor of Gabriel Johnston, who was Royal Governor at this period. He was a man of leaning, and did much to advance the interest of the colony over which he presided, and the happiness of the people.

It is situated about the centre of the State. Bounded on the north by Franklin, Wake and Nash, on the east by Nash, Wilson and Wayne, south by Wayne, Sampson and Harnett, and on the west by Harnett.

Its capital is Smithfield, and distant 27 miles south-east from Raleigh.

COUNTY OFFICERS.

Offices.	Names.
Superior Court Clerk....................	P. T. Massey.
Register of Deeds....................	J. A. Adams.
Sheriff....................	E. J. Holt.
Coroner....................	J. G. Rose.
Surveyor....................	J. C. Ellington.
Treasurer....................	Stephen Sneed.
Commissioners....................	Josephus Johnson, Chairman. J. T. Leach. Ed. S. Moore. Wm. Rains. Jno W. Lee.

JOHNSTON COUNTY—Continued.

JUSTICES OF THE PEACE.

Names.	Date of Qualification.	Post Office Address.
A. R. Duncan	Jan. 20th 1874.	Clayton.
S. S. O'Neal	Nov. 3rd, 1873.	Clayton.
A. P. Vinson	Sept. 1st, 1873.	Clayton.
Jno. R. Coats	" "	Smithfield.
E. R. Johnson	" "	Smithfield.
Jno. Q. Johnson	" "	Smithfield.
Elam Godwin	" "	Smithfield.
Bryant Williams	" "	Smithfield.
Jno. T. Atkinson	" "	Smithfield.
George Keen	" "	Smithfield.
Young J. Lee	" "	Smithfield.
Jno. D. Massey	" "	Smithfield.
Jno. H. Cotter	" "	Smithfield.
Jno. McC. Guy	" 3rd "	Smithfield.
Lovett Lewis	" 1st "	Princeton.
G. W. Britt	Nov. 3rd, 1873.	Princeton.
L. P. Creech	Sept. 1st, 1873.	Princeton.
Jno M. Stephenson	Feb. 3rd, 1874.	Selma.
R. W. Crumpler	Nov. 3rd, 1873.	Selma.
King Atkinson, (col.)		Selma.
B. R. Hinnant	Sept. 1st, 1873.	Selma.
James Hinnant	" "	Selma.
Joseph Hare	" "	Selma.
Clement Richardson	" "	Selma.
Jas. B. Reaves	" "	Clayton.
Wm. Hinnant	" 23, "	Clayton.

MEMBERS OF GENERAL ASSEMBLY.

Years.	Senate.	House.
1777	Needham Bryan	Henry Rains, Alexander Averyt.
1778	Arthur Bryan	William Ward, John Bryan, Jr.
1779	Arthur Bryan	Lewis Bryan, Philip Raiford.
1780	Arthur Bryan	James Lockhart, John Whitley.
1781	Benjamin Williams	Joseph Boon, Hardy Bryan.
1782	Hardy Bryan	Arthur Bryan, Nathan Williams.
1783	Hardy Bryan	Arthur Bryan, Nathan Williams.
1784	Benjamin Williams	Joseph Boon, Kedar Powell.
1785	Arthur Bryan	Hardy Bryan, Benjamin Williams.
1786	Benjamin Williams	William Averyt, Needham Bryan.
1787	Joseph Boon	Everett Pierce, Wm. Bridges.
1788	Arthur Bryan	Wm. Ward, John Bryan. Jr.
1789	Arthur Bryan	Benjamin Williams, John Bryan, Jr.
1790	Arthur Bryan	Matthias Handy, Hardy Bryan.
1791	Thomas Gray	Everett Pierce, Lovard Bryan.
1792	Hardy Bryan	Everett Pierce, Lovard Bryan.
1793	Hardy Bryan	Needham Bryan, Joseph Ingram.

JOHNSTON COUNTY—Continued.

MEMBERS OF GENERAL ASSEMBLY—Continued.

Years.	Senate.	House.
1794	Samuel Smith.............	John Whitley, Richard Rivers.
1795	Samuel Smith.............	Everett Pierce, John Whitley.
1796	Samuel Smith.............	Matthias Handy, Richard Rivers.
1797	Samuel Smith.............	Matthias Handy, John Williams.
1798	Samuel Smith.............	John Williams, Joseph Ingram.
1799	Samuel Smith.............	John Williams, Calvin Jones.
1800	Samuel Smith.............	John Williams, Joseph Ingram.
1801	John Williams.............	John A. Smith, Richard Rivers.
1802	John Williams.............	Calvin Jones, John A. Smith.
1803	John Williams.............	Edwin Smith, J. Sanders.
1804	John Williams.............	John A. Smith, Isaac Williams.
1805	John Williams.............	John A. Smith, Joseph Ingram.
1806	Samuel Smith.............	Robert Gulley, John Sanders.
1807	Robert Gulley, Jr...........	Joseph Richardson, John Boon, Jr.
1808	John Williams.............	Joseph Richardson, Joseph Boon.
1809	John Williams.............	Samuel Narsworthy, Joseph Richardson.
1810	John Williams.............	Samuel Narsworthy, Henry Guy.
1811	John Williams.............	Henry Guy, Samuel Narsworthy.
1812	Elick Sanders.............	Joseph Ingram, Wm. Bryan.
1813	John Williams.............	William Bryan, Jesse Adams.
1814	William Bryan.............	Jesse Adams, John A. Smith.
1815	William Hinton.............	Jesse Adams, Henry Bryan.
1816	John Williams.............	Jesse Adams, Henry Bryan.
1817	John Williams.............	Henry Bryan, Jesse Adams.
1818	Reuben Sanders.............	Robert H. Helme, John Atkinson.
1819	Jesse Adams.............	Philip Raiford, Henry Bryan.
1820	Jesse Adams.............	John McLeod, Jos. Richardson.
1821	Joseph Richardson..........	John McLeod, Hillory Wilder.
1822	Joseph Richardson..........	Hardy Adams, Samuel Lee.
1823	John McLeod.............	Robert H. Helme, Hillory Wilder.
1824	John McLeod.............	Hillory Wilder, Robert H. Helme.
1825	Reuben Sanders.............	Kenchen Q. Adams, Hillory Wilder.
1826	Reuben Sanders.............	Hillory Wilder, Josiah O. Watson.
1827	David Thomson.............	Hillory Wilder, K. Q. Adams.
1828	David Thomson.............	Hillory Wilder, K. Q. Adams.
1829	Reuben Sanders.............	Hillory Wilder, K. Q. Adams.
1830	Hillory Wilder.............	Josiah Houlder, Kedar Whitley.
1831	David Thomson.............	Josiah Houlder, Kedar Whitley.
1832	Hillory Wilder.............	John McLeod, Josiah Houlder.
1833	Hillory Wilder.............	John McLeod, Josiah Houlder.
1834	Hillory Wilder.............	James Tomlinson, Kedar Whitley.
1835	Josiah Houlder.............	James Tomlinson, Kedar Whitley.
1836	Josiah Houlder.............	James Tomlinson, Kedar Whitley.
1838	Josiah Houlder.............	John F. Ellington, James Tomlinson.
1840	Josiah Houlder.............	Jesse Adams, James Tomlinson.
1842	James Tomlinson............	Lunsford Richardson, Kedar Whitley.
1844	James Tomlinson............	Jesse Adams, Lunsford Richardson.
1846	James Tomlinson............	Lunsford Richardson, Ashly Saunders.
1848	William H. Watson..........	A. J. Leach, Linn. B. Sanders.
1850	William H. Watson..........	A. J. Leach, Linn B. Sanders.
1852	Wm. H. Watson............	W. H. Sanders, S. Goodwin.
1854	Wm. H. Watson............	S. Goodwin. ASA BARNES
1856	L. B. Sanders.............	B. H. Tomlinson, Asa Barnes.
1858	J. T. Leach.............	W. H. Sanders, B. H. Tomlinson.

JOHNSTON COUNTY—Continued.

MEMBERS OF GENERAL ASSEMBLY—Continued.

Years.	Senate.	House.
1860	J. W. B. Watson............	W. H. Watson, J. Mitchiner.
1862	C. B. Sanders..............	S. J. Woodall, W. H. Avera.
1864	Thos. D. Sneed.............	W. A. Smith, W. G. Banks.
1866	Thos. D. Sneed.............	Perry Goodwin, B. R. Hinnant.
1868	J. B. Cook.................	B. R. Hinnant, E. W. Pou.
1870	L. B. Waddell..............	Jesse Hinnant, W. H. Joyner.
1872	W. H. Avera................	Jesse Hinnant, W. H. Joyner.

Johnston forms 17th Senatorial District.

JONES COUNTY.

Jones County was formed in 1779, from Craven, and called in compliment of Willie Jones, who was so distinguished a patriot and useful a representative.

It is situated in the eastern part of the State, and bounded on the north and east by Craven and Carteret, south by Onslow, and west by Lenoir and Duplin.

Its capital is Trenton, and distant from Raleigh 120 miles east.

COUNTY OFFICERS.

Offices.	Names.
Superior Court Clerk....................	Jas. H. C. Bryan.
Register of Deeds.......................	Wm. W. Francks.
Sheriff.................................	Thos. E. Pritchett.
Coroner.................................	John Mercer.
Surveyor................................	None.
Treasurer...............................	Edward T. Franks.
Commissioners...........................	A. McDaniel, Chairman Benj. L. Bryan. Joseph Burney. Moses J. Green. J. H. Mattocks.

JUSTICES OF THE PEACE.

Names	Date of Qualification.	Post Office Address.
Amos Wetherington..............	Sept. 1, 1873.	Pollocksville.
J. H. Mattocks.................	" "	Pollocksville.
Samuel Hutson.	" "	Pollocksville.

JONES COUNTY—Continued.

JUSTICES OF THE PEACE—Continued.

Names.	Date of Qualification.	Post Office Address.
Sanders Kinsey........	Sept. 1st, "	Pollocksville.
Simon E. Koonce........	" "	Trenton.
James M. Pollock........	" "	Trenton.
Benjamin Brock, jr........	" "	Trenton.
H. C. Koonce........	" "	Comfort.
Isaac Brown........	" "	Comfort.
C. C. Fordham........	" "	Comfort.
Nathan McDaniel........	" "	Kinston.
D. H. Harrison........	" "	Trenton.

MEMBERS OF GENERAL ASSEMBLY.

Years.	Senators.	House.
1782		Abner Nash.
1783		Frederick Hargett, Wm. Randall.
1785		Abner Nash, John Isler.
1786	Fred. Hargett........	William Randall, John Isler.
1787	Fred. Hargett........	Nathan Bryan, Wm. Randall.
1788	Fred. Hargett........	William Randall, John H. Bryan.
1791	Fred. Hargett........	Nathan Bryan, Edward Bryan.
1792	Fred. Hargett........	Edward Bryan, Nathan Bryan.
1793	Fred. Hargett........	Nathan Bryan, Joseph Hatch.
1794	John Isler........	Nathan Bryan, George Pollock.
1795	John Isler........	William Bush, Benjamin Fordham.
1796	John Hatch........	William Bush, Benjamin Fordham.
1797	John Hatch........	William Bush, Amos Johnston.
1798	Edmund Hatch........	Amos Simmonds, Benj. Harrison.
1799	Edmund Hatch........	Benj. Fordham, Amos Johnston.
1800	Durant Hatch........	Amos Johnston, John T. Bryan.
1801	Durant Hatch........	Amos Johnston, Thomas Dudley.
1802	Durant Hatch........	Benjamin Fordham, John Isler.
1803	Durant Hatch........	Benjamin Fordham, Enoch Foy.
1804	Durant Hatch........	Benjamin Fordham, Enoch Foy.
1805	Durant Hatch........	Edward Bryan, Thos. P. Ives.
1806	Durant Hatch........	Thomas P. Ives, Frederick Foscue.
1807	Enoch Foy........	James C. Bryan, Edmund Hatch.
1808	Enoch Foy........	James C. Bryan, Edmund Hatch.
1809	Durant Hatch........	James C. Bryan, Leander Simmons.
1810	Benjamin Simmons........	Christopher Bryan, James C. Bryan.
1811	Durant Hatch........	Edmund Hatch, Christopher Bryan.
1812	Durant Hatch........	Josiah Howard, Christ. Bryan.
1813	Enoch Foy........	Jas. . Bryan, Christ. Bryan.
1814	Christ. Bryan........	Wm. Daniel, Hardy Perry.
1815	James Shine........	Hardy Perry, Wm. McDaniel.
1816	James Shine........	J. B. W. Smith, Wm. McDaniel.
1817	John Simmons........	Wm. McDaniel, J. B. W. Smith.
1818	Lewis Foscue........	Risden McDaniel, McLindall Jarman.
1819	Lewis Foscue........	R. McDaniel, Edmund Hatch.

JONES COUNTY—Continued.

MEMBERS OF GENERAL ASSEMBLY—Continued.

Years.	Senate.	House.
1820	Durant Hatch	R. McDaniel, Emanuel Jarman.
1821	Durant Hatch	Emanual Jarman, Risden McDaniel.
1822	Durant Hatch	R. McDaniel, Emanual Jarman.
1823	Durant Hatch	R. McDaniel, Emanual Jarman.
1824	Risden McDaniel	Emanual Jarman, L. H. Simmons.
1825	Risden McDaniel	L. H. Simmons, James N. Smith.
1826	Risden McDaniel	Owen B. Cox, Enoch Foy.
1827	Risden McDaniel	O. B. Cox, Enoch Foy.
1828	Risden McDaniel	O. B. Cox, Enoch Foy.
1829	Risden McDaniel	O. B. Cox, Alfred Stanly.
1830	Risden McDaniel	Nathan B. Bush.
1831	Risden McDaniel	O. B. Cox, James W. Howard.
1832	James Harrison	Nathan Foscue, John H. Hammond.
1833	James Harrison	Nathan Foscue, John H. Hammond.
1834	James Harrison	Nathan Foscue, John H. Hammond.
1835	James Harrison	John H. Hammond, Jas. W. Howard.
1836	James W. Bryan	James W. Howard.
1838	Enoch Foy	William Huggins.
1840	Isaac Hellen	William Huggins.
1842	Jas. W. Howard	Calvin Koonce.
1844	Isaac Hellen	Calvin Koonce.
1846	Jas. W. Howard	William Foy,
1848	E. S. Bell	Calvin Koonce.
1850	M. F. Arendell	B. F. Simmons.
1852	M. F. Arendell	W. P. Ward.
1854	Richard Oldfield	F. J. Simmonds.
1856	W. P. Ward	W. A. Cox.
1858	W. P. Ward	W. A. Cox.
1860	M. F. Arendell	W. P. Ward.
1862	C. D. Koonce	A. E. Rhodes.
1864	M. F. Arendell	F. G. Simmons.
1866	C. D. Koonce	Jacob F. Scott.
1868	D. D. Colgrove	L. D. Wilkie.
1870	W. R. King	B. L. Bryan.
1872	J. G. Scott	Jacob F. Scott.

Carteret, Jones and Onslow form the 9th Senatorial District.

LENOIR COUNTY.

Lenoir County was formed in 1791.

Dobbs County was formed from Johnston, in 1758, in honor of Arthur Dobbs, then the Royal Governor of the Province. In 1791, Dobbs was divided into Lenoir and Glasgow; the latter, in 1799, was changed into Greene. It was called in honor of Gen. William Lenoir, of Wilkes County.

It is situated in the eastern part of the State, and bounded on the north by Greene, east by Pitt and Jones, south by Duplin and Jones, and west by Duplin and Wayne Counties.

Its capital is Kinston, distant 80 miles east of Raleigh.

LENOIR COUNTY—Continued.

COUNTY OFFICERS.

Offices.	Names.
Superior Court Clerk	Wm. W. N. Hunter.
Register of Deeds	James K. Davis.
Sheriff	William R. Becton.
Coroner	Lewis H. Fisher.
Surveyor	Vacant.
Treasurer	Enoch F. Cox.
Commissioners	James L. Canaday, Chairman. Lemuel H. Aldridge. Wiley Lowery. James Wood. William A. Croom.

JUSTICES OF THE PEACE.

Names.	Date of Qualification.	Post Office Address.
Anthony Blount	Aug. 13th, 1873.	Kinston.
Wm. A. Coleman	" 9th, "	Kinston.
Allen Croom	" "	Kinston.
L. H. Davenport	" 14th, "	Kinston.
Wm. F. McCoy	" "	Fields.
Wm. B. Nunn	" 16th, "	Pink Hill.
J. S. W. Pearce	" "	Kinston.
H. J. Randolph	" "	Kinston.
Wm. J. Sutton	Sept. 1st, "	La Grange.
Frank Thomas	" 20th, "	Lenoir Institute.
George Turner	Aug. 12th, "	Pink Hill.
Wm. Henry West	" 9th, "	Kinston.
N. B. Whitefield	" "	La Grange.
Thomas H. Wood	Sept. 1st, "	La Grange.

MEMBERS OF GENERAL ASSEMBLY.

Years.	Senate.	House.
1792	Joshua Croom	Isaac Croom, Wm. White.
1793	William Croom	Isaac Croom, Wm. White.
1794	William Croom	Wm. White, Isaac Croom.
1795	William Croom	Henry Goodman, Simon Bruton.
1796	William White	Shadrach Wooten, Robert Collier.
1797	William White	Henry Goodman, Robert Collier.

LENOIR COUNTY—Continued.

MEMBERS OF GENERAL ASSEMBLY—Continued.

Years.	Senate.	House.
1798	William Bush	Benjamin Fordham, Amos Johnson.
1800	Simon Bruton	Hardy Croom, Wm. Easterling.
1801	Simon Bruton	Shadrach Wooten, Benj. Witherington.
1802	Simon Bruton	Benj. Witherington, Wm. Goodman.
1803	Simon Bruton	James Bright, Allen Wooten.
1804	Simon Bruton	James Bright, Lazarus Pierce.
1805	William Croom	James Bright, Lazarus Pierce.
1806	William Croom	James Bright, Lazarus Pierce.
1807	William Croom	Rigdon White, John Wooten.
1808	Simon Bruton	John Wooten, Wm. Branton.
1809	Simon Bruton	John Wooten, Lazarus Pierce.
1810	James Bright	Francis Kilpatrick, Alexander Mosely.
1811	James Bright	Francis Kilpatrick, Alexander Mosely.
1812	James Bright	Abraham Croom, Joseph Loften.
1813	Simon Bruton	Francis Kilpatrick, Joseph Loften.
1814	Simon Bruton	Joseph Loften, Nathan Byrd.
1815	Jesse H. Croom	Joseph Loften, Nathan Byrd.
1816	Joseph Loften	Joshua Mosely, Blount Coleman.
1817	Simon Bruton	James Cox, Joshua Moseley.
1818	Simon Bruton	John Whitfield, John Williams.
1819	Joseph Loften	James Cox, John Williams.
1820	Joseph Loften	Abraham Croom, John Cobb.
1821	Abraham Croom	Isaac Tull, Nathan B. Whitfield.
1822	Nathan B. Whitefield	Wm. B. Kilpratick, James Cox.
1823	Nathan B. Whitefield	Isaac Croom, W. B. Kilpatrick.
1824	John Williams	James Cox, R. W. Goodman.
1825	Nathan B. Whitefield	Jesse Lassiter, James Cox.
1826	Isaac Croom	Jas. Cox, W. B. Kilpatrick.
1827	Nathan B. Whitefield	W. B. Kilpatrick, Geo. Whitfield.
1828	Hardy B. Croom	Geo. Whitfield, W. B. Kilpatrick.
1829	Wm. D. Moseley	Allen W. Wooten, Council Wooten.
1830	Wm. D. Moseley	Allen W. Wooten, Council Wooten.
1831	Wm. D. Moseley	Council Wooten, A. W. Wooten.
1832	Wm. D. Moseley	A. W. Wooten, Council Wooten.
1833	Wm. D. Moseley	Blount Coleman, Pinckney Hardie.
1834	Wm. D. Moseley	Geo. Whitfield, Windall Davis.
1835	Wm. D. Moseley	Windall Davis, Council Wooten.
1836	Wm. D. Moseley	Windall Davis.
1838	Wm. D. Moseley	Windall Davis.
1840	James B. Whitefield	Windall Davis.
1842	Edwin G. Speight	Windall Davis.
1844	Edwin G. Speight	Jesse Jackson.
1846	Edwin G. Speight	Jesse Jackson.
1848	Edwin G. Speight	Council Wooten.
1850	Edwin G. Speight	William Sutton.
1852	J. P. Speight	William Sutton.
1854	J. P. Speight	William Sutton.
1856	J. P. Speight	S. W. Bright.
1858	J. P. Speight	N. B. Whitfield.
1860	J. P. Speight	W. C. Wooten.
1862	Edward Patrick	. W. Dunn.
1864	Jas. P. Speight	A. W. Wooten.
1866	J. H. Coward	B. F. Bright.
1868	D. D. Colgrove	Wallace Ames.
1870	R. W. King	B. F. Parrot.
1872	R. W. King	Stephen Lassiter.

Green and Lenoir form the 11th Senatorial District.

LINCOLN COUNTY.

LINCOLN COUNTY was formerly called Tryon, in honor of William Troy, the Royal Governor; but whose odious oppressions caused the General Assembly to blot out his name, and in 1779 to divide this territory into Lincoln and Rutherford.

Lincoln county was so called in honor of Benjamin Lincoln, who, at the time of its formation, was fighting the battles of his country against the British at Charleston.

Bounded on the north by Catawba, east by Catawba River, which separates it from Iredell and Mecklenburg, south by Gaston, and west by Cleaveland.

Its county seat, Lincolnton, is 172 miles distant from Raleigh.

COUNTY OFFICERS.

Offices.	Names.
Superior Court Clerk	S. P. Sherrill.
Register of Deeds	D. R. Hoover.
Sheriff	J. A. Robinson.
Coroner	P. S. Beal.
Surveyor	D. L. Beam.
Treasurer	J. C. Jenkins.
Commissioners	W. A. Thompson, Chairman.
	B. H. Sumner.
	J. R. Self.
	L. S. Camp.
	C. L. Hunter.

JUSTICES OF THE PEACE.

Names.	Date of Qualification.	Post Office Address.
A. G. Harrill	Sept. 1st, 1873.	Lincolnton.
M. L. Loftin	" "	Lincolnton.
Robert Nixon	" "	Lincolnton.
A. F. Barnett	" "	Beattie's Ford.
Henry Houser	" "	Lincolnton.
H. E. Ramsour	" "	Lincolnton.
W. A. Thompson	" "	North Brook.
J. A. Davis	" "	North Brook.
B. F. Grigg	" "	Lincolnton.
A. Alexander	" "	Lincolnton.
J. L. Wilkie	" "	Lincolnton.
J. G. Justice	" "	Lincolnton.
Melchi Rhodes	" "	Lincolnton.
Edward Beatty	" "	Lincolnton.

LINCOLN COUNTY—Continued.

MEMBERS OF GENERAL ASSEMBLY.

Years.	Senate.	House.
1780	James Johnston	Valentine Mauney, John Sloan.
1781	James Johnston	Robert Alexander, John Sloan.
1782	James Johnston	Robert Alexander, John Sloan.
1783	Robert Alexander	Daniel McKissick, John Sloan.
1784	Robert Alexander	Daniel McKissick, John Sloan.
1785	Robert Alexander	John Sloan, Daniel McKissick.
1786	Robert Alexander	Daniel McKissick, John Sloan.
1787	Robert Alexander	Daniel McKissick, Joseph Jenkins.
1788	Joseph Dixon	John Moore, Wm. McLean.
1789	Joseph Dixon	John Moore, Wm. McLean.
1791	Joseph Dixon	Wm. McLean, John Moore.
1792	Joseph Dixon	John Moore, Nathan Alexander.
1793	Joseph Dixon	John Moore, Nathan Alexander.
1794	Joseph Dixon	John Moore, Peter Forney.
1795	Joseph Dixon	Peter Forney, David Robeson.
1796	Wallace Alexander	Peter Forney, David Robeson.
1797	Wallace Alexander	Peter Forney, John Ramsour.
1798	Wallace Alexander	John Moore, John Ramsour.
1799	Wallace Alexander	John Moore, John Reinhardt.
1800	Peter Forney	John Moore, John Reinhardt.
1801	Peter Forney	Jesse Robeson, John Moore.
1802	Peter Forney	John Moore, Peter Hoyle.
1803	Henry Hoke	John Moore, Peter Hoyle.
1804	Henry Hoke	John Moore, Peter Hoyle.
1805	Ephraim Perkins	John Moore, Peter Hoyle.
1806	David Shufford	John Moore, Peter Hoyle.
1807	Andrew Hoyle	Peter Hoyle, Jones Abernathy.
1808	Andrew Hoyle	Peter Hoyle, Jones Abernathy.
1809	Andrew Hoyle	Daniel Hoke, Robert Patterson.
1810	John Reid	Peter Hoyle, Daniel Hoke.
1811	John Reid	Daniel Hoke, Peter Hoyle.
1812	David Shufford	Daniel Hoke, Peter Hoyle.
1813	David Shufford	Peter Hoyle, Daniel Hoke.
1814	William McLean	R. Patterson, John Ramsour.
1815	David Shufford	Peter Hoyle, Daniel Hoke.
1816	David Shufford	Peter Hoyle, Daniel Hoke.
1817	John Reid	Peter Hoyle, Henry Y. Webb.
1818	John Reid	Robert Williamson, J. F. Brevard.
1819	Peter Hoyle	Robert Williamson, D. Conrad.
1820	David Shufford	D. Conrad, William Johnson.
1821	Robert Williamson	Peter Hoke, Oliver W. Holland.
1822	Robert Williamson	Peter Hoke, Daniel Conrad.
1823	Daniel M. Forney	O. W. Holland, Daniel Conrad.
1824	Daniel M. Forney	Bartlett Shipp, Daniel Conrad.
1825	Daniel M. Forney	O. W. Holland, Daniel Conrad.
1826	Daniel M. Forney	O. W. Holland, Bartlett Shipp.
1827	Michael Reinhardt	Alex. J. M. Brevard, Daniel Conrad.
1828	Michael Reinhardt	Bartlett Shipp, Andrew H. Loretz.
1829	Daniel Hoke	Bartlett Shipp, Andrew H. Loretz.
1830	Daniel Hoke	Bartlett Shipp, Andrew H. Loretz.
1831	Daniel Hoke	Myles W. Abernathy, Henry Cansler.
1832	Daniel Hoke	Myles W. Abernathy, Henry Cansler.
1833	Daniel Hoke	P. Roberts, H. Cansler.
1834	Bartlett Shipp	Michael Hoke, Henry Cansler.

LINCOLN COUNTY—Continued.

MEMBERS OF GENERAL ASSEMBLY—Continued.

Years.	Senate.	House.
1835	John B. Harry..............	Henry Cansler, Michael Hoke.
1836	Michael Reinhardt..........	Michael Hoke, Henry Cansler, O. W. Holland, Thomas Ward.
1838	Michael Reinhardt..........	M. Hoke, John Killian, O. W. Holland, W. W. Monday.
1840	Thomas Ward..............	M. Hoke, O. W. Holland, W. W. Monday, John Killian.
1842	A. Ray......................	Larkin Stowe, Jas. H. White, Nathaniel Wilson, John Yount.
1844	Larkin Stowe..............	James H. White, Nathaniel Wilson, F. D. Reinhardt, Richard Rankin.
1846	Larkin Stowe	James H. White, Franklin D. Reinhardt, N. Wilson, John Webster.
1848	Henry W. Conner...........	J. H. White, Franklin D. Reinhardt, S. N. Stowe, Andrew H. Shuford.
1850	John F. Hoke..............	Richard Rankin, F. D. Reinhardt, S. N. Stowe, Henderson Sherrill.
1852	John F. Hoke..............	William Lander, H. Sherrill, J. H. Wheeler, J. A. Caswell.
1854	John F. Hoke..............	Henry Cansler.
1856	J. H. White................	A. P. Cansler.
1858	F. D. Reinhardt............	A. Costner.
1860	Jasper Stowe...............	J. F. Hoke.
1862	. H. White.................	A. Costner.
1864	L. M. McCorkle............	A. Costner.
1866	L. M. McCorkle............	M. L. Brown.
1868	L. A. Mason................	A. G. Wisewell.
1870	E. Crowell	David Kincaid.
1872	Jas. R. Ellis................	*A. J. Morrison, A. Costner.

*Resigned.

Catawba and Lincoln form the 37th Senatorial District.

MacDOWELL COUNTY.

MacDowell County was erected in 1842, and called in honor of Colonel Joseph MacDowell.

It was formed from portions of Rutherford and Burke Counties.

It is situated in the western part of the State, and bounded on the north by the Blue Ridge, which separates it from Yancey, east by Burke, south by Rutherford, and west by the Blue Ridge, which separates it from Yancey and Buncombe.

It is called in honor of Colonel Joseph MacDowell, who resided in this county. He was born at Pleasant Garden, on Feb. 25th, 1758. He was distinguished as a soldier and as a Statesman. He married Mary Moffet, by whom he had several children—among them, Colonel James MacDowell, of Yancey, John MacDowell, of Rutherford, and the wife of Captain Charles MacDowell. After his death, April, 1795, she married Colonel John Carson, of Pleasant Garden, and by him she had a number of children, among them the Hon. Samuel P. Carson.

Marion is the county seat, and called after the distinguished partisan general of South Carolina, Francis Marion, and is distant from Raleigh about 200 miles.

COUNTY OFFICERS.

Offices.	Names.
Superior Court Clerk	D. O. H. W. Gillespie.
Register of Deeds	A. L. Finley.
Sheriff	J. G. Neal.
Coroner	W. A. Goforth.
Surveyor	G. W. Crawford.
Treasurer	W. McD. Burgin.
Commissioners	J. W. Jarrett.
	J. W. Hunter.
	J. W. Bright.
	A. W. Crawfoad.
	J. M. Neal.

JUSTICES OF THE PEACE.

Names.	Date of Qualification.	Post Office Address.
James H. Duncan		Marion.
J. A. Scott		Marion.
J. C. Swann		Marion.
J. P. Swofford		North Cove.
A. H. McFalls		North Cove.
W. N. Thompson		Marion.
M. L. Kaylor		Marion.
J. H. Patton		Dysartsville.
W. L. Morrison		
G. R. Morgan		Sugar Hill.

MacDOWELL COUNTY—Continued.

JUSTICES OF THE PEACE—Continued.

Names.	Date of Qualification.	Post Office Address.
A. W. Crawford		Sugar Hill.
M. Burgin		Old Fort.
T. A. Davis		Old Fort.
T. A. Dalton		Stone Mountain.
Jesse Burgin		Stone Mountain.
R. H. Moore		Old Fort.
T. S. Greenlee.		Old Fort.
W. C. Tate		Marion.
A. C. Garden		Marion.

MEMBERS OF GENERAL ASSEMBLY.

Years.	Senate.	House.
1852	Anderson Mitchell	
1854	C. T. N. Davis	S. J. Neal.
1856	W. W. Avery	J. C. Whitson.
1858	E. P. Miller	A. Higgins.
1860	W. W. Avery	C. H. Burgin.
1862	S. J. Neal	W. F. Craig.
1864	S. F. Patterson	W. F. Craig.
1866	A. C. Avery	Jas. Neal.
1868	W. M. Moore	W. N. Gilbert.
1870	W. W. Fleming	J. C. Grayson.
1872	W. W. Fleming	G. W. Freeman.

Burke, Caldwell, McDowell, Mitchell and Yancey form the 36th Senatorial District.

MACON COUNTY.

Macon County was formed in 1828 from Haywood County, and called in honor of Hon. Nathaniel Macon, of Warren County, who was long the representative in Congress from the Warren District, Speaker of the House of Representatives, and Senator in Congress.

It is situated in the extreme western portion of North Carolina, and bounded on the north by Swain County, east by Jackson, south by the State line, and west by Clay County.

Its capital is Franklin, three hundred and thirty-one miles west from Raleigh, romantically situated on the Little Tennessee.

MACON COUNTY—Continued.

COUNTY OFFICERS.

Offices.	Names.
Superior Court Clerk	W. N. Allman.
Register of Deeds	William Sloan.
Sheriff	James Cansler.
Coroner	H. G. Trotter.
Surveyor	W. R. McDowell.
Treasurer	J. P. Moore.
Commissioners	J. B. Cunningham, Chairman. John Ammons. Joseph Morgan. J. N. Keener. L. Howard.

JUSTICES OF THE PEACE.

Names.	Date of Qualification.		Post Office Address.
Thomas Mashburn	Aug. 18th,	1873.	Franklin.
F. Poindexter	"	"	Franklin.
J. W. McGee	"	"	Franklin.
P. Howard	"	"	Franklin.
J. W. Cochran	"	"	Franklin.
W. H. Higdon	"	"	Franklin.
J. L. Strain	"	"	Franklin.
J. E. Peek	"	"	Franklin.
J. W. Wilson	"	"	Franklin.
S. V. Hill	"	"	Franklin.
Z. Barnes	"	"	Franklin.
J. M. Forester	"	"	Franklin.
G. W. Parrish	"	"	Franklin.
John Elmore	Sept. 1st,	"	Franklin.
E. H. Franks	"	"	Franklin.
Albert Siler	Aug. 9th,	"	Franklin.
W. H. Roane	"	"	Franklin.
Jno. H. Addington	Dec. 23d,	"	Franklin.

MEMBERS OF GENERAL ASSEMBLY.

Years.	Senate.	House.
1829	L. Lewis	Asaph Enloe, James Whitaker.
1830	Jas. W. Gwinn	Thomas Tatham, James Whitaker.
1831	James W. Gwinn	Thomas Tatham, James Whitaker.
1832	Benjamin S. Brittain	James Whitaker, Asaph Enloe.

MACON COUNTY—Continued.

MEMBERS OF GENERAL ASSEMBLY—Continued.

Years.	Senate.	House.
1833	Benjamin S. Brittain........	Jas. W. Gwinn, Thomas Tatham.
1834	Benjamin S. Brittain........	Jas. W. Gwinn, Thomas Tatham.
1835	Benjamin S. Brittain........	Jas. W. Gwinn, Jacob Siler.
1836	James Gudger.............	James W. Gwinn.
1838	Hodge Raburn.............	Jacob Siler.
1840	Thomas L. Clingman.......	Jacob Siler.
1842	I. Cathy.....................	James Whitaker.
1844	Michael Francis............	T. J. Roane.
1846	Michael Francis............	John Y. Hicks.
1848	William H. Thomas........	John Y. Hicks.
1850	William H. Thomas........	David W. Siler.
1852	William H. Thomas........	S. Munday.
1854	William H. Thomas........	A. J. Patton.
1856	William H. Thomas........	D. W. Siler.
1858	William H. Thomas........	—— Woodfin.
1860	William H. Thomas........	D. W. Siler.
1862	C. D. Smith.................	J. M. Lyle.
1864	S. C. Bryson.................	J. M. Lyle.
1866	R. M. Henry.................	W. G. Crawford.
1868	W. L. Love...................	Jas. L. Robinson.
1870	W. L. Love...................	Jas. L. Robinson.
1872	W. L. Love...................	Jas. L. Robinson.

Cherokee, Graham, Jackson, Macon and Swain form the 42d Senatorial District.

MADISON COUNTY.

Madison County was formed, in 1850, from Buncombe and Yancey counties, and called in honor of James Madison, the fourth President of the United States.

It is situated in the western portion of the State; and is bounded on the north by the Bald Mountain, which separates it from Tennessee, on the east by Yancey, and south by Buncombe, and on the west by Haywood.

Its county seat is Marshall, about two hundred and fifty miles from Raleigh.

COUNTY OFFICERS.

Offices.	Names.
Superior Court Clerk....................	D. F. Davis.
Register of Deeds........................	W. F. Runnion.
Sheriff..	A. G. Tweed.
Coroner..	

MADISON COUNTY—Continued.

COUNTY OFFICERS—Continued.

Offices.	Names.
Surveyor	Hiram Hunter.
Treasurer	Ira Proffit.
Commissioners	James K. Hardwick, Chairman. R. M. Farnsworth. J. C. Kilpatrick. John Rogers. J. D. Roberts.

JUSTICES OF THE PEACE.

Names.	Date of Qualification.	Post Office Address.
Louis Peek	Sept. 1st, 1873.	Marshall.
Burnett Footner	" "	Marshall.
James Ramsey	" "	Marshall.
Thomas McHargree	" "	White Rock.
Gilbert Tweed	" "	White Rock.
Stephen Ammons	" "	Halewood.
George Peek	" "	Halewood.
H. L. McLaine	" "	Mars Hill.
Joel B. Jervis	" "	Mars Hill.
Daniel Angell	" "	Mars Hill.
John M. Carver	" "	Marshall.
M. Teague	" "	Marshall.
Joseph Bradburn	" "	Marshall.
John Worley	" "	Marshall.
David Davis	" "	Spring Creek.
John Brown	" "	Spring Creek.
F. M. Lawson	" "	Warm Springs.
J. T. Ottinger	" "	Warm Springs.
Stephen Davis	" "	Big Laurel.
J. E. Rice	" "	Big Laurel.

MEMBERS OF GENERAL ASSEMBLY.

Years.	Senate.	House.
1854	David Coleman	John Yancey.
1856	David Coleman	John Yancey.
1858	B. W. Edney	John A. Fagg.
1860	M. Erwin	John A. Fagg.
1862	Wm. M. Shipp	D. Wallin.

MADISON COUNTY—Continued.

MEMBERS OF GENERAL ASSEMBLY—Continued.

Years.	Senate.	House.
1864	M. Patton	W. H. Brown.
1866	L. S. Gash	N. Kelsey.
1868	Wm. M. Moore	Nat. Kelsey.
1870	W. W. Fleming	Nat. Kelsey.
1872	Jas. H. Merrimon	H. A. Gudger.

Buncombe and Madison form the 40th Senatorial District.

MARTIN COUNTY.

Martin County was erected in 1774, from Halifax and Tyrrell counties, and called in honor of Josiah Martin, then the Royal Governor (and the last) of the Colony of North Carolina.

It is situated in the eastern portion of the State, and bounded on the north by Roanoke River, which separates it from Bertie, east by Washington county, south by Pitt, and west by Edgecombe county.

Its capital is Williamston, situated on the banks of Roanoke, 140 miles east of Raleigh.

COUNTY OFFICERS.

Offices.	Names.
Superior Court Clerk	Jos. M. Siterson.
Register of Deeds	W. A. Johnson.
Sheriff	W. W. Moore.
Coroner	Merick Gray.
Surveyor	None qualified.
Treasuer	John Watts.
Commissioners	A. A. Crookston, Chairman. P. W. Everett. J. W. Smith. Wm. A. Rogerson. Abner Eason.

MARTIN COUNTY—Continued.

JUSTICES OF THE PEACE.

Names.	Date of Qualification.	Post Office Address.
L. Z. Eborn	Sept. 1st, 1873.	Hamilton.
Jonathan G. Carroway	" "	Hamilton.
P. W. Everett	" "	Hamilton.
John S. Short	" "	Williamston.
John W. Groves	" "	Williamston.
Rubin S. Rogerson	" "	Williamston.
C. C. Coltrain	" "	Jamesville.
J. J. Smith	" "	Jamesville.
A. W. Powers	" "	Jamesville.

MEMBERS OF GENERAL ASSEMBLY.

Years.	Senate.	House.
1777	William Williams	Whitmel Hill, Wm. Slade.
1778	Whitmel Hill	Nathan Mayo, E. E. Smithwick.
1779	Whitmel Hill	Saml. Smithwick, Saml. Williams.
1780	Whitmel Hill	Edmund Smithwick, John Averit.
1781	K. McKenzie	Saml. Smithwick, Saml. Williams.
1782	K. McKenzie	Saml. Smithwick, Saml. Williams.
1783	K. McKenzie	Saml. Smithwick, Saml. Williams.
1784	Whitmel Hill	Nathan Mayo, John Ross.
1785	Whitmel Hill	Edmund Smithwick, Saml. Williams.
1786	Nathan Mayo	Joseph Bryan, Wm. McKenzie.
1787	Nathan Mayo	Joseph Bryan, Edmund Smithwick.
1788	Nathan Mayo	William Williams, Ebenezer Slade.
1789	Nathan Mayo	William Williams, John Mayo.
1790	Nathan Mayo	Ebenezer Slade, Jesse Cherry.
1791	Nathan Mayo	Ebenezer Slade, Jesse Cherry.
1792	Ebenezer Slade	Jesse Cherry, Ebenezer Smithwick.
1793	Ebenezer Slade	Ebenezer Smithwick, Wm. Griffin.
1794	Ebenezer Slade	Matthew Yarrell, John Kennedy.
1795	Ebenezer Slade	Joseph Bryan, Jesse Cherry.
1796	Ebenezer Slade	G. Sheppard, John Stewart.
1797	William McKenzie	Jeremiah Slade, John Hyman.
1798	William McKenzie	Jeremiah Slade, John Hyman.
1799	William McKenzie	Jeremiah Slade, John Hyman.
1800	William McKenzie	Jeremiah Slade, John Hyman.
1801	John Hyman	William Biggs, Jesse Cherry.
1802	John Hyman	Jeremiah Slade, Edmund Smithwick.
1803	Jeremiah Slade	Thomas Hyman, William Pierce.
1804	John Hyman	Stephen Fagan, Joel Cherry.
1805	John Stewart	James Burroughs, Joel Cherry.
1806	Jeremiah Slade	James Wiggins, James Burroughs.
1807	James Burroughs	Joel Cherry, James Sheppard.
1808	James Burroughs	Joel Cherry, James Sheppard.
1809	Jeremiah Slade	Henry G. Williams, Joel Cherry.
1810	Jeremiah Slade	Henry G. Williams, James Sheppard.

MARTIN COUNTY—Continued.

MEMBERS OF GENERAL ASSEMBLY—Continued.

Years.	Senate.	House.
1811	Jeremiah Slade	Joel Cherry, Andrew Joyner.
1812	Jeremiah Slade	Andrew Joyner, Joel Cherry.
1813	Jeremiah Slade	Andrew Joyner, Joel Cherry.
1814	Jeremiah Slade	Simmons J. Baker, John Guyther.
1815	Jeremiah Slade	Simmons J. Baker, Gabriel L. Stewart.
1816	Simmons J. Baker	Joel Cherry, Gabriel L. Stewart.
1817	Simmons J. Baker	Darling Cherry, Jos. J. Williams.
1818	Simmons J. Baker	Wm. Roulhac, Darling Cherry.
1819	William Darlett	J. R. Ballard, Darling Cherry.
1820	Lewellen Bowers	Jos. R. Ballard, Darling Cherry.
1821	Samuel Hyman	Alfred M. Slade, Jos. R. Ballard.
1822	Samuel Hyman	Jesse Cooper, Lawrence Cherry.
1823	Lewellen Bowers	L. Cherry, Gab. L. Stewart.
1824	John A. Smithwick	L. Cherry, Gabriel L. Stewart.
1825	John A. Smithwick	David Latham, Jesse Cooper.
1826	Jos. J. Williams	David Letham, Jesse Cooper.
1827	Jos. J. Williams	Gab. L. Stewart, Jesse Cooper.
1828	Jos. J. Williams	Jesse Cooper, David Latham.
1829	Jos. J. Williams	Jesse Cooper, Wm. Watts.
1830	Jos. J. Williams	Jesse Cooper, Wm. Watts.
1831	Jesse Cooper	Joseph Robinson, John Cloman.
1832	David Latham	Jas. L. G. Baker, Edwin S. Smithwick.
1833	David Latham	John Cloman, Edwin S. Smithwick.
1834	Jesse Cooper	Raleigh Roebuck, Alfred M. Slade.
1835	Jesse Cooper	Raleigh Roebuck, Alfred M. Slade.
1836	Jesse Cooper	Raleigh Roebuck.
1838	Jesse Cooper	Raleigh Roebuck.
1840	Jesse Cooper	Asa Biggs.
1842	Jesse Cooper	Asa Biggs.
1844	Asa Biggs	J. Woodard.
1846	Daniel Ward	A. H. Coffield.
1848	Daniel Ward	A. H. Coffield.
1850	W. R. W. Sherrod	Wm. L. Mizell.
1852	D. Ward	A. S. Moring.
1854	Asa Biggs	John Watts.
1856	A. Chesson	S. W. Outerbridge.
1858	D. C. Gaither	A. Moore.
1860	J. R. Stubbs	J. L. Ewell.
1862	Jas. G. Calloway	Jas. Robinson.
1864	J. R. Stubbs	S. W. Outerbridge.
1866	J. E. Moore	Abner S. Williams.
1868	F. G. Martindale	Jesse J. Smith.
1870	L. C. Lathum	George A. Gregory.
1872	J. B. Respess H. E. Stilly	J. R. Mizell.

Beaufort, Dare, Hyde, Martin, Tyrrell and Washington form the 2d Senatorial District.

MECKLENBURG COUNTY.

MECKLENBURG COUNTY was formed in 1762, from Anson county, and called in honor of the new queen, Princess Charlotte of Mecklenburg.

It is situated in the south-western portion of the State, and is bounded on the north by Iredell county, east by Cabarrus and Union, south by the South Carolina line, and west by the Catawba river, which separates it from Lincoln and Gaston counties.

Its capital is Charlotte, and distant 158 miles south-west of Raleigh.

COUNTY OFFICERS.

Offices.	Names.
Superior Court Clerk	E. A. Osborne.
Register of Deeds	Wm. Maxwell.
Sheriff	M. E. Alexander.
Coroner	Wm. P. Little.
Surveyor	John E. Moore.
Treasurer	S. E. Belle.
Commissioners	Thos. L. Vail, Chairman. R. L. DeArmon. Wm. H. Neal. M. M. Orr. Thos. Gluyas.

JUSTICES OF THE PEACE.

Names.	Date of Qalification.	Post Office Address.
S. B. Smith	Aug. 20th, 1874.	Rosevale.
A. H. Martin	" "	Charlotte.
M. W. Alexander	" "	Charlotte.
J. R. Kirkpatrick	" "	Pineville.
R. B. Hunter	" "	Charlotte.
H. Bryant	" "	Pineville.
B. H. Gaiusan	" "	Charlotte.
John Cathey	" "	Charlotte.
John B. Hood	" "	Charlotte.
W. F. Davidson	" "	Charlotte.
R. F. Blythe	" "	Cawan's Ford.
T. S. Cooper	" "	Charlotte.
Jno. G. Pates	" "	Charlotte.
R. B. Wallace	" "	Charlotte.
M. L. Wallis	" "	Pineville.
M. E. Kistler	" "	Charlotte.
W. M. Porter	" "	Charlotte.
J. M. Wilson	" "	Cawan's Ford.
C. W. McCoy	" "	Hopewell.
W P. Houston	" "	Fullwood's Store.

MECKLENBURG COUNTY—Continued.

JUSTICES OF THE PEACE—Continued.

Names.	Date of Qualification.	Post Office Address.
E. H. Hinson	Aug. 20th, 1874.	Mint Hill.
Thos P. Grier	" "	Steel Creek.
Thos. Gluyas	" "	Hopewell.
A. G. Reid	" "	Providence.
H. M. Dixon	" "	Query's Turnout.
J. H. Cheshire	" "	Charlotte.
T. B. Elliott	" "	Pineville.
W. P. Williams	Jan. 20th, 1874.	Davidson College.
Julius P. Alexander	Not qualified.	Charlotte.
W. G. Barnett	Not qualified.	Huntersville.

MEMBERS OF GENERAL ASSEMBLY.

Years.	Senate.	House.
1777	Jno. McK. Alexander	Martin Phifer, Waightstill Avery.
1778	Robert Irwin	Caleb Phifer, David Wilson.
1779	Robert Irwin	Caleb Phifer, David Wilson.
1780	Robert Irwin	Caleb Phifer, David Wilson.
1781	Robert Irwin	Caleb Phifer, David Wilson.
1782	Robert Irwin	Caleb Phifer, David Wilson.
1783	Robert Irwin	Caleb Phifer, David Wilson.
1784	James Harris	Caleb Phifer, David Wilson.
1785	James Harris	Caleb Phifer, George Alexander.
1786	James Mitchell	Caleb Phifer, George Alexander.
1787	Robert Irwin	William Polk, Caleb Phifer.
1788	Joseph Graham	Caleb Phifer, Joseph Douglass.
1789	Joseph Graham	Caleb Phifer, George Alexander.
1790	Joseph Graham	Robert Irwin, William Polk.
1791	Joseph Graham	Caleb Phifer, William Polk.
1792	Joseph Graham	Caleb Phifer, James Harris.
1793	Joseph Graham	Charles Polk, George Graham.
1794	Joseph Graham	Charles Polk, George Graham.
1795	Robert Irwin	Charles Polk, George Graham.
1796	George Graham	David McKee, William Morrison.
1797	Robert Irwin	James Conner, Nathaniel Alexander.
1798	Robert Irwin	James Conner, Hugh Parks.
1799	Robert Irwin	James Conner, Sherrod Gray.
1800	Robert Irwin	Charles Polk, Hugh Parks.
1801	Nathaniel Alexander	Alexander Morrison, Charles Polk.
1802	Nathaniel Alexander	Alexander Morrison, Thos. Henderson.
1803	George Graham	Alexander Morrison, Thos. Henderson
1804	George Graham	Thos. Henderson, Samuel Lowrie.
1805	George Graham	Sam'l Lowrie, Geo. W. Smart.
1806	George Graham	Sam'l Lowrie, Thos. Henderson.
1807	George Graham	John Harris, Thos. Henderson.
1808	George Graham	George W. Smart, John Harris.

MECKLENBURG COUNTY—Continued.

MEMBERS OF GENERAL ASSEMBLY—Continued.

Years.	Senate.	House.
1809	George Graham.............	Thos. Henderson, Hutchins G. Burton.
1810	George Graham.............	Thos. Henderson, H. G. Burton.
1811	George Graham.............	Jonathan Harris, Henry Massey.
1812	George Graham.............	Jonathan Harris, Henry Massey.
1813	William Davidson..........	Cunningham Harris, Jonathan Harris.
1814	Jonathan Harris............	William Beattie, Geo. Hampton.
1815	Wm. Davidson..............	John Ray, Abdon Alexander.
1816	Wm. Davidson..............	Joab Alexander, John Wilson.
1817	Wm. Davidson..............	John Rhea, John Wilson.
1818	Wm. L. Davidson...........	John Rhea, John Wilson.
1819	Michael McLeary...........	John Rhea, Miles J. Robinson.
1820	Michael McLeary...........	John Rhea, Miles J. Robinson.
1821	Michael McLeary...........	Samuel McCoombs, John Rhea.
1822	Michael McLeary...........	Matthew Baine, John Rhea.
1823	Michael McLeary...........	Thos. G. Polk, Matthew Baine.
1824	Michael McLeary...........	Thos. G. Polk, Matthew Baine.
1825	Wm. Davidson..............	Thos. G. Polk, Matthew Baine.
1826	Michael McLeary...........	Matthew Baine, Wm. J. Alexander.
1827	Wm. Davidson..............	Joseph Blackwood, Wm. J. Alexander.
1828	Wm. Davidson..............	Joseph Blackwood, Wm. J. Alexander.
1829	Wm. Davidson..............	Wm. J. Alexander, Evan Alexander.
1830	Joseph Blackwood..........	Wm. J. Alexander, Evan Alexander.
1831	Henry Massey..............	James Dougherty, John Harte.
1832	Henry Massey..............	John Harte, James Dougherty.
1833	Washington Morrison.......	Wm. J. Alexander, Andrew Grier.
1834	Wm. H. McLeary...........	Wm. J. Alexander, J. M. Hutchison.
1835	Stephen Fox................	J. M. Hutchison, J. A. Dunn.
1836	Stephen Fox................	Jas. M. Hutchison, G. W. Caldwell, J. A. Dunn.
1838	Stephen Fox................	G. W. Caldwell, Jas. T. J. Orr, Caleb Erwin.
1840	J. T. R. Orr................	G. W. Caldwell, John Walker, Benj. Morrow.
1842	John Walker................	John Kirk, Jas. W. Ross, Caleb Erwin.
1844	John Walker................	Robert Lemmons, J. A. Dunn, John Kirk.
1846	John Walker................	John W. Potts, John N. Davis, Robert Lemmons.
1848	John Walker................	—— Harrison, J. N. Davis, J. J. Williams.
1850	Green W. Caldwell..........	John K. Harrison, J. J. Williams, F. Constantine Davidson.
1852	Green W. Caldwell..........	W. Black, J. A. Dunn, J. Ingram.
1854	John Walker................	W. R. Myers, W. Black.
1856	W. R. Myers................	W. Matthews, W. F. Davidson.
1858	Wm. F. Davidson	[illegible]. M. Pritchard, W. Wallace.
1860	John Walker................	S. N. Davis, J. M. Potts.
1862	John A. Young.............	J. L. Brown, E. C. Grier.
1864	W. M. Grier................	J. L. Brown, E. C. Grier.
1866	J. H. Wilson...............	R. D. Whitely, J. M. Hutchison.
1868	Jas. W. Osborne............	D. D. Whitely, W. . Grier.
1870	H. C. Jones	R. P. Waring, J. W. Reid.
1872	R. P. Waring...............	John E. Brown, S. W. Reid.

MITCHELL COUNTY.

MITCHELL COUNTY was formed in 1861 out of the Counties of Yancey, Watauga, Caldwell, McDowell and Burke. It derives its name from Professor Mitchell, of the University of North Carolina, who lost his life exploring the mountains of North Carolina.

It is bounded on the north by Watauga, east by Caldwell and Burke, south by Yancey, and west by the Tennessee line.

Its county town is BAKERSVILLE.

COUNTY OFFICERS.

Offices.	Names.
Superior Court Clerk	David A. Bowman.
Register of Deeds	J. S. Garland.
Sheriff	A. A. Wiseman.
Coroner	Stephen Atkins.
Surveyor	T. D. Vance.
Treasurer	Reuben Young.
Commissioners,	Moses Young. James Greene. L. D. Anderson. Thomas Burleson. Jackson Short.

JUSTICES OF THE PEACE.

Names.	Date of Qualification.	Post Office Address.
J. B. Slagle	Aug. 6th, 1873.	Bakersville.
Isaiah Bradshaw	" "	Bakersville.
J. C. Blalock	" "	Grassy Creek.
Edmond Williams	" "	Grassy Creek.
T. D. Vance	" "	Yellow Mountain.
Wm. H. Ollis	" "	Yellow Mountain.
Wilson Burleson	" "	Yellow Mountain.
Adolphus Clarke	" "	Yellow Mountain.
J. R. Pritchard	" "	Cranberry.
J. M. Stafford	" "	Cranberry.
David Garland	" 8th, "	Fork Mountain.
Stephen Street	" "	Fork Mountain.
Samuel C. Phillips	" "	Red Hill.
George Beam	" "	Red Hill.
John M. Peterson	" "	Hollow Poplar.
James Bradshaw	" "	Hollow Poplar.
S. W. Blalock	" "	Ledger.
C. D. Stuard	" "	Ledger.

MITCHELL COUNTY—Continued.

MEMBERS OF GENERAL ASSEMBLY.

Years.	Senate.	House.
1868	Wm. M. Moore............	Jacob W. Bowman.
1870	W. W. Flemming...........	—— Collis.
1872	W. W. Flemming...........	Jacob W. Bowman.

Caldwell, Burke, McDowell, Mitchell and Yancey form the 36th Senatorial District.

MONTGOMERY COUNTY.

Montgomery County was formed in the year 1779 from Anson County, and called in honor of General Richard Montgomery, who was a distinguished officer of the Revolution, and who fell fighting her battles in his heroic attack upon Quebec, 31st December, 1775.

Montgomery County is situated in the southern part of the State, and bounded on the north by Randolph and Davidson, east by Moore, south by Richmond, and west by the Yadkin River which separates it from Stanly County.

Its capital is Troy, which preserves the name of the late John B. Troy, Esq., an eminent attorney at this county, and solicitor of this Judicial Circuit. Its distance from Raleigh one hundred and fifteen miles south-west.

COUNTY OFFICERS.

Offices.	Names.
Superior Court Clerk....................	C. C. Wade.
Register of Deeds......................	P. H. Morris.
Sheriff................................	P. C. Riley.
Coroner	J. M. Robinson.
Surveyor...............................	. G. Deberry.
Treasurer..............................	W. T. H. Ewing.
Commissioners..........................	John Robertson. Goodman ornelison. G. M. Ballard. J. G. Skinner.

MONTGOMERY COUNTY—Continued.

JUSTICES OF THE PEACE.

Names.	Date of Qualification.	Post Office Address.
Isaac Suggs	Aug. 9th, 1873.	Troy.
John B. Hurley	Feb. 6th, 1874.	Troy.
A. F. Rush	Aug. 15th, 1873.	Sulphur Springs.
Allen McLennan	" 16th, "	Sulphur Springs.
Calvin . Wooley	" 15th, "	Mount Gilead.
John H. Montgomery	" 16th, "	Swift Island.
D. C. McAulay	Jan. 30th, 1874.	Mount Gilead.
George M. Ballard	Aug. 9th, 1873.	Mount Gilead.
P. H. Turner	" 15th "	Pekin.
John G. Skinner	" 9th, "	Pekin.
M. M. Leach	" 15th, "	Hunsucker's Store.
G. W. Cagle	" 9th, "	Hunsucker's Store.
Peter ornelison	" "	Anson's Hill.
N. R. Blaton	" 15th, "	Anson's Hill.
N. W. Smart	" "	Swift Island.
Littleton Dennis	Jan. 17th, 1874.	Troy.
J. W. Reeves	Sept. 1st, 1873.	Sander's Hill.
A. S. Harris	Dec. 2nd, "	Sander's Hill.
James Reynolds	Aug. 9th, "	Sander's Hill.
P. C. Calicott	" "	Sander's Hill.
Daniel McAulay	" "	Ridge's Creek.
James McCaskill	" "	Ridge's Creek.

MEMBERS OF GENERAL ASSEMBLY.

Years.	Senate.	House.
1780	John Kimborough	James Roper, Edward Moore.
1781	Thomas Childs	Robert Moss, Peter Randle.
1782	Thomas Childs	Robest Moss, Peter Randle.
1783	Thomas Childs	James McDonald, Mark Allen.
1784	Samuel Parsons	Wm. Kendall, Mark Allen.
1785	Samuel Parsons	Jas. McDonald, Charles Robertson.
1786	John Stokes	Jas. McDonald, John Palmer.
1787	John Stokes	Thomas Childs, illiam Kendall.
1788	David Nesbit	James Tindall, Thomas Ussory.
1789	William Kendall	Wm. Johnson, James Tindall.
1790	Thomas Childs	Thomas Butler, John Ussory.
1791	James Turner	James Tindall. James Gray.
1792	James Turner	William Rush, West Harris.
1793	James Turner	William Rush, Wm. Loften.
1794	Thomas Childs	William Loften, Thos. Ussory.
1795	Thomas Childs	Thos. Ussory, Henry Deberry.
1796	Thomas Childs	Wm. Loften, Henry Deberry.
1797	West Harris	Henry Deberry, Arthur Harris.
1798	West Harris	Henry Deberry, Arthur Harris.
1799	West Harris	Henry Deberry, Thomas Childs, Jr.
1800	Thomas Blewet	Henry Deberry, Thomas Childs, Jr.
1801	West Harris	Thomas Childs, Silas Billingsfly.
1802	West Harris	Wm. R. Allen, James Saunders.

MONTGOMERY COUNTY—Continued.

MEMBERS OF GENERAL ASSEMBLY—Continued.

Years.	Senate.	House.
1803	Geo. W. Graham	John Maske, James Saunders.
1804	James Saunders	James Allen, John Maske.
1805	James Saunders	John Maske, James Allen.
1806	Edmund Deberry	James Allen, David Cochran.
1807	Edmund Deberry	David Cochran, Clement Lavier.
1808	Edmund Deberry	Claiborn Harris, Joseph Parsons.
1809	Edmund Deberry	Joseph Parsons, Wm. Crittenden.
1810	Edmund Deberry	George W. Davidson, Jos. Parsons.
1811	Edmund Deberry	James Legrand, Jos. Parsons.
1812	Geo. W. Davidson	James Legrand, John Randle.
1813	Edmund Deberry	John Crump, Thomas Butler.
1814	Edmund Deberry	J. Crump, John Randle.
1815	James Legrand	John Randle, John rump.
1816	James Legrand	John Crump, John Randle.
1817	John Crump	John Lilley, Andrew Wade.
1818	Geo. W. Davidson	John Kendall, John Lilley.
1819	Geo. W. Davidson	John Lilley, John Kendall.
1820	Edmund Deberry	John Dargan, John Lilley.
1821	Edmund Deberry	John Dargan, Hardy Morgan.
1822	James Legrand	Hardy Morgan, John Dargan.
1823	James Legrand	ardy Morgan, John Dargan.
1824	James Legrand	John Culpepper, John Dargan.
1825	James Legrand	John Dargan, Thos. C. Dunn.
1826	Edmund Deberry	John Dargan, James Allen.
1827	Edmund Deberry	James Allen, Jas. M. Lilley.
1828	Edmund Deberry	Reuben Kendall, Jas. M. Lilley.
1829	John Crump	Reuben Kendall, Jas. M. Lilley.
1830	John Crump	James M. Lilley, Reuben Kendall.
1831	Reuben Kendall	Geo. W. McClain, Pleasant M. Maske.
1832	James M. Lilley	Francis Locke, Pleasant M. Maske.
1833	Reuben Kendall	Francis Locke, Edmund F. Lilley.
1835	Reuben Kendall	William Harris, Peter R. Lilley.
1836	John B. Kelley	William Harris, Enoch Jordan.
1838	. H. Montgomery	illiam Harris, Thos. Pemberton.
1840	J. H. Montgomery	Thos. Pemberton, Edmund F. Lilley.
1842	J. M. Worth	Calvin J. Cochran, Francis Locke.
1844	J. M. Worth	Calvin J. Cochran.
1846	Alexander Kelly	Zebedee Russell.
1848	J. M. Worth	Zebedee Russell.
1850	Angus R. Kelly	Zebedee Russell.
1852	Angus R. Kelly	S. V. Simmons.
1854	S. H. Christian	Zebedee Russell.
1856	S. H. Christian	J. M. Crump.
1858	A. B. McDonald	—— Chambers.
1860	W. D. Dowd	Alex. Kelly.
1862	Calvin W. ooley	Allen Jordan.
1864	J. M. Crump	Allen Jordan.
1866	m. B. Richardson	Geo. A. Graham.
1868	John H. Davis	Geo. A. Graham.
1870	J. M. Worth	J. G. Morgan.
1872	R. T. Long	Allen Jordan.

Montgomery and Richmond form the 26th Senatorial District.

MOORE COUNTY.

MOORE COUNTY was formed in 1784, from Cumberland county, and named in compliment of Hon. Alfred Moore, late one of the Associate Justices of the Supreme Court of the United States.

Moore county is near the centre of the State, being bounded on the north by Chatham and Randolph, east by Cumberland and Harnett, south by Richmond, and west by Montgomery.

Its capital is Carthage, 79 miles south-west of Raleigh.

COUNTY OFFICERS.

Offices.	Names.
Superior Court Clerk	A. H. McNeill.
Register of Deeds	W. P. Willcox.
Sheriff	J. M. Monger.
Coroner	A. M. D. illiamson.
Surveyor	J. J. Wicker.
Treasurer	G. A. McRae.
Commissioners	J. B. Graham, Chairman. J. O. A. Kelley. W. P. Cameron. B. Coffin. Hugh Leach.

JUSTICES OF THE PEACE.

Names.	Date of Qualification.	Post Office Address.
M. M. Fry	Aug. 16th, 1873.	Carthage.
M. M. Fergurson	" "	arthage.
Jesse Muse	" "	Carthage.
Daniel B. Currie	" "	Carriersville.
Kenneth Matheson	" 25th "	Caledonia.
E. T. Williams	" 16th "	arter's Mills.
Richard Street	" "	Carthage.
A. W. Cable	" "	Carter's Mills.
William McLeod	" "	rain's Creek.
William Arnold	" "	Jonesboro'.
D. B. McIver	" "	Jonesboro'.
A. E. Kelly	" "	Jonesboro'.
John McNeill	" 22d, "	Crain's reek.
John A. Walker	" "	Swan's Station.
M. A. Munroe	" "	arthage.
D. C. Blue	" "	McKenzie's Bridge.
M. G. McKenzie	" "	McKenzie's Bridge.
D. B. Caddell	" "	McKenzie's Bridge.
C. W. Shaw	Nov. 15th, 1873.	Solemn Grove.

MOORE COUNTY—Continued.

MEMBERS OF GENERAL ASSEMBLY.

Years.	Senate.	House.
1785	Philip Alston..............	John Carroll, John Cox.
1786	Philip Alston..............	ohn Cox, Charles Crawford.
1787	Thomas Overton............	John Cox, Thomas Tyson.
1788	Thomas Overton............	William Martin, William Mears.
1789	Thomas Overton............	William Martin, William Mears.
1790	Thomas Overton.	William Martin, William Mears.
1791	Thomas Tyson..............	Cornelius Dowd, William artin.
1792	Thomas Overton............	William Barrett, William Dunn.
1793	William Martin............	William Dunn, Daniel McIntosh.
1794	Daniel McIntosh	Thomas H. Perkins, Malcolm Gilchrist.
1795	Daniel McIntosh	Malcolm Gilchrist, William Gilchrist.
1796	Malcolm Gilchrist..........	Jacob Gastor, Murdock Martin.
1797	Daniel McIntosh	Cornelius Dowd, Jacob Gastor.
1798	Malcolm Gilchrist..........	William Barrett, Cornelius Dowd.
1799	Malcolm Gilchrist..........	John McIvor, Jacob Gastor.
1800	Malcolm Gilchrist..........	Murdock artin, Jacob Gastor.
1801	Duncan Brice...............	Allen McLellan, Archibald Dalrymple.
1802	Murdock McKenzie.........	Jacob Gastor, Allen McLellan.
1803	Duncan Brice...............	John Atkinson, Cornelius Dowd.
1804	Jacob Gastor...............	Allen McLellan, Francis Bullock.
1805	Thomas Tyson..............	Allen McLellan, Francis Bullock.
1806	Jacob Gastor...............	William Barrett, Cornelius Dowd.
1807	Benjamin Williams.........	Cornelius Dowd, Allen McLellan.
1808	Thomas Tyson	Archibald McNeill, William Brice.
1809	Benjamin Williams.........	Archibald McNeill, Edmund Wade.
1810	Allen McClennan...........	William Brice, David Reid.
1811	Archibald McNeill..........	Atlas Jones, John cLennan.
1812	Jacob Gastor...............	James Seawell, Atlas Jones.
1813	Archibald McBryde.........	James Seawell, Josiah Tyson.
1814	Archibald McBryde.........	Jonathan Tyson, Malone Brice.
1815	Archibald McNeill..........	Jacob Gastor, Josiah Tyson.
1816	Atlas Jones................	Josiah Tyson, John Murchison.
1817	Atlas Jones................	John Murchison, Josiah Tyson.
1818	John B. Kelly..............	Benjamin Person, John Murchison.
1819	Josiah Tyson...............	Malcolm Bryce, Alexander McNeill.
1820	Benjamin Person............	Alexander McNeill, Josiah Tyson.
1821	Benjamin Person............	Josiah Tyson, Alexander McNeill.
1822	Benjamin Person............	Josiah Tyson, Alexander McNeill.
1823	William Jackson...........	Gideon Seawell, Angus Martin.
1824	Benjamin W. Williams......	Jos. A. Hill, Jos. Lamb.
1825	Cornelius Dowd............	John Murchison, William Crawford.
1826	Josiah Tyson...............	Gideon Seawell, William Wadsworth.
1827	Alexander McNeill..........	Gideon Seawell, William Wadsworth.
1828	Alexander McNeill..........	Josiah Tyson, William Wadsworth.
1829	Alexander McNeill..........	William Hancock, Duncan Murchison.
1830	Alexander McNeill..........	William Wadsworth, Willis D. Dowd.
1831	Josiah Tyson...............	William Wadsworth, Gideon Seawell.
1832	osiah Tyson...............	Wm. Wads orth, Jno. H. Montgomery.
1833	Duncan Murchison..........	Wm. Wadsworth, Jno. . Montgomery.
1834	Cornelius Dowd............	Wm. Wadsworth, Angus McDonald.
1835	Cornelius Dowd............	John B. Kelly, John A. D. McNeill.
1838	John H. Montgomery.......	John A. D. McNeill.
1840	John H. Montgomery.......	Duncan Murchison.
1842	J. M. Worth................	William D. Harrington.

MOORE COUNTY—Continued.

MEMBERS OF GENERAL ASSEMBLY—Continued.

Years.	Senate.	House.
1844	J. M. Worth	Donald Street.
1846	Alexander Kelly	M. B. Person.
1848	J. M. Worth	Samuel J. Person.
1850	Angus R. Kelly	Samuel J. Person.
1852	A. R. Kelly	Wm. Barrett.
1854	S. H. Christian	Hugh Leach.
1856	S. H. Christian	Wm. B. Richardson.
1858	A. B. McDonald	John Shaw.
1860	W. D. Dowd	Alexander Kelly.
1862	Calvin W. Wooley	Alexander Kelly.
1864	J. M. Crump	E. G. Harrington.
1866	Wm. B. Richardson	Wm. M. Black.
1868	Wm. B. Richardson	Abel Kelly.
1870	R. S. Ledbetter	——— Morgan.
1872	J. M. Worth	J. Shaw.

Moore and Randolph form the 25th Senatorial District.

NASH COUNTY.

Nash County was formed from Edgecombe county, in 1777, and named in compliment of General Francis Nash, of Orange, who fell this year at the battle of Germantown, bravely fighting for the liberties of his country.

It is situated in the eastern part of the State, and bounded on the north by Halifax, east by Edgecombe and Wilson, south by Wilson and Johnston, and west by Franklin.

Its capital is Nashville, and is distant 44 miles east from Raleigh.

COUNTY OFFICERS.

Offices.	Names.
Superior Court Clerk	Josiah P. Jenkins.
Register of Deeds	William T. Griffin.
Sheriff	George N. Lewis.
Coroner	Vacant.
Surveyor	Alexander Hilliard.
Treasurer	Orren Cobb.
Commissioners	W. P. Walker. G. D. Langley. Willis Eason. Kinchen H. Bailey. B. C. Strickland.

NASH COUNTY—Continued.

JUSTICES OF THE PEACE.

Names.	Date of Qualification.	Post Office Address.
James Harper	Aug. 12th, 1873.	Castalia.
Richard F. Drake	" "	Hilliardston.
T. P. Braswell	" "	Battleboro'.
W. H. Harrison	" "	Battleboro'.
Manriah Lucas	" "	Rocky Mount.
John C. Harper	" "	Nashville.
Willie H. Robbins	" "	Nashville.
G. D. Langley	" "	Nashville.
J. J. E. Deans	" "	Nashville.
Z. R. Hinton	" "	Nashville.
H. M. Warren	" "	Nashville.
Z. R. Bissett	" "	Stanhope.
D. H. Finch	" "	Stanhope.
John T. Morgan	" "	Stanhope.
H. H. Williams	" "	Wilson.
S. Fountain	" "	Rocky Mount.
George W. Robbins	" "	Sharpsburg.
James Viverett	" "	Toisnot.
J. W. Thompson	" "	Whitaker's.
McBrantley	Sept. 2d, 1873.	Stanhope
H. H. Medlin	" "	Stanhope.

MEMBERS OF GENERAL ASSEMBLY.

Years.	Senators.	House.
1778	Hardy Griffin	Thomas Huester, Hardy Griffin.
1780	Hardy Griffin	Joseph Arrington, Edward Nicholson.
1781	Hardy Griffin	Joseph Arrington, Edward Nicholson.
1782	Hardy Griffin	Joseph Arrington, Edward Nicholson.
1783	Hardy Griffin	Micajah Thomas, Thomas Pounds.
1784	Hardy Griffin	Micajah Thomas, Thomas Pounds.
1785	Hardy Griffin	John Bonds, Micajah Thomas.
1786	Hardy Griffin	John Bonds, Jos. J. Clinch.
1787	Hardy Griffin	Micajah Thomas, John Bonds.
1788	Red. Bunn	Wilson Vick, John Bonds.
1789	Hardy Griffin	Wilson Vick, John Bonds.
1790	Hardy Griffin	James Battle, John Bonds.
1791	Hardy Griffin	Howell Ellen, Joseph Arrington.
1792	Hardy Griffin	John H. Drake, Joseph Arrington.
1793	Hardy Griffin	John H. Drake, John Bonds.
1794	Hardy Griffin	John H. Drake, Arch'd Hunter.
1795	Hardy Griffin	John H. Drake, Arch'd Hunter.
1796	William Arrington	John H. Drake, Arch'd Hunter.
1797	Archibald Griffin	Redmond Bunn, Arch'd Hunter.
1798	John Arrington	Redmond Bunn, John H. Drake.
1799	John Arrington	Redmond Bunn, Arch'd Hunter.
1800	John H. Drake	George Boddie, Redmond Bunn.

NASH COUNTY—Continued.

MEMBERS OF GENERAL ASSEMBLY—Continued.

Years.	Senate.	House.
1801	John Arrington	George Boddie, Arch'd Hunter.
1802	John Arrington	John Hilliard, Arch'd Griffin.
1803	John Arrington	Arch'd Griffin, John Hilliard.
1804	John Arrington	Arch'd Griffin, Nathan Whitehead.
1805	John H. Drake	Nathan Whitehead, Henry Hines.
1806	John Arrington	Arch'd Griffin, Redmond Bunn.
1807	John Arrington	Arch'd Griffin, Redmond Bunn.
1808	William Arrington	Amos Grandy, Redmond Bunn.
1809	William Arrington	Michael Collins, Exum Phillips.
1810	William Arrington	Amos Grandy, Michael Collins.
1811	William Arrington	Michael Collins, Exum Phillips.
1812	William Arrington	George Boddie, Michael Collins.
1813	George Boddie	R. C. Hilliard, Michael Collins.
1814	George Boddie	R. C. Hilliard, Michael Collins.
1815	George Boddie	R. C. Hilliard, Michael Collins.
1816	Michael Collins	Bartley Deans, David Ricks.
1817	Robert C. Hilliard	Arch'd Lamon, Joseph Terrell.
1818	Michael Collins	Wm. W. Boddie, Arch'd Lamon.
1819	Joseph Terrell	Wm. W. Boddie, Arch'd Lamon.
1820	Wm. W. Boddie	Arch'd Lamon, Henry Blount.
1821	Wm. W. Boddie	Henry Blount, Arch'd Lamon.
1822	Wm. W. Boddie	Arch'd Lamon, Thos. N. Mann.
1823	Wm. W. Boddie	Arch'd Lamon, Thos. N. Mann.
1824	Wm. W. Boddie	Arch'd Lamon, N. J. Drake.
1825	Wm. W. Boddie	Nicholas Drake, Major A. Wilcox.
1826	Wm. W. Boddie	Duncan York, Joseph Arrington.
1827	Nicholas Drake	Frederick Battle, Jas. N. Mann.
1828	Wm. W. Boddie	Frederick Battle, Gideon Bass.
1829	Wm. W. Boddie	Duncan York, Joseph Arrington.
1830	Wm. W. Boddie	Jos. Arrington, Robert C. Hilliard.
1831	Wm. W. Boddie	Jos. Arrington, George Boddie.
1832	Wm. W. Boddie	Jos. Arrington, George Boddie.
1833	Samuel L. Arrington	George Boddie, Ford Taylor.
1834	Samuel L. Arrington	George Boddie, Ford Taylor.
1835	Samuel L. Arrington	Samuel Brown, Ford Taylor.
1836	Samuel L. Arrington	Henry Blount.
1838	Samuel L. Arrington	Ford Taylor.
1840	Samuel L. Arrington	Ford Taylor.
1842	Samuel L. Arrington	Ford Taylor.
1844	John H. Drake	W. D. Harrison.
1846	John H. Drake	W. D. Harrison.
1848	John H. Drake	Dr. Taylor.
1850	John H. Drake	Ford Taylor.
1852	John H. Drake	J. W. Bryant.
1854	John H. Drake	J. W. Bryant.
1856	L. N. B. Battle	G. N. Lewis.
1858	L. N. B. Battle	G. N. Lewis.
1860	A. G. Taylor	H. G. Williams.
1862	A. G. Taylor	H. G. Williams.
1864	A. G. Taylor	H. G. Williams.
1866	L. N. B. Battle	George N. Lewis.
1868	Joshua Barnes	W. W. Boddie.
1870	Lawrence F. Battle	—— Woodard.
1872	John W. Dunham William K. Davis	John E. Lindsay.

Franklin, Nash and Wilson form the 7th Senatorial District.

NEW HANOVER COUNTY.

NEW HANOVER COUNTY was formed in 1728, and called in honor of the House of Hanover, then on the English throne.

It is situated in the south-eastern part of North Carolina; and bounded on the north by Duplin, east by Onslow, south by the Atlantic Ocean, and west by the Cape Fear and South Rivers, which separate it from Brunswick and Bladen counties.

Its capital is Wilmington, called in compliment to the Earl of Wilmington, the nobleman to whose patronage Governor Johnston (in 1739) was indebted for his office. It was originally called Newton. Distance from Raleigh 148 miles.

On April 30th, 1844, a large portion of this beautiful town was destroyed by fire.

COUNTY OFFICERS.

Offices.	Names.
Superior Court Clerk	James C. Mann.
Register of Deeds	Joseph C. ill.
Sheriff	Archd. R. Black.
Coroner	Edward D. Hewlett.
Surveyor	Henry A. Colvin.
Treasurer	Edwin E. Buruess.
Commissioners	Silas H. Martin, Chairman.
	Lawson E. Rice.
	Aug. H. Morris.
	Deleware Nixon.
	Jas. H. Chadbourn.

JUSTICES OF THE PEACE.

Names.	Date of Qualification.	Post Office Address.
W. M. Harris		
Stacey Van Amringe		
Thomas M. Gardner		
Anthony Howe		
W. H. Moore		
W. A. Green		
Jesse J. Cassiday		
Solomon Reaves		
W. H. Montgomery		
Elijah Hewlett		
John G. Wagner		
W. W. Humphrey		
Deleware Nixon		
Andrew Nixon		
Alfred Lloyd		
Henry E. Scot		

NEW HANOVER COUNTY—Continued.

JUSTICES OF THE PEACE—Continued.

Names.	Date of Qualification.	Post Office Address.
Murphy Wood		
G. F. Jordan		
W. T. Bannerman		
Jas. B. McPherson		
August Gernburg		
Geo. W. Bordeuax		
C. M. Galloway		
James Thompson		
James I. Pridgen		
S. C. Fillyan		
Rufus Garris		
Thomas Williams		
John L. Mashbourne		
Wm. J. Birins		
Samuel C. Larkins		
A. J. McIntyre		

LIST OF MEMBERS TO THE HOUSE OF COMMONS FROM WILMINGTON.

Years.	House of Commons.	Years.	House of Commons.
1776	William Hooper.	1806	J. G. Wright.
1778	William Hooper.	1807	J. G. Wright.
1779	Wm. Hooper.	1808	J. G. Wright.
1780	Wm. Hooper.	1809	J. G. Wright.
1781	Wm. Hooper.	1810	Wm. W. Jones.
1782	Wm. Hoopor.	1811	Wm. W. Jones.
1783	Arch'd McLean.	1812	Wm. W. Jones.
1784	Arch'd McLean.	1813	Wm. W. Jones.
1785	Arch'd McLean.	1814	Wm. W. Jones.
1786	Arch'd McLean.	1815	Wm. W. Jones.
1787	Joshua Potts.	1816	Edward B. Dudley.
1788	Edward Jones.	1817	Eaward B. Dudley.
1789	Edward Jones.	1818	Wm. B. Meares.
1790	Edward Jones.	1819	John D. Jones.
1791	Edward Jones.	1820	John D. Jones.
1792	Joshua G. Wright.	1821	John D. Jones.
1793	J. G. Wright.	1822	John D. Jones.
1794	J. G. Wright.	1823	M. W. Campbell.
1795	J. G. Wright.	1824	Robert H. Cowan.
1796	J. G. Wright.	1825	Robert H. Cowan.
1797	J. G. Wright.	1826	Joseph A. Hill.
1798	J. G. Wright.	1827	Joseph A. Hill.
1799	J. G. Wright.	1828	John Walker.
1801	J. G. Wright.	1830	Joseph A. Hill.
1802	J. G. Wright.	1831	Daniel Sherwood.
1803	J. G. Wright.	1832	Daniel Sherwood.
1804	J. G. Wright.	1833	John D. Jones.
1805	J. G. Wright.	1834	Edward B. Dudley.

The Convention of 1835 abolished the Borough representation.

NEW HANOVER COUNTY—Continued.

MEMBERS OF GENERAL ASSEMBLY.

Years.	Senate.	House.
1777	John Ashe	Alexander Lillington, Samuel Swann.
1778	John Ashe	John Devane, Timothy Bloodworth.
1779	John Devane	John A. Campbell, Timothy Bloodworth.
1780	John Devane	John A. Campbell, Timothy Bloodworth.
1781	John Devane	Thomas Bloodworth, Caleb Granger.
1782	Caleb Granger	Timothy Bloodworth, Jas. Bloodworth.
1783	John A. Campbell	Timothy Bloodworth, Jas. Bloodworth.
1784	John A. Campbell	Timothy Bloodworth, Jas. Bloodworth.
1785	John A. Campbell	Jas. Bloodworth, John Pugh Williams.
1786	John A. Campbell	Jas. Bloodworth, John Pugh Williams.
1787	John A. Campbell	Thomas Devane, Jr., Timothy Bloodworth
1788	Timothy Bloodworth	John Pugh Williams, Thomas Devane.
1789	Timothy Bloodworth	John A. Campbell, John Pugh Williams.
1791	John A. Campbell	John G. Scull, Timothy Bloodworth.
1792	John A. Campbell	Thomas Devane, George Moore.
1793	John A. Campbell	Timothy Bloodworth, James Larkins.
1794	William H. Hill	Timothy Bloodworth, James Larkins.
1795	Jas. Bloodworth	David Jones, John Gambier Scull.
1796	Jas. Bloodworth	Samuel Ashe, Alexander D. Moore.
1797	John Hill	Samuel Ashe, Alex. D. Moore.
1798	John Hill	Alex. D. Moore, James Larkins.
1799	John Hill	Thomas Hill, Samuel Ashe.
1800	John Hill	Alex. D. Moore, Samuel Ashe.
1801	Samuel Ashe	Timothy Bloodworth, Richard Nixon
1802	Samuel Ashe	Richard Nixon, James Larkins.
1803	Samuel Ashe	James Foy, Franklin T. Bloodworth
1804	John Bloodworth	Jas. Foy, F. T. Bloodworth.
1805	John Hill	Richard Nixon, F. T. Bloodworth.
1806	Samuel Ashe	Richard Nixon, Roger Moore.
1807	Samuel Ashe	Wm. W. Jones, Hinton James.
1808	F. T. Bloodworth	Wm. W. Jones, Hinton James.
1809	F. T. Bloodworth	Hinton James, David Jones.
1810	Thomas Devane	David Jones, Joseph Lamb.
1811	William Hill	Joseph Lamb, John D. Jones.
1812	David Jones	Joseph Lamb, George Fennell.
1813	David Jones	Geo. Fennell, Joseph Parrish.
1814	David Jones	Joel Parrish, Geo. Fennell.
1815	James Larkins	Geo. Fennell, Joel Parrish.
1816	Richard Nixon	Owen Fillyaw, Joel Parrish.
1817	Samuel Ashe	Joseph Lamb, Ed. St. George.
1818	M. W. Campbell	Joseph Lamb, John Bunting.
1819	George Fennell	Jos. Lamb, John Bunting.
1820	George Fennell	John Walker, Abel Morgan.
1821	M. W. Campbell	Abel Morgan, Eli L. Larkins.
1822	Thomas Devane	Joseph Lamb, S. Sidbury.
1823	Thomas Devane	Stokely Sidbury, Jos. A. Hill.
1824	Thomas Devane	Jos. A. Hill, Jos. Lamb.
1825	Thomas Devane	Jos. Lamb, Wm. Watts Jones.
1826	Thomas Devane	John Kerr, Wm. Watts Jones.
1827	Thomas Devane	John Kerr, Wm. Watts Jones.
1828	Wm. B. Meares	John Kerr, Wm. S. Larkins.
1829	Wm. B. Meares	Wm. S. Larkins, Patrick Murphey.
1830	Wm. B. Meares	Wm. S. Larkins, Thomas Hill.
1831	M. W. Campbell	Wm. S. Larkins, Wm. J. Wright.

NEW HANOVER COUNTY—Continued.

MEMBERS OF GENERAL ASSEMBLY—Continued.

Years.	Senate.	House.
1832	Jos. H. Lamb	Thomas Hill, Louis H. Marsteller.
1833	Wm. B. Meares	L. H. Marsteller, Stephen Register.
1834	Owen Holmes	L. H. Marsteller, Stephen Register.
1835	L. H. Marsteller	Charles Henry, John R. Walker.
1836	Louis H. Marsteller	John R. Walker, Charles Henry.
1838	Charles Henry	Jas. T. Miller, Evans Larkins.
1840	Wm. S. Larkins	Jas. T. Miller, James Kerr.
1842	Wm. S. Larkins	Jeremiah Nixon, David McIntire.
1844	Owen Holmes	Jeremiah Nixon, David McIntire.
1846	Wm. S. Ashe	Edward Hall, Thomas H. Williams.
1848	Wm. S. Ashe	Thomas H. Williams, N. N. Nixon.
1850	N. N. Nixon	Wm. Hill, J. D. Powers.
1852	J. Kerr	Robt. Strange, Jr., J. A. Corbett.
1854	Owen Fennel	S. J. Person, Thos. H. Williams, D. McMillan.
1856	Owen Fennel	T. H. Tate, S. H. Holmes.
1858	Wm. S. Ashe	R. K. Bryan, G. J. Moore.
1860	Eli W. Hall	S. J. Person, Daniel Shaw.
1862	Eli W. Hall	S. J. Person, J. R. Haws.
1864	Edward D. Hall	S. J. Person, J. R. Haws.
1866	Edward D. Hall	R. H. Cowan, C. W. McClammy.
1868	Edwin Legg, A. H. Galloway	Jos. C. Abbott, Llewellen C. Estes, Geo. W. Price.
1870	Charles McClammy, A. H. Galloway	S. A. Ashe, Geo. Z. French, G. L. Mabson
1872	Geo. L. Mabson	James Heaton, Wm. H. McLaurin, Alfred Lloyd.

New Hanover is the 12th Senatorial District.

NORTHAMPTON COUNTY.

Northampton County was formed in 1741, from Bertie; but history and tradition are alike silent as to the origin of its name. Martin, in his History, merely states that the Legislature met "at Wilmington, in the latter part of 1741, and the session was of short duration; the county of Bertie was divided, and the upper part of it established as a new county, to which the name of Northampton was given.

It is situated in the north-eastern part of the State; and bounded on the north by the Virginia line, east by Hertford and Bertie, south by Halifax, and west by the Roanoke River, which separates it from Halifax.

Its capital is Jackson, and preserves the name of Andrew Jackson, the hero of New Orleans, and sixth President of the United States.

NORTHAMPTON COUNTY—Continued.

COUNTY OFFICERS.

Offices.	Names.
Superior Court Clerk	Noah R. Odom.
Register of Deeds	Wm. T. Buxton.
Sheriff	Jas. W. Newsum.
Coroner	. A. Parker.
Surveyor	E. W. Conner.
Treasurer	Jas. W. Copeland.
Commissioners	Jas. W. Grant. Lemuel H. Boyce. Thos. C. Peele. Samuel N. Buxton. Thos. Kee.

JUSTICES OF THE PEACE.

Names.	Date of Qualification.	Post Office Address.
William J. Maddery	Aug. 18th, 1878.	Seaboard.
Joseph W. Coker	" "	Garysburg.
Andrew E. Peele	" "	Jackson.
Joseph N. Seldon	" "	Jackson.
Isaac Peele	" "	Jackson.
Mate. Calvert	" "	Jackson.
T. F. Moore	" "	Gaston.
James W. Grant	" "	Garysburg.
Ira W. Futicle	" "	Murfreesboro.
E. A. Martin	" "	Boykin's Depot.
A. J. Harrell	" "	Rich Square.
William T. Peele	" "	Rich Square.
Jacob D. Hill	" "	Garysburg.
James L. Lassiter	" "	Jackson.
William H. Parker	" "	Margarettsville.
William Grant	Sept. 19th, "	Jackson.

MEMBERS OF GENERAL ASSEMBLY.

Years.	Senate.	House.
1777	James Vaughan	Robert Peeples, Jeptha Atherton.
1778	James Vaughan	Robert Peoples, Joseph Bryan.
1779	James Vaughan	Robert Peoples, Joseph Bryan.
1780	James Vaughan	Robert Peoples, John Dawson.
1781	James Vaughan	John Dawson, Jas. Sikes.
1782	Samuel Lockhart	John Dawson, Jas. Sikes.

NORTHAMPTON COUNTY—Continued.

MEMBERS OF GENERAL ASSEMBLY—Continued.

Years.	Senate.	House.
1783	Samuel Lockhart	James Vaughan, Drury Gee.
1784	Allen Jones	James Vaughan, Wm. R. Davie.
1785	Allen Jones	Howell Edmunds, Augustin Wood.
1786	Allen Jones	James Vaughan, Nehemiah Long.
1787	Allen Jones	Robert Peebles, John Vaughan.
1788	John M. Benford	John Knox, Robert Peebles.
1789	John M. Benford	Samuel Peete, Halcott Briggs Pride.
1791	John M. Benford	William Amis, Samuel Tarver.
1792	John M. Benford	William Amis, Nicholas Edmunds.
1793	John M. Benford	William Amis, Nicholas Edmunds.
1794	John M. Benford	Benjamin Williamson, Nicholas Edmunds.
1795	John M. Benford	Benjamin Williamson, Henry Cotten.
1796	John M. Benford	Benjamin Williamson, Henry K. Peterson.
1797	John M. Benford	Benjamin Williamson, William Edmunds.
1798	John M. Benford	William Edmunds, James Benford.
1799	John M. Benford	Henry Cotten, James Long.
1800	John M. Benford	Howell Peebles, Henry Cotten.
1801	John M. Benford	Henry Cotten, Howell Peebles.
1802	John M. Benford	Henry Cotten, William Edmunds.
1803	Henry Cotton	Peter Woodlief, William Edmunds.
1804	Richard W. Freear	Green Turner, William Edmunds.
1805	John M. Benford	Green Turner, Samuel Tarver.
1806	John M. Benford	William Edmunds, John Peebles.
1807	John M. Benford	Charles Harrison, Francis A. Bynum.
1808	Wm. Edmunds	Charles Harrison, Francis A. Bynum.
1809	Wm. Edmunds	Green Turner, Andrew Jones.
1810	Wm. Edmunds	Andrew Jones, John Peebles.
1811	Wm. Edmunds	Peter Woodlief, Cornelius Moore.
1812	Wm. Edmunds	Peter Woodlief, Cornelius Moore.
1813	Francis Dancy	Henry Boon, Richard Freear.
1814	Howell Peebles	Henry Boon, —— Jenkins.
1815	Howell Peebles	John R. Moore, Henry Boon.
1816	Howell Peebles	Henry Boon, John R. Moore.
1817	Cornelius Moore	Henry Boon, William Moody.
1818	Henry Boon	Henry Abingdon, B. C. Smith.
1819	Henry Boon	W. Sandiford, A. Deberry.
1820	Henry Boon	Allen Deberry, T. Barrow.
1821	John Peebles	Roderick B. Gary, Thomas Peete.
1822	John Peebles	L. P. Williamson, R. B. Gary.
1823	John Peebles	R. B. Gary, L. P. Williamson.
1824	John Peebles	R. B. Gary, Thomas Bynum.
1825	John Peebles	Thomas Bynum, Roderick B. Gary.
1826	Exum Holliman	R. B. Gary, J. H. Patterson.
1827	Exum Holliman	R. B. Gary, J. H. Patterson.
1828	John H. Patterson	R. B. Gary, Jos. M. S. Rogers.
1829	Collin W. Barnes	Jas. T. Hayley, R. B. Gary.
1830	Collin W. Barnes	R. B. Gary, James T. Hayley.
1831	James T. Haylay	Richard Crump, John M. Moody.
1832	Herod Faison	R. B. Gary, Allen Pierce.
1833	Herod Faison	Allen Pierce, Samuel Calvert.
1834	Wm. B. Lockhart	A. B. Smith, Wm. E. Crump.
1835	William Moody	Wm. E. Crump, R. B. Gary.
1836	William Moody	R. B. Gary, Herod Faison.
1838	William Moody	Junius Amis, H. Faison.

NORTHAMPTON COUNTY—Continued.

MEMBERS OF GENERAL ASSEMBLY—Continued.

Years.	Senate.	House.
1840	Herod Faison..............	Samuel B. Spruill, Edmund Jacobs.
1842	Jos. M. S. Rogers..........	John B. Odom, Thomas Bragg, Jr.
1844	John M. Moody............	John B. Odem, David A. Barnes.
1846	John M. Moody............	E. J. Peebles, David A. Barnes.
1848	Jos. M. S. Rogers..........	T. J. Person, E. J. Peebles.
1850	Jos. M. S. Rogers..........	T. J. Person, David A. Barns.
1852	T. J. Pearson..............	J. B. Bynum, B. F. Lockhart.
1854	J. B. Bynum................	M. W. Smallwood.
1856	M. W. Smallwood..........	J. Mason.
1858	M. W. Smallwood..........	M. W. Ransom.
1860	Jos. M. S. Rogers..........	M. W. Ransom, W. W. Peeples.
1862	[illegible]. S. Copeland.............	W. W. Peoples, H. Stancil.
1864	J. B. Odem..................	S. B. Calvert, S. T. Stancil.
1866	H. C. Edwards...............	R. B. Peebles, D. A. Martin.
1868	Wm. Barrow..................	Rosendell C. Parker, [illegible]. T. Grant.
1870	Jesse Blythe................	Samuel N. Buxton, R. Buxton Jones.
1872	Geo. D. Holloman..........	Benton H. Jones.

Bertie and Northampton form the third Senatorial District.

ONSLOW COUNTY.

Onslow County was formed in 1734, from New Hanover county, and named in honor of Arthur Onslow, then the Speaker of the British House of Commons.

Onslow is situated in the extreme eastern part of the State, and is bounded on the north and east by Jones and Carteret, south by Core Sound and the Atlantic Ocean, and west by New Hanover and Duplin.

Its Court House is 145 miles south-east from Raleigh.

COUNTY OFFICERS.

Offices.	Names.
Superior Court Clerk....................	A. C. Huggins.
Register of Deeds.......................	J. O. Frazel.
Sheriff..................................	Elijah Murrill.
Coroner..................................	Thomas Jarman.
Surveyor	None.
Treasurer................................	L. W. Hargett.
Commissioners..........................	A. J. Murrill. B. [illegible]. Trott. John Shepard. Harvey Cox. W. P. Ward.

ONSLOW COUNTY—Continued.

JUSTICES OF THE PEACE.

Names.	Date of Qualification.	Post Office Address.
Jere W. Yopp	Aug. 11th, 1873.	Sneeds Ferry.
Andrew J. Sheperd	" "	Jacksonville.
James Gurganus	" "	Jacksonville.
Andrew J. Johnston	" "	Jacksonville.
John W. Thompson	Aug. 16th, "	Haw Branch.
Elijah J. Newbold	" "	Gum Branch.
Wm. J. Montfort	Aug. 23d, "	Ward's Mills.
Richard Canaday	" 25th, "	Swansboro'.
Louis O. Fonvielle	" "	Ward's Mills.
Samuel L. Gerock	Jan. 5th, 1874.	Palo Alto.
John Sheperd	" "	Jacksonville.
William P. Ward	Aug. 25th. 1873.	Swansboro'.

MEMBERS OF GENERAL ASSEMBLY.

Years.	Senators.	House.
1777	Henry Rhodes	John King, Benejah Doty.
1778	Henry Rhodes	Benejah Doty, George Mitchell.
1779	Henry Rhodes	James Howard, Edward Starkey.
1780	Henry Rhodes	Edward Starkey, George Mitchell.
1781	Henry Rhodes	Edward Starkey, Lewis Williams.
1782	Henry Rhodes	Edward Starkey, Lewis Williams.
1783	John Spicer	Edward Starkey, James Howard.
1784	Thomas Johnson	Edward Starkey, David Yeates.
1785	John Spicer	Reuben Grant, Edward Starkey.
1786	George Mitchell	Daniel Yates, Reuben Grant.
1787	George Mitchell	Daniel Yates, Reuben Grant.
1788	Thomas Johnson	Daniel Yates, Reuben Grant.
1789	David Yeates	Robert W. Sneed, John Spicer.
1790	Robert W. Sneed	John Spicer, Christopher Dudley.
1791	Robert W. Sneed	Reuben Grant, Christopher Dudley.
1792	Reuben Grant	John Spicer, Joseph S. Cray.
1793	Robert Sneed	Joseph S. Cray, Christopher Dudley.
1794	John Spicer	Zachariah Barrow, Joseph S. Cray.
1795	John Spicer	Zachariah Barrow, Joseph S. Cray.
1796	John Spicer	Zachariah Barrow, Nathaniel Loomis.
1797	John Spicer	Nathaniel Loomis, Joseph S. Cray.
1798	John Spicer	Joseph S. Cray, Nathaniel Loomis.
1799	John Spicer	Jesse Williams, Nathaniel Loomis.
1800	John Spicer	Jesse Williams, William Russell.
1801	Christopher Dudley	Geo. W. Mitchell, George Ward.
1802	George Ward	Stephen Williams, Geo. W. Mitchell.
1803	Christopher Dudley	George W. Mitchell, John Fullwood.
1804	John Fullwood	Stephen Williams, William French.
1805	John Fullwood	William French, Stephen Williams.
1806	Wm. French	Lemuel Doty, Edward Ward.
1807	Wm. French	Edward Williams, Benjamin Farnell.
1808	Stephen Williams	Edward Williams, John E. Spicer.

ONSLOW COUNTY—Continued.

MEMBERS OF GENERAL ASSEMBLY—Continued.

Years.	Senate.	House.
1809	Christopher Dudley	Edward Williams, William Jones.
1810	John E. Spicer	Edward Ward, Edward Williams.
1811	Edward Ward, jr	Edward B. Dudley, Geo. W. Noble.
1812	Edward Williams	Lott Humphrey, William Jones.
1813	Brice Bender	Edward B. Dudley, Jas. Thompson.
1814	Edward B. Dudley	Jason Gregory, G. E. Grant.
1815	Edward Ward	William Mitchell, Jason Gregory.
1816	Christopher Dudley	Eli W. Ward, Solomon E. Grant.
1817	Christopher Dudley	Eli W. Ward, Basil R. Smith.
1818	Christopher Dudley	Eli W. Ward, Basil R. Smith.
1819	Eli W. Ward	Basil R. Smith, Edward Williams.
1820	Eli W. Ward	Edward Williams, D. M. Dulany.
1821	Basil R. Smith	Daniel M. Dulany, W. D. Humphreys.
1822	Edward Ward	Eli W. Ward, Daniel M. Dulany.
1823	Edward Ward	L. T. Oliver, Eli W. Ward.
1824	Edward Ward	Frederick Foy, Lewis T. Oliver.
1825	Edward Ward	Edward Williams, Frederick Foy.
1826	Edward Ward	John Giles, Wm. P. Ferrand.
1827	Edward Ward	Edward Williams, Frederick Foy.
1829	Edward Ward	Richard H. Hatch, John B. Thompson.
1830	Edward Ward	Frederick Foy, James Rowe.
1831	Lewis Dishong	John B. Thompson, Geo. A. Thompson.
1832	Lewis Dishong	Geo. A. Thompson, Jos. D. Ward.
1833	Thomas Foy	Daniel Thompson, Thomas Ennett.
1834	Thomas Ennett	Nathan'l L. Mitchell, Dan'l S. Sanders.
1835	David W. Simmons	Dan'l S. Saunders, Dan'l Thompson.
1836	Daniel S. Saunders	John A. Averitt.
1838	Joshua Foy	John B. Pollock.
1840	John B. Pollock	Thomas Ennett.
1842	Thomas Ennett	Timothy Haskins.
1844	W. Ennett	Edward W. Saunders.
1846	William Ferrand	Harvey Cox.
1848	John F. Spicer	E. D. Foy.
1850	Geo. H. McMillan	E. W. Fonville.
1852	Geo. H. McMillan	E. W. Fonville.
1854	E. W. Fonville	Lott W. Humphrey.
1856	E. W. Fonville	Lott W. Humphrey.
1858	Lott W. Humphrey	J. H. Foy.
1860	Lott W. Humphrey	J. H. Foy.
1862	A. J. Murrell	J. H. Foy.
1864	Isaac V. Saunders	A. G. Murrell.
1866	Jasper Etheridge	A. G. Murrell.
1868	Wm. A. Allen	Franklin Thomas.
1870	Wm. A. Allen	Jas. G. Scott.
1872	J. G. Scott	J. W. Shackelford.

Carteret, Jones and Onslow form the 9th Senatorial District.

ORANGE COUNTY.

ORANGE COUNTY was formed in 1751, from Granville, Johnston and Bladen Counties, and called in compliment to the House of Orange, which, in the persons of William and Mary, in 1692, filled the English throne.

It is located in the centre of the State, and bounded on the north by Person and Caswell, on the east by Granville and Wake, south by Chatham, and west by Alamance.

Its capital is HILLSBORO', 40 miles north-west of Raleigh.

Hillsboro' was laid out in 1759, by W. Churton, and was first called Childsburg, in honor of the Attorney General of the Colony; but altered to Hillsboro', in compliment to Earl of Hillsboro', the English Secretary of State for America.

COUNTY OFFICERS.

Offices.	Names.
Superior Court Clerk	George Laws.
Register of Deeds	John La s.
Sheriff	Thomas H. Hughes.
Coroner	Vacant.
Surveyor	A. M. Leathers.
Treasurer	David C. Parks.
Commissioners	William N. Patterson. Nelson P. Hall. John F. Lyon. Wm. S. Kirkland. Jos. W. Latta.

JUSTICES OF THE PEACE.

Names.	Date of Qualification.	Post Office Address.
William W. Allison	Sept. 1st, 1873.	Cedar Grove.
John F. Atwater	" "	Chapel Hill.
Merrett Cheek	" "	Chapel Hill.
John P. Forrest	" "	Cedar Grove.
Hugh B. Guthrie	" "	Chapel Hill.
Asa B. Gunter	" "	Durham.
Archabald C. Hunter	" "	Hillsboro'.
George M. Harden	" "	Hillsboro'.
Addison L. Holden	" "	Hillsboro'.
Richard M. Jones	" "	Hillsboro'.
Samuel H. Jordan	" "	Hillsboro'.
Asahael M. Latta	" "	South Lowell.
William H. Lloyd	" "	Chapel Hill.
John A. McMannen	" "	Durham.

ORANGE COUNTY.—Continued.

JUSTICES OF THE PEACE—Continued.

Names.	Date of Qualification.	Post Office Address.
W. C. Mason	Sept. 1st, 1873.	Durham.
Daniel F. Morrow	" "	Oaks.
Addison Mangum	Nov. 3rd, "	Flat River.
Doctor C. Parrish	Sept. 1st, "	Durham.
Calvin E. Smith	" "	Hillsboro'.
William W. Woods	" "	Durham.

MEMBERS OF THE HOUSE OF COMMONS FROM THE ADOPTION OF THE CONSTITUTION IN 1776 TO 1835, FROM HILLSBORO'.

Years.	House of Commons.	Years.	House of Commons.
1777	William Courtney.	1806	William Norwood.
1778	William Courtney.	1807	William Norwood.
1779	Thomas Tullock.	1808	Catlett Campbell.
1780	Thomas Tullock.	1809	Catlett Campbell.
1781	Thomas Tullock.	1810	Henry Thompson.
1782	Thomas Farmer.	1811	Henry Thompson.
1783	Thomas Farmer.	1812	John Street.
1784	Archibald Lytle.	1813	Thomas Ruffin.
1785	John Taylor.	1814	James Child.
1786	John Taylor.	1815	Thomas Ruffin.
1787	John Taylor.	1816	Thomas Ruffin.
1788	Absalom Tatom.	1817	William Lockhart.
1789	Wm. Nash.	1818	John Scott.
1790	Wm. Nash.	1819	John Scott.
1791	David Ray.	1820	John Scott.
1792	Samuel Benton.	1821	James S. Smith.
1793	Alexander D. Moore.	1822	Thomas Clancy.
1794	John Hogg.	1823	Thomas Clancy.
1795	Samuel Benton.	1824	John Scott.
1796	John Hogg.	1825	John Scott.
1797	Absalom Tatom.	1826	John Scott.
1798	Absalom Tatom.	1827	John Scott.
1799	Absalom Tatom.	1828	Frederick Nash.
1800	Absalom Tatom.	1829	Frederick Nash.
1801	Absalom Tatom.	1830	Wm. H. Phillips.
1802	Absalom Tatom.	1831	Thomas J. Faddis.
1803	Barnaby O'Farrel, (Catlett Campbell resigned.)	1832	Thomas J. Faddis.
		1833	William A. Graham.
1804	Catlett Campbell.	1834	William A. Graham.
1805	Catlett Campbell.	1835	William A. Graham.

In 1835 the Convention abolished the Borough representation.

ORANGE COUNTY—Continued.

MEMBERS OF GENERAL ASSEMBLY.

Years.	Senate.	House.
1777		Thomas Burke, John Butler.
1778		John Butler, Wm. McCauley.
1779		Wm. McCauley, Mark Patterson.
1780		Wm. McCauley, Mark Patterson.
1781	John Butler................	Jesse Benton, Robert Campbell.
1782	William Mebane............	Wm. McCauley, Mark Patterson.
1783	William McCauley..........	Alexander Mebane, Thomas Burke.
1784	Wm. McCauley............	Alexander Mebane, Wm. Hooper.
1785	Wm. McCauley............	William Courtney, William Cain.
1786	Wm. McCauley............	Jonathan Lindlay, Wm. Hooper.
1787	Wm. McCauley............	Alexander Mebane, Jonathan Lindlay.
1788	Wm. McCauley............	Alexander Mebane, Jonathan Lindlay.
1789	Joseph Hodge.............	Alexander Mebane, Jonathan Lindlay.
1790	William Courtney.........	Alexander Mebane, John Carrington.
1791	Joseph Hodge..............	Alexander Mebane, Jonathan Lindlay.
1792	Wm. F. Strudwick..........	Alexander Mebane, William Nash.
1793	William Sheppard..........	Walter Alves, Wm. Nash.
1794	William Cain...............	William Lytle, Walter Alves.
1795	William Cain...............	Walter Alves, Wm. Lytle.
1796	William Cain...............	Samuel Benton, John Cabe.
1797	Wm. F. Strudwick..........	Samuel Benton, John Cabe.
1798	David Ray.................	James Mebane, John Cabe.
1799	David Ray.................	Samuel Benton, William F. Strudwick.
1800	David Ray.................	Samuel Benton, John Cabe.
1801	William Sheppard..........	Wm. F. Strudwick, James Mebane.
1802	William Cain...............	Wm. F. Strudwick, Duncan Cameron.
1803	William Sheppard..........	James Mebane, Wm. F. Strudwick.
1804	David Ray..................	John Thompson, Michael Holt.
1805	Jonathan Lindlay...........	John Thompson, David Mebane.
1806	David Ray..................	Duncan Cameron, David Mebane.
1807	David Ray..................	Duncan Cameron, John Thompson.
1808	James Mebane..............	John Thompson, David Mebane.
1809	James Mebane..............	John Thompson, David Mebane.
1810	James Mebane..............	John Thompson, David Mebane.
1811	James Mebane..............	John Craig, John Thompson.
1812	Arch'd D. Murphey.........	Duncan Cameron, John Craig.
1813	A. D. Murphey.............	Duncan Cameron, John Craig.
1814	A. D. Murphey.............	J. Craig, Frederick Nash.
1815	A. D. Murphey.............	Frederick Nash, John Craig.
1816	A. D. Murphey.............	William Holt, Frederick Nash.
1817	A. D. Murphey.............	William Holt, Frederick Nash.
1818	A. D. Murphey.............	James Mebane, Willie P. Mangum.
1819	Duncan Cameron...........	W. Barbee, Willie P. Mangum.
1820	Michael Holt...............	Willie Shaw, James Mebane.
1821	Michael Holt...............	Willie Shaw, James Mebane.
1822	Duncan Cameron...........	James Mebane, John McCauley.
1823	Duncan Cameron...........	James Mebane, John McCauley.
1824	Wm. Montgomery..........	William McCauley, James Mebane.
1825	Wm. Montgomery..........	William McCauley, John Boon.
1826	Wm. Montgomery..........	John Boon, John Stockard.
1827	Wm. Montgomery..........	John Boon, John Stockard.
1828	James Mebane..............	Hugh Waddell, John Stockard.
1829	Wm. Montgomery..........	Thomas H. Taylor, John Stockard.
1830	Wm. Montgomery..........	John Stockard, Joseph Allison.
1831	Wm. Montgomery..........	Joseph Allison.

ORANGE COUNTY—Continued.

MEMBERS OF GENERAL ASSEMBLY—Continued.

Years.	Senate.	House.
1832	Wm. Montgomery..........	Joseph Allison, Priestley H. Mangum.
1833	Wm. Montgomery..........	Joseph Allison, John Stockard.
1834	Wm. Montgomery..........	Joseph Allison, John Stockard.
1835	Jos. Allison................	John Stockard, James Forest.
1836	Hugh Waddell............	Wm. A. Graham, Nathaniel J. King, Jno. Boon, John Stockard.
1838	Joseph Allison.............	B. Trollinger, J. Stockard, H. Sims, Wm. A. Graham.
1840	Willie P. Mangum..........	Wm. A. Graham, Nathan J. King, M. W. Holt, Cadwallader Jones, Jr.
1842	Joseph Allison..............	Cadwallader Jones, Jr., J. S. Bracken, Jno. Stockard, Henry K. Nash.
1844	Hugh Waddell.............	J. B. Leathers, Loften K. Pratt, Giles Mebane, C. F. Faucett.
1846	Hugh Waddell.............	Giles Mebane, C. F. Faucett, J. B. Leathers, Sidney Smith.
1848	John Berry.................	Cadwallader Jones, Jr., P. H. McDade, J. Stockard, Giles Mebane.
1850	John Berry.................	Cadwallader Jones, Jr., D. A. Montgomery, B. A. Durham, George Patterson.
1852	John Berry.................	S. F. Phillips, Josiah Turner, Jr., B. A. Durham, J. F. Lyon.
1854	Wm. A. Graham............	S. F. Phillips, Josiah Turner, Jr.
1856	P. H. Cameron..............	Wm. F. Strayhorn, J. F. Lyon.
1858	Josiah Turner, Jr...........	P. Jones J. W. Norwood.
1860	Josiah Turner, Jr...........	H. B. Guthrie, W. N. Patterson.
1862	Wm. A. Graham............	John Berry, W. N. Patterson.
1864	John Berry.................	S. F. Phillips, W. N. Patterson.
1866	John Berry.................	W. W. Guess, S. D. Umsted.
1868	Josiah Turner, Jr...........	E. M. Holt, J. W. Graham.
1870	J. W. Graham.............	F. N. Strudwick, C. C. Atwater.
1872	John W. Norwood...... John W. Cunningham..	Pride Jones, Jones Watson.

Caswell, Person and Orange form the 20th Senatorial District.

PAMLICO COUNTY.

Pamlico County formed in 1872, from Craven and Beaufort; bounded north by Beaufort and Hyde, east by Pamlico Sound, south by Craven, and west by Beaufort.

(Votes with Beaufort.)

PAMLICO COUNTY—Continued.

COUNTY OFFICERS.

Offices.	Names.
Superior Court Clerk	James H. Miller.
Register of Deeds	James R. Jewell.
Sheriff	Frederic E. Alfred.
Coroner	Wm. T. Caho.
Surveyor	Thos. Campen.
Treasurer	Charles H. Fowler.
Commissioners	Joseph M. Caho, Chairman. Adam Barrington. Henry H. Muse. Aquilla T. Aldridge. Frederic B. Miller.

JUSTICES OF THE PEACE.

Names.	Date of Qualification.	Post Office Address.
John B. Martin	Aug. 16th, 1873.	Bay River.
Charles Harper	" "	Bay River.
Thomas Campen	" "	Vandemere.
George Whealton	" "	Vandemere.
William T. Paul	" "	Grantsboro.
R. B. Hardison	Sept. 1st. 1873.	Grantsboro.
J. M. Caho	Nov. 13th, 1873.	Bay River.

PASQUOTANK COUNTY.

Pasquotank County existed in 1729, one of the original precincts of ancient Albemarle.

It derives it name from the tribe of Indians who once owned the soil.

It is situated in the north-eastern part of the State, and bounded on the north by the Virginia line, east by Camden, south by the Albemarle Sound, and west by Perquimans and Gates.

Its capital is Elizabeth City, which is two hundred and fifteen miles north-east of Raleigh.

PASQUOTANK COUNTY—Continued.

COUNTY OFFICERS.

Offices.	Names.
Superior Court Clerk	Wm. F. Vaughan.
Register of Deeds	Jno. T. Price.
Sheriff	Jno. L. Wood.
Coroner	None.
Surveyor	None.
Treasurer	Thos. P. Wilcox.
Commissioners	C. W. Smith. James S. Wilcox. Edmond Dodry. Emanuel Davis. Abram Morris.

JUSTICES OF THE PEACE.

Names.	Date of Qalification.			Post Office Address.
Geo. W. Brothers	Aug.	20th,	1873.	Elizabeth City.
Sam'l J. Halsted	"	26th,	"	Elizabeth City.
Elijah Overton	"	27th,	"	Elizabeth City.
B. C. Brothers	"	14th,	"	Elizabeth City.
Joseph Eves	"	"	"	Elizabeth City.
J. M. White	"	9th,	"	Rosedale P. O.
P. A. Hinton	"	15th,	"	Rosedale P. O.
Wm. B. Pritchard	"	26th,	"	Elizabeth City.
Wm. J. Munden	"	23rd,	"	Elizabeth City.
A. W. Morgan	"	29th,	"	Elizabeth City.
W. S. Temple	"	29th,	"	Elizabeth City.
Geo. [illegible]. Cobb	"	9th,	"	Elizabeth City.
Robert Fearing	"	18th,	"	Elizabeth City.
G. B. Thompson	"	16th,	"	Elizabeth City.
Henry Starke	"	18th,	"	Elizabeth City.
Hugh Cale	"	18th,	"	Elizabeth City.
J. S. Wilcox	Sept.	4th,	"	Elizabeth City.
Emanuel Davis	Oct.	7th,	"	Elizabeth City.

MEMBERS OF GENERAL ASSEMBLY.

Years.	Senate.	House.
1777		James Ferebee, Thos. Harvey.
1778		Thos. Harvey, Thos. Relfe.
1779		John Blackstock, Thos. Reading.
1780		John Blackstock. Thos. Havey.
1781		

PASQUOTANK COUNTY—Continued.

MEMBERS OF GENERAL ASSEMBLY—Continued.

Years.	Senate.	House.
1782	Edward Everigen	Thomas Reading, Wm. Lane.
1783	Edward Everigen	Thomas Reading, Wm. Lane.
1784	Thomas Relfe	Thomas Reading, John Smithson.
1785	Thomas Relfe	Edward Everigen, Abraham Jones.
1786	Thomas Relfe	Thomas Reading, Edward Everigen.
1787	Thomas Relfe	Caleb H. Koen, Edward Everigen.
1788	Joseph Keaton	Edward Everigen, Devotion Davis.
1790	Joseph Keaton	Edward Everigen, —— Reading.
1791	Joseph Keaton	Thaddeus Freshwater.
1792	John Swann	Thomas Harvey, Devotion Davis.
1793	Thomas Reading	John Lane, John Hamilton.
1794	Joseph Keaton	Devotion Davis, Thomas Banks.
1795	Joseph Keaton	Bailey Jackson, John Lane.
1796	Thomas Banks	John Lane, Bailey Jackson.
1797	Thomas Banks	Wm. Ferange, Bailey Jackson.
1798	Thomas Banks	John Shaw, Wm. S. Hinton.
1799	Bailey Jackson	John Shaw, Wm. S. Hinton.
1800	Bailey Jackson	Thomas Banks, Wm. S. Hinton.
1801	Bailey Jackson	Thomas Banks, Wm. S. Hinton.
1802	Thomas Banks	Timothy Cotter, F. B. Sawyer.
1803	Timothy Cotter	F. B. Sawyer, Jesse Reading.
1804	Timothy Cotter	F. B. Sawyer, Jesse Reading.
1805	Thaddeus Freshwater	F. B. Sawyer, Marmaduke Scott.
1806	Wm. S. Hinton	F. B. Sawyer, Marmaduke Scott.
1807	Wm. S. Hinton	John Hamilton, Marmaduke Scott
1808	Wm. S. Hinton	Marmaduke Scott, John Mullen.
1809	Wm. S. Hinton	Wm. T. Relfe, James Carver.
1810	Thaddeus Freshwater	Wm. T. Relfe, Marmaduke Scott.
1811	Thaddeus Freshwater	Marmaduke Scott, Wm. T. Relfe.
1812	Samuel Warner	Wm. T. Relfe, James Carver.
1813	Wm. S. Hinton	Wm. T. Relfe, Thos. Jordan.
1814	Wm. S. Hinton	Wm. T. Relfe, Wm. Martin.
1815	Wm. T. Relfe	John Mullen, James Jennings.
1816	Wm. Martin	Leonard Martin, Thomas Jordan.
1817	Asa Sanderlin	John Pool, Jr., Henry P. Overman.
1818	Wm. Martin	John Pool, Jr., Leonard Martin.
1819	Wm. Martin	John C. Eringhaus, Leonard Martin.
1820	Wm. Martin	John C. Eringhaus, Leonard Martin.
1821	John Pool	Leonard Martin, Thomas Bell.
1822	Wm. C. George	Thomas Bell, Leonard Martin.
1823	John Pool	Carter Barnard, Thomas Bell.
1824	John Pool	John L. Bailey, Carter Barnard.
1825	John Pool	Wm. J. Hardy, Thomas Bell.
1826	Thomas Bell	Wm. J. Hardy, Thomas Jordan.
1827	John L. Bailey	John Pool, William J. Hardy.
1828	John L. Bailey	John Pool, Wm. Gregory.
1829	John Pool	Thomas Jordan, Thomas Bell.
1830	Lemuel Jennings	Thomas Bell, John M. Skinner.
1831	John Pool	Thomas Bell, John M. Skinner.
1832	John L. Bailey	Wm. T. Relfe, Frederick A. Sawyer.
1833	John M. Skinner	Wm. T. Relfe, Nathan M. Roper.
1834	Frederick Whitehurst	John C. Blatchford, Thos. C. Matthews.
1835	Frederick Whitehurst	Thomas Bell, John B. Muse.
1836	John M. Skinner	David H. Kenyan.

PASQUOTANK COUNTY—Continued.

MEMBERS OF GENERAL ASSEMBLY—Continued.

[illegible]

PERQUIMANS COUNTY.

[illegible]

PERQUIMANS COUNTY—Continued.

COUNTY OFFICERS—Continued.

Offices.	Names.
[illegible]	[illegible]
[illegible]	[illegible]
	[illegible]
	[illegible]
Commissioners	[illegible]
	[illegible]
	[illegible]

JUSTICES OF THE PEACE.

Names.	Date of Qualification.	Post Office Address.
[illegible]	[illegible]	[illegible]
[illegible]	[illegible]	[illegible]
[illegible]	[illegible]	[illegible]
[illegible]	[illegible]	[illegible]
[illegible]	[illegible]	[illegible]
[illegible]	[illegible]	[illegible]
[illegible]		[illegible]
[illegible]		[illegible]
[illegible]	[illegible]	New Hope.
[illegible]	[illegible]	[illegible]
[illegible]		[illegible]

MEMBERS OF GENERAL ASSEMBLY.

Year.	Senate.	House.
[illegible]	[illegible]	[illegible]
[illegible]	[illegible]	[illegible]
[illegible]	[illegible]	[illegible]
[illegible]	[illegible]	[illegible]
[illegible]	[illegible]	[illegible]
[illegible]	[illegible]	[illegible]
[illegible]	[illegible]	[illegible]
[illegible]	[illegible]	[illegible]
[illegible]	[illegible]	[illegible]
[illegible]	[illegible]	[illegible]
[illegible]	[illegible]	[illegible]
[illegible]	[illegible]	[illegible]
[illegible]	[illegible]	[illegible]
[illegible]	[illegible]	[illegible]

PERQUIMANS COUNTY—Continued.

MEMBERS OF GENERAL ASSEMBLY—Continued.

Years.	Senate.	House.
1792	Joshua Skinner............	Robert Reddick, Gosby Toms.
1793	Joshua Skinner............	Charles Harvey, Robert Reddick.
1794	Robert Reddick	John Skinner, Joseph Harvey.
1795	Robert Reddick	Francis Newby, Joseph Harvey.
1796	Joseph Harvey............	harles Harvey, William Blount.
1797	Joseph Harvey............	John Skinner, Joseph White.
1798	Joseph Harvey............	Charles Harvey, Joseph White.
1799	Joseph Harvey............	Charles Harvey, Charles W. Blount
1800	Joseph Harvey............	John Nixon, Charles W. Blount.
1801	Joseph White............	William Blount, Josiah Jordan.
1802	Joseph White............	Wm. Robinson, Wm. Blount.
1803	Joseph White............	Joseph B. Skinner, Thomas Harvey.
1804	Joseph White............	Erie Barrow, Thomas H. Harvey.
1805	Joseph White............	Willis Reddick, Thomas Nicholson.
1806	William Blount............	Thomas Nicholson, Willis Reddick.
1807	Joseph White............	Willis Reddick, Josiah Townsend.
1808	Willis Reddick............	Isaac Barber, Josiah Townsend.
1809	Willis Reddick............	Isaac Barber, John Clary.
1810	Willis Reddick............	Isaac Barber, Jesse Copeland.
1811	Willis Reddick............	Isaac Barber, Jesse Copeland.
1812	Willis Reddick............	Isaac Barber, Henry Copeland.
1813	Willis Reddick............	Isaac Barber, Henry Copeland.
1814	Willis Reddick............	William Jones, F. Toms.
1815	Willis Reddick............	Francis Toms, William Jones.
1816	Willis Reddick............	William Jones, F. Toms.
1817	Willis Reddick............	Robert Perry, William Reddick.
1818	Willis Reddick............	Robert Perry, James Leigh.
1819	Willis Reddick............	T. Barrow, Robert Perry.
1820	Willis Reddick............	Theophilus Barrow, J. Nixon.
1821	Willis Reddick............	John Nixon, Matthew Jordan.
1822	Jona. H. Jacocks............	Theo. Barrow, H. Skinner.
1823	Willis Reddick............	Theo. Barrow, M. Elliott.
1824	Willis Reddick............	Theo. Barrow, Henry Skinner.
1825	Willis Reddick............	enry Skinner, Elisha Burke.
1826	Willis Reddick............	Elisha Burke, Robert Perry.
1827	Willis Reddick............	Elisha Burke, Robert Perry.
1828	Willis Reddick............	Thos. Wilson, Daniel Rogerson.
1829	Willis Reddick............	Thomas Wilson, Benjamin, Mullen.
1830	Henry Skinner	Jos. W. Townsend, Thomas Wilson.
1831	Henry Skinner	Benjamin Mullen, Thomas Wilson.
1832	Henry Skinner	Jos. W. Townsend, Benjamin Mullen.
1833	Henry Skinner	Benjamin Mullen, Thos. Wilson.
1834	Jesse Wilson............	Benjamin Mullen, Josiah Perry.
1835	Jesse Wilson............	Jona. H. Jacocks, J. T. Granberry
1836	John M. Skinner............	Josiah T. Granberry.
1838	Wm. B. Shepard............	Thomas Wilson.
1840	Wm. B. Shepard............	Thomas Wilson.
1842	Jona. H. Jacocks............	Thomas Wilson.
1844	Wm. B. Shepard............	Thomas Wilson.
1846	J. C. B. Eringhaus............	T. L. Skinner.
1848	Wm. B. Shepard............	T. L. Skinner.
1850	Wm. B. Shepard............	Thomas Wilson.
1852	Thomas F. Jones............	B. Albertson.
1854	Nathan Winslow............	J. P. -oadan.

PERQUIMANS COUNTY—Continued.

MEMBERS OF GENERAL ASSEMBLY—Continued.

Years.	Senate.	House.
1856	John Pool	J. M. Cox.
1858	John Pool	N. Newby.
1860	J. M. Whedbee	N. Newby.
1862	W. H. Bagley	Jos. H. Riddick.
1864	Wm. H. Bagley	Jos. H. Pickard.
1866	R. K. Speed	Thomas Wilson.
1868	E. A. White Jas. W. Etheridge	Jeptha White.
1870	Rufus K. Speed Jas. C. Skinner	T. E. Darden.
1872	John L. Chamberlain C. W. Grandy	J. R. Darden.

Camden, Chowan, Currituck, Hertford, Gates, Pasquotank and Perquimans form the 1st Senatorial District.

PERSON COUNTY.

Person County was formed in 1791, from Caswell, and called in honor of General Thomas Person, of Granville county, who was a distinguished friend of popular rights.

It is located in the northern part of the State, bounded on the north by the Virginia line, east by Granville, south by Orange, and west by Caswell.

Roxboro', its county seat, is 54 miles north of Raleigh.

COUNTY OFFICERS.

Offices.	Names.
Superior Court Clerk	N. N. Tuck.
Register of Deeds	John W. Hunt.
Sheriff	John L. Harris.
Coroner	Robert A. Williams.
Surveyor	John H. Clay.
Treasurer	Josephus Younger.
Commissioners	J. T. Yancey. W. R. Webb. J. T. Noell. Jas. O. Bradsher. W. G. Winstead.

PERSON COUNTY—CONTINUED.

JUSTICES OF THE PEACE.

Names.	Date of Qualification.	Post Office Address.
C. Pamlin	Aug. 18th, 1873.	Roxboro'.
A. R. Foushee	" "	Roxboro'.
Richard Springfield	" "	Woodsdale.
A. M. Long	" "	Hurdle's Mills.
J. T. · atis	" "	Hurdle's Mills.
· alvin Hawkins	" "	Hurdle's Mills.
J. J. Brooks	" "	Woodsdale.
J. B. Pleasant	" "	Roxboro'.
Nathan Lunsford	" "	Centre Grove.
J. T. Yancey	" "	Allensville.
W. T. Noell	" "	Mt. Tirzah.
Henry J. Montgomery	" "	Mt. Tirzah.
W. H. Royster	" "	Allensville.
Jesse D. Walker	" "	Roxboro'.
J. J. Jones	" "	Cunningham's Store.
Jas. T. Sergeant	" "	Winstead's.
J. P. Williams	" "	Cunningham's Store.
J. M. Burton	" "	Winstead's.
W. F. Reade.	" "	Mt. Tirzah.

MEMBERS OF GENERAL ASSEMBLY.

Years.	Senate.	House.
1792	James Jones	John Wommach, George Lea.
1793	William Cocke	George Lea, Herndon Harralson.
1794	James Jones	Herndon Harralson, George Lea.
1795	James Jones	Edward Atkinson, Herndon Harralson.
1796	John ampbell	Edward Atkinson, George Lea.
1797	John Campbell	George Lea, John Hall.
1798	John Campbell	George Lea, Jos. D. McFarland.
1799	John Campbell	George Lea, John Hall.
1800	John Wommach	George Lee, Herndon Harralson.
1801	Samuel Smith	James Williamson, Wm. Mitchell.
1802	Samuel Smith	James Williamson, James Cochran.
1803	Samuel Smith	James Cochran, William Mitchell.
1804	George Lea	James Cochran, William Mitchell.
1805	George Lea	James Cochran, William Mitchell.
1806	George Lea	James Cocoran, Richard Atkinson.
1807	James Cochran	Robert Vanhook, Richard Atkinson.
1808	Richard Atkinson	Robert Vanhook, John Paine.
1809	Richard Atkinson	Robert Vanhook, Benjamin Chambers.
1810	Richard Atkinson	Robert Vanhook, John Paine.
1811	Alex. Cunningham	Robert Vanhook, Benjamin Chambers.
1812	Richard Atkinson	Robert Vanhook, Lawrence Vanhook.
1813	Richard Atkinson	Benjamin Chambers, Samuel Dickens.
1814	Richard Atkinson	Samuel Dickens, R. Vanhook.
1815	Robert Vanhook	Sampson M. Glenn, Samuel Dickens.

PERSON COUNTY—Continued.

MEMBERS OF GENERAL ASSEMBLY—Continued.

Years.	Senate.	House.
1816	Robert Vankook	Thomas Webb, Sampson M. Glenn.
1817	Richard Atkinson	Thomas Webb, Ira Lea.
1818	Richard Atkinson	William A. Lea, Samuel Dickens.
1819	Richard Atkinson	L. Rainey, B. Chambers.
1820	Richard Atkinson	Benjamin hambers, Thomas Snead.
1821	Robert Vanhook	Thomas Webb, Thomas Sneed.
1822	Robert Vanhook	Thomas Sneed, Thomas Webb.
1823	Robert Vanhook	Thomas Webb, J. G. A. Williamson.
1824	Robert Vanhook	J. G. A. Williamson, Thomas Webb.
1825	Robert Vanhook	Thomas Webb, J. G. A. Williamson.
1826	Robert Vanhook	Thomas McGehee, Thomas Webb.
1827	Robert Vanhook	Thomas Lawson, Thomas Webb.
1828	Maurice Smith	Thomas Webb, Elijah Hester.
1829	Maurice Smith	Thomas Webb, Thomas M. McGehee.
1830	Robert Vanhook	Thomas McGehee, Thomas Lawson.
1831	Robert Vanhook	Benjamin Sumner, Thomas McGehee.
1832	Robert Vanhook	Benjamin Sumner, Robert Jones.
1833	Robert Vanhook	Robert Jones, Thomas McGehee.
1834	Isham Edwards	Robert Jones, Jas. M. Williamson.
1835	Isham Edwards	Jas. M. Williamson, Robert Jones.
1836	John Barnett	Moses Chambers, Jas. M. Williamson.
1838	John W. Williams	Robert Jones, Moses Chambers.
1840	John W. Williams	Robert Jones, Moses Chambers.
1842	John W. Williams	John A. olloway, Hiram Satterfield.
1844	Robert H. Hester	John W. Cunningham.
1846	Robert H. Hester	James Holeman.
1848	Robert H. Hester	C. H. K. Taylor.
1850	Robert H. Hester	C. S. Winstead.
1852	John W. Cunningham	James Holloman.
1854	John W. Cunningham	Major Green.
1856	John W. Cunningham	R. H. Hester.
1858	John W. Cunningham	R. H. Hester.
1860	C. S. Winstead	J. D. Wilkerson.
1862	Jas. Holeman	M. D. C. Bumpass.
1864	C. S. Winstead	J. W. Cunningham.
1866	J. W. Cunningham	. H. Bradshaw.
1868	C. S. Winstead R. W. Lassiter	Sam'l C. Barnett.
1870	R. W. Lassiter J. Barnett	H. T. Jordan.
1872	John W. Norwood John W. Cunningham	Montford McGehee.

Caswell, Orange and Person form the 30th Senatorial District.

PITT COUNTY.

Pitt County was formed from Beaufort as early as 1760, and called in compliment to William Pitt, Earl of Chatham, who was so distinguished and devoted a friend to America in the English Parliament.

It is situated in the eastern part of the State, and bounded on the north by Edgecombe and Martin, east by Hyde and Beaufort, south by Craven, and west by Greene and Lenoir.

Greenville, its capital, is 102 miles east of Raleigh.

COUNTY OFFICERS.

Offices.	Names.
Superior Court Clerk	W. L. Cherry.
Register of Deeds	James L. Langley.
Sheriff	William A. Quimby.
Coroner	None.
Surveyor	None.
Treasurer	John Peebles.
Commissioners	T. R. Cherry, Chairman. B. L. T. Barnhill. James H. Forbs. . E. Nelson. W. M. King.

JUSTICES OF THE PEACE.

Names.	Date of Qualification.	Post Office Address.
W. L. Cherry	Sept. 1st, 1873.	Greenville.
James L. Langley	" "	Greenville.
Eason James	" "	Bethel.
J. J. Walston	" "	Bethel.
Guilford Mooring	Sept. 30th, "	Pactolus.
W. W. Little	Jan. 24th, "	Pactolus.
Dennis Atkinson	Sept. 1st, "	Falkland.
W. A. Barrett	" "	Farmville.
J. W. May	" "	Farmville.
Caleb Cannon	" "	Ridge Spring.
John B. Worsley	" "	Greenville.
Arch Cox	" "	Coxville.
Allen Johnson	" "	Johnson's Mills,
J. B. Stickney	" "	Greenville.
Geo. W. Venters	" "	Greenville.

PITT COUNTY.—Continued.

MEMBERS OF GENERAL ASSEMBLY.

Years.	Senate.	House.
1777	Edward Salter..............	William Robeson, John Williams.
1778	Edward Salter..............	William Robeson, John Williams.
1779	Edward Salter..............	James Gorham, John Williams.
1780	Edward Salter..............	George Moye, John Williams.
1781	Edward Salter..............	James Gorham, George Evans.
1782	John Williams..............	James Gorham, John Simpson.
1783	John Williams..............	John Jordan, Richard Moye.
1784	John Williams..............	John Jordan, Richard Moye.
1785	John Williams..............	Richard Moye, John Jordan.
1786	John Simpson..............	Reading Blount, Robert Williams.
1787	John Williams..............	Reading Blount, Robert Williams.
1788	William Blount............	John Moye, Shadrach Allen.
1789	William Blount............	James Armstrong, Shadrach Allen.
1790	William Blount............	John Moye, Robert Williams.
1791	John Moye.................	Robert Williams, Richard Moye.
1792	Stephen Brooks............	Benjamin Bell, Samuel Simpson.
1793	Robert Williams...........	Wm. Grimes, Richard Moye.
1794	Robert Williams...........	Benjamin Bell, illiam Grimes.
1795	Robert Williams...........	Holland Johnston, Frederick Bryan.
1796	Samuel Simpson............	Frederick Bryan, Holland Johnston.
1797	Samuel Simpson............	Holland Johnston, Frederick Bryan
1798	Frederick Bryan...........	Richard Evans, Holland Johnston.
1799	Frederick Bryan...........	William Moye, Holland Johnston.
1800	Frederick Bryan...........	William Moye, Richard Evans.
1801	Frederick Bryan...........	William Moye, Wm. Eastwood.
1802	Robert Williams...........	William Moye, Wm. Eastwood.
1803	Robert Williams...........	m. Eastwood, George Eason.
1804	Robert Williams...........	John Mooring, Benjamin May.
1805	Robert Williams...........	John Mooring, Benjamin May.
1806	Robert Williams...........	Benjamin May, John Mooring.
1807	William Moye..............	John Mooring, Benjamin May.
1808	Robert Williams...........	John Mooring, Benjamin May.
1809	Benjamin May..............	Benjamin May, John Mooring.
1810	Benjamin May..............	Elias Carr, Hardy Smith.
1811	Benjamin May..............	Franklin Gorham, Hardy Smith.
1812	Benjamin May..............	Hardy Smith, James Sheppard.
1813	Robert Williams...........	Hrady Smith, James Sheppard.
1814	Robert Williams...........	Hardy Smith, James Sheppard.
1815	Hardy Smith...............	Oliver Prince, Luke Albritton.
1816	Luke Albritton.............	Roderick Cherry, Oliver Prince.
1817	Luke Albrittsn.............	Roderick Cherry, Oliver Prince.
1818	Luke Albritton.............	Oliver Prince, Roderick Cherry.
1819	Luke Albritton.............	Joel Patrick, Marshall Dickinson.
1820	Robert Williams...........	m. Clark, Gideon Bynum.
1821	Luke Albritton.............	Lanier Daniel, John Joyner.
1822	Luke Albritton.............	John Cherry, Lanier Daniel.
1823	Luke Albritton.............	John Cherry, Wilkes Brooks.
1824	John Joyner...............	S. P. Allen, Jno. C. Gorham.
1825	John Joyner...............	John C. Gorham, Shadrach P. Allen.
1826	John Joyner...............	Marshall Dickinson, Wm. W. Andrews.
1827	John Joyner...............	John Cherry, Marshall Dickinson.
1828	ohn Joyner................	Marshall Dickinson, Alfred Moye.
1829	Marshall Dickinson.........	Alfred Moye, William Clark.
1830	Marshall Dickinson.........	William Clark, William Clemmons.

PITT COUNTY—Continued.

MEMBERS OF GENERAL ASSEMBLY—Continued.

Years.	Senate.	House.
1831	Alfred Moye................	Henry Toole, Roderick Cherry.
1832	Alfred Moye................	Thomas Jordan, James Blow.
1833	Alfred Moye................	J. L. Foreman, Roderick Cherry.
1834	Alfred Moye................	Luke Albritton, J. L. Foreman.
1835	Alfred Moye................	J. L. Foreman, Macon Moye.
1836	Alfred Moye................	Macon Moye, John Spiers.
1838	Alfred Moye................	J. L. Foreman, John C. Gorham.
1840	Alfred Moye................	J. L. Foreman, Isaac Joyner.
1842	Alfred Moye................	J. L. Foreman, Isaac Joyner.
1844	J. L. Foreman..............	H. F. Harris, C. Perkins.
1846	B. F. Eborn................	Elias J. Blount, H. F. Harris.
1848	B. F. Eborn................	—— Satterthwait, Wm. J. Blow.
1850	William Eborn..............	Marshall Dickinson, Wm. J. Blow.
1852	B. G. Albritton............	W. J. Blow, J. J. Foreman.
1854	B. F. Eborn................	G. E. B. Singeltary, Wm. J. Blow.
1856	M. L. Kerr.................	Wm. J. Blow, Edward Moore.
1858	E. J. Blount...............	C. McCotter, —— Cox.
1860	E. J. Blount...............	B. J. Albritton, Churchill Perkins.
1862	E. J. Blount...............	B. J. Albritton, Churchill Perkins.
1864	E. J. Blount...............	B. J. Albritton, Churchill Perkins.
1866	C. Perkins.................	W. R. Williams, John Galloway.
1868	W. A. Cherry...............	Byron Laflin, Richard Short.
1870	Jacob McCotter.............	—— Atkinson, —— Joyner.
1872	Jacob McCotter.............	Wm. P. Bryant, Guilford Cox.

Pitt is the 6th Senatorial District.

POLK COUNTY.

Polk County was formed in 1855 out of Henderson and Rutherford, called in compliment to Colonel William Polk, of the Revolution.

It is bounded on the north and east by Rutherford, south by the State line, and west by Henderson.

Its county seat is Columbus, called after the discoverer of America, distant from Raleigh about 220 miles.

It voted with Rutherford until 1868.

COUNTY OFFICERS.

Offices.	Names.
Superior Court Clerk....................	R. S. Abrams.
Register of Deeds.......................	S. Waldrop.
Sheriff.................................	G. B. Arledge.
Coroner.................................	Vacant.

POLK COUNTY—Continued.

COUNTY OFFICERS.—Continued.

Offices.	Names.
Surveyor	C. W. Watkins.
Treasuer	J. W. Hampton.
Commissioners	W. B. Walker. M. V. Edwards. Jno. Jackson. Berry Thompson. G. H. Blackwell.

JUSTICES OF THE PEACE.

Names.	Date of Qualification.	Post Office Address.
David Foster	September, 1873.	Columbus.
James F. Rains	" "	Columbus.
H. Waldrop	" "	Mill's Spring.
J. E. A. Waldrop	" "	Mill's Spring.
James Jackson	" "	Mill's Spring.
Nesbit Deinsdale	" "	Mill's Spring.
Berry Thompson	" "	Tryon.
B. T. Morris	" "	Columbus.
R. M. Farland	" "	Columbus.
D. F. Greenway	" "	Columbus.

MEMBERS OF GENERAL ASSEMBLY.

Years.	Senate.	House.
1868	J. B. Eaves	Ashburry Waldrop.
1870	J. M. Whitesides	John Gartison.
1872	Martin Walker	N. B. Hampton.

Polk and Rutherford form the 39th Senatorial District.

RANDOLPH COUNTY.

RANDOLPH COUNTY was formed in 1779 from Guilford and Rowan, and named in compliment to the Randolph family in Virginia, distinguished for patriotism and talents.

It presents on the map, in nearly the centre of the State, a beautiful compact square, and is bounded on the north by Guilford County, east by Chatham, south by Moore and Montgomery, and west by Davidson.

Its capital is ASHBORO', called in compliment to Governor Samuel Ashe, and is nearly due west from Raleigh, seventy-two miles distant.

COUNTY OFFICERS.

Offices.	Names.
Superior Court Clerk	A. M. Diffie.
Register of Deeds	W. J. Page.
Sheriff	W. R. Asheworth.
Coroner	D. N. Barrow.
Surveyor	Levi Cox.
Treasurer	Benj. Moffitt.
Commissioners	A. H. Kendall, Chairman.
	H. T. Moffitt.
	Samuel Walker.
	R. M. Free.
	Isaac Lee.

JUSTICES OF THE PEACE.

Names.	Date of Qualification.	Post Office Address.
W. . Wilborne	Aug. 9th, 1873.	Trinity College.
W. S. Bradshaw	Mar. 28th, 1872.	Trinity College.
R. L. Coltrane	Aug. 16th 1873.	New Market.
James N. Caudle	" 15th, "	New Salem.
Wm. Branson	" "	New Salem.
J. W. Burgess	" 8th, 1871.	Liberty.
John Frint	" 30th, 1873.	Sandy Creek.
Henry Craven	" 15th. "	Reed reek.
John Hays	" 9th, "	Reed Creek.
J. W. Bean	" 15th, "	Franklinsville.
D. B. Julian	Sept. 1st, "	Asheboro'.
Alfred Bulla	" 2d, "	Asheboro'.
W. A. Dougan	" 1st, "	Sawyersville.
F. Pearce	Aug. 16th "	Hoover Hill.
Isaac Spencer	" 9th, "	Eden.
B. W. Steed	" 3rd, 1871.	Hill's Store.
L. G. B. Bingham		Jackson's Creek.
Peter Vuncannon	Aug. 15th 1873.	Science Hill.
Thomas Walker	Sept. 20th, "	Science Hill.
Riley Wright	" 2d, "	Asheboro'.

RANDOLPH COUNTY—CONTINUED.

JUSTICES OF THE PEACE—CONTINUED.

Names.	Date of Qualification.	Post Office Address.
R. M. Free	Aug. 9th, 1873.	Asheboro'.
James A. Cole	Sept. 1st, "	Cole's Mills.
Hugh T. Moffitt	Aug. 9th, "	Moffitt's Mills.
Alfred Maness	Sept. 1st, "	Moffitt's Mills.
John Brady	" 15th, "	Moffitt's Mills.
Alfred L. Yow	Aug. 9th, "	Asheboro'.
W. D. King	" 14th, "	Asheboro'.
R. M. Cox	" 15th, 1871.	Auman Hill.
George Auman	" 28th, 1873.	Auman Hill.
O. C. Brewer	" 19th, "	Hill's Store.
Jesse F. Lyndon	" 14th, "	Hill's Store.

MEMBERS OF GENERAL ASSEMBLY.

Years.	Senate.	House.
1780	John Collier	Andrew Balfour, Jeduthan Harper.
1781	John Collier	J. Harper, Absalom Tatom.
1782	John Collier	Edward Williams, A. Tatom.
1783	Thomas Dougan	Robert McLean, J. Harper.
1784	Thomas Dougan	James Robins, Aaron Hill.
1785	Edward Sharpe	Aaron Hill, Joseph Robbins.
1786	Edward Sharpe	William Bell, Zebedee Wood.
1787	Jesse Hendley	John Stanfield, Edmund Waddell.
1788	Thomas Dougan	Zebedee Wood, William Bell.
1789	John Arnold	Zebedee Wood, Aaron Hill.
1791	Zebedee Wood	William Bell, Reuben Wood.
1792	Zebedee Wood	William Bailey, Henry Branson.
1793	Edmund Waddell	William Bailey, Henry Branson.
1794	Edmund Waddell	Henry Branson, William Bailey.
1795	Edmund Waddell	William Bailey, Henry Branson.
1796	Edmund Waddell	William Bailey, Henry Branson.
1797	Edmund Waddell	William Bailey, Henry Branson.
1798	Edmund Waddell	William Bailey, Michael Harvey.
1799	Alexandor Gray	William Bailey, Simon Green.
1800	Henry Branson	William Bailey, Michael Harvey.
1801	Henry Branson	Michael Harvey, John Brower.
1802	Henry Branson	William Bailey, Michael Harvey.
1803	Henry Branson	John Brower, Michael Harvey.
1804	Alexander Gray	Whitlock Arnold, Colin Sneed.
1805	Alexander Gray	John Brower, Michael Harvey.
1806	Alexander Gray	Colin Sneed, Whitlock Arnold.
1807	Alexander Gray	Whitlock Arnold, Seth Wade.
1808	Colin Steed	Whitlock Arnold, Seth Wade.
1809	Michael Harvey	John Brower, Solo. K. Goodman.
1810	Michael Harvey	Solo. K. Goodman, Josiah Lyndon.
1811	Lewis Spinks	John Long, Jasiah Lyndon.
1812	Alexander Gray	John Long, Josiah Lyndon.

RANDOLPH COUNTY—Continued.

MEMBERS OF GENERAL ASSEMBLY—Continued.

Years.	Senate.	House.
1813	Whitlock Arnold	William Hogan, Seth Wade.
1814	John Long, Jr.	Josiah Lyndon, John Lane, Jr.
1815	John Long, Jr.	Solo. K. Goodman, Joshua Craven.
1816	Seth Wade	Joshua Craven, Shubal Gardner.
1817	Seth Wade	Joshua Craven, West Armistead.
1818	Charles Steed	Shubal Gardner, West Armistead.
1819	Seth Wade	Shubal Gardner, J. Brower.
1820	William Hogan	Charles Steed, Joshua Craven.
1821	Seth Wade	Abraham Brower, Tidance Lane.
1822	Seth Wade	A. Brower, Benjamin Marmon.
1823	Alexander Gray	A. Brower, George Hoover.
1824	William Hogan	A. Brower, George Hoover.
1825	William Hogan	George Hoover, Abraham Brower.
1826	Alexander Gray	Abraham Brower, Robert Walker.
1827	Alexander Gray	Hugh Walker, John B. Troy.
1828	Alexander Gray	Thomas Hancock, Hugh Walker.
1829	Abraham Brower	Alexander Cunningham, A. Brower.
1830	Abraham Brower	Jonathan Worth, A. Brower.
1831	Benjamin Elliott	Jona. Worth, Alex. Cunningham.
1832	Hugh Moffitt	A. Cunningham, A. Brower.
1833	Henry B. Elliott	A. Brower, Benjamin Hawkins.
1834	Alfred Staley	Zebedee Rush, Benjamin Hawkins.
1835	Alfred Staley	William B. Lane, Zebedee Rush.
1836	Jonathan Redding	Michael Cox, William B. Lane.
1838	Jonathan Redding	Zebedee Rush, Wm. B. Lane.
1840	Jonathan Worth	William B. Lane, Alfred Brower.
1842	Henry B. Elliott	Alfred Brower, Julian E. Leach.
1844	Henry B. Elliott	Alfred Brower, Zebedee Rush.
1846	Alexander Hogan	A. Brower, Isaac White.
1848	Dr. Wm. B. Lane	Allen Skinner, Isaac White.
1850	Dr. Wm. B. Lane	Jesse Thornberg, J. M. A. Drake.
1852	Wm. B. Lane	Wm. A. Long, Jesse Thornberg.
1854	Wm. B. Lane	John A. Craven, Jesse Thornberg.
1856	M. W. Holt	H. B. Elliott, A. G. Forster.
1858	J. Worth	John A. Craven, Jesse Thornberg.
1860	J. Worth	A. H. Foust, Thos. S. Winslow.
1862	Giles Mebane	Jonathan Worth, M. S. Robbins.
1864	Giles Mebane	Joel Ashworth, E. T. Blair.
1866	M. S. Robbins	Joel Ashworth, E. T. Blair.
1868	J. H. Davis	Joel Ashworth, E. T. Blair.
1870	J. M. Worth	Jonathan Lassiter, S. F. Tomlinson.
1872	J. M. Worth	J. W. Bean, Geo. W. Reed.

Moore and Randolph form the 25th Senatorial District.

RICHMOND COUNTY.

RICHMOND COUNTY was formed in 1779 from Anson. It is called in honor of the Duke of Richmond, who was an able advocate of the cause of America in the House of Lords.

It is located in the southern part of the State, and bounded on the north by Montgomery county, east by Moore, Cumberland and Robeson, south by the South Carolina line, and west by the Pee Dee River, which separates it from Anson county.

Its capital is Rockingham, distant 135 miles southwest of Raleigh.

COUNTY OFFICERS.

Offices.	Names.
Superior Court Clerk	Dugald Stewart.
Register of Deeds	William R. Terry.
Sheriff	Stephen T. Cooper.
Coroner	Vacant.
Surveyor	Jesse A. Baldwin.
Treasurer	Rev. R. S. Ledbetter.
Commissioners	Thomas M. Wright, Chairman. George W. McKinnon. Harry Snead. James W. O'Bryan. James L. Yates.

JUSTICES OF THE PEACE.

Names.	Date of Qualification.	Post Office Address.
James S. Matheson	Aug. 16th, 1873.	Mangum.
Saunders M. Ingram	" 12th, "	Little's Mills.
Tristiam Bostick	" 27th, "	Bostick's Mills.
Daniel W. Gibson	" 23d, "	Bear Branch.
James L. Yates	" 9th, "	Rockingham.
William W. Graham	" "	Rockingham.
William W. Dunn	" "	Rockingham.
Thomas J. Covington	" 15th, "	Rockingham.
Elisha C. Terry	" 16th, "	Rockingham.
Louis H. Shortridge	" 9th, "	Rockingham.
John B. ovington	" "	Rockingham.
Elbridge Millikin	" "	Rockingham.
Marshal Leviner*	" "	Rockingham.
James P. Smith	" 18th "	Laurel Hill.
Malcolm D. McNeill	" "	Laurel Hill.
John McKay	Sept. 1st, 1873.	Shoe Heel.
Samuel J. Gibson	Aug. 18th, "	Laurel Hill.
James J. McCallum	Sept. 23rd, "	Laurinburgh.
Peter McRae	" 20th, "	Laurinburgh.

*Resigned. One to be appointed.

RICHMOND COUNTY—Continued.

MEMBERS OF GENERAL ASSEMBLY.

Years.	Senate.	House.
1780	Charles Medlock	Henry Wm. Harrington, Robert Webb.
1781	Charles Medlock	Edward Williams, Robert Webb.
1782	Charles Medlock	Robert Webb, Thomas Crawford.
1783	Charles Medlock	John Childs, Robert Webb.
1784	Charles Medlock	Robert Webb, Charles Robertson.
1785	Charlas Medlock	Robert Webb, Benjamin Covington.
1786	Charles Medlock	Robert Webb, Benjamin Covington.
1787	William Crawford	Wm. Pickett, Robert Webb.
1788	Robert Webb	Miles King, Edward Williams.
1789	Robert Webb	Wm. Robeson, Thomas Blewitt.
1790	Robert Webb	Wm. Robeson, Thomas Blewitt.
1791	Edward Williams	Thomas Blewitt, John McAllister.
1792	James Terry	James Coleman, Duncan McFarland.
1793	Duncan McFarland	Malcolm Smith, Wm. Robinson.
1794	William Wall	Malcolm Smith, Wm. Robinson.
1795	William Wall	Malcolm Smith, Joseph Hines.
1796	Robert Webb	James Coleman, James Sandford.
1797	Robert Webb	William Robinson, Jas. T. Sandford.
1798	Robert Webb	Lauchlin McKenan, Jas. Stewart.
1800	Duncan McFarland	John Speed, Stephen Cole.
1801	Peter H. Cole	John Clarke, Moses Knight.
1802	James Stewart	John Clarke, Moses Knight.
1803	John Wall, jr	Moses Knight, John Clarke.
1804	James Stewart	Moses Knight, Robert Webb.
1805	Thomas Blewitt	John Clarke, John McFarland.
1806	Moses Knight	John Clarke, Robert Webb.
1807	Duncan McFarland	James Speed, John Smith, jr.
1808	Duncan McFarland	John Smith, Jas. A. Harrington.
1809	Duncan McFarland	John Smith, Thoroughgood Pate.
1810	Alex. McMillan	William Thomas, Neill Smith.
1811	Alex. McMillan	John R. Buie, Neill Smith.
1812	Alex. McMillan	Allen Stewart, Wm. P. Leake.
1813	James Stewart	Robert Powell, Wm. McLeod.
1814	James Stewart	Edward Williams, Wm. Thomas.
1815	James Stewart	Thomas Steele, Wm. McLeod.
1816	Thomas Steele	Henry W. Harrington, Wm. Thomas
1817	Thomas Steele	H. W. Harrington, Neill McNair.
1818	Wm. McLeod	J. L. Vaughan, John McAllister, jr.
1819	Thomas Steele	J. L. Vaughan, W. Thomas.
1820	Wm. McLeod	Robert Powell, Wm. Thomas.
1821	William Thomas	J. L. Vaughan, W. F. Leake.
1822	Stephen Wall	Duncan McLauren, A. Dockery.
1823	Stephen Wall	John Cole, Tryan McFarland.
1824	Wm. L. Cole	Tryan McFarland, S. Meredith.
1825	Francis T. Leak	Henry Dockery, Arch. McNair.
1826	Francis T. Leak	Arch. McNair, Henry Dockery.
1827	Erasmus Love	George Thomas, Arch. McNair.
1828	Tregan McFarland	Neill Nicholson, Nathan Gibson.
1829	Tregan McFarland	Neill Nicholson, James Murphey.
1830	Tregan McFarland	James Murphey, Isham A. Dumas.
1831	Tregan McFarland	Walter F. Leake, Duncan McLaurin
1832	Walter F. Leake	Isaac Dockery, Duncan McLaurin.
1833	Alexander Martin	James Williams, Duncan Malloy.
1834	John Fairley	James Williams, Isaac Dockery.

RICHMOND COUNTY—Continued.

MEMBERS OF GENERAL ASSEMBLY.

Years.	Senate.	House.
1835	Alex. Martin	George Thomas, John R. Buie.
1836	Alfred Dockery	John McAllister, George Thomas.
1838	Alfred Dockery	Duncan McLaurin, George Thomas.
1840	Alfred Dockery	Duncan McLaurin, John W. Covington.
1842	Alfred Dockery	Alexander Martin, Isaac Dockery.
1844	Alfred Dockery	Neill McNair.
1846	John Gilchrist	Walter L. Steele.
1848	J. A. Rowland	Walter L. Steele.
1850	J. Malloy	Walter L. Steele.
1852	Walter L. Steele	D. C. McIntyre.
1854	T. J. Morrisey	W. L. Steele.
1856	Alfred Dockery	W. L. Steele.
1858	W. L. Steele	O. H. Dockery.
1860	Giles Leitch	Sanders M. Ingram.
1864	Giles Leitch	B. F. Little.
1866	M. McRae	Peter McRae.
1868	W. B. Richardson	Richmond T. Long.
1870	R. S. Ledbetter	Robert Fletcher, col.
1872	R. T. Long	Robt. Fletcher, col.

Montgomery and Richmond form the 26th Senatorial District.

ROBESON COUNTY

Was formed in 1786, from Bladen county, and called in compliment of Colonel Robeson, who distinguished himself in the battle of Elizabethtown, in Bladen county, (fought in July, 1781.)

It is situated in the southern part of the State, and bounded on the north by Cumberland, east by Bladen and Columbus, south by the South Carolina line, and west by Richmond county.

Its capital is Lumberton, on Lumber river, and is 91 miles south-west of Raleigh.

COUNTY OFFICERS.

Offices.	Names.
Superior Court Clerk	Wm. A. Dick.
Register of Deeds	S. E. Ward.
Sheriff	R. McMillan.
Coroner	None.
Surveyor	None.

ROBESON COUNTY—Continued.

COUNTY OFFICERS—Continued.

Offices.	Names.
Treasurer	P. P. Smith.
Commissioners	Daniel S. Morrison, Chairman. H. F. Pitman. Meill McNeill. John T. Pope. L. W. Thompson.

JUSTICES OF THE PEACE.

Names.	Date of Qualification.			Post Office Address.
Charles McRae	Aug.	13th,	1873.	Red Banks.
John H. Morrison	"	30th,	"	Morrisonian.
James McMillan	"	23rd,	"	Moss Neck.
A. A. McLean	"	18th,	"	Moss Neck.
D. C. McIntyre	"	13th,	"	Lumberton.
A. J. Thompson	Sept.	2nd,	"	Lumberton.
David Currie	"	1st,	"	Dundarrach.
Thos. M. Watson	"	"	"	Melrose.
W. A. Stone	Aug.	21st	"	Lumberton.
Alvin G. Lewis	"	22nd,	"	Lumberton.
Thos. Allen	Sept.	1st,	"	Lumberton.
Arch'd M. White	"	"	"	Lumberton.
James Sinclair	Aug.	8th,	"	Lumberton.
E. K. Proctor	"	13th,	"	Lumberton.
Joshua Wingate	"	11th,	"	Lumberton.
A. M. Cobb	"	16th,	"	Shoe Heel.
C. E. Barton	"	"	"	Red Banks.
R. R. Barnes	"	14th,	"	Brooklin.
John F. Britt	"	15th,	"	Brooklin.
Neill NcNeill	"	16th,	"	St. Pauls.
Daniel McMillan	Sept.	1st,	"	St. Pauls.
M. C. McNair	Aug.	15th,	"	Shoe Heel.
Oliver George	"	"	"	Shoe Heel.
John [illegible]. McEachin	"	16th,	"	Dundarrach.
Neill C. Graham	Sept.	1st,	"	Dundarrach.
Jas. C. McKeller	Aug.	13th,	"	Lumberton.
John Taylor	"	"	"	Lumberton.
W. G. Oliver	Nov.	3rd,	"	Fair Bluff, Columbus Co.
Allen Inman	Aug.	13th,	"	Lumberton.
B. Stansel	"	9th,	"	Bear Bay.
Edward R. Phillips	"	"	"	Bear Bay.
A. H. McLeod	May	9th,	"	Lumberton.
Daniel S. Morrison	Aug.	8th,	"	Shoe Heel.
James Rozier	"	"	"	Lumberton.

ROBESON COUNTY—Continued.

MEMBERS OF GENERAL ASSEMBLY.

Years.	Senate.	House.
1787	John Willis	Elias Barnes, Neill Brown.
1788	John Willis	Elias Barnes, Neill Brown.
1789	John Willis	Elias Barnes, Neill Brown.
1791	John Willis	Elias Barnes, Jacob Alford.
1792	Elias Barnes	Ralph Rogan, John Gilchrist.
1793	Elias Barnes	Jacob Alford, John Gilchrist.
1794	Elias Barnes	James McQueen, John Willis.
1795	Elias Barnes	John Willis, Joseph Wade.
1796	John Gilchrist	Joseph Wood, James McQueen.
1797	John Gilchrist	John Regan, Joseph Wood.
1799	Elias Barnes	John Regan, Neill Brown.
1800	Elias Barnes	Robert Haills, Hugh Brown.
1801	Elias Barnes	Hugh Brown, James McQueen.
1802	Elias Barnes	Benjamin Lee, James McQueen.
1803	Elias Barnes	Benjamin Lee, James McQueen.
1804	Benjamin Lee	Zachariah Jordan, Hugh Brown.
1805	Benjamin Lee	Zachariah Jordan, Duncan McNeill.
1806	Benjamin Lee	Zachariah Jordan, Duncan McNeill.
1807	Benjamin Lee	Hugh Brown, Alexander Rowland.
1808	Benjamin Lee	Alexander Rowland, Hugh Brown.
1809	Benjamin Lee	Hugh Brown, Wm. Sterling.
1810	Benjamin Lee	Hugh Brown, John Gilchrist.
1811	Alfred Rowland	John Gilchrist, Duncan McAlpin.
1812	Alfred Rowland	Duncan McAlpin, Isaac Sullivan.
1813	Alfred Rowland	Archibald S. Brown, Kenneth Black.
1814	Alfred Rowland	Murdock McLean, Wm. Sterling.
1815	Kenneth Black	Archibald S. Brown, Murdock McLean.
1816	Kenneth Black	John Gilchrist, Wm. Sterling.
1817	William Brown	John Gilchrist, Francis L. Haynes.
1818	William Brown	Francis L. Haynes, Kenneth Black.
1819	William Sterling	John Guinn, Isaac Sullivan.
1820	Kenneth Black	Archibald McEachin, Willis Pope.
1821	Kenneth Black	Jacob Alford, Archibald McEachin.
1822	Isaac Sullivan	John Gilchrist, Jacob Alford.
1823	M. D. Murphey	Jacob Alford, Shad. Howell.
1824	Isaac Sullivan	Warren Alford, Shad. Howell.
1825	John Gilchrist	Shadrach Howell, Warren Alford.
1826	John Gilchrist	Shadrach Howell, Warren Alford.
1827	Arch'd McEachin	R. C. Rhodes, Malcolm Purcell.
1828	Arch'd McEachin	Warren Alford, Malcolm Purcell.
1829	Neill B. Johnson	John Purcell, John Brown.
1830	Shadrach Howell	John Purcell, John Brown.
1831	Shadrach Howell	Wm. L. Miller, Alexander Watson.
1832	Shadrach Howell	Alexander Watson, Benjamin Lee.
1833	Shadrach Howell	Alexander Watson, Giles S. McLean.
1834	Shadrach Howell	Benjamin Lee, Giles S. McLean.
1835	Malcolm Patterson	Oliver K. Tuton, Alexander Watson.
1836	Alfred Dockery	Alexander Watson, O. K. Tuton.
1838	Alfred Dockery	O. K. Tuton, James Blount.
1840	Alfred Dockery	Daniel A. Graham, Neill Regan.
1842	Alfred Dockery	Neill Regan, Alexander Watson.
1844	Alfred Dockery	Neill Regan, John McNeill.
1846	John Gilchrist	Neill Regan, John McNeill.
1848	J. A. Rowland	Neill Regan, John McNeill.

ROBESON COUNTY—Continued.

MEMBERS OF GENERAL ASSEMBLY—Continued.

Years.	Senate.	House.
1850	J. Malloy	Wm. McNeill, Neal McNeill.
1852	Walter L. Steele	Wm. D. McNeill, Jacob Alford.
1854	Thos. Morrisey	Thos. A. Norment, Neill Regan.
1856	Alfred Dockery	Giles Leitch, —— Harrison.
1858	W. L. Steele	—— Blount, Alex. Watson.
1860	A. Dockery	Alex. McMillan, Eli Wishart.
1862	Giles Leitch	Murdock McRae, D. McNeill.
1864	Giles Leitch	Thomas J. Morrisey.
1866	M. McRae	R. McNair, J. A. McArthur.
1868	D. S. Hayes	Jas. Sinclair, Edward K. Procter.
1870	R. M. Norment	Thos. A. McNeill, H. B. Regan.
1872	J. W. Ellis	W. S. Norment, Thos. A. McNeill.

Columbus and Robeson form the 15th Senatorial District.

ROCKINGHAM COUNTY.

Rockingham County was formed in 1785 from Guilford County, and derives its name from Charles Watson Wentworth, Marquis of Rockingham, who was a distinguished friend of America in the English Parliament, and acted in concert with William Pitt, Earl of Chatham, in opposition to Lord North. In 1782 he was the Premier of England.

It is located in the north-western part of the State, and bounded on the north by the Virginia line, east by Caswell, south by Guilford, and west by Stokes.

Its capital is Wentworth, in honor of the family name of the House of Rockingham, and is distant one hundred and sixteen miles north-west of Raleigh.

COUNTY OFFICERS.

Offices.	Names.
Superior Court Clerk	R. H. Wray.
Register of Deeds	D. W. Brusick.
Sheriff	John S. Johnston.
Coroner	Vacant.
Surveyor	E. W. Hancock.
Treasurer	A. J. Boyd.
Commissioners	H. P. Lomax. J. H. Hall. Geo. W. Peay. Dr. W. R. Smith.

ROCKINGHAM COUNTY—Continued.

JUSTICES OF THE PEACE.

Names.	Date of Qualification.	Post Office Address.
T. K. Cummings	Sept. 1st, 1873.	Aspen Grove.
Wm. M. Ellington	" "	Wentworth.
R. A. Holderby	" "	Rutlin.
H. P. Lomax	" "	Aspen Grove.
Thos. Price	" "	Madison.
John A. Ratliff	" "	Wentworth.
Charles A. Reynolds	" 9th, "	Leaksville.
John A. Vernon	" 1st, "	Madison.
T. McWoodburn	" "	Madison.
Abram Womack	" "	Reidsville.
C. J. L. Williams	Oct. 6th, "	Reidsville.
Jones W. Burton	Sept. 1st, "	Leaksville.
E. P. Barnes	" "	Douglas.
M. D. King	Jan. 5th, 1874.	Wentworth.

W. S. Allen elected and not qualified.

MEMBERS OF GENERAL ASSEMBLY.

Years.	Senate.	House.
1786	James Galloway	William Bethell, Peter Perkins.
1787	James Galloway	William Bethell, Peter Perkins.
1788	James Galloway	William Bethell, Abram Phillips.
1789	James Galloway	Wm. Bethell, Abram Phillips.
1790	William Bethel	Abram Phillips, James Taylor.
1791	Charles Galloway	Henry Scales, John Leak.
1792	Robert Williams	Thomas Henderson, James Taylor.
1793	Robert Williams	Henry Scales, George Peay.
1794	Robert Williams	Thomas Henderson, George Peay.
1795	Robert Williams	George Peay, Alexander Joyce.
1796	Thomas Henderson	Alexander Joyce, Henry Scales.
1797	Abraham Phillips	John Peay, Henry Scales.
1798		
1799		
1800	Henry Scales	Drury Smith, Joshua Smith.
1801	Abraham Phillips	Theo. Lacey, Nathl. Williams.
1802	Abraham Phillips	Samuel Hill, Nathaniel Williams.
1803	Abraham Phillips	Nathl. Scales, Alexander Sneed.
1804	Alexander Martin	Alexander Sneed, Joseph Gentry.
1805	Alexander Martin	Alex. Sneed, Sampson Lanier.
1806	Nath. Scales	Alex. Sneed, Mark Harden.
1807	Nath. Scales	Mark Harden, Sampson Lanier.
1808	Nath. Scales	Thos. Wortham, Mark Harden.
1809	Nath. Scales	Mark Harden, Hugh C. Mills.
1810	Nath. Scales	William Douglas, Jos. S. Gentry
1811	Nath. Scales	William Douglas, Jos. S. Gentry.

ROCKINGHAM COUNTY—Continued.

MEMBERS OF GENERAL ASSEMBLY—Continued.

Years.	Senate.	House.
1812	Abraham Phillips	Samuel Hill, John Odeneal.
1813	Abraham Phillips	Samuel Hill, Wm. Douglas.
1814	Abraham Phillips	Wm. Douglas, Thomas Blackwell.
1815	Wm. Bethell	Wm. Douglas, Thomas Blackwell.
1816	Wm. Douglas	Thos. Settle, Thomas Blackwell.
1817	Wm. Bethell	Thomas Hill, Nathaniel Scales.
1818	Wm. Bethell	Richard W. Micheaux, Nathl. Scales, Jr.
1819	Wm. Bethell	H. Baughn, W. Donnell.
1820	Wm. Bethell	Thomas Blackwell, W. Donnell.
1821	Nathaniel Scales	John M. Moorehead, James Miller.
1822	Thos. Blackwell	Robert Martin, E. T. Broadnax.
1823	Nathaniel Scales	E. T. Broadnax, Robert Martin.
1824	Thomas Blackwell	Wm. Donnell, Robt. Martin.
1825	Henry Baughn	Robert Martin, James Barnett.
1826	Thomas Blackwell	James Barnett, Thomas Settle.
1827	Thomas Blackwell	James Barnett, Thomas Settle.
1828	Edwd. T. Broadnax	Thomas Settle, Wm. Bethell.
1829	Robert Martin	Wilson S. Hill, Wm. Bethel.
1830	Robert Martin	Philip Irion, William Donnell.
1831	Robert Martin	Wilson S. Hill, Benjamin Settle.
1832	Robert Martin	Benjamin Settle, Philip Irion.
1833	Robert Martin	Benjamin Settle, Philip Irion.
1834	Robert Martin	Philip Irion, Blake W. Brasswell.
1835	David S. Reid	Philip Irion, Blake W. Brasswell.
1836	David S. Reid	Philip Irion, Blake W. Brasswell.
1838	David S. Reid	R. P. Cardwell, B. W. Brasswell.
1840	David S. Reid	R. P. Cardwell, Geo. D. Boyd.
1842	Geo. D. Boyd	R. P. Cardwell, Peter Scales.
1844	George D. Boyd	Peter Scales, R. P. Williamson.
1846	George D. Boyd	Danl. W. Courts, Joseph Neal.
1848	Wm. D. Bethell	Danl. W. Courts, T. W. Keen.
1850	Daniel W. Courts	Thomas Ruffin, Jr., Horatio Kallam.
1852	Geo. D. Boyd	A. M. Scales, Alfred Reid.
1854	Geo. D. Boyd	Thos. Smith, Jr., Jos. W. Neal.
1856	Geo. D. Boyd	A. M. Scales, Thos. Settle, Jr.
1858	Geo. D. Boyd	Thos. Settle, Jr., F. L. Simpson.
1860	F. L. Simpson	Rawley Galloway, Thomas Slade.
1862	F. L. Simpson	W. J. Gilliam, Jas. Reynolds.
1864	D. W. Courts	John Strong, A. G. Boyd.
1866	W. Hand	J. Holderby, R. B. Henderson.
1868	Jno. M. Lindsay	Henry Barnes, D. S. Ellington.
1870	James T. Morehead	A. B. Johns, David Settle.
1872	James T. Morehead	A. B. Johns, David Settle.

Rockingham forms the 23d Senatorial District.

ROWAN COUNTY.

ROWAN COUNTY was formed in 1753 from Anson county, and until Surry (in 1770), and Burke (in 1777), were taken off, comprehended much of the western part of the State of North Carolina and Tennessee. The history of Rowan then is the history of Western North Carolina.

Rowan is situated in the western part of the State, bounded on the north by Davie county, one of her daughters, east by the Yadkin River, which separates her from Davidson, (another daughter,) south by Stanly and Cabarrus, and west by Iredell, another daughter.

Salisbury, her capitol, is nearly west from Raleigh 118 miles. It derives its name from a town in England about seventy miles west from London. It is a word of Saxon origin, meaning *a dry town.*

COUNTY OFFICERS.

Offices.	Names.
Superior Court Clerk	John A. Boyden.
Register of Deeds	Horatio N. Woodson.
Sheriff	Charles F. Waggoner.
Coroner	Benjamin F. Fraley.
Surveyor	Thomas P. Johnston.
Treasurer	James S. McCubbin.
Commissioners	M. L. Holmes, Chairman. D. A. Davis. George M. Bernhardt. J. G. Fleming. Ephraim Mauney.

JUSTICES OF THE PEACE.

Names.	Date of Qalification.	Post Office Address.
T. W. Keen		Salisbury.
R. W. Price		Salisbury.
D. L. Bringle		Salisbury.
Philip Sowers		Salisbury.
Adam M. Brown		Salisbury.
T. G. Haughton		Salisbury.
W. M. Kincaid		Salisbury.
A. L. Hall		Salisbury.
J. O. C. Graham		Salisbury.
John A. Bailey		Salisbury.
W. A. Luckey		Rowan Mills.
Joseph A. Hawkins		Rowan Mills.
Michael W. Goodman		Salisbury.
Jesse W. Miller		Salisbury.
W. F. Watson		Salisbury.
C. H. McKenzie		Salisbury.

ROWAN COUNTY—Continued.

JUSTICES OF THE PEACE—Continued.

Names.	Date of Qualification.	Post Office Address.
S. M. Furr		China Grove.
J. L. Sloan		China Grove.
John Sloop		China Grove.
P. A. Sloop		Salisbury.
A. W. Klutts		Gold Hill.
Wiley Bean		Salisbury.
John W. Miller		Salisbury.
David Barringer		Salisbury.
Alfred M. Peeler		Salisbury.

LIST OF MEMBERS TO THE HOUSE OF COMMONS FROM SALISBURY.

Years.	House of Commons.	Years.	House of Commons.
1777	David Nesbett,	1807	Archibald Henderson,
1778	Matthew Troy,	1808	Archibald Henderson,
1779	Maxwell Chambers,	1809	Archibald Henderson,
1780	Anthony Newman,	1810	Joseph Chambers,
1781	Anthony Newman,	1811	John Steele,
1782	Anthony Newman,	1812	John Steele,
1783	Anthony Newman,	1813	John Steele,
1784	Anthony Newman,	1814	Archibald Henderson,
1785	Thomas Frohock,	1815	John L. Henderson,
1786	Thomas Frohock,	1816	John L. Henderson,
1787	John Steele,	1817	Stephen L. Ferrand.
1788	John Steele,	1818	John Beard, jr.
1789	Maxwell Chambers,	1819	Archibald Henderson,
1791	Lewis Beard,	1820	Archibald Henderson,
1792	Lewis Beard,	1821	Charles Fishet,
1793	Lewis Beard,	1822	Alfred McKay,
1794	John Steele,	1823	John L. Henderson.
1795	John Steele,	1824	John L. Henderson,
1796	Evan Alexander,	1825	David F. Caldwell,
1797	John Newman,	1826	Charles Fisher,
1798	Evan Alexander,	1827	Charles Fisher,
1799	Evan Alexander,	1828	Charles Fisher,
1800	Evan Alexander,	1829	Charles Fisher,
1801	Evan Alexander,	1830	Charles Fisher,
1802	Evan Alexander,	1831	Charles Fisher,
1803	Evan Alexander,	1832	Burton Craige,
1804	Joseph Pearson,	1833	Richard H. Alexander,
1805	Joseph Pearson,	1834	Richard H. Alexander,
1806	John Steele,	1835	William Chambers.

The Borough representation was abolished by the Convention of 1835.

ROWAN COUNTY—Continued.

MEMBERS OF GENERAL ASSEMBLY.

Years.	Senate.	House.
1777	Griffith Rutherford	Matthew Lock, James Smith.
1778	Griffith Rutherford	Matthew Lock, Moses Winslow.
1779	Griffith Rutherford	Matthew Lock, Moses Winslow.
1780	Griffith Rutherford	Matthew Lock, George H. Berger.
1781	Matthew Lock	Wm. Sharpe, Samuel Young.
1782	Matthew Lock	Wm. Sharpe, Samuel Young.
1783	Griffith Rutherford	Matthew Lock, George H. Berger.
1784	Griffith Rutherford	Wm. Sharpe, James Kerr.
1785	Griffith Rutherford	Matthew Locke, George H. Berger.
1786	Griffith Rutherford	Thomas Carson, Richard Pearson.
1787	George H. Berger	Richmond Pearson, Thomas Carson.
1788	Basil Gaither	David Caldwell, Thomas Carson.
1789	Geo. H. Berger	Matthew Lock, John Stokes.
1790	Geo. H. Berger	Matthew Lock, Basil Gaither.
1791	Geo. H. Berger	Matthew Lock, Basil Gaither.
1792	Geo. H. Berger	Matthew Lock, Basil Gaither.
1793	Lewis Beard	Thomas Carson, Basil Gaither.
1794	William Cathey	Basil Gaither, Thomas Carson.
1795	William Cathey	Basil Gaither, Thomas Carson.
1796	Basil Gaither	Matthew Brandon, Thomas Carson.
1797	Basil Gaither	Matthew Brandon, Thomas Carson.
1798	Basil Gaither	Samuel Dusenbury, George Fisher.
1799	Basil Gaither	Matthew Brandon, George Fisher.
1800	Basil Gaither	George Fisher, Samuel Dusenbury.
1801	Basil Gaither	George Fisher, John Munro.
1802	Basil Gaither	Matthew Brandon, Daniel Leatherman.
1803	George Fisher	Daniel Leatherman, Daniel Hunt.
1804	Jacob Fisher	John Hunt, George Fisher.
1805	Matthew Brandon	Daniel Leatherman, Daniel Hunt.
1806	Jacob Fisher	Daniel Leatherman, Daniel Hunt.
1807	Jacob Fisher	Daniel Leatherman, Jesse A. Pearson.
1808	Jacob Fisher	Jesse A. Pearson, John Smith.
1809	Jacob Fisher	Jesse A. Pearson, Wm. Wellborn.
1810	Jacob Fisher	Alexander Cladcleugh, George Mumford.
1811	Jacob Fisher	Daniel Leatherman, George Mumford.
1812	Wm. Bodenhamer	Jesse A. Pearson, John Lindsay.
1813	Wm. Bodenhamer	George McCulloh, Jesse A. Pearson.
1814	Wm. Bodenhamer	Jesse A. Pearson, George McCulloh.
1815	Wm. Bodenhamer	George McCulloh, Jesse A. Pearson.
1816	Jesse A. Pearson	Henry Chambers, Joel McCorkle.
1817	Daniel Leatherman	Michael Holdshouser, Ransom Powell.
1818	Charles Fisher	Michael Holdshouser, Ransom Powell.
1819	Francis Locke	George Smith, Samuel Jones.
1820	Francis Locke	Samuel Jones, Thomas Hampton.
1821	John Lindsay	John Clements, Henry Rats.
1822	Joseph Spurgen	Charles Fisher, George Smith.
1823	James Martin, jr.	Charles Fisher, John Clements.
1824	Jacob Fisher	John Linn, George Andrews.
1825	Samuel Jones	George Andrews, John Clements.
1826	John Beard	John Clements, John Linn.
1827	John Scott	Hamilton C. Jones, John Clements.
1828	John Scott	John Clements, H. C. Jones.
1829	David F. Caldwell	Thomas G. Polk, Richmond M. Pearson.
1830	David F. Caldwell	Thomas G. Polk, Richmond M. Pearson.
1831	David F. Caldwell	Thomas G. Polk, Richmond M. Pearson.

ROWAN COUNTY—Continued.

MEMBERS OF GENERAL ASSEMBLY—Continued.

Years.	Senate.	House.
1832	Archd. G. Carter...........	Thomas G. Polk, Richmond M. Pearson.
1833	John Beard, jr..............	John Clements, Charles Fisher.
1834	John Beard, jr..............	Burton Craig, John Clements.
1835	Thomas G. Polk............	John Clements, Jesse W. Wharton.
1836	Thomas G. Polk............	John Clements, Charles Fisher, William D. Crawford.
1838	Samuel Ribelin.............	William D. Crawford, H. C. Jones, J. A. Clements.
1840	Samuel Ribelin.............	H. C. Jones, Isaac Burns, F. Williams.
1842	Samuel Ribelin.............	Alexander W. Brandon, F. Williams, Jno. B. Lord.
1844	Nathaniel Boyden..........	John B. Lord, Jno. W. Ellis.
1846	Samuel E. Kerr	Isaac Ribelin, Jno. W. Ellis.
1848	John A. Lillington	John W. Ellis, Wilie Bean.
1850	John A. Lillington	A. H. Caldwell, O. G. Foard.
1852	John A. Lillington	Wm. A. Walton, Levi Trexler.
1854	Charles F. Fisher...........	A. H. Caldwell, C. A. Rose.
1856	J. G. Ramsay...............	N. F. Hall, W. A. Henck.
1858	J. G. Ramsay...............	N. N. Fleming, N. F. Hall.
1860	J. G. Ramsay...............	N. N. Fleming, N. F. Hall.
1862	J. G. Ramsay...............	F. E. Shober, N. N. Fleming.
1864	Wm. B. Marsh	W. H. Crawford, F. E. Shober.
1866	Robert F. Johnston.........	O. G. Foard, W. H. Crawford.
1868	Wm. M. Robbins...........	Jos. Hawkins, Isaac M. Shaver.
1870	Wm. M. Robbins...........	Wm. H. Crawford, F. N. Lucky.
1872	Charles Price...............	F. N. Lucky, Kerr Craige.

Davie and Rowan form the 30th Senatorial District.

RUTHERFORD COUNTY.

Rutherford County was erected in 1779 out of Tryon County, which was in this year abolished, and its territory divided into Lincoln and Rutherford, and called in honor of Griffith Rutherford, who was a Brigadier-General in the Revolutionary war.

It is located in the western part of the State, and bounded on the north by McDowell, east by Cleaveland, south by the South Carolina line and Polk County, and west by Henderson and Buncombe.

Its capital, Rutherfordton, is two hundred and sixteen miles west of Raleigh.

RUTHERFORD COUNTY—Continued.

COUNTY OFFICERS.

Offices.	Names.
Superior Court Clerk	J. B. Carpenter.
Register of Deeds	R. J. Williams.
Sheriff	J. E. McFarland.
Coroner	A. P. Hollifield.
Surveyor	W. P. Watson.
Treasurer	J. P. Bradley.
Commissioners	E. D. Hawkins. R. L. Gilkey. M. J. Harrill. Jno. Hampton. C. J. Sparks.

JUSTICES OF THE PEACE.

Names.	Date of Qualification.	Post Office Address.
John H. Bradley	Aug. 8th, 1873.	Rutherfordton.
James M. Allen	" "	Rutherfordton.
R. J. Williams	Not qualified.	Rutherfordton.
Noah H. Hampton	Aug. 8th, 1873.	Green Hill.
William B. Wilson	" 11th, "	Green Hill.
Martin Champion	" 13th, "	Rutherfordton.
Issac D. McClure	Sept. 1st, "	Rutherfordton.
John Owens	Aug. 8th, "	Island Ford.
E. J. Henson	" "	Island Ford.
D. D. Scruggs	" "	Hicksville.
Leander A. Holland	" "	Hicksville.
A. S. Harrill	" 12th, "	Webb's Ford.
B. B. Byers	" "	Oak Springs.
Wm. G. Price	" 11th, "	Duncan's Creek.
Thomas Stroud	" "	Duncan's Creek.
James M. Mode	" 20th, "	First Broad.
Alford Jones	Sept. 22d, "	First Broad.
W. B. Freeman	Aug. 8th, "	Logan's Store.
L. L. Peck	" 11th, "	Logan's Store.
William Mentuth	" "	Brittain.
Robt. L. Gilkey	Sept. 1st, "	Rutherfordton.
A. W. aynes	Aug. 8th, "	Otter Creek.
P. Wilkerson	" "	Otter Creek.
Jerry Jackson	" 23rd, "	Grassy Knob.
William M. Henderson	" "	Chimney Rock.

RUTHERFORD COUNTY—Continued.

MEMBERS OF GENERAL ASSEMBLY.

Years.	Senate.	House.
1780	William Porter	David Whitesides, Wm. Gilbert.
1781	William Porter	James Withrow, David Miller.
1782	James Miller	William Gilbert, David Dickey.
1783	James Holland	William Gilbert, Richard Singleton.
1784	James Miller	Richard Singleton, James Withrow.
1785	James Miller	George Moore, Richard Singleton.
1786	James Whiteside	James Withrow, James Holland.
1787	James Miller	Richard Singleton, James Withrow.
1788	Richard Singleton	William Porter, Jomes Withrow.
1789	Richard Singleton	William Porter, James Holland.
1790	Richard Singleton	Wm. Porter, Wm. Davidson.
1791	Richard Singleton	Wm. Davison, Wm. Porter.
1792	Richard Singleton	Wm. Porter, Felix Walker.
1793	Richard Singleton	Felix Waker, Wm. Porter.
1794	Richard Singleton	William Porter, Samuel Carpenter.
1795	Charles Wilkins	Samuel Carpenter, Jonas Bedford.
1796	William Porter	Jonas Bedford, Samuel Carpenter.
1797	James Holland	Samuel Carpenter, Jonas Bedford
1798	Samuel Carpenter	William Greene, Chas. Lewis.
1799	Samuel Carpenter	Wm. Porter, Felix Walker.
1800	William Greene	Felix Walker, Arthur Clarke.
1801	William Greene	Felix Walker, John Miller.
1802	Jonathan Hampton	Felix Walker, James Withrow.
1803	William Greene	William Porter, John Miller.
1804	Jonathan Hampton	James Withrow, Housen Harrell.
1805	Jonathan Hampton	Wm. Porter, James Withrow.
1806	William Greene	Felix Walker, James Terrell.
1807	William Greene	Wm. Porter, James L. Terrell.
1808	William Greene	James L. Terrell, John Carson.
1809	William Greene	Daniel Gold, George Camp.
1810	William Carson	Daniel Gold, George Camp.
1811	William Greene	William Porter, Daniel Gold.
1812	Jonathan Hampton	William Porter, Joseph Carson.
1813	Jonathan Hampton	Jos. M. Carson, Abram Crow.
1814	William Greene	J. M. D. Carson, William Porter.
1815	William Greene	William Porter, John Carson.
1816	John Moore	William Porter, John Carson.
1817	William Greene	John H. Alley, Robert H. Taylor.
1818	William Greene	John H. Alley, James L. Terrell.
1819	George Walton	Daniel Gold, John Carson.
1820	George Walton	John Carson, John McDowell.
1821	Benj. H. Bradley	John Carson, John McDowell.
1822	William Greene	James Graham, John Carson.
1823	Elias Alexander	John Carson, James Graham.
1824	William Greene	John Carson, James Graham.
1825	Martin Shuford	John Carson, Joseph Greene.
1826	Martin Shuford	John Carson, Wm. Richardson.
1827	Martin Shuford	Daniel Gold, Joseph Greene.
1828	Martin P. Shuford	James Graham, James Webb.
1829	John McIntyre	James Graham, James M. Carson.
1830	John McIntyre	Robert McAfee, James Webb.
1831	John McIntyre	James M. Webb, Joseph Greene.
1832	Jos. M. D. Carson	Thomas Dewes, A. B. Irvine.
1833	Martin P. Shuford	A. B. Irvine, Alanson W. Moore.

RUTHERFORD COUNTY—Continued.

MEMBERS OF GENERAL ASSEMBLY—Continued.

Years.	Senate.	House.
1834	Bremen H. Durham........	David Hannick, John H. Bedford.
1835	Alanson W. Moore..........	J. H. Bedford, Jos. M. D. Carson.
1836	Jos. M. D. Carson..........	W. J. T. Miller. T. Jefferson, J. H. Bedford
1838	Jos. M. D. Carson..........	W. J. T. Miller, W. E. Mills, J. H. Bedford.
1840	John G. Bynum.............	W. J. T. Miller, W. E. Mills, Thos. Jefferson
1842	W. J. T. Miller.............	Thos. Jefferson, W. E. Mills, John Baxter.
1844	Thomas Jefferson..........	m. E. Mills, Tollevis Davis.
1846	Columbus Mills............	Wm. F. Jones, Simon McCurry.
1848	Wm. J. T. Miller...........	A. G. Logan, m. ilkins.
1850	John G. Bynum.............	C. J. Webb, Jesse B. Sloan.
1852	John G. Bynum.............	T. J. Webb, L. A. Mills.
1854	Columbus Mills............	Wm. M. Shipp, John G. Bynum.
1856	Columbus Mills............	Ed. Toms, L. Harrell.
1858	L. A. Mills.................	B. Washburne, O. P. Gardner.
1860	A. W. Burton..............	. T. N. Davis, B. H. Paget.
1862	M. O. Dickson..............	A. R. Bryan, J. B. Carpenter.
1864	W. J. T. Miller..............	A. R. Bryan, Jos. L. Carson.
1866	C. L. Harris.................	Geo. W. Logan, N. Scoggin.
1868	John B. Eaves..............	Jas. M. Justice.
1870	G. M. Whitesides...........	Jas. M. Justice.
1872	Martin Walker.............	Eli Whisnant.

Rutherford and Polk form the 39th Senatorial District.

SAMPSON COUNTY.

Sampson County was formed in 1784, from Duplin, named in compliment to Colonel John Sampson.

It is situated in the eastern part of the State, and bounded on the north by Johnson and Wayne, on the east by Duplin, south by Bladen and New Hanover, west by Cumberland.

Its capital is Clinton, and ninety-four miles south from Raleigh.

COUNTY OFFICERS.

Offices.	Names.
Superior Court Clerk...................	Jas. K. Morisey.
Register of Deeds.......................	Oliver Blackburn.
Sheriff..................................	Clifton Ward.
Coroner..................................	Henry B. Giddens.

SAMPSON COUNTY—Continued.

COUNTY OFFICERS—Continued.

Offices.	Names.
Surveyor	Arthul Lee.
Treasurer	Jas. Oates.
Commissioners	M. J. Faison. O. L. Chesnutt. Owen Fennell. Amos Bullard. Wm. Daughtry.

JUSTICES OF THE PEACE.

Names.	Date of Qualification.	Post Office Address.
Amos Royal	Aug. 15th, 1873.	Clinton.
G. W. Highsmith	" "	Clinton.
N. B. Barefoot	" 16th, "	Newton Grove.
Josiah Baggett	" "	Newton Grove.
L. R. Carroll	" "	Clinton.
J. M. Moseley	" 18th, "	Clinton.
J. E. Barden	" "	Clinton.
C. H. Crumpler	" 20th, "	Clinton.
W. A. Anders	" 28th, "	Clinton.
J. D. Carter	" 29th, "	Lisbon.
Columbus G. Robinson	Sept. 1st, 1873.	Lisbon.
R. C. Holmes	" "	Clinton.
E. C. Smith	" "	Harrell's Store.
Luther R. Millard	" "	Clinton.
G. Spell	" "	Clinton.
William Sessoms	" "	Clinton.
Thomas B. Hall	" "	Dismal.
A. T. Herring	" "	Clinton.
Daniel Robinson	" "	Harrell's Store.
Hardy Daughtry	" "	Newton Grove.
Wilson Lockamy	" "	Clinton.
Robinson Ward	" "	Newton Grove.
M. B. Crumpler	" "	Clinton.
Albert Johnson	" 15th "	Harrell's Store.
J. R. Maxwell	Oct. 6th "	Dismal.

SAMPSON COUNTY—CONTINUED.

MEMBERS OF GENERAL ASSEMBLY.

Years.	Senate.	House.
1785	Richard Clinton............	John Hay, David Dodd.
1786	Richard Clinton............	David Dodd, Lewis Holmes.
1787	Richard Clinton............	David Dood, Lewis Holmes.
1788	Hardy Holmes..............	Lewis Holmes, William King.
1789	Richard Clinton............	James Speller, James Thompson.
1790	Richard Clinton............	William King, James Thompson.
1791	Richard Clinton............	William King, James Thompson.
1792	Richard Clinton............	James Thompson, Wm. King.
1793	Richard Clinton............	Laban Taylor, Gabriel Holmes.
1794	Richard Clinton............	Gabriel Holmes, James Thompson.
1795	Richard Clinton............	James Thompson, Gabriel Holmes.
1796	Josiah Blackman...........	Claiborn Ivey, James Thompson.
1797	Gabriel Holmes............	James Thompson, Kedar Bryan.
1798	Gabriel Holmes............	Kedar Bryan, James Thompson.
1799	Gabriel Holmes............	Wm. S. Clinton, James Thompson.
1800	Gabriel Holmes............	Wm. S. Clinton, James Thompson.
1801	Gabriel Holmes............	Wm. Robeson, Joab Blackman.
1802	Gabriel Holmes............	Joab Blackman, Wm. Robeson.
1803	Joab Blackman.............	Raiford Crumpler, Allen Mobley.
1804	Joab Blackman.............	Thomas King, Allen Mobley.
1805	Joab Blackman.............	Allen Mobley, Thomas King.
1806	Joab Blackman.............	W. R. King, Allen Mobley.
1807	Joab Blackman.............	John Bryan, William Blackman.
1808	Joab Blackman.............	Wm. R. King, Jesse Darden.
1809	Joab Blackman.............	James Matthews, Wm. R. King.
1810	Joab Blackman.............	James Matthews, Hardy Royal.
1811	Allen Mobley..............	Hardy Royal, James Matthews.
1812	Gabriel Holmes............	James Matthews, Thomas King.
1813	Gabriel Holmes............	James Matthews, William Blackman.
1814	Allen Mobley..............	Wm. Blackman, J. Matthews.
1815	Allen Mobley..............	Wm. Blackman, J. Matthews.
1816	John Ingram..............	Wm. Blackman, J. Matthews.
1817	Michael J. Kenan..........	James Matthews, Wm. Blackman.
1818	Michael J. Kenan..........	James Matthews, Thomas Sutton.
1819	James Holmes..............	Thomas Sutton, John Sellers.
1820	Edward C. Gavin...........	J. Crumpler, D. Underwood.
1821	Edward C. Gavin...........	John Sellers, Thomas Boykin.
1822	William Robinson..........	Alexander Fleming, Thomas Boykin.
1823	Edward C. Gavin...........	John Sellers, D. Underwood.
1824	Thomas Boykin	J. Crumpler, D. Underwood.
1825	Thomas Boykin	Daniel Joyner, D. Underwood.
1826	Thomas Boykin	D. Underwood, Thomas Sutton.
1827	Hardy Royal...............	D. Underwood, Thomas Boykin.
1828	Hardy Royal...............	D. Underwood, Thomas Boykin.
1829	David Underwood..........	Dickson Sloan, Arch'd Monk.
1830	Edward C. Gavin...........	Arch'd C. Monk, Dickson Sloan.
1831	Thomas Boykin	Arch'd C. Monk, Dickson Sloan.
1832	Edward C. Gavin...........	Arch'd C. Monk, Dickson Sloan.
1833	Edward C. Gavin...........	Arch'd C. Monk, Dickson Sloan.
1834	Edward C. Gavin...........	Arch'd C. Monk, Dickson Sloan.
1835	Edward C. Gavin...........	Dickson Sloan, Isaac W. Lane.
1836	Thomas Bunting............	Isaac W. Lane, Dickson Sloan.
1838	Thomas Bunting............	Timothy Underwood, Dickson Sloan.
1840	Dickson Sloan.............	Joseph Herring, Isaac W. Lane.

SAMPSON COUNTY—Continued.

MEMBERS OF GENERAL ASSEMBLY—Continued.

Years.	Senate.	House.
1842	John Boykin	Joseph Herring, E. C. Gavin.
1844	Edward C. Gavin	—— Beaman, David Murphy.
1846	Edward C. Gavin	David Murphy, Arthur Brown.
1848	Matthew J. Faison	Arthur Brown, Amos Herring.
1850	Thomas Bunting	Amos Herring, J. L. Boykin.
1852	Thos. Bunting	E. B. Chesnut, Hardy Fleming.
1854	Thos. J. Faison	Geo. H. Daughtry, E. F. Shaw.
1856	T. H. Holmes	O. P. White, J. M. Mosely.
1858	A. A. McKay	F. J. Faison, —— Kirby.
1860	Thos. J. Faison	N. C. Faison, Geo. W. Autrey.
1862	Thos. J. Faison	Wm. Kirby, Thos. H. Holmes.
1864	Wm. Kirby	L. A. Powell, P. Murphy.
1866	John C. Williams	John Barden, Geo. W. Autrey.
1868	Jas. S. Harrington D. L. Hall	John C. Williams.
1870	W. C. Troy	J. R. Maxwell.
1872	C. Tate Murphy	W. R. Maxwell, W. H. Bryan.

Sampson forms the 14th Senatorial District.

STANLY COUNTY.

Stanly County was formed in 1841, from the western portion of Montgomery, as divided by the Pee Dee River, and is called in honor of Hon. John Stanly, of Newbern.

It is situated in the western part of the State, and bounded on the north by Rowan county, east by Montgomery, south by Anson and Union, and west by Cabarrus.

Its capital is Albemarle, and preserves the name of one of its Lords Proprietors.

COUNTY OFFICERS.

Offices.	Names.
Superior Court Clerk	J. M. Redwine.
Register of Deeds	J. W. Snuggs.
Sheriff	Joseph Marshall.
Coroner	N. P. Efird.
Surveyor	W. H. Randle.
Treasurer	M. B. Howell.
Commissioners	E. W. Davis, Chairman. W. R. McSwain. W. F. Moss. George C. Smith. Daniel Ritchey.

STANLY COUNTY—Continued.

JUSTICES OF THE PEACE.

Names.	Date of Qualification.	Post Office Address.
F. A. Lowder	Sept. 1st, 1873.	Norwood.
Eli Kendall	" "	Norwood.
Dr. A. J. Shankle	" "	Albemarle.
John A. Moody	" "	Albemarle.
A. S. Moss	" "	Albemarle.
R. J. Stone	" "	Albemarle.
Solomon Ritc[illegible]	" "	Kendall's Store.
William Moody	" "	Kendall's Store.
R. A. Almond	" "	Albemarle.
R. Almond	" "	Albemarle.
C. H. Brooks	" "	Big Lick.
C. W. Honeycutt	" "	Big Lick.
S. H. Efird	" "	Big Lick.
J. W. Honeycutt	" "	Big Lick.
W. H. D. Greene	" "	Albemarle.
D. S. Morton	" "	Albemarle.

MEMBERS OF GENERAL ASSEMBLY.

Years.	Senate.	House.
1844	Walter F. Pharr	Francis J. Locke.
1846	Christopher Melchor	D. A. G. Palmer.
1848	R. Kendall	D. A. G. Palmer.
1850	Rufus Barringer	Francis Locke.
1852	E. C. Freeman	John Farr.
1854	E. C. Freeman	John Farr.
1856	E. R. Gibson	M. P. Waddell.
1858	—— Davis	M. P. Waddell.
1860	Victor C. Barringer	Lafayette Green.
1862	J. W. Smith	Lafayette Green.
1864	J. E. McEachen	Richard Harris.
1866	—— Marshall	L. C. Morton.
1868	C. Melchor	Lafayette Green.
1870	Valentine Mauney	John Farr.
1872	J. C. Barnhardt	M. T. Waddell.

Cabarrus and Stanly form the 28th Senatorial District

STOKES COUNTY.

STOKES COUNTY was formed in 1789, from Surry county, and called in honor of Hon. John Stokes.

Stokes county is located in the north-western part of the State, and bounded on the north by the Virginia Line, east by Rockingham, south by Forsyth, and west by Surry.

Its capital is Danbury, 110 miles north-west from Raleigh.

COUNTY OFFICERS.

Offices.	Names.
Superior Court Clerk	Squire Venable.
Register of Deeds	J. T. W. Davis.
Sheriff	Wm. H. Gentry.
Coroner	None.
Surveyor	Giden George.
Treasurer	Thomas M. Baker.
Commissioners	S. B. Taylor, Chairman. Thomas Martin. J. M. Martin. John W. Spainhour. C. W. Lasley.

JUSTICES OF THE PEACE.

Names.	Date of Qualification.	Post Office Address.
Martin Venable	August, 1873.	Pilot Mountain.
William Newsom	" "	Little Yadkin.
Joel Y. Allen	" "	Wilson's Store.
Lafayette Smith	" "	Danbury.
William Lash, jr.	" "	Walnut Cove.
W. B. Vaughan	" "	Walnut Cove.
J. G. H. Mitchell	" "	Red Shoals.
Jonathan Flynn	" "	Red Shoals.
John Martin	" "	Martin's Limekiln.
P. D. Watkins	" "	Crooked Creek.
W. V. Shelton	" "	Danbury.
James M. Hill	" "	Danbury.
George Pearce	" "	Westfield.
J. T. Joyce	" "	Francisco.

STOKES COUNTY—Continued.

MEMBERS OF GENERAL ASSEMBLY.

Years.	Senate.	House.
1790	Joseph Winston	George Houser, Absalom Bostick.
1791	Joseph Winston	James Martin, Absalom Bostick.
1792	Peter Harston	James Martin, George Houser.
1793	Matthew Brooks	George Houser, Absalom Bostick.
1794	Matthew Brooks	Absalom Bostick, George Houser.
1795	Matthew Brooks	Absalom Bostick, George Houser.
1796	Peter Harston	Wm. Hughlet, George Houser.
1797	Matthew Brooks	Wm. Hughlet, Charles Banner.
1798	Matthew Brooks	John Martin, Charles Banner.
1799	Peter Harston	John Martin, Charles Banner.
1800	Peter Harston	Henry B. Dobson, Charles Banner.
1801	Wm. T. Hughlett	John Bostick, Charles Banner.
1802	Joseph Winston	Charles Banner, Henry B. Dobson.
1803	Joseph Cloud	Henry B. Dobson, John Bostick.
1804	Wm. Hughlett	John Bostick, Henry B. Dobson.
1805	Gotlieb Shober	Henry B. Dobson, Isaac Dalton.
1806	Johnston Clements	John Bostick, Isaac Dalton.
1807	Joseph Winston	Jacob Salmons, Benjamin Forsythe.
1808	Gotleib Shober	Jona. Dalton, Banjamin Forsythe.
1809	Henry B. Dobson	Jona. Dalton, Charles Banner.
1810	Henry B. Dobson	Joseph Wilson, Isaac Nelson.
1811	Henry B. Dobson	James Martin, Joseph Wilson.
1812	Joseph Winston	James Martin, Joseph Wilson.
1813	Edward Moore	Thos. Longina, Charles F. Bagge.
1814	Andrew Bowman	Wm. P. Dobson, Isaac Dalton.
1815	Andrew Bowman	Isaac Dalton, Joseph Allen.
1816	Isaac Nelson	Joseph Allen, William Hughes.
1817	Joseph Allen	John L. Houser, Joseph Winston
1818	Charles Banner	Jacob Salmons, Samuel Welch.
1819	Emmanuel Shober	Edward Tatum, John Hill.
1820	Emmanuel Shober	John Hill, Salathiel Stone.
1821	Arch'd R. Ruffin	John Hill, Jos. M. Flynt.
1822	Emmanuel Shober	Augustine H. Shepherd, John Hill.
1823	John Hill	Augustine H. Shepherd, Jos. M. Flynt.
1824	Emmanuel Shober	Augustine H. Shepherd, Jos. M. Flynt.
1825	Johu Hill	A. H. Shepherd, Wm. Carter.
1826	John Hill	A. H. Shepherd, Wm. Carter.
1827	Emmanuel Shober	Jacob Salmons, Elisha Plummer.
1828	Emmanuel Shober	Gab. T. Moore, Henry A. Martin.
1829	Gab. T. Moore	John Banner, John Butner.
1830	John Hill	Leonard Zigler, Jos. W. Winston.
1831	John Hill	Jos. W. Winston, Leonard Zigler.
1832	Gab. T. Moore	John F. Poindexter, Leonard Zigler.
1833	Matthew R. Moore	Leonard Zigler, John F. Poindexter.
1834	William Flynt	John F. Poindexter, Leonard Zigler.
1835	Matthew R. Moore	Caleb H. Matthews, John F. Poindexter.
1836	Matthew R. Moore	Caleb H. Matthews, James M. Covington, Peter Critz.
1838	Matthew R. Moore	Caleb H. Matthews, James M. Covington, James Stafford.
1840	Matthew R. Moore	James M. Covington, Leon. Zigler, William Withers.
1842	Jas. Stafford	Jacob Shulzt, John F. Nelson, William A Mitchell.

STOKES COUNTY—Continued.

MEMBERS OF GENERAL ASSEMBLY—Continued.

Years.	Senate.	House.
1846	John F. Poindexter.........	R. Golding, H. Marshall, M. Martin.
1848	John ill Reich	Andrew M. Gamble, John Blackburn, Anderson Nicholson.
1850	Philip Barrow..............	Allen Flynt, Henry Marshall, J. A. Waugh.
1852	Philip Barrow..............	J. A. Waugh, H. Marshall, J. Matthews.
1854	J. J. Martin................	J. F. Hill.
1856	J. J. Martin................	J. F. Hill.
1858	J. J. Martin................	J. F. Hill.
1860	Jesse A. Waugh............	H. C. McKallum.
1862	J. E. Matthews............	William Flynt.
1864	J. E. Matthews............	William Flynt.
1866	J. E. Matthews............	Silas Westmoreland.
1868	Peter A. Wilson............	W. W. McCandless.
1870	—— Adams	T. G. H. Mitchell.
1872	John M. Stafford...........	T. G. H. Mitchell.

Forsythe and Stokes form the 32d Senatorial District.

SURRY COUNTY.

Surry County was formed in 1770, from Rowan county; which until this date comprehended a large portion of Western North Carolina, from beyond the Yadkin to the Mississippi river.

It derives its name from the county of Surry in the south of England. Its name is Saxon, and signifies "the South river."

Surry county is situated in the north-western portion of North Carolina.

It is bounded on the north by the Virginia line, east by Stokes county, south by Yadkin, and west by Wilkes and Alleghany counties.

Its capital is Rockford, and is distant from Raleigh 110 miles north-west.

COUNTY OFFICERS.

Offices.	Names.
Superior Court Clerk.....................	A. H. Freeman.
Register of Deeds........................	J. W. Martin.
Sheriff..................................	Wm. Haymore.
Coroner..................................	
Surveyor.................................	S. W. Roberts.

SURRY COUNTY—Continued.

COUNTY OFFICERS—Continued.

Offices.	Names.
Treasurer	M. L. Patterson.
Commissioners	M. Sparger, Chairman. J. C. Dodson. D. F. Holcomb. L. W. Bryan. A. H. Kapp.

JUSTICES OF THE PEACE.

Names.	Date of Qualification.	Post Office Address.
Thomas L. Gwyn		Elkin.
James H. Maxwell		Elkin.
William H. Wolfe		Judesville.
Columbus Thompson		Judesville.
Jackson Lowe		Lowe Gap.
James S. Pedigo		Edwardsville.
John T. Johnson		Mount Airy.
Hasten Beamer		Mount Airy.
James W. Jackson		Mount Airy.
Isaac Armfield		Mount Airy.
John H. Lowe		Flat Shoal.
Joseph White		Mount Airy.
Abram Whitaker		Siloam.
Martin L. Patterson		Tom's Creek.
Vestal Hutchens		Mount Airy.
Joseph Flippin		Flat Shoal.
John Brown		Rockford.
John H. Cornelius		Siloam.
Rom. S. Folger		Rockford.
John J. Setleff		Rush.
John E. Stanly		Rusk.
Lacy J. Norman		Dobson.
James M. Gordon		Dobson.
Thomas V. Hamlin		Dobson.
James W. Davis		Mount Airy.

MEMBERS OF GENERAL ASSEMBLY.

Years.	Senate.	House.
1777	Wm. Sheppard	Jos. Winston, Charles Gordon.
1778	Wm. Sheppard	Matthew Brooks, Frederick Miller.
1779	Wm. Sheppard	Gray Bynum, Frederick Miller.
1780	Wm. Sheppard	Samuel Cummings, Samuel Freeman.
1781	Wm. Sheppard	Samuel Cummings, Wm. T. Lewis.

SURRY COUNTY—Continued.

MEMBERS OF GENERAL ASSEMBLY—Continued.

Years.	Senate.	House.
1782	Wm. Sheppard	Samuel Cummings, Trangott Bagge.
1783	Martin Armstrong	Wm. T. Lewis, James Martin.
1784	John Armstrong	Joel Lewis, James Martin.
1785	John Armstrong	James Martin, William Lewis.
1786	John Armstrong	James Martin, William Lewis.
1787	Joseph Winston	Jas. Gaines, Seth Coffee.
1788	John Armstrong	George Houser, Wm. T. Lewis.
1789	Joseph Winston	Gideon Edwards, Absolam Bostick.
1790	Joseph Winston	Jonathan Haines, Jacob Sheppard.
1791	Gideon Edwards	Jonathan Haines, Jacob Sheppard.
1792	Gideon Edwards	Jonathan Haines, Jacob Sheppard.
1793	Gideon Edwards	Henry Speer, Jesse Franklin.
1794	Gideon Edwards	Jesse Franklin, Micajah Oglesby.
1795	Gideon Edwards	Micajah Oglesby, Hugh Armstrong.
1796	Gideon Edwards	Hugh Armstrong, Francis Poindexter.
1797	Gideon Edwards	Jesse Franklin, Hugh Armstrong.
1798	Gideon Edwards	Jesse Franklin, Thomas Wright.
1799	Gideon Edwards	Martin Armstrong, Joseph Williams, Jr.
1800	Gideon Edwards	Meshach Franklin, Thomas Wright.
1801	Gideon Edwards	Thomas Wright, Meshach Franklin.
1802	Gideon Edwards	Thomas Wright, Nicholas Horn.
1803	Gideon Edwards	Thomas Wright, Nicholas Horn.
1804	Peter Eaton	Micajah Oglesby, Nicholas Horn.
1805	Jesse Franklin	Nicholas Horn, David Davis.
1806	Jesse Franklin	Nicholas Horn, Nathan Chaffin.
1807	Thomas Wright	Nicholas Horn, Daniel Scott.
1808	Thomas Wright	Nicholas Horn, Micajah Oglesby.
1809	Gideon Edwards	Nicholas Horn, William Dowling.
1810	Thomas Wright	Nicholas Horn, Matthew M. Hughes.
1811	Thomas Wright	Nicholos Horn, Charles Taliaferro.
1812	Thomas Wright	Nicholas Horn, Charles Taliaferro.
1813	Thomas Wright	Lewis Williams, Charles Taliaferro.
1814	Thomas Wright	Lewis Williams, Nicholas Horn.
1815	Thomos Wright	Edward Sweatt, Gabriel Hanby.
1816	Thomas Wright	Gabriel Hanby, Josiah Hatley.
1817	Thomas Wright	Josiah Hatley, Edward Sweatt.
1818	Wm. P. Dobson	Solomon Graves, H. B. Poindexter.
1819	Wm. P. Dobson	Solomon Graves, Edward Lovell.
1820	Solomon Graves	Henry B. Poindexter, P. B. Roberts.
1821	Solomon Graves	Thomas Hampton, Pleasant B. Roberts.
1822	Solomon Graves	E. Thompson, P. B. Roberts.
1823	Solomon Graves	T. B. Wright, E. Thompson.
1824	Pleasant B. Roberts	David Durrett, W. C. Martin.
1825	Henry B. Poindexter	David Durrett, Golihu Moore.
1826	Pleasant B. Roberts	Elisha Arnold, Golihu Moore.
1827	Wm. P. Dobson	Wm. Douglas, Ephraim Hough.
1828	Meshach Franklin	Mordecai Fleming, Alfred C. Moore.
1829	Meshach Franklin	Alfred C. Moore, Ephraim Hough.
1830	Wm. P. Dobson	Mordecai Fleming, Alfred C. Moore.
1831	Wm. P. Dobson	Daniel W. Courts, Mordecai Fleming.
1832	Wm. P. Dobson	Thomas J. Word, Daniel W. Courts.
1833	Wm. P. Dobson	Daniel W. Courts, Harrison M. Waugh
1834	Wm. P. Dobson	H. M. Waugh, Pleasant Henderson.
1835	Harrison M. Waugh	Thomas L. Clingman, Mordecai Fleming.

SURRY COUNTY—Continued.

MEMBERS OF GENERAL ASSEMBLY—Continued.

Years.	Senate.	House.
1836	Wm. P. Dobson	Daniel W. Courts, P. B. Roberts, James Calloway.
1838	Mesbach Franklin	R. C. Puryear, Nathaniel Boyden, M. Oglesby.
1840	R. C. Puryear	Nathaniel Boyden, Columbus Franklin, H. B. Poindexter.
1842	Wm. P. Dobson	Dickson Taliaferro, Theo. C. Houser, Jno. J. Conrad.
1844	A. B. McMillan	R. C. Puryear, G. W. Brown, D. Taliaferro.
1846	A. B. McMillan	R. C. Puryear, Hugh Gwynn, James Sheek.
1848	George Bower	James Sheek, C. W. Williams, A. A. Oglesby.
1850	George Bower	J. R. McLean, James Sheek, Joseph Cockerham.
1852	George Bower	R. C. Puryear, J. Gwynn, Jos. H. Dobson.
1854	George Bower	Charles Whitlock.
1856	A. Brant	R. E. Reeves.
1858	Jos. Dobson	R. E. Reeves.
1860	Jos. Dobson	P. Waugh.
1862	Isaac Garrett	Jos. Hollingsworth.
1864	Jonathan Horton	H. M. Waugh.
1866	A. C. Cowles	H. M. Waugh.
1868	S. Forkner	A. L. Hendricks.
1870	A. C. Cowles	H. C. Hampton.
1872	A. C. Cowles	H. M. Waugh.

Surry and Yadkin form the 33rd Senatorial District.

SWAIN COUNTY.

Formed in 1871 from portions of Macon and Jackson, called in compliment to Gov. Swain, formerly Governor of the State and President of the University.

It is bounded on the north by the Tennessee Line, east by Haywood, south by Jackson and Macon, and west by Graham.

Its capital, Charleston, is distant 325 miles from Raleigh.

COUNTY OFFICERS.

Offices.	Names.
Superior Court Clerk	Henry J. Beck.
Register of Deeds	T. H. Parish.
Sheriff	E. Everett.

SWAIN COUNTY—Continued.

COUNTY OFFICERS—Continued.

Offices.	Names.
Coroner	Vacant.
Surveyor	A. A. J. McCoy.
Treasurer	B. McHan.
Commissioners	W. J. D. Hart. W. M. Enloe. J. S. Conner. S. A. Monteith.

MEMBERS OF GENERAL ASSEMBLY.

Years.	Senate.	House.
1872	W. L. Love	T. D. Bryson.

Cherokee, Clay, Graham, Jackson, and Macon form the 42d Senatorial District.

TRANSYLVANIA COUNTY.

Formed in 1861, from Henderson and Jackson. It is bounded on the north by Haywood and Buncombe, east by Henderson, south by State line, and west by Jackson. Its name from the Latin means "Beyond the woods."

Brevard is its county town. Its name is of revolutionary fame.

COUNTY OFFICERS.

Offices.	Names.
Superior Court Clerk	George C. Neill.
Register of Deeds	B. C. Lankford.
Sheriff	J. H. Lanning.
Coroner	None.
Surveyor	J. E. Merrell.
Treasurer	W. P. Poor.
Commissioners	T. G. Henson. B. F. Akins. G. F. Justus. J. B. Hefner. J. E. Galloway.

TRANSYLVANIA COUNTY—Continued.

JUSTICES OF THE PEACE.

Names.	Date of Qualification.	Post Office Address.
E. B. Clayton	Sept. 1st, 1874.	Davidson's River.
J. C. Ownbey	" "	Davidson's River.
Alex. Gray	" "	alhoun.
J. S. Heath	" "	Cedar Mountain.
M. J. Orr	" "	Brevard.
Samuel King	" "	Brevard.
H. C. Gillespie	" "	Brevard.
B. F. Aiken	" "	Brevard.
G. F. Justus	" "	Brevard.
J. F. Paxton	" "	Cherry Field.
H. E. Mull	" "	Cherry Field.
C. M. Gillespie	" "	Cherry Field.
J. B. Galloway	" "	Cherry Field.
J. B. Hefner	" "	Cherry Field.
J. W. McCall	" "	Cherry Field.
J. L. Fisher	" "	Cherry Field.
Wesley Patterson	" "	Cherry Field.

MEMBERS OF GENERAL ASSEMBLY.

Years.	Senate.	House.
1864	M. Patton	M. N. Patton.
1868	James Blythe	James W. Clapton.
1870	James Merrimon	—— Duckworth.
1872	W. P. Welch	F. J. Whitmire.

Haywood, Henderson and Transylvania form the 41st Senatorial District.

TYRRELL COUNTY.

Tyrrell County is one of the oldest counties in the State, and one of the original precincts of the Lords Proprietors.

It derives its name from Sir John Tyrrell, who owned that part of the province originally granted to Lord Ashly.

Tyrrell County is located in the eastern part of the State, and is bounded on the north by the Albemarle Sound, east by Dare County, south by Hyde, and west by Washington County.

Its capital, Columbia, is two hundred miles east of Raleigh.

TYRRELL COUNTY.—Continued.

COUNTY OFFICERS.

Offices.	Names.
Superior Court Clerk	Eli Spruill.
Register of Deeds	B. F. Sikes.
Sheriff	R. I. Hassell.
Coroner	Vacant.
Surveyor	J. R. Richardson.
Treasurer	John B. Combs.
Commissioners	J. . Meekins. B. T. Sikes. A. D. Litchfield. enderson Lewis. Samuel Norman.

JUSTICES OF THE PEACE.

Names.	Date of Qualification.	Post Office Address.
T. B. Myers	August, 1873.	Columbia.
R. D. Woodly	" "	Columbia.
M. D. L. Newberry	" "	Columbia.
James E. Graves	" "	Columbia.
William Reynolds	" "	Columbia.
Thos. L. Jones	" "	Gum Neck.
Lemuel Basnight	" "	Gum Neck.
Jas. A. Spruill	" "	Fort Landing.
W. G. Melson	" "	Fort Landing.

MEMBERS OF GENERAL ASSEMBLY.

Years.	Senate.	House.
1777	Archibald Currie	Benjamin Spruill, John Hooker.
1778	Jeremiah Frazier	Joshua Swain, Benjamin Spruill.
1779	Jeremiah Frazier	Benjamin Spruill, Joshua Swain.
1780	Jeremiah Frazier	John Warrington, Edmund Blount.
1781	Jeremiah Frazier	Isham Webb, Nehemiah Norman.
1782	Jeremiah Frazier	Nehemiah Norman, Nathan Hooker.
1783	Jeremiah Frazier	Nehemiah Norman, Nathan Hooker.
1784	Jeremiah Frazier	Benjamin Spruill, Nathan Hooker.
1785	John Warrington	Nehemiah Norman, Nathan Hooker.
1786	John Warrington	Simon Spruill, Nathan Hooker.
1787	John Warrington	Simon Spruill, Benjamin Spruill.
1788	Thomas Stewart	Simon Spruill, Samuel Chesson.

TYRRELL COUNTY—Continued.

MEMBERS OF GENERAL ASSEMBLY—Continued.

Years.	Senate.	House.
1790	Thomas Stewart	Simon Spruill, Samuel Chesson.
1791	Thomas Stewart	Hezekiah Spruill, Richard Howett.
1792	John Warrington	Simon Spruill, Charles Spruill.
1793	John Warrington	Simon Spruill, Charles Spruill.
1794	Richard Howett	Charles Spruill, Levi Blount.
1795	Richard Howett	Charles Spruill, Robert Cushing.
1796	Richard Howett	Charles Spruill, John Guyther.
1797	Charles Spruill	John Guyther, James Hoskins.
1798	Charles Spruill	Martin R. Byrd, James Hoskins.
1799	Charles Spruill	John Clayton, Samuel Spruill.
1800	Samuel Spruill	John Clayton, Thomas Hoskins.
1801	Samuel Spruill	John Clayton, Thomas Hoskins.
1802	Richard Davis	Elijah Warrington, John Clayton.
1803	Richard Davis	John Clayton, Jesse Alexander.
1804	Richard Davis	Jesse Alexander, Moses E. Cator.
1805	Richard Davis	Jeremiah Wynne, Benjamin Spruill.
1806	Richard Davis	Jeremiah Wynne, Levi Bateman.
1807	Richard Davis	Jeremiah Wynne, Moses E. Cator.
1808	Jesse Alexander	Levi Bateman, Moses E. Cator.
1809	James Alexander	Thomas Garrett, Moses E. Cator.
1810	Jesse Alexander	Levi Bateman, Solomon Hassell.
1811	Zebulon Tarkington	Solomon Hassell, Levi Bateman.
1812	Zebulon Tarkington	Solomon Hassill, Daniel Sawyer.
1813	Charles Hoskins	Solomon Hassell, Daniel Sawyer.
1814	Charles Hoskins	Solomon Hassell, Daniel Sawyer.
1815	Charles Hoskins	Daniel Bateman, Daniel Sawyer.
1816	Charles Hoskins	Solomon Hassell, Thomas Leigh.
1817	Zebulon Tarkington	Thomas Leigh, Daniel Bateman.
1818	Zebulon Tarkington	Thomas Leigh, Daniel Bateman.
1819	Richard Davis	Daniel Bateman, Enoch Hassell.
1820	Richard Davis	Daniel Bateman, Enoch Hassell.
1821	John B. Beasley	Daniel Bateman, Enoch Hassell.
1822	John B. Beasley	Daniel Bateman, Enoch Hassell.
1823	John B. Beasley	Enoch Hassell, Ephraim Mann.
1824	John B. Beasley	Frederick Davenport, Enoch Hassell.
1825	John B. Beasley	Daniel N. Bateman, Frederick Davenport.
1826	John B. Beasley	Daniel N. Bateman, Frederick Davenport.
1827	John B. Beasley	Daniel N. Bateman, Frederick Davenport.
1828	John B. Beasley	Daniel N. Bateman, Frederick Davenport.
1829	John B. Beasley	Daniel N. Bateman, Frederick Davenport.
1830	John B. Beasley	Daniel N. Bateman, Benjamin Sikes.
1831	Daniel N. Bateman	H. G. Spruill, Charles McCleese.
1832	Daniel N. Bateman	Charles McCleese, Samuel B. Spruill.
1833	Ephraim Mann	Charles McCleese, George H. Alexander.
1834	Ephraim Mann	Charles McCleese, George P. Alexander.
1835	George H. Alexander	Charles McCleese, Thomas Hassell.
1836	Hez. G. Spruill	Silas Davenport.
1838	Hez. G. Spruill	Charles McCleese.
1840	Hez. G. Spruill	Charles McCleese.
1842	Hez. G. Spruill	Joseph Halsey.
1844	Joseph Halsy	Silas Davenport.
1846	Joseph Halsy	Silas Davenport.
1848	Joseph Halsy	Charles McCleese.
1850	Thomas E. Pender	Joseph McCleese.

TYRRELL COUNTY—Continued.

MEMBERS OF GENERAL ASSEMBLY—Continued.

Years.	Senate.	House.
1852	Charles McClure	Jordan L. Jones.
1854	Charles Mc lure	Jordan L. Jones.
1856	Francis M. Burgess	John A. Benbury.
1858	—— Basnight	John A. Benbury.
1860	Jones Spencer	C. McCleese.
1862	Charles McClure	Eli Spruill.
1864	E. L. Mann	L. L. Harrell.
1866	Jones Spencer	W. W. Walker.
1868	F. C. Martindale	T. J. Jarvis.
1870	L. C. Latham	T. J. Jarvis.
1872	J. R. Respass H. E. Stilley	B. Jones.

Beaufort, Dare, Hyde, Martin, Tyrrell and Washington Counties form the second Senatorial District.

UNION COUNTY.

Union County was formed in 1842, from the south-eastern part of Mecklenburg, and western part of Anson counties.

It is situated in the south-western part of the State, and is bounded on the north by Cabarrus and Stanly, east by Anson, south by the South Carolina line, and west by Mecklenburg.

Its capital, Munroe, is 160 miles south-west from Raleigh; named in compliment to James Munroe, fifth President of the United States.

COUNTY OFFICERS.

Offices.	Names.
Superior Court Clerk	G. W. Flow.
Register of Deeds	W. J. C. McCauley.
Sheriff	A. F. Stevens.
Coroner	H. S. Presson.
Surveyor	J. F. Austin.
Treasurer	T. W. Griffin.
Commissioners	W. H. Fitzgerald, Chairman. William Crow. T. E. Ashcraft. T. W. Griffin. G. W. McCain.

UNION COUNTY—Continued.

JUSTICES OF THE PEACE.

Names.	Date of Qualification.	Post Office Address.
S. S. S. McCauley	Sept. 1st, 1873.	Munroe.
Abel Helms	" "	Munroe.
Jonathan Trull	" "	Munroe.
James O. Griffin	" "	Beaver Dam.
John W. Smith	" "	Beaver Dam.
V. T. Chears	" "	Lane's Creek.
Jacob S. Little	" "	Lane's Creek.
T. C. Eubanks	" "	Munroe.
J. E. Irby	" "	Munroe.
J. J. C. Steele	" "	Walkersville.
Alex. McIlwaine	" "	Walkersville.
A. J. Price	" "	Wolfesville.
E. S. Harkness	" "	Indian Trail.
John D. Williams	" "	Munroe.
N. M. Beckham	Feb. 5th, 1874.	Coburn's Store.

MEMBERS OF GENERAL ASSEMBLY.

Years.	Senate.	House.
1854	Thomas S. Ashe	J. A. Dunn.
1856	A. Myers	D. Rushing.
1858	S. W. Walkup	——— Wilson.
1860	S. W. Walkup	C. Q. Lemmonds.
1862	W. C. Smith	C. Q. Lemmonds.
1864	W. C. Smith	C. Austin.
1866	D. A. Covington	Jonathan Trull.
1868	B. T. Beaman	Hugh Downing.
1870	Atlas J. Dargan	C. M. T. McCauley.
1872	C. M. T. McCauley	Lemuel Presson.

Anson and Union form the 27th Senatorial District.

WAKE COUNTY

Was erected in 1770, from Orange, Johnston and Cumberland.

The troubles arising from the oppression and extortion in this war, induced Governor Tryon to divide Orange county into three divisions: Guilford, Chatham and Wake. Wake was so called in compliment to the maiden name of Governor Tryon's wife.

Wake is bounded on the north by Granville and Franklin counties, on the east by Franklin and Johnston, on the south by Johnston and Harnett, and on the west by Chatham and Orange.

In this county is Raleigh, the capital of the State of North Carolina.

Most appropriately does it preserve the name of the statesman and soldier, under whose anspices was fitted out the first expedition that ever landed in the United States. His name is illustrious as a gallant warrior, as a sagacious statesman, and as a faithful and accurate historian; he was born in 1552. Under the smiles of the "Virgin Queen" Elizabeth, he rose to favor and honors, but after her death, from the pusillanimous policy of James I, he was condemned for offences of which he was innocent, and was beheaded in 1618.

COUNTY OFFICERS.

Offices.	Names.
Superior Court Clerk	John N. Bunting.
Register of Deeds	W. W. White.
Sheriff	T. F. Lee.
Coroner	Paul Lineke.
Surveyor	J. P. H. Adams.
Treasurer	Albert Magnin.
Commissioners	R. W. Wynne, Chairman. William Jinks. Moses G. Todd. Henry C. Jones. Samuel Rayner.

JUSTICES OF THE PEACE.

Names.	Date of Qualification.	Post Office Address.
J. H. Hutchison	Aug. 23d, 1873.	Raleigh.
L. B. Seagraves	" "	New Hill.
W. H. Burt	" "	Apex.
J. P. H. Adams	" "	Carey.
J. R. Page	" "	Carey.
R. H. Slater	" "	Morrisville.
O. H. Page	" "	Morrisville.
Isaiah King	" "	Raleigh.
C. S. Jinks	" "	Raleigh.

WAKE COUNTY—CONTINUED.

JUSTICES OF THE PEACE—CONTINUED.

Names.	Date of Qalification.	Post Office Address.
B. T. Strickland	Aug. 30th, 1873.	Wakefield.
A. J. Montague	" 23d, "	Wakefield.
M. G. Todd	" "	Raleigh.
W. A. Rhodes	" "	Raleigh.
G. H. Alford	" "	Raleigh.
J. A. Norris	" "	Raleigh.
J. O. Harrison	" "	New Light.
J. P. Beck	" "	New Light.
J. T. Coleleugh	" "	Fish Dam.
H. W. Nichols	" "	Fish Dam.
J. H. Adams	" "	Raleigh.
S. M. Williams	" "	Raleigh.
G. A. Keith	" "	Raleigh.
N. B. Williams	" "	Raleigh.
John G. Andres	" "	Auburn.
Eli Dupre	" "	Auburn.
L. D. Stephenson	" "	Raleigh.
S. G. Hayes	" "	Raleigh.
T. C. Smith	" "	Raleigh.
A. L. Davis	" "	Forestville.
J. M. Flemming	" "	Rolesville.
W. R. Suitt	" "	Apex.
A. M. Betts	" "	Apex.
Wesley Whitaker	" "	Raleigh.
J. P. Prairie	" "	Raleigh.
Handy Lockhart	" "	Raleigh.
O. F. Alston	" "	Raleigh.
A. H. Temple	" "	Raleigh.
J. D. Allen	" "	Neuse.

MEMBERS OF GENERAL ASSEMBLY.

Years.	Senate.	House.
1777	James Jones	John Rand, Tignal Jones.
1778	Michael Rodgers	Lodwick Alford, Hardy Saunders.
1779	Michael Rodgers	Thomas Hines, John Hinton, jr.
1780	Michael Rodgers	Nathaniel Jones, John Humphries.
1781	Michael Rodgers	Burwell Pope, James Hinton.
1782	Joel Lane	James Hinton, Burwell Pope.
1783	Joel Lane	Theophilus Hinton, Hardy Saunders
1784	Joel Lane	James Hinton, William Hayes.
1785	Joel Lane	James Hinton, William Hayes.
1786	Joel Lane	John Humphries, James Hinton.
1787	Joel Lane	Nathaniel Jones, Brittain Saunders.
1788	Joel Lane	James Hinton, Brittain Saunders.
1789	Joel Lane	Brittain Saunders, Thomas Hines.
1790	Joel Lane	Brittain Saunders, Ransom Sutherland.

WAKE COUNTY—Continued.

MEMBERS OF GENERAL ASSEMBLY—Continued.

Years.	Senate.	House.
1791	Joel Lane	Ransom Sutherland, Brittain Saunders.
1792	Joel Lane	Brittain Saunders, William Hinton.
1793	James Hinton	Wyatt Aawkins, Wm. Person.
1794	Joel Lane	William Hinton, Michael Rogers.
1795	Joel Lane	Nathaniel Jones, William Hinton.
1796	ThomasHines	Nathaniel Jones, John Rogers.
1797	Tignall Jones	m. Hinton, Solomon Rogers.
1799	Thomas Hines	Wm. Hinton, Henry Seawell.
1800	Nathaniel Jones	Matthew McCullers, Henry Seawell.
1801	Nathaniel Jones	Henry Seawell, Matthew McCullers.
1802	William Hinton	Henry H. Cook, Henry Seawell.
1803	William Hinton	Allen Rogers, Henry H. Cooke.
1804	William Hinton	Nathaniel Jones. Henry H. Cooke.
1805	Nathaniel Jones	Nathaniel Jones, Henry H. Cooke.
1806	Allen Rogers	Walter Rand, Henry H. Cooke.
1807	Allen Rogers	Calvin Jones, Henry H. Cooke.
1808	Allen Rogers	Nathaniel Jones, Allen Gilchrist.
1809	William Hinton	Nathaniel Jones, Kimbro Jones.
1810	William Hinton	Henry Seawell, Kimbro Jones.
1811	William Hinton	Nathaniel Jones, Kimbro Jones.
1812	Allen Rogers	Henry Seawell, Kimbro Jones.
1813	John Hinton, jr	Wm. Boylan, Daniel L. Barringer.
1814	John Hinton	Wm. Boylan, Seth Jones.
1815	John Hinton	Wm. Boylan, Seth Jones.
1816	John Hinton, jr	William Boylan, Seth Jones.
1817	Nathaniel Jones	Seth Jones, Stephen Haywood.
1818	Nathaniel Jones	Seth Jones, Stephen Haywood.
1819	Stephen Haywood	Kimbro Jones, D. L. Barringer.
1820	Josiah Crudup	Daniel L. Barringer, C. L. Hinton.
1821	Henry Seawell	Charles L. Hinton, D. L. Barringer.
1822	Henry Seawell	D. L. Barringer, Samuel Whitaker.
1823	Henry Seawell	James F. Taylor, Samuel Whitaker.
1824	Henry Seawell	Samuel Whitaker, Johnson Busbee.
1825	Henry Seawell	Samuel Whitaker, Nathaniel G. Rand.
1826	Henry Seawell	Samuel Whitaker, N. G. Rand.
1827	Charles L. Hinton	Samuel Whitaker, Johnson Busbee.
1828	Charles L. Hinton	Wesley Jones, Samuel Whitaker.
1829	Charles L. Hinton	Samuel Whitaker, N. G. Rand.
1830	Charles L. Hinton	Samuel Whitaker, N. G. Rand.
1831	Henry Seawell	Wm. H. Haywood, jr., N. G. Rand.
1832	Henry Seawell	Nathaniel G. Rand, Charles L. Hinton.
1833	Charles L. Hinton	Nathaniel G. Rand, Wesley Jones.
1834	Samuel Whitaker	Wm. H. Haywood, jr.. Wesley Jones.
1835	Samuel Whitaker	Wm. H. Haywood, jr., Allen Rogers.
1836	Samuel Whitaker	Western R. Gales, Wm. H. Haywood, jr., N. G. Rand.
1838	Samuel Whitaker	N. G. Rand, D. B. Massey, J. M. Mangum.
1840	Samuel Whitaker	N. G. Rand, D. B. Massey, J. M. Mangum.
1842	James B. Shepard	N. G. Rand, Gaston H. Wilder, D. B. Massey.
1844	George W. Thompson	J. M. Mangum, Gaston H. Wilder, James B. Shepard.
1846	George W. Thompson	Berry D. Sims, G. H. Wilder, W. W. Holden.
1848	George W. Thompson	Berry D. Sims, James D. Newsom, Rufus H. Jones.

WAKE COUNTY—Continued.

MEMBERS OF GENERAL ASSEMBLY—Continued.

Years.	Senate.	House.
1850	Wesley Jones	R. M. Saunders, James D. Newsom, Burwell Rollins.
1852	Wesly Jones	R. M. Saunders, G. H. Wilder, W. A. Allen.
1854	G. H. Wilder	N. G. Rand, .W. Whitaker, J. Mordecai.
1856	G. H. Wilder	N. G. Rand, A. M. Lewis, M. A. Bledsoe.
1858	M. A. Bledsoe	G. H. Farribault, Fabius J. Hutchins.
1860	M. A. Bledsoe	Sion H. Rogers, J. P. H. Russ.
1862	J. P. H. Russ	H. W. Miller, G. H. Alford, Wm. Laws.
1864	Wilie D. Jones	D. G. Fowle, J. H. Alford, C. J. Rogers.
1866	Wilie D. Jones	C. J. Rogers, J. P. H. Russ, R. S. Perry.
1868	Wilie D. Jones, R. J. Wynne	Joseph W. Holden, S. D. Franklin, F. J. Moring, Jas. H. Harris.
1870	L. P. Olds, P. B. Hawkins	Henderson Hodge, T. W. Young, Willis Morgan, Stewart Ellison.
1872	James H. Harris	M. V'B. Gilbert, John C. Gorman, R. S. Perry, Stewart Ellison.

Wake is the 18th Senatorial District.

WARREN COUNTY.

Warren County was formed in 1779. In this year Bute county was divided, and the counties of Franklin and Warren formed from it.

Warren is bounded on the north by the Virginia line, on the east by Northampton and Halifax counties, on the south by Franklin county, on the west by Granville.

It derives its name from Joseph Warren, of Massachusetts.

COUNTY OFFICERS.

Offices.	Names.
Superior Court Clerk	William A. White.
Register of Deeds	Isham H. Bennett.
Sheriff	Nathaniel R. Jones.
Coroner	
Surveyor	

WARREN COUNTY—CONTINUED.

COUNTY OFFICERS—CONTINUED.

Offices.	Names.
Treasurer	John C. McCraw.
Commissioners	B. D. Williams. Alex. L. Steed. John Read. John M. Paschall. Alexander Wright.

JUSTICES OF THE PEACE.

Names.	Date of Qualification.	Post Office Address.
John W. Allen	Aug. 18th, 1873.	Brookston.
Robt. W. Alston	" "	Warrenton.
Phill G. Alston, Sr	" "	Warrenton.
John M. Brame	" "	Macon Depot.
Wm. H. Brehon	" "	Warrenton.
George R. Clements	" "	Warrenton.
Richard A. Davis	" "	Warren Plains.
Henry B. Hunter, Sr	" "	Ridgeway.
Landon Johnston	" "	Littleton.
Wm. Drew Jones	" "	Warrenton.
Samuel D. King	" "	Littleton.
James H. Mayfield	" "	Ridgeway.
J. W. H. Paschall	" "	Macon Depet.
John M. Paschall	" "	Manson.
Thomas P. Paschall	" "	Manson.
W. G. Plummer	" "	Warrenton.
John W. Riggan	" "	Littleton.
Solon Southerland	" "	Henderson.
Robt. B. Thornton	" "	Macon Depot.
Alexander Wright	" "	Littleton.
John H. White	" "	Ridgeway.
B. D. Williams	" "	Warrenton.
Dr. Sol G. Ward	" "	Warrenton.

MEMBERS OF GENERAL ASSEMBLY.

Years.	Senate.	House.
1780	Nathaniel Macon	John Macon, Jason Hawkins.
1781	Nathaniel Macon	Jason Hawkins, John Macon.
1782	Nathaniel Macon	Joseph Hawkins, John Macon.
1783	Herbert Haynes	Joseph Hawkins, John Macon.

WARREN COUNTY—Continued.

MEMBERS OF GENERAL ASSEMBLY—Continued.

Years.	Senate.	House.
1784	Nathaniel Macon...........	James Paine, John Macon.
1785	Nathaniel Macon...........	Henry Montfort, Wyatt Hawkins.
1786	John Macon................	Wyatt Hawkins, Sol. Green.
1787	John Macon................	Philemon Hawkins.
1788	John Macon................	Wyatt Hawkins, Henry Montfort.
1789	John Macon................	Philemon Hawkins, Wyatt Hawkins.
1790	John Macon................	Ransome Southerland, Brittain Sanders.
1791	John Macon................	Wyatt Hawkins, Sol. Green.
1792	John Macon................	Wyatt Hawkins, Henry Montfort.
1793	John Macon................	Wyatt Hawkins, William Person.
1794	John Macon................	William Person, Kemp Plummer.
1795	John Macon................	William Person, Wyatt Hawkins.
1796	James Payne...............	James Collier, William Person.
1797	Solomon Green.............	James Collier, William Person.
1798	James Collier.............	James Turner, Oliver Fitts.
1799	James Collier.............	James Turner, Oliver Fitts.
1800	James Collier.............	James Turner, Thos. E. Sumner.
1801	James Turner..............	Thos. E. Sumner, Robert Parke.
1802	James Turner..............	John Macklin, Robert Parke.
1803	Solomon Green.............	Philemon Hawkins, John Harwell.
1804	William P. Little.........	William Hawkins, John Harwell.
1805	Wm. P. Little.............	William Hawkins, Philemon Hawkins.
1806	Wm. P. Little.............	Philemon Hawkins, John Harwell.
1807	Philemon Hawkins..........	Blake Baker, Wm. R. Johnson.
1808	Philemon Hawkins..........	Wm. R. Johnson, John Harwell.
1809	Henry Fitts...............	John H. Hawkins, Wm. Miller.
1810	Philemon Hawkins..........	William Miller, Wm. R. Johnson.
1811	Philemon Hawkins..........	William Miller, Wm. R. Johnson.
1812	Joseph Hawkins............	Wm. R. Johnson, William Miller.
1813	Joseph Hawkins............	Wm. Miller, Wm. R. Johnson.
1814	Wm. Williams..............	Wm. Miller, Wm. R. Johnson.
1815	Kemp Plummer..............	Welden N. Edwards, John H. Walker
1816	Kemp Plummer..............	Robt. H. Jones, John H. Walker.
1817	Robert R. Johnson.........	Robt. H. Jones, Philemon Hawkins.
1818	Robert R. Johnson.........	Robt. H. Jones, Philemon Hawkins.
1819	Robert R. Johnson.........	Daniel Turner, M. T. Hawkins.
1820	Robert R. Johnson.........	Micajah T. Hawkins, Daniel Turner.
1821	William Miller............	Francis A. Thornton, Daniel Turner.
1822	William Miller............	Daniel Turner, F. A. Thornton.
1823	M. T. Hawkins.............	Daniel Turner, Robt. H. Jones.
1824	M. T. Hawkins.............	Gideon Alston, R. H. Jones.
1825	M. T. Hawkins.............	Gideon Alston, Ransom Walker.
1826	M. T. Hawkins.............	Robt. H. Jones, Thomas J. Green.
1827	M. T. Hawkins.............	Robt. H. Jones, Ransom Walker.
1828	Richard Davis.............	Wm. G. Jones, Ransom Walker.
1829	Richard Davis.............	Wm. G. Jones, John H. Green.
1830	John H. Hawkins...........	John Bragg, Ransom Walker.
1831	John H. Hawkins...........	John Bragg, Thomas I. Judkins.
1832	John H. Hawkins...........	John Bragg, Thos. I. Judkins.
1833	Weld. N. Edwards..........	John Bragg, Thos. I. Judkins.
1834	W. N. Edwards.............	John Bragg, Thos. I. Judkins.
1835	W. N. Edwards.............	John H. Hawkins, Thos. I. Judkins.
1836	W. N. Edwards.............	John H. Hawkins, Thos. I. Judkins.
1838	W. N. Edwards.............	Wm. Eaton, Jr., Samuel A. Williams.

WARREN COUNTY—Continued.

MEMBERS OF GENERAL ASSEMBLY—Continued.

Years.	Senate.	House.
1840	W. N. Edwards	Wm. Eaton, Jr., John H. Hawkins.
1842	W. N. Edwards	John H. Hawkins, Oliver D. Fitts.
1844	W. N. Edwards	John H. Hawkins, A. C. Brame.
1846	M. T. Hawkins	A. A. Austin, John H. Hawkins.
1848	A. B. Hawkins	J. L. Mosely, F. A. Thornton.
1850	W. N. Edwards	F. A. Thornton, Wm. Eaton, Jr.
1852	W. N. Edwards	T. A. Christmas, S. A. Williams.
1854	Wm. Eaton, Jr.	Wm. A. Jenkins, S. A. Williams.
1856	Wm. Eaton, Jr.	Wm. A. Jenkins, Thos. J. Pitchford.
1858	Thomas J. Pitchford	D. C. Hall, E. D. Drake.
1860	Thomas J. Pitchford	G. B. Batchelor, W. H. Clark.
1862	Thomas J. Pitchford	Thos. I. Judkins, L. Henderson.
1864	Thomas J. Pitchford	T. Alston, Thos I. Judkins.
1866	Frank A. Thornton	John B. Turnbull, Thos. I. Judkins.
1868	John A. Hyman	Wm. Cawthorn, Richard Falkner.
1870	John A. Hyman	Wm. Cawthorn, Richard Falkner.
1872	John A. Hyman	Geo. H. King, J. W. H. Pascal.

Warren forms the 19th Senatorial District.

WASHINGTON COUNTY.

Washington County was formed in 1799 from Tyrrell County, and called in honor of the Father of his Country, General George Washington, who was born on the 22d of February, 1732, and who died on the 13th December, 1799.

It is located in the north-eastern part of the State, on the south side of the Albemarle Sound; and is bounded on the north by the Sound, east by Tyrrell County, south by Hyde and Beaufort, and west by Martin and Bertie Counties.

Its capital is Plymouth, and is distant one hundred and sixty-two miles from Raleigh.

COUNTY OFFICERS.

Offices.	Names.
Superior Court Clerk	James A. Melson.
Register of Deeds	W. F. Sanderson.
Sheriff	John M. Bateman
Coroner	Vacant.
Surveyor	Vacant.
Treasurer	Levi Jackson, Jr
Commissioners	Jas. E. Jackson. Enoch H. Leary. Jesse P. Newberry. J. J. Woodley. George McDonald.

WASHINGTON COUNTY—Continued.

JUSTICES OF THE PEACE.

Names.	Date of Qualification.	Post Office Address.
A. N. Vail	Aug. 15th, 1873.	Plymouth.
N. H. Spruill	" "	Plymouth.
R. S. Goetel	" 16th, "	Plymouth.
M. C. McNamara	" 22d, "	Plymouth.
Samuel Wiggins	Sept. 1st, "	Plymouth.
Joshua B. Davenport	" "	Scuppernong.
Franklin Spruill	" "	Scuppernong.
B. B. Phelps	Aug. 25th, "	Scuppernong.
L. M. Phelps	" 16th, 1874.	Scuppernong.

MEMBERS OF GENERAL ASSEMBLY.

Years.	Senate.	House.
1800	Benj. Davenport	Miles Hardy, Isaac Long.
1801	Samuel Chesson	John Guyther. Miles Hardy.
1802	Samuel Chesson	Miles Hardy. John Guyther.
1803	Daniel Davenport	Edmund Blount, Miles Hardy.
1804	Daniel Davenport	Levin Bozman, Joseph hristopher.
1805	Daniel Davenport	Levin Bozman, Joseph Christopher.
1806	Daniel Davenport	Levin Bozman, Joseph Christopher.
1807	Daniel Davenport	Levin Bozman. John Frazer.
1808	Miles Hardy	Joseph hristopher, Edmund Blount.
1809	Ebenezer Pettigrew	James Freeman. Josiah Flowers.
1810	Ebenezer Pettigrew	Josiah Flowers. Samuel Blount.
1811	Levin Boyman	Samuel Blount, William Garrett.
1812	Thomas Johnson	James Freeman, Daniel Bateman.
1813	William Garrett	Ezekiel Hardison. Daniel Bateman.
1814	Thomas Johnson	Miles Hardy, Daniel Bateman.
1815	Thomas Norman	James Freeman, Daniel Bateman.
1816	Thomas Norman	Daniel Bateman, Taylor B. Walker.
1817	Downing Leary	Daniel Bateman, Thos. B. Haughton.
1818	Downing Leary	Daniel Bateman, Thos. B. Haughton.
1819	Charles Phelps	B. Tarkinton, Thos. B. Haughton.
1820	Charles Phelps	Benj. Tarkinton, Aaron Harrison.
1821	Thomas Walker	Wm. A. Bozman, Abner N. Vail.
1822	Benjamin Phelps	T. H. Walker, S. Davenport.
1823	Thomas Cox	T. H. Walker, S. Davenport.
1824	Thomas Johnson	A. N. Vail, P. O. Picott.
1825	Samuel Davenport	Peter O. Picott, Wm. A. Bozman.
1826	Samuel Davenport	Wm. A. Bozman, Wm. J. Armistead.
1827	Samuel Davenport	Wm. A. Bozman. Abner N. Vail.
1828	Samuel Davenport	Abner N. Vail, Thos. Sanderson.
1829	Samuel Davenport	James A. Chesson, Uriah W. Swanner.
1830	Samuel Davenport	James A. Chesson, U. W. Swanner.
1831	Samuel Davenport	Watrus Beckwith, U. W. Swanner.
1832	Josiah Collins	Samuel Hardison, Jos. A. Norman.
1833	Josiah Collins	Samuel Hardison, Charles Phelps.
1834	Charles Phelps	U. W. Swanner, A. Davenport.

WASHINGTON COUNTY—CONTINUED.

MEMBERS OF GENERAL ASSEMBLY—CONTINUED.

Years.	Senate.	House.
1835	John B. Beasley	U. W. Swanner, A. Davenport.
1836	Hezekiah G. Spruill	Joshua T. Swift.
1838	Hezekiah G. Spruill	David C. Guyther.
1840	Hezekiah G. Spruill	David C. Guyther.
1842	Hezekiah G. Spruill	Joseph C. Norcum.
1844	Joseph Halsey	David C. Guyther.
1846	Joseph Halsey	Thomas B. Nichols.
1848	Joseph Halsey	Thomas B. Nichols.
1850	Thomas E. Pender	Uriah W. Swanner.
1852	Charles McCleese	Charles Phelps.
1854	Asa Biggs	H. A. Gilliam.
1856	A. C. Chesson	H. A. Gilliam.
1858	D. C. Guyther	Jos. Norcum.
1860	J. R. Stubbs	. Latham.
1862	Jas G. Calloway	C. Latham.
1864	Jesse R. Stubbs	L. C. Latham.
1868	F. G. Martindale	J. G. Rea.
1870	L. C. Latham	D. C. Guyther.
1872	J. B. Respass H. E. Stilley	D. C. Guyther.

Beaufort, Dare, Hyde, Martin, Tyrrell and Washington County form the 2d Senatorial District.

WATAUGA COUNTY.

WATAUGA COUNTY was formed in 1849, from Ashe, Caldwell, Wilkes and Yancey, and derives its name from the river that runs through it, which is an Indian name, and signifies "the River of Islands.

It is situated in the extreme north-western part of the State, and is bounded on the north by Ashe county, east by Wilkes and Caldwell, south by Mitchell and Caldwell, and west by the Yellow Mountain, which separates it from the State of Tennessee.

Its capital is Boone, and is called in remembrance of the celebrated Daniel Boone, who once lived near Holeman's Ford, on the Yadkin River, about eight miles from Wilkesboro'.

JUSTICES OF THE PEACE.

Names.	Date of Qualification.	Post Office Address.
William Horton	Aug. 9th, 1873.	Boone.
D. B. Dougherty	" 11th, "	Boone.
William H. Dugger	" 18th, "	Boone.
Solomon Green	" 11th, "	Stony Fork.

WATAUGA COUNTY.—Continued.

JUSTICES OF THE PEACE—Continued.

Names.	Date of Qalification.	Post Office Address.
D. B. Wagner	Aug. 11th, 1873.	Stony Fork.
S. W. Cook	" 16th, "	Sugar Grove.
H. Hagamm	" 18th, "	Sugar Grove.
John McGuire	" "	McBride's Mills.
J. C. Lewis	" "	McBride's Mills.
Jacob Younce	" "	Watauga Falls.
Jacob Vuncannon	" "	Valleerusis.
John J. L. Church	Feb. 2d, 1874.	Elk X Roads.
H. A. Dobbin	Aug. 18th, 1873.	Elk X Roads.
J. W. McClaird	" "	Shull's Mills.
W. F. Shull	" "	Valleerusis.
Joel Norris	" "	Moretz's Mill.
John Ragan	" "	Moretz's Mill.
O. M. Hamlet	" "	Blowing Rock.
L. W. Estes	" "	Blowing Rock.
J. Y. Caloway	" "	Boone.
L. M. Hodges	" "	Boone.
Benjamin Greer	Sept. 8th, 1873.	Sugar Grove.

MEMBERS OF GENERAL ASSEMBLY.

Years.	Senate.	House.
1854	George Bower	Jonathan Horton.
1856	A. Brant	G. N. Folk.
1858	Joseph Dobson	—— Holtsclaw.
1860	Joseph Dobson	George N. Folk.
1862	Isaac Garrett	Wm. Horton.
1864	Jonathan Horton	Wm. Horton.
1866	A. C. owles	Wm. Horton.
1868	Edmond Jones	Lewis B. Banner.
1870	W. B. Council	W. F. Shull.
1872	J. W. Todd	J. B. Todd.

Alleghany, Ashe and Watauga form the 35th Senatorial District.

WAYNE COUNTY.

WAYNE COUNTY was formed in 1779 from Dobbs county, (now divided into Greene and Lenoir.)

Wayne is bounded on the north by Wilson county, on the east by Greene and Lenoir, on the south by Duplin and Sampson, on the west by Johnston county.

Its capital is Goldsboro', fifty-one miles south-east of Raleigh.

Its name is derived from Anthony Wayne, of Pennsylvania, distinguished in the Revolutionary War.

COUNTY OFFICERS.

Offices.	Names.
Superior Court Clerk	Geo. Jno. Robinson.
Register of Deeds	D. J. Ezzell.
Sheriff	W. A. Deans.
Coroner	James Williams.
Surveyor	Jas. M. Gardner.
Treasurer	L. J. Moore.
Commissioners	E. B. Jordan. Washington Winn. J. K. Smith. N. G. Holland.

JUSTICES OF THE PEACE.

Names.	Date of Qualification.	Post Office Address.
J. A. Washington	Aug. 12th, 1873.	Goldsboro.
J. B. Whitaker	" " "	Goldsboro.
John Robinson	" " "	Goldsboro.
A. B. Williams	" " "	Goldsboro.
Jackson Pate	" 16th, "	Goldsboro.
D. A. Grantham	" 13th, "	Goldsboro.
C. J. McCullen	" 11th, "	Goldsboro.
Geo. H. Grantham	" 16th, "	Dudley.
Geo. W. Simmons	" 30th, "	Dudley.
Thomas W. Brogden	" 30th, "	Dudley.
Jno. A. Kornegay	" 9th, "	Mt. Olive.
J. C. Price	" 9th, "	Mt. Olive.
Aaran Parks	" 16th, "	Goldsboro.
Jesse Benton	" 18th, "	Goldsboro.
C. C. Peacock	" 25th, "	Fremont.
Wm. E. Fountain		Fremont.
H. J. Sauls	Oct. 3rd, 1873.	Fremont.
W. H. Edgerton	Aug. 28th, 1873.	Fremont.
Jesse Hooks	Nov. 3rd, "	Fremont.
W. R. Perkins	Aug. 12th, "	Pikeville.
Wm. H. Ham	" 13th, "	Pikeville.
Hillory Hastings	" 16th, "	Goldsboro.
E. G. Copeland	" 18th, "	Goldsboro.

WAYNE COUNTY—CONTINUED.

MEMBERS OF GENERAL ASSEMBLY.

Years.	Senate.	House.
1780		Stephen Cobb, Burwell Mooring.
1781		Joseph Green, Burwell Mooring.
1782		Burwell Mooring, Richard McKinnie.
1783	Burwell Mooring	Richard McKinnie, Needham Whitfield.
1784	Burwell Mooring	William Alford, John Handley.
1785	Burwell Mooring	William Taylor, John Handley.
1786	Burwell Mooring	William Taylor, Richard McKinnie.
1787	Burwell Mooring	Richard McKinnie, William Taylor.
1788	Richard McKinnie	William Taylor, James Handley.
1789	Richard McKinnie	James Handley, Burwell Mooring.
1790	Burwell Mooring	John Coor Pender, Richard McKinnie.
1791	Richard McKinnie	John Coor Pender, Benjamin Fort.
1792	Richard McKinnie	John Coor Pender, William Taylor.
1793	Richard McKinnie	John Coor Pender, William Taylor.
1794	Richard McKinnie	William Taylor, John Coor Pender.
1795	Richard McKinnie	John Garland, John Coor Pender.
1796	Richard McKinnie	John Garland, Benjamin Fort.
1797	Richard McKinnie	John Coor Pender, Richard Croom.
1798	Richard McKinnie	John Coor Pender, Richard Croom.
1799	Richard McKinnie	Joseph Everett, Barnabas McKinnie.
1800	Richard Croom	Joseph Everett, Barnabas McKinnie.
1801	Richard Croom	Abram Simons, Ezekiel Slocumb.
1802	John C. Pender	William Smith, James Rhodes.
1803	Needham Whitfield	James Rhodes, William Smith.
1804	Richard McKinnie	James Rhodes, William Smith.
1805	Richard McKinnie	William Smith, James Rhodes.
1806	Richard McKinnie	James Rhodes, William Smith.
1807	James Rhodes	William Smith, James Deans.
1808	James Rhodes	William Smith, Ezekial Slocumb.
1809	James Rhodes	William Smith, James Deans.
1810	John Davis	Cullen Blackman, James Deans.
1811	John Davis	Cullen Blackman, James Deans.
1812	Barnabas McKinnie	Joab Newsom, Ezekial Slocumb.
1813	Barnabas McKinnie	Ezekial Slocumb, Stephen Cook.
1814	Barnabas McKinnie	Ezekial Slocumb, J. Cook.
1815	Barnabas McKinnie	Ezekial Slocumb, Stephen Cook.
1816	Barnabas McKinnie, Jr	Ezekial Slocumb, Stephen Cook.
1817	Barnabas McKinnie	Stephen Smith, Ezekial Slocumb.
1818	Michael J. Kennan	Ezekial Slocumb, Lewis C. Pender.
1819	Barnabas McKennie	Ephraim Daniel, Sampson Lane.
1820	Josiah Garland	Joshua Hastings, Arthur Bardin.
1821	Ephraim Daniel	Joshua Hastings, Arthur Bardin.
1822	Jethro Howell	Joshua Hastings, Stephen Smith.
1823	Richard B. Hatch	Joshua Hastings, Stephen Smith.
1824	Gabriel Sherard	Philip B. Raiford, Arthur Barden.
1825	Jethro Howell	Philip B. Raiford, John Wasden.
1826	John Wasden	Philip B. Raiford, Joshua Hastings.
1827	Gabriel Sherard	Joshua Hastings, James Rhodes.
1828	Gabriel Sherard	James Rhodes, John W. Sasser.
1829	Gabriel Sherard	James Rhodes, John W. Sasser.
1830	Gabriel Sherard	James Rhodes, John W. Sasser.
1831	Gabriel Sherard	John W. Sasser, John Broadhurst.
1832	James Rhodes	John B. Hurst, P. S. Cromwell.
1833	Gabriel Sherard	Cullen A. Blackman, P. S. Cromwell.

WAYNE COUNTY—Continued.

MEMBERS OF GENERAL ASSEMBLY—Continued.

Years.	Senate.	House.
1834	Gabriel Sherard	Calvin Coor, William B. Frost.
1835	John Exum	alvin Coor, Giles Smith.
1836	John Exum	Calvin Coor, Raiford Whitney.
1838	John Exum	Curtis H. Brogden, Elias Barnes.
1840	John Exum	Curtis H. Brogden, Elias Barnes.
1842	John Exum	Curtis H. Brogden, Elias Barnes.
1844	John Exum	Curtis H. Brogden, Elias Barnes.
1846	John Exum	Curtis H. Brogden, Elias Barnes.
1848	John Exum	Curtis H. Brogden, John V. Sherard.
1850	William Thompson	Curtis H. Brogden, John V. Sherard.
1852	William Thompson	W. T. Dortch, Etheldred Sauls.
1854	William Thompson	W. T. Dortch, Lewis Whitfield.
1856	William Thompson	E. Sauls, E. A. Thompson.
1858	Wm. K. Lane	W. T. Dortch, E. A. Thompson.
1860	Wm. K. Lane	Wm. T. Dortch, M. K. Thompson.
1862	Wm. K. Lane	B. B. Reeves, M. K. Crawford.
1864	Benj. Aycocke	J. M. Caho, M. K. Crawford.
1866	Wm. A. Thompson	J. H. Everett. J. C. Jones.
1868	C. H. Brogden	John T. Person, John C. Rhodes.
1870	C. H. Brogden	D. E. Smith, E. J. Copeland.
1872	Wm. A. Allen Lott W. Humphrey	D. E. Smith, E. J. Copeland.

Wayne and Duplin form the 10th Senatorial District.

WILKES COUNTY.

Wilkes County was formed in the year 1777 from Surry, and called in honor of John Wilkes, a distinguished English statesman and member of Parliament. He was ejected by the ministerial party from Barliament on account of his liberal political views; and as often he was returned by the people. He died in 1797.

Wilkes County is situated in the extreme north-west portion of our State; and bounded on the north by the Blue Ridge, which separates it from Ashe County, east by Surry, south by Alexander, and west by Ashe and Watauga Counties.

Its capital, Wilkesboro', is one hundred and seventy-two miles north-west of Ralegh.

Its population in 1850 was 10,746 whites; 211 free negroes; 1,142 slaves; 11,642 representative population.

Its products in 1840 were 463,793 bushels of corn; 64,210 bushels of oats: 30,268 bushels of wheat; 24,567 pounds of tobacco; 12,468 pounds of cotton; 19,634 pounds of wool.

WILKES COUNTY—CONTINUED.

COUNTY OFFICERS.

Offices.	Names.
Superior Court Clerk	Geo. H. Brown.
Register of Deeds	S. P. Smith.
Sheriff	J. T. Ferguson.
Coroner	G. F. McNiel.
Surveyor	J. F. Somers.
Treasurer	Isaac S. Call.
Commissioners	James H. Foote, Chairman.
	A. Wiles.
	Harrison Church.
	Asa Triplett.
	H. Hays.

JUSTICES OF THE PEACE.

Names.	Date of Qualification.	Post Office Address.
F. A. Harris	Aug. 9th, 1873.	Elkin.
J. C. Armstrong	" "	Newcastle.
C. L. Cook	" "	Hunting Creek.
Elisha Porter	" "	Dellaplane.
D. F. Shepherd	" "	Wilbar.
Adam Staley	" "	Wilbar.
W. H. Hubbord	" "	Wilkesboro'.
W. A. Broghill	" "	Wilkesboro'.
O. D. Dancy	" "	Perlier's Creek.
A. Warren	Sept. 1st, "	Zimmerman.
Henry Jennings	" "	Mulberry.
J. T. Mastin	" "	Dellaplane.
E. M. Redding	" "	Newcastle.
J. S. Holbrook	" "	Trap Hill.
Ansel Parks	" "	Trap Hill
G. F. McNiel	" "	Perlier's Creek.
J. L. Church	" "	Wilkesboro'.
W. H. Somers	" "	Hunting Creek.
J. K. Hendix	" "	Elkville.
N. D. Alexander	" "	Wilkesboro'.
Wm. Porter	" "	Wilkesboro'.
J. H. Thompson	" "	Maple Springs.
E. E. Hudson	" "	Wilkesboro'.
H. Hays	" "	Wilkesboro'.
J. A. Mathias	" "	Newcastle.
J. T. Alexander	" 2d, "	Trap Hill.
E. B. Phillips	" "	Warrier Creek.
R. F. Hackett	" "	Wilkesboro'.
Solomon Key	" "	Elkville.
Thomas Foster	Aug. 9th, "	Dellaplane.
J. U. Myer	Sept. 2d, "	Dockery.
D. R. Edwards	Jan. 5th, 1874.	Dellaplane.

WILKES COUNTY—CONTINUED.

MEMBERS OF GENERAL ASSEMBLY.

Years.	Senate.	House.
1778		Benjamin Cleaveland, Elisha Isaacs.
1779	Benj. Cleaveland	Benjamin Thornton, Elisha Isaacs.
1781	Charles Jordon	Joseph Herndon, William Lenoir.
1782	Elijah Isaacs	William Lenoir, Joseph Herndon.
1783	Elijah Isaacs	Benjamin Herndon, William Lenoir.
1784	Elijah Isaacs	Benjamin Herndon, Jesse Franklin.
1785	Benjamin Herndon	Jesse Franklin, Wm. T. Lewis.
1786	Benjamin Herndon	Jesse Franklin, John Brown.
1787	William Lenoir	Jesse Franklin, John Brown.
1788	William Lenoir	John Brown, Joseph Herndon.
1791	William Lenoir	Jesse Franklin, Benjamin Jones.
1792	William Lenoir	Jesse Franklin, Benjamin Jones.
1793	William Lenoir	Richard Allen, Joseph Herndon.
1794	William Lenoir	Benjamin Jones, Theophilas Evans.
1795	William Lenoir	Jesse Robinett, David Witherspoon.
1796	James Wellborn	David Witherspoon, Jesse Robinett.
1797	James Wellborn	Jesse Robinett, James Burgarner.
1798	James Wellborn	Jesse Robinett, Edmund Jones.
1799	James Wellborn	Jesse Robinett, George Koonce.
1800	James Wellborn	Andrew Erwin, William Hulme.
1801	James Wellborn	William Hulme, Andrew Erwin.
1802	James Wellborn	Edmund Jones, William Hulme.
1803	James Wellborn	Robert Martin, Edmund Jones.
1804	James Wellborn	Edmund Jones, William Hulme.
1805	James Wellborn	Edmund Jones, William Hulme.
1806	James Wellborn	William Hulme, John Martin.
1807	James Wellborn	William Hulme, Edmund Jones.
1808	James Wellborn	William Hulme, Edmund Jones.
1809	James Wellborn	Edmund Jones, Benjamin Parks.
1810	James Wellborn	Edmund Jones, William Hulme.
1811	James Wellborn	Jesse Allen, Edmund Jones.
1812	James Waugh	Edmund Jones, Jesse Allen.
1813	James Waugh	John Martin, Wm. Davenport.
1814	Wm. Hulme	Jesse Allen, John Saintclair.
1815	Wm. Hulme	Jesse Allen, John Saintclair.
1816	Wm. Hulme	John Saintclair, Jesse Allen.
1817	James Wellborn	John Saintclair, John Witherspoon.
1818	James Wellborn	John Saintclair, John Witherspoon.
1819	James Wellborn	M. Stokes, Nathaniel Gordon.
1820	James Wellborn	William Horton, John Isbell.
1821	James Wellborn	John Isbell, Nathaniel Gordon.
1822	Edmund Jones	William Horton, Nathaniel Gordon.
1823	James Wellborn	Nathaniel Gordon, William Horton.
1824	James Wellborn	William Miller, Thomas W. Wilson.
1825	Edmund Jones	Thomas W. Wilson, Nathaniel Gordon.
1826	Montford Stokes	Nathaniel Gordon, John Saintclair.
1827	Edmund Jones	Malachi Roberts, Nathaniel Gordon.
1828	James Wellborn	John Saintclair, Nathaniel Gordon.
1829	James Wellborn	William Horton, Moutfort Stokes.
1830	Edmund Jones	William Horton, Moutfort Stokes.
1831	John Martin	Eli Petty, William C. Emmett.
1832	James Wellborn	William C. Emmett, John Sinclair.
1833	Edmund Jones	Benjamin F. Martin, William Horton.
1834	James Wellborn	William Horton, Benj. F. Martin.

WILKES COUNTY—Continued.

MEMBERS OF GENERAL ASSEMBLY—Continued.

Years.	Senate.	House.
1836	Edmund Jones	William Horton, John Watts.
1838	Edmund Jones	William Horton, Eli Petty.
1840	Anderson Mitchell	Eli Petty, William W. Peden.
1842	Edmund W. Jones	John J. Bryan, David Gray.
1844	B. S. Gaither	Robert L. Steel, John J. Bryan.
1846	B. S. Gaither	J. J. Gambell, —— Church.
1848	S. F. Patterson	James Wellborn, J. J. Gambill.
1850	Tod R. Caldwell	J. B. Gordon, A. M. Forster.
1852	A. Mitchell	L. B. Carmichael, C. L. Cook.
1854	A. Mitchell	L. B. Carmichael, C. L. Cook.
1856	R. H. Parks	A. . Martin, P. Eller.
1858	L. B. Carmichael	A. W. Martin, P. Eller.
1860	L. Q. Sharp	A. H. Martin, F. S. Horton.
1862	L. Q. Sharp	E. M. Wellborn, A. H. Hampton.
1864	A. M. Bogle	A. S. Calloway, P. T. Horton.
1866	J. [illegible] Hill	P. T. Horton, Tyre York.
1868	S. P. Smith	Wm. B. Segrist.
1870	C. L. Cook	Tyre York.
1872	J. W. Todd	Thomas J. Dula, A. C. Bryan.

Alleghany, Ashe and Watauga form the 35th Senatorial District.

WILSON COUNTY

Was formed in 1855, from the counties of Edgecombe, Johnston, Nash and Wayne, called in memory of General Louis D. Wilson, long a member of the Legislature, and who died in Mexico in the service of his country.

Its county seat, Wilson, is about 50 miles from Raleigh.

COUNTY OFFICERS.

Offices.	Names.
Superior Court Clerk	Arthur Barnes.
Register of Deeds	Thomas J. Rowe.
Sheriff	Benjamin F. Briggs.
Coroner	Henry W. Peel.
Surveyor	E. M. Nadal.
Treasurer	John W. Farmer.
Commissioners	Willie D. Rountree, Chairman. Marcellus J. Edwards. Sidney P. Clark. William Hinnant. Newit D. Owens.

WILSON COUNTY—Continued.

JUSTICES OF THE PEACE.

Names.	Date of Qualification.	Post Office Address.
Calvin Barnes	Aug. 1st, 1872.	Wilson.
P. M. Briggs	" "	Wilson.
K. H. Winstead	" "	Wilson.
Alvin Bagley	" "	Wilson.
G. W. Stanton	" "	Wilson.
Elbert Felton	" "	Wilson.
G. R. Owens	" "	Wilson.
A. C. Burnett	" "	Wilson.
A. J. Moore	" "	Wilson.
James Wiggins	" "	Toisnott.
John L. Bailey	" "	Toisnott.
M. M. Matthews	" "	Wilson.
W. W. Farmer	" "	Wilson.
Frank Eatman	" "	Wilson.
James Mercer	Jan. 30th, 1874.	Wilson.
Thomas A. Thompson	Aug. 1st, 1873.	Black Creek.
Solomon Lamom	" "	Black Creek.
A. G. Brooks	" "	Black Creek.
T. J. Meacham	" "	Black Creek.
William Watson	" "	Wilson.
Simon Barnes	" "	Wilson.
R. J. Taylor	" "	Wilson.

MEMBERS OF GENERAL ASSEMBLY.

Years.	Senate.	House.
1868	Joshua Barnes	George W. Stanton.
1870	Lawrence F. Battle	J. W. Dunham.
1872	John W. Dunham Wm. K. Davis	H. C. Moss.

Franklin, Nash and Wilson form the 7th Senatorial District.

YADKIN COUNTY.

Yadkin County was formed in 1850-'51, from the southern portion of Surry, and derives its name from the river which runs through it.

It is situated in the north-western part of the State, and bounded on the north by Surry, east by Forsythe, south by Davie and Iredell, and West by Wilkes.

Yadkinville, its county seat, is distant about 175 miles from Raleigh.

YADKIN COUNTY—Continued.

COUNTY OFFICERS.

Offices.	Names.
Superior Court Clerk	James A. Martin.
Register of Deeds	Thos. L. Sulburt.
Sheriff	Isaac N. Vestal.
Coroner	Vacant.
Surveyor	B. R. Brown.
Treasurer	Wm. W. Patterson.
Commissioners	Aquilla Speer. George Lang. Leroy Hampton. B. C. Myers. W. F. Shores.

JUSTICES OF THE PEACE.

Names.	Date of Qualification.	Post Office Address.
P. M. Neeks	Sept. 1st, 1873.	Hamptonville.
A. D. Gentry	" "	Hamptonville.
Thomas Haynes	" "	Jonesville.
E. D. Swaine	" "	Jonesville.
S. S. Arnold	" "	Jonesville.
W. S. Arnold	" "	Hamptonville.
J. B. Holcomb	" "	Chesnutt Ridge.
J. M. Speer	" "	Boonville.
E. R. Reece	" "	Boonville.
P. G. Russell	" "	Yadkinville.
W. L. Macey	" "	Yadkinville.
W. F. Hoots	" "	Yadkinville.
C. H. Adams	" "	Mt. Nebo.
J. H. Myers	" "	Mt. Nebo.
David Smitherman	" "	East Bend.
J. W. Fleming	" "	East Bend.
J. T. Conrad	" "	Huntsville.
W. J. Dickson	" "	Huntsville.
B. D. Fauser	" "	Panther Creek.
B. F. Jones	" "	Panther Creek.

MEMBERS OF GENERAL ASSEMBLY.

Years.	Senate.	House.
1854	George Bower	C. W. Williams.
1856	A. Brant	W. H. Spear.
1858	Jos. Dobson	W. H. Spear.

YADKIN COUNTY—Continued.

MEMBERS OF GENERAL ASSEMBLY—Continued.

Years.	Senate.	House.
1860	Jos. Dobson................	A. C. Cowles.
1862	Isaac Garrett..............	A. C. Cowles.
1864	Jonathan Horton...........	A. C. Cowles.
1866	A. C. Cowles...............	T. N. Vestal.
1868	Samuel Forkner............	T. N. Vestal.
1870	A. C. Cowles...............	J. G. Marler.
1872	A. C. Cowles...............	J. G. Marler.

Surry and Yadkin form the 33d Senatorial District.

YANCY COUNTY.

Yancy County was formed in 1833, from Burke and Buncombe, and called in honor of Hon. Bartlett Yancey.

It is an extreme western county, bounded on the north by the Iron Mountains which separate it from Tennessee and Mitchell, east by Caldwell county, south by Yancey, and west by the Tennessee line and Madison county.

Its capital is Burnsville, called in honor of Captain Otway Burns, who resided at Beaufort, Carteret county, and is distant from Raleigh 245 miles.

COUNTY OFFICERS.

Offices.	Names.
Superior Court Clerk......................	John W. Burton.
Register of Deeds..........................	Lowell B. Briggs.
Sheriff..	N. M. Wilson.
Coroner...	None.
Surveyor..	John O. Griffith.
Treasurer.......................................	John A. Hensley.
Commissioners..............................	William M. Moore, Chairman. Wm. H. Deyton. Z. Horton. James W. Gibbs. J. K. Blankenship.

YANCY COUNTY—CONTINUED.

JUSTICES OF THE PEACE.

Names.	Date of qualification.	Post Office Address.
William C. Woodfin	Aug. 15th, 1873.	Burnsville.
L. H. Delinger	" "	Burnsville.
M. P. Hampton	" "	Ball Creek.
Joshua Horton	" "	Ball Creek.
L. S. Phillips	Sept. 1st, "	Ball Creek.
Silas B. Hensley	Aug. 15th, "	Ball Creek.
James F. Byrd	" "	Ramseytown.
J. W. Peck	" "	Ramseytown.
Z. McConry	" "	Day Book.
E. M. Honeycutt	" "	Day Book.
B. S. L. Deyton	" "	Day Book.
Jeremiah Hughes	" "	Day Book.
John O. Griffith	" "	Burnsville.
John Cox	" "	Burnsville.
William Hutchins	" "	Burnsville.
Charles F. Gibbs	Oct. 20th, "	Burnsville.
B. Riddle	Aug. 15th, "	Burnsville.
Milton P. Ray	Jan. 5th, 1874.	Burnsville.

MEMBERS OF GENERAL ASSEMBLY.

Years.	Senate.	House.
1834	Thomas Baker	Tilman Blalock, Wm. Dayton.
1835	Thomas Baker	May Jervis, Samuel Byrd.
1836	Thomas Baker	Samuel Byrd.
1838	Thomas Baker	Tilman Blalock.
1840	Burgess S. Gaither	Samuel Fleming.
1842	Alney Burgen	Samuel Byrd.
1844	N. W. Woodfin	Samuel Fleming.
1846	N. W. Woodfin	Samuel Fleming.
1848	N. W. Woodfin	Calvin Edney.
1850	N. W. Woodfin	Samuel Fleming.
1852	N. W. Woodfin	Neely Byrd.
1854	David Coleman	C. . Williams.
1856	David Colemane	Isaac A. Pearson.
1858	B. M. Edney	Thomas Byrd.
1860	Marcus Erwin	John W. Bowman.
1862	Wm. M. Shipp	D. M. Young.
1864	M. Patton	D. M. Young.
1866	L. S. Gash	—— Williams.
1868	W. M. Moore	David Proffitt.
1870	W. W. Fleming	—— Young.
1872	W. W. Fleming J. M. Gudger	J. C. Byrd.

Caldwell, Burke, Macon, McDowell, Mitchell and Yancy form the 36th Senatorial District.

No. XXIV.

List of Commissioners of Affidavits.

LIST OF COMMISSIONERS OF AFFIDAVITS, &C.,

FOR THE

STATE OF NORTH CAROLINA.

List of Commissioners of Affidavits in the several States and Territories, and in the District of Columbia, for the State of North Carolina, appointed since July 4th, 1868, together with residence, date of commission and qualification of each.

STATE OR TERRITORY.	NAME.	RESIDENCE.	DATE OF APPOINTMENT.	DATE OF QUALIFICATION.
Arkansas,	Jas. M. Alexander,	Helena,	February 10, 1871,	March 8, 1871,
"	E. J. Brooks,	Fort Smith,	November 23, 1870,	March 25, 1872,
"	Rufus V. M'Cracken,	Pine Bluff,	June 12, 1873,	July 3, 1873,
California,	N. Proctor Smith,	San Francisco,	June 1, 1869,	November 19, 1866,
"	Frank V. Scudder,	"	August 25, 1869,	November 19, 1869,
"	C. M. Arnold,	San Diago,	January 18, 1871,	February 6, 1871,
"	P. Crittendon,	San Francisco,	January 5, 1871,	January 20, 1871,
"	Edward Cadwalader,	Sacramento,	October 27, 1868,	December 26. 1872,
Connecticut,	Julius Twiss,	New Haven,	May 23, 1870,	May 18, 1870,
"	Edward Goodman.	Hartford.	May 23, 1871,	May 26, 1871,

LIST OF COMMISSIONERS OF AFFIDAVITS—(*Continued.*)

STATE OR TERRITORY.	NAME.	RESIDENCE.	DATE OF APPOINTMENT.		DATE OF QUALIFICATION.	
Connecticut,	David G. Gordon,	Hartford,	March	14, 1872,	March	21, 1872,
"	Henry E. Taintor,	"	April	12, 1873,	April	23, 1873,
"	John C. Hollister,	New Haven,	September	16, 1873,	September	20, 1873,
Deleware,	Albert W. Smith,	Wilmington,	July	2, 1873,	July	8, 1873,
District of Columbia,	Joseph T. K. Plant,	Washington,	August	4, 1869,	November	18, 1870,
"	M. Willingsford,	"	February	21, 1870,	March	4, 1869.
Florida,	Charles B. Graybill,	Jacksonville,	July	17, 1870,	August	3, 1871.
"	George Lewis,	Tallahassee,	October	23, 1871,	November	4, 1871.
"	J. H. Norton,	Jacksonville.	October	24, 1871,	March	12, 1871.
"	Joseph H. Durkee,	"	May	11, 1872,	May	15, 1872.
Georgia,	Frank H. Miller,	Augusta,	June	1, 1870,	November	12, 1869.
"	Allen Fort,	Americus,	May	7, 1869,	November	13, 1869.
"	John W. Burroughs.	Savannah,	March	21, 1871,	March	23, 1871.
"	Raphael J. Moses, Jr.,	Columbus,	April	10, 1871,	April	28, 1872.
"	Thomas J. Perry,	Rome,	January	25, 1872,	January	29, 1872.
"	R. J. Moses,	Columbus,	February	21, 1873,	February	27, 1873.
"	Samuel Levy,	Augusta,	September	15, 1873,	September	20, 1873.
Illinois,	John B. Hicks,	Metropolis,	March	10, 1870,	April	2, 1869.
"	Simeon W. King,	Chicago,	June	1, 1870,	June	23, 1869.
"	Philip A. Hayne,	"	June	1, 1870,	November	15, 1869.
Louisiana,	James Graham,	New Orleans,	June	1, 1870,	November	15, 1869.
"	John G. Eustis,	"	April	7, 1873,	April	12, 1873.
"	Andrew Hero, Jr.,	"	March	25, 1873,	April	1, 1873.
Maine,	James O'Dónell,	Portland,	June	1, 1870,	June	19, 1869.
Maryland,	Herman L. Emmons,	Baltimore,	June	1, 1869,	July	6, 1869.
"	W. M. Lattimer,	"	May	19, 1869,	May	24, 1869.
"	George Philpot,	"	June	1, 1869,	December	14, 1869.
"	H. R. Dulany,	"	June	1, 1869,	December	27, 1869.
"	William Quarlmeyer,	"	August	17, 1872,	August	28, 1872.
"	W. J. Waterman,	"	September	25, 1872,	September	26, 1872.

Maryland,	Thomas R. Purnell,†	Baltimore,	February	16, 1871,	February	27, 1871.
"	Wm. B. Hill,	"	September	29, 1873,	October	1, 1873.
"	Henry Brock,	"	January	22, 1874,	January	27, 1874.
Massachusetts,	Charles B. F. Adams,	Boston,	June	1, 1869,	July	14, 1869.
"	James B. Bell,	"	June	1, 1869,	July	22, 1869.
"	Samuel Jennison,	"	May	13, 1870,	May	21, 1870.
"	George A. Drury,	"	April	23, 1872,	April	26, 1872.
"	Charles H. Adams,	"	October	1, 1872,	October	4, 1872.
"	S. A. B. Abbott,	"	October	4, 1869,	December	6, 1870.
"	Edward J. Jones,	"	March	21, 1873,	March	24, 1873.
"	George J. Angel,	"	December	8, 1873,	December	11, 1873.
Missouri,	Theodore Papin,	St. Louis,	June	1, 1869,	July	3, 1869.
"	Austin Drake,	"	February	16, 1871,	March	4, 1871.
"	John R. Boas,	"	November	22, 1872,	March	16, 1872.
Mississippi,	E. W. Upshaw,	Holly Springs,	January	1, 1870,	February	7, 1870.
"	H. M. Sullivan,	Oxford,	August	9, 1872,	August	13, 1872.
Minnesota,	Cyrus Aldrich,	Minneapolis,	March	31, 1870,	June	20, 1870.
"	C. McReeve,	"	March	12, 1872,	March	23, 1872.
North Carolina,	Charles Hibbard,	Newbern,	May	7, 1869,	April	7, 1870.
New Jersey,	Garrett B. Adrian,	New Brunswick,			April	27, 1869.
New York,	Nathaniel Gill,	New York City,	August	20, 1868,	June	1, 1869.
"	Charles H. Hatch,	"			February	16, 1869.
"	W. E. Osborn,	Brooklyn,	April	16, 1869,	April	19, 1869.
"	Horace Andrews,	New York City,	May	20, 1869,	May	26, 1869.
"	Lucius W. How,	"	April	28, 1873,	May	3, 1873.
"	Moses B. McClay,	"	June	1, 1869,	June	29, 1869.
"	David McAdams,	"	May	20, 1869,	July	16, 1869.
"	James M. Slevin,	"	August	18, 1869,	September	13, 1869.
"	Michael Jacobs,	"	April	6, 1869,	May	15, 1869.
"	Henry C. Banks,	"			June	10, 1869.
"	A. C. Anderson,	"			November	16, 1869.
"	G. W. Collis,	"	May	20, 1869,	November	11, 1869.
"	Joseph B. Nones,	"	May	20, 1869,	September	14, 1869.
"	Louis Hurst,	"	June	14, 1869,	December	7, 1869.
"	Alex. Ostrander,	"	May	20, 1869,	November	11, 1869.
"	Charles I. Bushnell,	"	June	1, 1869,	December	21, 1869.
"	Segismond Lasar,	"	June	1, 1869,	December	21, 1869.
"	Sylvester Lay,	"			November	25, 1869.
"	John Bizzell,	"	June	5, 1869,	November	12, 1869.

LIST OF COMMISSIONERS OF AFFIDAVITS—*Continued.*

STATE OR TERRITORY.	NAME.	RESIDENCE.	DATE OF APPOINTMENT.		DATE OF QUALIFICATION.	
New York,	Fred. R. Anderson,	New York City,	June	15, 1869,	November	12, 1869.
"	Rufus K. M. Hay,	"			October	10, 1868.
"	Edwin F. Carey, Sr.,	"	April	1, 1870,	April	2, 1870.
"	Daniel P. Bible,	"	February	22, 1870,	February	23, 1870.
"	Edwin F. Carey, Jr.,	"	September	1, 1871,	June	4, 1870
"	Arthur W. Knapp,	"			November	23, 1869.
"	Walter S. Poor,	"	March	10, 1871,	March	13, 1871.
"	Alfred B. Smith,	Poughkeepsie,	March	20, 1871,	March	23, 1871.
"	Charles W. Anderson,	New York City,	April	1, 1871,	April	5, 1871.
"	W. J. Hildreth,	"	April	6, 1871,	April	12, 1871.
"	Edward E. Burr,	"	February	10, 1871,	May	16, 1871.
"	Jacob DeBois,	"	May	23, 1871,	May	25, 1871.
"	J. Spencer Smith,	"	May	27, 1871,	June	2, 1871.
"	Alex. H. Nones,	"	March	17, 1871,	March	22, 1871.
"	Jos. T. Brown,	"	November	25, 1871,	November	28, 1871.
"	J. D. Morrell,	"	March	13, 1871,	February	16, 1872,
"	Thomas Kilvert,	"	February	13, 1872,	February	17, 1872,
"	C. H. Smith, Jr.,	"	December	12, 1871,	December	15, 1871,
"	E. Bissell,	"	March	12, 1872,	March	15, 1872,
"	W. H. Clarkson,	"	March	21, 1872,	April	16, 1872,
"	W. S. Oliver,	"	March	12, 1872,	May	1, 1872,
"	Isaac N. Hall,	"	June	10, 1869,	May	28, 1872,
"	D. W. Esmond.	Newburg,			September	6, 1870,
"	F. P. Burke,	New York City,	August	4, 1872,	August	13, 1872.
"	Charles T. Bruen,	"	September	25, 1872,	October	2, 1872,
"	Andrew W. Kent,	"	October	23, 1872,	October	25, 1872.
"	William F. Lett,	"	June	22, 1869,	December	11, 1869,
"	Thomas Sadler,	"	January	6, 1873,	January	9, 1873.
"	S. B. Goodale,	"	January	13, 1873,	January	15, 1873.
"	harles Edgar Mills,	"	January	8, 1873,	January	20, 1873.

New York,	W. H. Melich,	New York City	March	21, 1870,	January	25, 1873.
"	John A. Hillory,	"	February	21, 1873,	February	24, 1873.
"	George W. Brown,	"	February	21, 1873,	February	24, 1873.
"	John Burt,	Warwich,	September	26, 1873,	October	1, 1873.
"	Harold A. Bagley,	New York City,	December	8, 1873,	December	13, 1873.
"	Fred. R. Anderson,	"	February	9, 1874,	February	9, 1874.
"	Charles Nettleton,	"	July	22, 1873,	March	4, 1874.
"	James Taylor,	"	February	28, 1874,	March	12, 1874.
Ohio,	James Wade, Jr.,	Cleveland,			November	11, 1869.
"	J. B. Conklin,	Cincinnati,	April	10, 1869,	December	16, 1869.
"	A. H. McGuffey,	"	June	1, 1869,	November	12, 1869.
"	Samuel S. Carpenter,	"	June	1, 1869,	December	27, 1869.
"	Samuel E. Crawford,	"	October	28, 1869,	May	6, 1870.
Pennsylvania,	Kinely J. Tener,	Philadelphia,	June	1, 1869,	June	10, 1869.
"	Joshua Sperring,	"	June	1, 1869,	June	18, 1869.
"	Charles Chauncey,	"	June	1, 1869,	July	2, 1869.
"	Edward Shippin,	"	June	1, 1869,	September	1, 1869.
"	Theo. D. Rand,	"	May	20, 1869,	December	14, 1869.
"	Samuel S. Taylor,	"	May	20, 1869,	November	11, 1869.
"	John McClaren,	Pittsburg,	June	1, 1869,	November	19, 1869.
"	F. Herbut Janvier,	Philadelphia,	January	6, 1870,	January	10, 1870.
"	Henry Phillips, Jr.,	"			December	6, 1869.
"	George W. Thurston,	"	May	8, 1873,	May	9, 1873.
"	G. W. Barton,	"	March	5, 1870,	March	21, 1870.
"	Samuel B. Huay.	"	May	20, 1870,	May	25, 1870.
"	Joseph Frankish,	"	April	25, 1870,	April	28, 1870.
"	Judson R. Sprague,	"	July	6, 1871,	July	11, 1871.
"	Alexander Ramsey,	"	October	3, 1871,	October	7, 1871.
"	John Sparhawk,	"	November	25, 1871,	November	28, 1871.
"	J. P. Diver,	"	November	24, 1871,	November	28, 1871.
"	J. D. Reinboth,	"	March	20, 1873,	March	22, 1873.
"	H. E. Hindmarsh,	"	March	12, 1872,	March	14, 1872.
"	C. H. Krumbnaar,	"	March	12, 1872,	March	16, 1872.
"	Samuel M. Grice,	"	February	1, 1871,	February	8, 1871.
"	Henry Reed,	"	April	1, 1873,	April	3, 1873.
"	Cyrus R. Lantz,	Lebanon,	September	18, 1873,	September	22, 1873.
South Carolina,	J. W. Stone,	Bradford,	June	10, 1873,	December	13, 1873.
"	V. J. Tobias,	Charleston,	June	1, 1869,	November	13, 1869.
"	Thomas Frost,	"	February	23, 1870,	March	19, 1870.

LIST OF COMMISSIONERS OF AFFIDAVITS—*Continued.*

STATE OR TERRITORY.	NAME.	RESIDENCE.	DATE OF APPOINTMENT.	DATE OF QUALIFICATION.
South Carolina,	A. V. Horton,	Cheraw,	March 12, 1872,	April 1, 1872.
"	C. J. Iredell,	Columbia,	October 14, 1872,	October 17, 1872.
"	John H. Schofield,	Greenville,	November 11, 1872,	November 20, 1872.
Tennessee,	Henry P. Woodard,	Memphis,	October 28, 1868,	January 27, 1869.
"	Josiah W. Westcott,	"	March 31, 1871,	April 7, 1871.
"	James E. Temple,	"		November 13, 1869.
"	John C. Reeves,	Summerville,	August 25, 1868,	December 30, 1869,
"	Hudson Carey,	Memphis,	November 6, 1869,	November 12, 1869.
"	Henry F. Dix,	"	August 22, 1871,	August 31, 1871.
"	R. Dudley Frayser,	"	December 23, 1868,	December 29, 1868.
"	Jas. K. Stephens,	Jackson,	August 14, 1873,	August 19, 1873.
Texas,	R. D. Johnson,	Galveston County,	June 1, 1869,	November 17, 1869.
"	J. M. Long,	Paris,	March 21, 1872,	April 19, 1872.
"	E. C. Chambers,	Montgomery,	December 19, 1870,	January 2, 1871.
Virginia,	S. B. Ginn,	Norfolk,		January 5, 1869.
"	Alexander Donnan,	Petersburg,	May 20, 1869,	May 26, 1869.
"	John R. Kilby,	Suffolk,		May 20, 1869.
"	Warren G. Elliott,	Norfolk,	September 10, 1869,	September 20, 1869.
"	Frank A. Wilcox,	"	May 20, 1869,	November 16, 1869.
"	T. R. Borland,	"	**May** 3, 1869,	May 5, 1869.
"	Gilbert Elliott,	"	June 22, 1869,	November 13, 1869.
"	Thomas W. Upshur,	Richmond,	September 1, 1869,	November 11, 1869.
"	E. R. Hunter,	County of Norfolk,	August 28, 1869,	December 14, 1869.
"	E. M. Garrett,	Richmond,	June 1, 1869,	November 10, 1869.
"	W. B. Martin,	Norfolk,		October 21, 1868.
"	George M. Peck,	Hampton,	September 21, 1871,	October 11, 1871.
"	William W. Smith,	Norfolk,	November 29, 1870,	December 6, 1870.
"	W. M. Chaplin,	"	October 23, 1871,	May 19, 1871.
"	John S. Rady,	Richmond,	September 5, 1872,	November 13, 1872.
"	William Wise Smith,	Norfolk,	November 29, 1870,	December 6, 1870.

Virginia,	I. B. Prince,	Jerusalem,	April 9, 1873,	May 20, 1873.
"	Lucien D. Starke,	Norfolk,	August 13, 1873,	August 15, 1873.
West Virginia,	A. M. Warner,	Huntingdon,	September 25, 1873,	September 29, 1873.
France,	Emile B. Morrell,	City of Paris,		February 19, 1874.

†Resigned.

NOTE.—Under chapter 73, public laws of 1873 and 1874, all appointments of commissions made previous to February 2nd, 1874, must be renewed on or before the 1st of January, 1875, otherwise they will be void. All commissions since February 2nd, 1874, will expire in two years after date of issue.

No. XXV.

Index.

INDEX.

ERRATA.

On page 10. for "Andrew Jackson born 3d April, 1767, read 15th March, 1767.

On page 13, for "capitatl," read capital.

On page 41, for "Thomas Bragg in U. S. Senate in 1849, 1851," read 1859, 1861.

On page 41. for "Thomas L. Clingman in U. S. Senate in 1859," read 1858.

On page 41, for "Robert Strange, 1837," read 1836.

On page 15, for "A. S. Merrimon born 28th September, 1830," read 15th September.

On page 16, for "Matt W. Ransom born 5th October, 1826," read 8th October.

On page 42, for "Wm. S. Bleckledge," read Blackledge.

On page 42, for "C. L. Cobb 1871," read 1869.

On page 42, for "Cocaran," read Cochran.

On page 42, for "Crane Butler," read Burton Craige.

On page 42, for "John R. French 1871," read 1867.

On page 42, for "James Holland 1891," read 1800.

On page 42. for "Nathaniel Macon 1805," read 1815.

On page 42, for "George Momford," read George Mumford.

On page 42, for "Robert B. Vance 1812," read Robert B. Vance 1823—1825.

On page 50, for "Movement of population west by counties from 1790 to 1870," read Movement, &c., from 1790 to 1860.

On page 50, for "900,000," read 500,000.

On page 53, for "Wisconsin 1," read Wisconsin 8.

On page 88, for "John W. Ellis Governor in 1858," read 1859.

On page 88, for "Z. B. Vance Governor in 1861," read 1862.

On page 88, for "Tod R. Caldwell 1871," read 1870.

On page 90, for "John B. Neathery salary \$75," read \$750.

On page 90, for "J. Howerton Bailey," read T. Howerton Bailey.

On page 90, for "Wm. B. Wetherel, salary \$900," read Wm. P. Wetherel, salary \$1,000.

On page 90, for "Secretery of State," read Secretary of State.

On page 95, for "Neil McKay, Solicitor," read A. R. McDonald.

On page 97, for "Wm. G. Chandler, Solicitor," read W. G. Candler.

On page 100, for "1859, R. R. Heath," read 1858.

On page 100, for "1858, James W. Osborne," read 1860.

On page 100, for "1870, C. C. Pool," read 1868.

On page 100, for "John L. Henry," read James L. Henry.

On page 101, for "Wm. A. Bailey," read William H. Bailey.

On page 106, for "Stephen Cabarras," read Stephen Cabarrus.

On page 106, for "1823, Alfred Moore, Speaker," read 1824.

On page 106, for "1862, M. S. Robbins," read M. S. Robins.

On page 119, for "Bruswick county," read Brunswick.

On page 125, for "1825 to 1929," read 1825 to 1829.
On page 129, for "Cladwell," read Caldwell.
On page 158, for "1823, Wm. Marshatl," read Wm. Marshall.
On page 163, for "Beaufort county C," read Beaufort county.
On page 163, for "1831, David O. Freeman," read David C. Freeman.
On page 164, for "Richard S. Donnells," read Richard S. Donnell.
On page 164, for "Cashier River," read Cashie.
On page 166, for "1824, Wm. H. Roseoe," read Wm. H. Rascoe.
On page 179, for "Christophor Melchor," read Christopher.
On page 195, for "which," read and.
On page 197, for "1823, Joshua Mewborn," read Joshua Newbern.
On page 210, for "1831, John D. Toomar," read Toomer.
On page 235, for "1799, for Sterling Youneey," read Yancey.
On page 247, for "I. Gra. Sterling," read S. R. Grady.
On page 269, for "William Troy," read William Tryon.
On page 271, for "1852, James A. Caswell," read Caldwell.
On page 279, for "1870, L. C. Lathum," read Latham.
On page 280, for "Cawan's Ford," read Cowan's Ford.

www.ingramcontent.com/pod-product-compliance
Lightning Source LLC
Chambersburg PA
CBHW022256280326
41932CB00010B/883

9783744728744